THE PRICE OF AMENITY

Five Studies in Conservation and Government

By the same author

The Miners and British Politics, 1906–1914

THE PRICE OF AMENITY

Five Studies in Conservation and Government

ROY GREGORY

Lecturer in Politics
University of Reading

Macmillan

St. Martin's Press

First published 1971 by
THE MACMILLAN PRESS LTD
London and Basingstoke
Associated companies in New York Toronto
Dublin Melbourne Johannesburg and Madras

Library of Congress catalog card no. 78–154022

SBN 333 03098 2

Printed in Great Britain by
WESTERN PRINTING SERVICES LTD
Bristol

Contents

List of Maps

He had no eyes for beauty, which was a thing beyond price, and therefore worthless.

HUGH WALPOLE, *The Inquisitor*

Acknowledgements

THIS BOOK of case-studies is based upon research made possible by a grant from the Social Science Research Council. I am very glad to acknowledge their support.

Many of those with first-hand knowledge of these cases were kind enough to discuss them with me. Some of them went to a great deal of trouble to read and correct material in draft. I am particularly grateful to Mr J. R. C. Boys, formerly head of the Development and Market Division of the Iron and Steel Board, and Mr W. J. A. Knibbs, formerly Managing Director, Richard Thomas and Baldwins (Mineral Recovery) Ltd, both now of the British Steel Corporation; Major J. B. Schuster; Mr F. R. Hunt, of the Central Electricity Generating Board; Mr Michael Clark; Mr G. F. Seymour; Mr G. E. G. Rodgers; Mr J. Cattermole, Labour Party Regional Organiser for the East Midlands; Mr C. F. Thring and Dr J. A. Cooper of Imperial Chemical Industries; Mr A. S. Hughes, Clerk and Chief Executive Officer of the Tees Valley and Cleveland Water Board, and his predecessor Mr E. A. Morris; Mr J. V. D. Webb; Dr M. E. D. Poore, Dr M. W. Holdgate, and Dr J. F. D. Frazer of the Nature Conservancy; Mr Max Nicholson; Mr J. E. Lousley; Mr F. H. B. Layfield, Q.C.; Mr C. R. L. Clarke of Shell U.K. Ltd; Mr Max Davies; Mr F. E. Dean of the Gas Council; Mr J. E. Mottram; Mr D. P. Welman; Mr Richard West; Mr Airey Neave, M.P.; Mr Reginald Freeson, M.P., formerly Parliamentary Secretary, Ministry of Power, and Joint Parliamentary Secretary, Ministry of Housing and Local Government; and Lord Kennet, formerly Joint Parliamentary Secretary, Ministry of Housing and Local Government.

My thanks are due to the Clerks and other officers of the following local authorities: the Oxfordshire County Council; the Nottinghamshire County Council; the Carlton Urban District Council; the West Bridgford Urban District Council; the Norfolk County Council; the Smallburgh Rural District Council;

the Berkshire County Council; and the Abingdon Borough Council. I am also grateful for the help of officers of the Southern Gas Board and the Nottingham Area of the National Union of Mineworkers.

I should like to acknowledge the kindness of all those officers of the former Ministry of Housing and Local Government and the former Ministry of Power who helped me to avoid many pitfalls and answered my questions so patiently.

Dr E. J. Mishan of the London School of Economics and Mr M. F. B. Bell of the Countryside Commission were good enough to talk to me at some length about a number of the problems discussed in later chapters. I also had the benefit of numerous conversations with Mr R. E. Wraith and Mr G. B. Lamb. For his help and advice in the early stages of the research I am very much indebted to Mr D. N. Chester, Warden of Nuffield College, Oxford.

In collecting the material for these case-studies I had the assistance of Mrs Anne Brown; I am grateful for the hard work she put into what was often a tedious job. Miss C. M. Davy helped with the preparation of the text. Mrs M. E. Chick typed and re-typed numerous drafts with speed and good humour.

Any errors of fact, and all expressions of opinion, are, of course, the responsibility of the author alone.

R.G.G.

Preface

THE FIVE case-studies that make up the bulk of this book are concerned with the impact of industrial development on amenity and the natural environment. It is an important theme, and one that steadily attracts more attention and discussion. It is also a subject that stirs deep feelings. Understandably, there is a good deal more partisan over-simplification than dispassionate analysis. The result is that the intractable problems facing developers, conservationists, administrators and politicians are often lost to sight in the turmoil of argument and recrimination.

In a complex society nothing changes without disturbing the existing arrangements and affronting someone or some group. And in a much governed country like this, little of importance happens that is not sanctioned or set in motion by public bodies under political control. Wherever they go, the politician and the administrator almost inevitably leave a trail of aggrieved citizens in their wake. Not everyone loses, of course; but even those who are satisfied today will be outraged by some other decision to-morrow. In recent years the British system of government and politics has come in for a great deal of criticism. No doubt it is deficient in many ways. Yet much of the current discontent may be unavoidable: a large and growing output of unwelcome decisions is not necessarily a sign of inefficiency or ineptitude. This is something that everyone finds it difficult to accept, and there is not much to be done about it.

Alienation that springs from lack of understanding is another matter. True, a dogged determination to see the other man's point of view and understand his difficulties can go too far. *Tout comprendre, c'est tout pardonner*: an excess of sympathy can easily give rise to paralysis or a sense of Panglossian complacency. On balance, however, the dangers of uninformed cynicism look the more serious. Whatever conclusions the general reader may reach about the performance and motives of the men involved in the planning cases described in this book, I should be surprised if, even with the wisdom of hindsight, he judges many of them to have been knaves or fools, confronted with easy questions, but too wicked or too stupid to see the right answers. As for professional administrators, I am inclined to believe that most of them have less to learn from common-room critics than some academics like to think. All the same, it can sometimes be illuminating to look at our own problems through the eyes of others. For this reason alone, those who earn their bread and butter in the world of planning may find something of interest in these reconstructions of five of the more celebrated amenity disputes in the last decade. They are likely to be typical of many more to come.

The value of case-studies for teaching purposes is now widely acknowledged, particularly in the field of public administration.[1] This is not surprising, because 'administration' is an activity that can be extraordinarily difficult to describe, except in terms so abstract and generalised that they convey little or nothing unless the reader already knows what it is. I suspect that for many students of government, what administrators actually do remains obscure long after all the ills in the system are diagnosed and appropriate remedies confidently prescribed. Nor do most aspects of public administration readily lend themselves to a style of writing that grips the attention, for by its very nature, administration lacks the drama and the clash of persons and principles that characterise the more familiar world of politics. Formal accounts of the continuing processes of government often have a good deal in common with instructions for the use of domestic appliances: they are necessary, practical and useful, but they are not designed to stimulate interest, and they are rarely read for

---

[1] The case method has been in general use for some years in the United States, where the theory of case writing has attracted considerable attention. See, for example, Harold Stein (ed.), *Public Administration and Policy Development: A Case Book* (New York: Harcourt, Brace, 1952), and Edwin A. Bock, *Essays on the Case Method in Public Administration* (Brussels: International Institute of Administrative Sciences, 1962). For another collection of overseas cases, see B. B. Schaffer and D. C. Corbett (eds), *Decisions: Case Studies in Australian Administration* (Melbourne: Cheshire, 1966). Most of the case-studies so far written on British administration are scattered throughout the specialist journals. The best-known collections in book form are two volumes in the *Administrators in Action* series (London: Allen & Unwin), vol. I (1961) by F. M. G. Willson, and vol. II (1965) by Gerald Rhodes.

enjoyment. The advantage of the case-study is that it can bring administration alive in a way that abstractions obviously cannot.[1] Uninformative though it might at first sound, Dwight Waldo's description of administration as 'a man in a situation having to make a decision' prompts the questions that every student of government must at some time have asked himself. What kinds of situation? What sort of decisions?

How much to include, and what to leave out, is a constant problem in case writing. Over-elaboration clogs the narrative, and too much detail soon makes for tedious reading. But if they are to succeed in imparting what has been described as 'a sense of vicarious living', case-histories cannot afford to go too far in the other direction. The object, after all, is to re-create situations as they looked to the men on the job at the time. To put himself in the shoes of those involved in a controversy, the reader must know something of their institutional responsibilities and perspectives; he must take account of the pressures and constraints that they had to contend with, and he must himself grapple with the facts and arguments presented to the men who had to make the decisions. Because of the conveniently Olympian vantage point occupied by the story teller, it is difficult enough anyway to re-capture the feel of bygone dilemmas. Tempting though it is, it really serves no purpose to make complex cases look simple merely in the interests of easier going.

Although the case writer may in some respects get to know more about a situation than many of the individual participants knew at the time, there is almost always a good deal of information that is denied him. No one who writes about contemporary British government from the outside is likely to be given access to

[1] Whether it will ever be possible to use case-studies for the more grandiose purposes of 'theory building' must be very debatable. They may well suggest hypotheses of considerable interest, and of course the single contrary case may serve to destroy 'proverbs' that pose as universal laws. But it is hard to see how the somewhat indeterminate variables that characterise administrative situations could ever be rigorously and scientifically controlled, or how hypotheses could ever be systematically tested without replicating an enormous number of cases so much alike as to become insufferably boring. This problem is discussed by Dwight Waldo, 'Five Perspectives on the Cases of the Inter-University Case Program', and James W. Fesler, 'The Case Method in Political Science', in Bock, op. cit.

as much documentary material as he would wish, and this is particularly true if the episodes that he chooses to examine are not only recent but controversial too. There are compensations, however. Provided that allowances are made for the frailties and selective tendencies of human memory, interviews can be used to supplement the public record; with luck and perseverance a great deal may come the writer's way that was never committed to paper at all. Cases that develop into disputes between organisations make especially good subjects for research purposes, because in these circumstances the protagonists are very often required to explain, justify and defend their positions, an exercise that obliges them to describe how and why they reached their decisions. And what they do not volunteer, opponents will sometimes manage to extract under cross-examination.

There are also dangers. Information produced in the course of making a case cannot always be taken at its face value. After all, it is not being provided for the benefit of contemporary historians. An organisation's spokesmen naturally describe its internal processes with the object of improving their chances of success, treading lightly over anything that might not. Indeed, to judge from their own versions of what occurred as they moved towards a decision, it would often seem that some divine presence hovered over their logical and orderly deliberations, guiding them inexorably to conclusions that no reasonable body of men could possibly have failed to reach. The fact is, of course, that what may be said for the purposes of advocacy is by no means always a wholly accurate record of what actually happened. Internal divisions and differences of opinion are not advertised once an organisation has gone into battle against another, and at this stage, decisions that could very easily have gone either way are made to appear virtually inevitable. On occasions, it can be difficult to distinguish between what was really relevant to a decision and what is brought in afterwards by way of justification. A reasonably accurate reconstruction of the true picture almost invariably calls for some careful excisions.

Case-studies are certainly not without their limitations and drawbacks. Because they frequently portray exceptional or unusual episodes in the life of the administrator, rather than his everyday work, they can easily convey a very misleading impression. The controversies described in this book, for example, may be representative of a whole class of planning disputes. But for few of the individuals concerned were they merely routine occurrences, and many of those involved, I know, would add their heartfelt thanks for that. Battles make good stories, and when one institution is pitted against another the element of conflict helps to heighten the interest and suspense. At the same time, pitched battles with other agencies make up only a fraction of the total activity of most public bodies. And sometimes the case-history may do less than justice to the administrator and his difficulties, in that it isolates a vertical slice of his work for the reader's inspection. In reality, officials are usually occupied with more than one case at a time, and whereas the observer can devote the whole of his attention to the problem set before him, the administrator may well be dealing with other matters, some of which, at the time, appear to be of greater urgency and importance. Unlike the case writer, officials never start with the advantage of knowing the end of the story. It may be only one case in a hundred that eventually becomes a matter of public interest and concern. Yet however obvious it may look afterwards, in the early and often crucial stages it is not always so easy to see which that case will be. The better the administrators the more sensitive they are to trouble on the horizon, and the more of these potentially controversial cases they will spot. But they cannot always be right, and in the nature of things they tend to be judged by their handling of that one case which turns out to be exceptionally difficult. Good news is no news, and all the others that pass off smoothly go unnoticed and without comment.

Nor do case-studies in one area of public administration necessarily tell us much about life in other parts of the forest. Many of the organisations that appear in the following chapters are responsible for supplying a physical product. Capital investment decisions are a major part of their business. Whilst it is true that, as with all administrative agencies, their concern is with means rather than ends, it is nevertheless a far cry from planning power stations, reservoirs, or natural gas terminals, to administering a pensions scheme, collecting taxes, or running a hospital or a school meals service. There is no point in pretending that cases concerned with amenity problems and the use of land tell us much about the more traditional aspects of public administration. Nevertheless, there is no doubt that as the public sector expands, both absolutely and in relative terms, what Professor Peter Self has described as the 'transformative' content of public administration will become steadily more significant. Increasingly, Government departments, public corporations and local authorities find themselves responsible for managing, or supervising the management of, physical resources on a hitherto unprecedented scale. Changing the face of the earth and regulating the environment we live in may not be the very first activities that come to mind when we think of public administrators and their work. All the same, there can be few responsibilities that are more important.

1 Naming the Parts

> The attachment for his territory is as profound as in
> any species . . . So far as defence is concerned, it is
> continual and inviolable. The wasp will repel an
> intruder by threat, or by a chase if threat is not
> enough, or by butting him in mid-air if chasing will
> not do, or, in the last resort, grappling with him,
> tumbling to earth and trying if possible to bite out his
> eyes. It is a rough game.
>
> Robert Ardrey, *The Territorial Imperative*

DISPUTES ABOUT the use of land are nothing new in British experience. In their time, enclosures, canals, turnpikes, railways, nineteenth-century public utilities and schemes for municipal improvement all occasioned controversies hardly less ferocious than battles over what we now call 'development'. Nor is a concern for the preservation of the countryside and the conservation of wild life an altogether modern phenomenon. But it is chiefly in the last twenty years or so that 'amenity' has regularly and conspicuously come to be part of the stuff of conflict between developers and their opponents.[1] All the signs suggest that as a result of a growing preoccupation with 'the quality of life', it will figure even more prominently in the annals of future decades.

The origins of this continuing conflict are familiar enough. An expanding population insists upon higher standards of material comfort and convenience. To satisfy these demands a limited supply of land must be developed or redeveloped to provide both

---

[1] The *Oxford English Dictionary* defines amenity as 'the quality of being pleasant; of places, their situation, aspect, climate, etc.' Paradoxically enough, in ordinary usage practical utilities such as a supply of electricity, gas and water, roads, shops, schools and employment are also commonly described as 'amenities'. Life would certainly be much less pleasant without them. But, of course, it is the provision of some of these utilities that frequently destroys or impairs 'amenity' in the more intangible and immaterial sense of the word.

the apparatus of production and distribution and also the opportunities for people to enjoy in their everyday lives the benefits of a rising national income. The result is a well-known catalogue of developments, so often chanted nowadays as almost to sound hackneyed. Motorways and airports, power stations and overhead transmission lines, mineral workings and reservoirs, gasholders and natural gas terminals, New Towns and housing estates, factories and oil refineries, all invade the countryside and change the face of cities and towns. Necessary and desirable they may be; but, as often as not, these developments interfere with the amenities of the locality chosen for the project. Indeed, their impact is frequently felt far beyond the particular patch or strip of land on which they are situated. They may spoil the natural beauty of the countryside and coastline, ruin the appearance of part of a town, destroy buildings of historic and architectural value, or wipe out precious reserves of wild life. In their wider effects, they may create noise and disturbance, or pollute the atmosphere, rivers and lakes.[1]

When they learn what is afoot, those who see their values and interests threatened naturally resent, and frequently resist the proposed development. Sometimes a compromise agreement is possible, and no one not directly involved is any the wiser. But when neither side feels that it can give enough ground to satisfy the other, the outcome may be a spectacular battle, attracting nation-wide, or occasionally even international, attention. When it comes to an open fight, who are the parties to these amenity disputes? And when the battle lines are drawn, how are such conflicts resolved?

[1] Much of the growing body of literature on this theme takes the form of scattered periodical and newspaper articles. But for more readily available surveys, see for example H. E. Bracey, *Industry and the Countryside. The Impact of Industry on Amenities in the Countryside* (London: Faber, for the Acton Society Trust, 1963); Garth Christian, *Tomorrow's Countryside* (London: Murray, 1966); Robert Arvill, *Man and Environment* (Harmondsworth: Penguin Books, 1967); Max Nicholson, *The Environmental Revolution: A Guide for the New Masters of the Earth* (London: Hodder & Stoughton, 1970); and Nan Fairbrother, *New Lives, New Landscapes* (London: Architectural Press, 1970). Brief accounts of many of the more controversial proposals are to be found in the Annual Reports of the Countryside Commission (formerly the National Parks Commission) and the Council for the Protection of Rural England (formerly the Council for the Preservation of Rural England).

The organisations principally responsible for promoting major physical projects are well enough known. They may be Government departments, such as the Department of the Environment, which in October 1970 took over the powers formerly vested in the Ministry of Transport and the Ministry of Housing and Local Government. They may be public corporations, like the Central Electricity Generating Board, the Gas Council, Area Gas and Electricity Boards, the British Airports Authority, or the National Coal Board. Sometimes they are local statutory undertakers, such as district Water Boards; sometimes they are local authorities, initiating housing and highway schemes. Or they may be private firms, seeking to establish all manner of commercial and industrial installations.

Ranged against them, the organised guardians of amenity take many forms. There are elected councils, this time in their role as Local Planning Authorities. There are statutory or charter bodies, such as the Countryside Commission, the Nature Conservancy and the Royal Fine Art Commission. There are voluntary and non-official bodies, dedicated to preserving rural and urban amenities, conserving wild life, combating nuisances, or promoting recreational and leisure activities. Some of these organisations, such as the Council for the Protection of Rural England, the Commons, Open Spaces and Footpaths Preservation Society, the Ramblers' Association, and the Council for Nature, are permanent organisations operating on a national basis. Others have achieved permanence, but they interest themselves only in preserving or enhancing the amenities of their own locality. They include, for example, the County Naturalist Trusts, county branches of the C.P.R.E., Civic Societies in individual cities and towns, and societies concerned with particular areas of the countryside, such as the Lake District, the Chilterns or Dartmoor. Others again are ephemeral and *ad hoc* bodies, established to fight a specific development, and disbanding after their local battle is won or lost.[1] If a scheme is sufficiently controversial, all kinds of organisa-

---

[1] Since the late fifties there has been a rapid increase in the number of local amenity societies. According to one observer, by 1968 over 600 were in existence. See John Barr, 'The Amenity Protesters', *New Society*, 1 Aug 1968. An earlier estimate suggests that between 1957 and 1962 over a hundred local societies were formed, a high proportion of them in the predominantly middle-class areas of the Home Counties and south-east

tions normally concerned with entirely different matters may be drawn into a dispute alongside the regular troops. As we shall see, local councils other than planning authorities, Hospital Management Committees, Ratepayers' Associations, universities, Women's Institutes, and professional and sports clubs and societies have all from time to time entered the lists in opposition to what they considered obnoxious developments in their area. And lastly, since so many land-use conflicts involve good-quality farmland, more often than not local branches of the National Farmers' Union and the Country Landowners' Association are also prominent among the objectors, though of course their interest is primarily in agriculture rather than amenity.

Amenity conflicts are usually settled through one of two processes, both of which are illustrated in the case-studies that follow. Firstly, there is the Parliamentary process. Though much less frequently employed than in its heyday in the middle of the nineteenth century, in certain circumstances developers seeking powers and benefits in addition to those already conferred on them under existing public law still resort to Private Bill procedure. Like measures sponsored by Government departments and back-bench Members of Parliament, Private Bills must be examined and approved by both Houses in the usual way. The crucial hurdle for a Private Bill, however, is the Committee hearing, which takes an altogether different form from the Committee stage of a Public Bill. After its Second Reading, a Private Bill is referred to a small Select Committee, consisting usually of four Members of the House of Commons or five Members of the Lords. If the Bill is opposed, the Committee sits in a semi-judicial capacity. Evidence for both sides is marshalled by counsel, witnesses are called and cross-examined, and Government departments with an interest in the outcome may present written reports on the merits of the proposal. At the close of the proceedings the Committee recommends that the Bill be rejected or approved. This recommendation is usually accepted, though if the scheme is particularly controversial there may be further opposition on

England (Bracey, op. cit., p. 200). These figures apparently include both permanent and ephemeral associations. It is, of course, true that societies formed to oppose one development sometimes remain in being after the storm has passed, and interest themselves in other threats to local amenities.

the floor of the House, and possibly a division at the end of the debate.[1]

Secondly, and far more commonly nowadays, the developer may go by way of an administrative process, beginning with an application to a Local Planning Authority or a Minister, continuing (where there are objections) with a public local inquiry, and ending with a Ministerial decision. Planning law is a highly complex subject, and it must be emphasised that the very brief and rudimentary sketch that follows is intended merely to outline the procedures relevant to the cases described in this book.[2] The main purpose and effect of post-war planning legislation was, of course, to transfer the control of development and re-development to the State. Applications to develop are usually submitted in the first instance to the Local Planning Authority in which the land is situated; alternatively, where the proposal is thought to be of national rather than local importance, or is especially controversial, the Secretary of State for the Environment may 'call in' the application for his own decision. In certain circumstances, for example under the Electricity Acts, where the authorisation of a Government department is required for development, the developer applies direct to the appropriate Minister, in this case the Secretary of State for Trade and Industry;[3] if the Minister's authorisation is forthcoming, he directs that planning permission shall be deemed to be granted for the development.

When an application is refused by the Local Planning Authority, an aggrieved developer may appeal to the Secretary

[1] For Private Bill procedure, see Erskine May, *Parliamentary Practice*, 17th ed. (London: Butterworth, 1964), chaps xxxiv–xxxviii; and O. Cyprian Williams, *The Historical Development of Private Bill Procedure and Standing Orders in the House of Commons*, 2 vols (London: H.M.S.O., 1948–9). Many of the more celebrated battles fought out in this arena are described in Frederick A. Clifford, *A History of Private Bill Legislation*, 2 vols. (London: Butterworth, 1885–7).

[2] For a full and up-to-date description, see Desmond Heap, *An Outline of Planning Law*, 5th ed. (London: Sweet & Maxwell, 1969). The mechanics of development control are described in J. A. G. Griffith, *Central Departments and Local Authorities* (London: Allen & Unwin, 1966).

[3] In October 1969 the Minister of Technology took over the Ministry of Power, which had previously dealt with planning applications made under the Electricity Acts (see Chapter 3). Subsequently, in October 1970, the Ministry of Technology (with the exception of its Aviation Group) merged with the Board of Trade, to form the Department of Trade and Industry.

of State for the Environment. In this event, before reaching his decision, the Minister is obliged to give both the would-be developer and the Local Planning Authority the opportunity of a hearing conducted by a person appointed by himself. Similarly, where a case is called in, where the developer is seeking consent direct from a Minister, or where a Minister is himself the developer, those who oppose the project are usually given the chance to make their views known. If there is a hearing, other parties affected by the proposed scheme are customarily permitted to express their feelings; they may include local authorities other than the planning authority, statutory bodies concerned with amenity, national and local amenity societies, and local residents.

It is usual for the hearing to take the form of a local inquiry, held in public, and conducted by an Inspector appointed by the Minister concerned. Two departments, the Department of the Environment and the Department of Trade and Industry, are provided with their own Inspectorates.[1] Though it is generally felt that public inquiries ought to be kept as informal as possible, the procedure adopted is to some extent patterned on that of a court of law, and in the more important and complex cases the developers are almost invariably represented by counsel, who are often employed by the more important objectors too. The Inspector opens the proceedings with a statement about the purpose of the inquiry. Developers and objectors deploy their arguments, both calling witnesses to support their own case, and challenging in cross-examination evidence marshalled by the other side. At the close of the inquiry (and sometimes informally

---

[1] Within the Department of the Environment there are two Inspectorates which hold planning inquiries. By far the largest is the Housing and Planning Inspectorate, with over 160 Inspectors in the field, all of whom are engaged on full-time inquiry work. For the most part, they have already established careers for themselves in such professions as surveying, town planning, civil engineering, architecture or the overseas civil service before they are recruited. The pressure of work is too great to permit specialisation; but some attempt is made to match Inspectors with particular types of case, so that they may be reasonably at home with the technical substance of a problem. The Engineering Inspectorate, about forty strong, is only partly concerned with public inquiries, and deals chiefly with water supply, sewerage and the collection and disposal of refuse. In the Department of Trade and Industry, the Inspectorate consists of professional electrical engineers, and deals with public inquiries into power stations and overhead transmission lines.

before or during the hearings) the Inspector visits the site of the proposed development to try to weigh up for himself its probable effect on the locality. The proceedings over, he ponders what he has seen and heard, and submits his report to the Minister. This report consists of a description of the area affected, a resumé of what was said, his own findings (including sometimes an assessment of the strength of local feeling), and finally his recommendation as to what decision the Minister should take.

After examination in the appropriate branch or section of the department concerned, straightforward cases that appear to raise no special difficulties are often decided at the level of Senior or Chief Executive Officer. The more complex cases, and those which raise issues of national importance, are considered at a higher level in the administrative hierarchy, and in these circumstances the decision-letter will be signed by an Assistant Secretary or Deputy Secretary. The department is under no obligation to endorse an Inspector's recommendation. But since he has heard the evidence first-hand, and seen the site or route for himself (whereas usually Ministers and civil servants have not), there is a strong presumption in favour of his judgement, and it usually requires a consensus of opinion among the most senior and experienced officials in the department before any question of rejecting his recommendation arises. In the last resort, of course, it is always open to the Minister personally to overrule both the Inspector and his civil servants if he so chooses.

More planning cases go to Ministers and junior Ministers for their personal consideration than is commonly thought. Briefly, the general principle is this: when policy is firmly established and the precedents are clear, cases are decided by the department without reference to Ministers. In other words, when civil servants feel they know what decision the Minister would take, they take it themselves. When they are unsure, they do not. A case might reach the Minister's desk for a variety of reasons. It may raise new issues, not precisely covered by existing policy. There may have been talk of a change of policy. A case may have aroused widespread public controversy and attracted the notice of Members of Parliament. Or it may simply be so unlike anything that has gone before that it clearly calls for a personal judgement on the part of the Minister. As one Permanent Secretary has put it, 'Whatever he wants to see, he sees, and whatever we think he

ought to see, again he sees.'[1] Some cases, of course, are so controversial that they are plainly destined for the Minister's attention
almost from the moment the development is conceived. Long
before the Inspectors' reports were completed, it was quite obvious
to everyone concerned that the cases described in Chapters 2, 3
and 5 could be settled only at ministerial level.

It is not so long ago that public inquiries and the subsequent
departmental processes were the subject of a good deal of criticism
and disquiet. Thanks largely to the administrative changes that
followed the publication of the Report of the Franks Committee
in 1957, and the work of the Council on Tribunals, there is now
considerably less dissatisfaction with the fairness of planning procedures, though, as we shall see, the doubts and fears had
certainly not disappeared in the early sixties at the time of the
cases described in Chapters 2 and 3. Government departments
themselves draw a clear distinction between the quasi-judicial
role of a Minister in deciding planning applications and appeals,
where he is called on to adjudicate between two contending
parties, and his administrative function in relation to projects
sponsored by the Government itself, such as New Towns
and motorways. However, the term 'quasi-judicial' is itself open
to somewhat different interpretations, and not surprisingly there
are different views as to the nature and purpose of a public
inquiry. The parties to a dispute see it as a contest, in which they
hope to outpoint their opponents. In their view, the whole process is essentially adjudicatory; the Minister's decision ought to
be a verdict that is based upon and follows solely from the evidence submitted at the hearing. If they go away convinced that
they have had the better of the exchanges, but then lose the case,
not so much because of what was said at the inquiry, but 'for
reasons of policy fought out in the Department after the enquiry',[2]
they naturally feel cheated of a verdict which (they think) ought
by rights to have been theirs. By the same token, of course, from
time to time there will be some who lose the argument but win

---

[1] *Report from the Select Committee on the Parliamentary Commissioner
for Administration*, H.C. 385 (1968–9), *Minutes of Evidence*, Q. 69.

[2] The phrase is that of Dame Evelyn Sharp, a former Permanent Secretary at the Ministry of Housing and Local Government. See Franks Committee, *Report on Administrative Tribunals and Enquiries: Minutes of
Evidence*, Third Day, Q. 661.

the battle; they will have reason to be grateful to 'the unknown hands and voices',[1] that come into play when the inquiry is over.

The Ministry, on the other hand, sees the inquiry in another light. For the Minister and his officials it is a source of information, not only about the project itself, why it is necessary and why it has to be sited in one spot rather than somewhere else, but also about the feelings and interests of those most affected by the proposed development. Because it takes place in public and is adversative in character, a local inquiry certainly differs from the usual administrative methods of collecting data. But the fact remains that from the Ministry's point of view, its central purpose is to 'inform the Minister's mind', to explore every facet of the problem, and to provide him with the maximum of knowledge, so that he has the best possible chance of reaching the right decision. It is true that this decision is, in a sense, a verdict awarded to one side or the other. And what is said at the inquiry is naturally of great importance in helping the Minister to make up his mind. Nevertheless, the inquiry can never be more than a part of the decision-making process, at least where major planning disputes are concerned.

This is not just because the Minister alone is in a position to assess the significance of any one case in terms of national policy; as we shall see, some of the most difficult and controversial cases are virtually *sui generis*, and 'policy' is not really involved at all. Such cases neither have, nor are they likely to set precedents, for although the ingredients may frequently recur, they are never twice mixed in exactly the same proportions. They are, as one observer puts it, 'unique and political'.[2] When it is a question of

[1] Sir Oliver Franks, ibid., Q. 662.
[2] Denys Munby, 'The Procedures of Public Inquires', *Public Administration*, xxxiv (spring 1956). See also H. W. R. Wade, 'Are Public Inquiries a Farce?', *Public Administration*, xxxiii (winter 1955); Geoffrey Marshall, 'The Franks Report on Administrative Tribunals and Enquiries', *Public Administration*, xxxv (winter 1957); J. A. G. Griffith, 'Tribunals and Inquiries', *Modern Law Review*, xxii, 2 (1959); W. A. Robson, 'Public Inquiries as an Instrument of Government', in *Politics and Government at Home and Abroad* (London: Allen & Unwin, 1967); and H. R. Burroughes, 'Electricity Supply and the Public Enquiry', M.A. thesis (University of Manchester, 1966). A comprehensive survey by R. E. Wraith and G. B. Lamb, *Public Inquiries as an Instrument of Government*, is to be published in 1971 (London: Allen & Unwin).

choosing between competing and conflicting aspects of the public good, or taking decisions the effect of which will be to allocate costs and benefits among various sections of the community, an Inspector's report, based upon the evidence presented at a public local inquiry, can never be the last word. And as we shall see, planning is a field where important decisions can sometimes turn upon a special kind of value-judgement. Emphatically, they are personal decisions for responsible politicians.

No one who reflects upon the implications of a second industrial revolution for a small and crowded island is likely to underrate the importance of these encounters between developers and the guardians of amenity. But it is more than a little misleading to portray them as dramatic conflicts between amenity on the one hand and utility on the other. This is not usually the form which these battles take. The disputed development is very often required in order to provide benefits which, rightly or wrongly, are generally considered essential, such as additional electricity, gas and water, better housing, or raw materials for exporting industries. If, for technical reasons, the only alternative to the destruction of amenity were to forgo altogether benefits of this kind, objectors would seldom get their case on its feet at all, and when they did, the resulting contests would be so one-sided as to be hardly worth fighting. However, objectors are rarely forced into this position, for it is hardly ever a question of this or that, all or nothing. More often, at a price, it is possible both to preserve amenity (or at least to avoid the worst that might befall it) *and* to provide the required goods and services. In practice, therefore, the arguments are about how much preservation would cost, and whether or not the amenity in jeopardy is worth the price of saving it.[1] What is at issue comes out more clearly if we examine the origins of amenity disputes, and see how they look to the parties typically involved.

Take firstly the developers. Obviously they do not become

[1] It is of course true that if industrialists were compelled to incur the full social costs of their operations, under rigorously competitive conditions output would be reduced or restricted to a level at which their substantially higher *social* marginal costs were covered by prevailing market prices. In these circumstances, the effect might indeed be to rule out entirely many industrial projects. For a cogent exposition of this argument, see E. J. Mishan, *The Costs of Economic Growth* (London: Staples Press, 1967).

embroiled in what are frequently expensive and protracted public inquiries or Private Bill hearings just for the joy of it. No doubt there are still plenty of 'greedy men, prowling over the face of Britain and devastating it';[1] but the executives who launch their organisations into these controversial planning battles are by no means always insensitive philistines. In private life many of them probably shake their heads over pollution, the destruction of wild life, and the ruination of the countryside and coastline as much as anyone else; in their own suburb or village they may even be active members of the local amenity society. Moreover, under Section 11 of the 1968 Countryside Act, all public bodies are now under a statutory obligation to 'have regard to the desirability of conserving the natural beauty and amenity of the countryside'. In one important industry, namely electricity supply, this so-called 'amenity clause' has been operative for considerably longer.[2] And whilst legislation of this kind does not extend to private developers, it would nevertheless be widely agreed that most of the better-known and larger companies at least are anxious to uphold a reputation for enlightened and socially responsible behaviour. Nor do developers, public and private, usually blunder unsuspecting into these controversies. Occasionally, they may be taken unawares by the depth and intensity of national and local hostility to their proposals. But anyone who plans to develop land in a National Park, a Nature Reserve, an Area of Outstanding Natural Beauty, an Area of Great Landscape Value, a Green Belt, or a Site of Special

---

[1] C. A. R. Crosland, *The Conservative Enemy* (London: Cape, 1962), p. 183.

[2] There are differences of opinion as to the practical value of this clause. If challenged, it would presumably always be open to a public body to reply that it had indeed 'had regard for' amenity, however little weight had in fact been given to the desirability of conserving natural beauty. To that extent, it may indeed be 'pious and toothless', as one critic has put it. On the other hand, a clause on these lines does give freer rein to those organisations which genuinely do wish to spend money in the interests of amenity. It also precludes the attitude adopted, for example, by the Iron and Steel Board in the case described in Chapter 2. For a history of the 'amenity clause', see Bracey, *Industry and the Countryside*, pp. 214–16. It made its first appearance as Section 9 of the Hydro-Electric Development Act (Scotland), 1943, and was subsequently included as Section 37 of the Electricity Act, 1957, Section 43 of the Pipelines Act, 1962, and Section 101 of the Water Resources Act, 1963.

Scientific Interest knows very well that he can safely bank on some kind of reaction.[1]

Virtue apart, worldly calculations of expediency also discourage too offhand or cavalier an attitude towards amenity. If the project is designed to meet what is generally considered to be an essential need, then somehow it must go forward. Nevertheless, a range of options usually remains open to the developer. It is true that some of the possibilities advocated by objectors are urged more in desperation than with any real sense of expectation; to underground the whole of the supergrid would certainly put an end to disputes about pylons and cables, and desalination would indeed eliminate the need for new reservoirs. But at present, developers have little difficulty in convincing themselves and most others that these 'painless' alternatives are still far too expensive to be worth serious consideration.[2] Setting them aside, very often the developer can still choose from a set of more practicable possibilities. There is almost always more than one possible site for an airport, a power station, a natural gas terminal or a reservoir. Motorways and transmission lines must go from A to B; but there is usually more than one feasible route. Town gas must be stored in something; but traditional gasholders are not the only possible containers. And even minerals can usually be worked in one part of the country rather than another, or imported from abroad.

If he can, the developer naturally wants to avoid the expense and delay of a battle. And if he concludes that there has to be a battle, he naturally chooses his ground with care, so as to give himself the best possible chance of winning. However admirable

[1] In 1963 it was estimated that about 40 per cent of total land area in Great Britain was protected under one or other of these classifications. See *Report from the Select Committee on Nationalised Industries (The Electricity Supply Industry)*, H.C. 236 – 1 (1962–3), 157. The then chairman of the C.E.G.B., in what has since become a widely quoted remark, told the Committee that throughout the year he spent more time on thinking about amenity problems than any other subject. Ibid., II (*Minutes of Evidence*) Q. 973.

[2] According to the C.E.G.B.'s calculations in 1963, to underground all future transmission lines would have required additional capital expenditure of the order of £100 to 150 million a year, the equivalent of 6d. on the standard rate of income tax or a 20 per cent increase in the price of electricity.

a scheme may be from his own point of view, simple prudence will often make him think twice about putting it forward if it is known to be open to powerful amenity objections. Though objectors may not believe it, the projects that so outrage planning authorities and amenity societies are by no means always just the first and cheapest that happen to have entered the developer's head. Only a fool would propose something which he knows will probably be rejected out of hand; consequently, the developer must try to judge what is likely to be acceptable to those with the power of decision. As he well knows, *their* judgement will be to some extent conditioned by what they think public opinion will consider reasonable. In short, a great deal depends upon the prevalent standards of acceptability, and this is an important point to which we will return at a later stage.

But if developers are not necessarily villains or fools as far as amenity is concerned, it would of course be quite unrealistic to suppose that the environmental implications of their projects are the first, or anything like the first, considerations taken into account when they make their decisions. In cases of the kind described in later chapters, the developer is planning a major capital investment. At this stage and for his purposes, the need or demand is already established and specific: so many tons of iron ore are required, a generating station of a certain capacity has to be built, or a reservoir with a particular yield is needed. Whether he is discharging a statutory duty, or planning to supply a commercial market, usually there is also a target date to be met. The developer sees it as his main task to achieve a given objective at the least cost to himself. When the possible means have been identified, his next step is to assess and compare the costs and timetables of the various alternative methods of reaching his goal. In principle at least, this calls for no more than straightforward commercial calculations. Because there is a market for the necessary factors of production, such as land, raw materials, transport, equipment and labour, they all have known money prices. And since these prices are all expressed in terms of a common unit of measurement, there is no difficulty in combining them as a preliminary to choosing the least costly among the alternatives that will satisfy his requirements.

At this point, however, an increasingly familiar problem emerges. The developer is not concerned with the *total* cost that his project inflicts on the community as a whole; his objective is simply to minimise the private costs that fall upon his own budget and which he himself must bear. This distinction between 'social' and 'private' costs has obvious consequences. From the developer's point of view, site A may be considerably cheaper than site B; but the side-effects of developing site A may impose substantially higher costs on others, and typically, one of these side-effects is loss of amenity. There is no market in which amenity changes hands, and therefore it has no money price. And even if the developer is prepared to acknowledge that a monetary cost ought to be ascribed to the destruction of amenity, there is no financial incentive for him to take it into account. His choice between sites A and B is bound to be made chiefly on the basis of private and quantifiable costs, for these are the only costs that appear on his balance-sheet.

None of this is to suggest that public bodies and responsible private companies consistently and systematically display a total disregard for the wider effects of their activities. This would be patently untrue. As we have already observed, our hypothetical site A may not be the very cheapest possibility: that may well have been passed over at an early stage, not just for the reasons of prudence mentioned earlier, but also because the developer sincerely believed that some additional costs ought to be accepted in the interests of amenity. Decisions, after all, are made by individuals, or by small groups of men, and not by impersonal entities called firms or organisations. And there is no obvious reason why those who happen to work in Government departments, nationalised industries or private industry should set a lower value on amenity than anyone else.

In practice, however, the scope for personal judgement is often restricted. There are always some individuals, of course, who identify so completely with an organisation and its interests that private values become irrelevant. Whatever appears to be right for the organisation is right for them. But even those of a more independent turn of mind do not have much room for manœuvre. Every role has its own requirements, binding on anyone who occupies a particular position. As an experienced observer of organisations at work points out, 'the individuals concerned are acting as governors, directors, controllers of some institution and their decisions are approved or criticised for their effect on the regulation of the institution they control, rather than for their effect on the personal fortunes of those who take them'.[1] In other words, institutional imperatives set limits on what a man in a job will feel free to do. The pressures and constraints will be the same, whoever the individual and whatever his personal views.

Moreover, in any area of activity where interests and values are very much bound up together, a subtle process of self-justification almost always reinforces the initial predisposition to do what is best for ourselves. It can hardly be denied that, to some extent at least, the values we profess are rationalisations; they do not always impress others, but they often serve to sustain or enhance our own self-respect. Naturally, in an argument we all claim that what suits us best is also right in terms of more disinterested and high-minded standards. Not only do we claim it, usually we also believe it.[2] Their objectives and interests being what they are, it is hardly surprising that developers adopt a scale of values rather different from that of other sections of the community intensely preoccupied with the problems of preserving amenity. If the difference in cost to the developer between sites A and B is £x, it is not long before he honestly and genuinely comes to believe that the loss of amenity entailed in choosing A really is not worth £x, the additional expense that would be incurred in avoiding it by going to B instead.

There is one further consideration that may also subconsciously influence the developer's outlook. In the nature of things, he knows that he will get little credit for passing over projects that

[1] Sir Geoffrey Vickers, *The Art of Judgment: A Study of Policy Making* (London: Chapman & Hall, 1965), p. 17. It is because individuals behave in ways that can very often be predicted once we understand the interests and objectives of the organisations they serve that it makes sense to use the conventional shorthand, and talk of a country, or an institution, 'deciding' this or that. We need to examine personal idiosyncrasies and backgrounds only when decisions are patently at variance with what might have been expected of those who make them. See, for example, James N. Rosenau, 'The Premises and Promises of Decision-Making Analysis', in James C. Charlesworth (ed.), *Contemporary Political Analysis* (New York: The Free Press; London: Collier-Macmillan, 1967).

[2] This is, of course, a well-worn academic theme, familiar to all social scientists. For examples of recent discussion, see Robert A. Dahl, *Modern Political Analysis* (Englewood Cliffs, N.J.: Prentice-Hall, 1963), pp. 107 ff.; and William E. Connolly, *Political Science and Ideology* (New York: Atherton Press, 1967), *passim*.

might suit him very well, but which would inflict a good deal of damage on amenity or the natural environment. Indeed, if he makes such a decision voluntarily, quite often nobody outside the organisation even knows that he has done so. On the other hand, as he very well knows, everybody feels the impact of increased taxation or the higher prices that may have to be charged as a result of such good deeds. And anything that takes more money out of the pockets of the public is as likely to be put down to profiteering, inefficiency, or a perverse political philosophy as to civic virtue.

When we turn to those whose interests and amenities are threatened by new physical projects, it is clear that they too must pause for reflection before involving themselves in an open fight. Like the developers, potential objectors do not relish the prospect of spending their time, money and energy on public inquiries or Private Bill proceedings.

In terms of personal sacrifice, local residents and unofficial amenity societies face the most serious problems. Whatever money they spend, they must raise by their own efforts, and any time they devote to fighting a case is their own time. On the other hand, the knowledge that they have most to lose, should the project be approved, may help to strengthen their resolve; if students of animal behaviour are to be believed, there is nothing like a threat to personal territory for generating fresh reserves of energy and determination. They can also afford to be more single-minded than others contemplating whether or not to start or join a resistance movement. Members of a local amenity society usually have only one object, and that is to keep the development away from their own doorsteps. They need have no inhibitions about suggesting or supporting alternative routes or sites, because from their point of view anywhere else is preferable, provided it is outside their own bailiwick.

National organisations, whether they are statutory bodies like the Countryside Commission or voluntary societies like the C.P.R.E., are frequently in a more difficult position. True, their full-time officials do not pay the costs of expensive public inquiries out of their own pocket; and fighting undesirable developments is part of their job. But organisations of this kind must pick their battles carefully. They certainly cannot afford to oppose indiscriminately everything they dislike, because a reputation for automatic and irresponsible opposition will serve only to reduce their chances of success when the really crucial case comes along.[1] Moreover, there is always the disquieting possibility that if a project is turned down, partly as a consequence of their efforts, the developer may turn his attention to some other spot, even more objectionable from their point of view.[2]

Local authorities are in a different position again. They, of course, have public funds at their disposal, and if they feel that a development really ought to be opposed there is no difficulty about raising the money. Responsible as they are for planning and that alone, planning officers are not likely to be subject to conflicting pressures and agonising political dilemmas. But planning *committees* are another matter, for they consist of aldermen and councillors, members of elected bodies with responsibilities that go wider than the preservation of amenity. When a new development is proposed it may at once be obvious that some local ratepayers will stand to gain a good deal without being adversely affected in the slightest. Even some of those whose amenities patently will be impaired may feel that their losses in this respect are likely to be more than offset in other directions. Development often brings or safeguards employment, and in an area where jobs are scarce, where there is anxiety about the future, or where there are vivid recollections of the depression, local politicians may have to think twice before opposing industrialisation in the interests of natural beauty, or in order to preserve those invisible and intangible qualities associated with a satisfactory environment, and taken for granted until they are damaged or destroyed. It is true that where a planning authority

[1] Describing the attitude of the C.P.R.E., one observer has written: 'In this country it is not a realistic policy to oppose all objectionable developments, and the Council appears to be, above all else, a realistic body. It may be untrammelled by statutory obligations, but it appreciates that a national group that has to persuade Ministers and others of the strength of its case must know when to fight and when not to, and it has no desire to give hostages to its enemies and allow the latter to represent it as reactionary and irresponsible. Some development, industrial and otherwise, in rural areas is unavoidable. The Council knows this, and it goes into action only when success appears reasonably possible or when the proposal seems so monstrous that the Council feels it cannot but protest and campaign'. Bracey, *Industry and the Countryside*, pp. 190–1.

[2] See, for example, the turn of events described in Chapter 3.

covers a large area, the local council will sometimes disapprove only of the particular spot or route chosen. They may be quite prepared to see the project located somewhere else within their boundaries. However, where the developer has a measure of freedom to please himself, there can be no guarantee that if his application is rejected, he will come back with an alternative proposal, more costly to himself, but less obnoxious to the local authority. He may prefer to take his scheme to some other part of the country, or even abandon it altogether.[1]

These are important constraints. But just as the logic of his situation almost inevitably leads the developer to select the cheapest and most convenient scheme among the reasonable possibilities (even in face of certain opposition), so there are powerful forces of self-interest at work driving potential opponents to press their hostility to the point of a formal objection and an open fight. Confronted with a proposal that will obviously inflict a great deal of damage on the local environment, they must first ask themselves whether there is any other way in which the developer's requirements could be met. Is there any feasible alternative which would spare the amenities that are in danger, or at least do considerably less harm? Sometimes there is not. In this event, if the developer is providing or producing something generally considered essential, there is little point in fighting what would obviously be a lost cause. Very often, however, there are alternatives. Almost invariably, they will be more costly; probably the developer has already rejected them for this very reason.

It is now that the familiar symmetry of these conflicts of interest begins to appear. Just as the developer has a natural incentive to minimise his private costs (whatever the consequences in terms of social costs), so his opponents have every reason to try to translate social costs that fall chiefly upon themselves into private costs for the developer. Reverting to our hypothetical sites A and B, they can cheerfully urge the merits of B (which is more expensive but less damaging to amenity), secure in the knowledge that the difference in cost will be met not by themselves, but by the developer, or rather by those who eventually pay the difference through increased taxation or higher prices.[2] The objectors, like

[1] For a Local Planning Authority faced with this dilemma in a particularly acute form, see the case described in Chapter 3.

[2] More rarely, when higher money costs cannot be passed on to the

the developer, are bound to be concerned not so much with the total cost to the community as with that part of it which falls upon themselves; in other words, with the part that takes the form of their lost amenities. And once again there is the same natural tendency to justify self-regard by reference to apparently more disinterested standards and values. If the difference in cost (to the developer) between sites A and B is established to be £x, it will not be long before the objectors are honestly convinced in their own minds that it would be nothing short of a national scandal if, for the sake of a mere £x, the Minister or Parliament were to permit the wanton destruction of amenity that would be entailed by the choice of site A when B is a perfectly feasible alternative.

The symmetrical character of these conflicts is now reflected in the pattern of advocacy that constantly recurs in cases of this kind. Whether they see it in this light or not, both sides, it should be remembered, are bent upon showing that the total cost to the community of what they are proposing is less than that of the scheme or schemes advocated by their opponents. The appropriate strategy, therefore, is to argue that the other side is underestimating the costs of its own proposals, and exaggerating the cost of any alternatives it is resisting.

For their part, the developers begin by explaining why their project is necessary, and why they have selected the particular site, route or method of development that is the subject of dispute. Partly in order to forestall their opponents, they will also describe the alternatives that were examined but rejected, emphasising the advantages of their own proposals, and drawing attention to the drawbacks of these other possibilities. Usually, they will have no difficulty in demonstrating that in money terms their scheme is indeed cheaper than any other, though by how much will often become an important part of the dispute. Of course, if the developers do fail at this first hurdle, their chances of success are likely to be very much diminished; for then, in order to establish that on balance their plan ought to be preferred, the objectors

---

consumer, they may be borne by the shareholders in a commercial company. This is a situation that could have occurred in the case described in Chapter 5; but the circumstances were unusual in that the developer concerned had already contracted to sell his product at a fixed price to a monopoly buyer.

have only to show that it will inflict less damage on the environment, generally a simple enough task because it is for just this
reason that they have put it forward.[1] Often, the developers will
concede that there are indeed valid amenity objections to what
they are proposing; but, they will suggest, the prospective loss of
amenity is not really as serious as it being made out. And since
hardly any scheme will be entirely free from some degree of
objection on amenity grounds, the odds are that the objectors'
alternative proposal will also have something to be said against it
on this score, besides being more expensive. Finally, the developers
will claim that even though their scheme may damage amenity
in the locality affected, this damage is not so great that they ought
to be put to all the expense of avoiding it, especially if (as is
likely) the alternative being pressed upon them is itself open to
criticism on account of its effect on amenity or the local environment.

On the other side, the objectors will draw attention to the
exceptional value of the amenity they are defending, at the same
time emphasising the extent of the damage that the proposed
development would inflict upon it. They will point out that if the
developers were prepared to pay more attention to amenity, and
spend a little more on preserving it, no insuperable obstacles would
prevent them from achieving their objective in some other way,
less harmful to amenity. Usually, the objectors will specify the
alternatives that they have in mind. They will often concede that
the alternatives suggested by themselves are indeed more expensive; but, they will claim, the additional costs are nothing like so
great as is being made out by the developers, who are taking
altogether too rosy a view of their own scheme and deliberately
exaggerating the difficulties associated with the objectors' counter-
proposals. Even allowing that their alternative may be somewhat
more expensive, and may itself inflict a measure of damage on
the environment, so important is the amenity endangered by the
developers, they will argue, that in the public interest this extra
cost ought to be accepted.

What lies at the heart of the argument is now clear. The
objectors are in effect trying to persuade those with the power to
recommend or decide, that something which is never bought and
sold, and therefore has no market price, is worth in money terms

[1] For an example of a case that took this turn, see Chapter 2.

at least as much as the probable difference between the cost of the developer's scheme and that of the alternative proposed by themselves. This is precisely what the developers will not accept, and their object is to persuade the decision-makers that the amenity at risk simply is not worth the price required to save it.

At the end of the line, we come to the Inspectors, civil servants and Ministers. How do they see these conflicts of interest and value, and what do they take into account when it falls to them to decide whether consent should be given or withheld for a project of the kind we have been discussing? What follows must be in part conjectural, for no one on the outside can ever be certain of exactly what happens inside a Government department, or, for that matter, in the privacy of someone else's mind. It is true that Ministers are under a statutory obligation to give reasons for their decisions, and they must say what they have and have not taken into consideration. But 'reasons' as they appear in a decision-letter may not always tell the full story, not because anything is being concealed or falsified, but simply because there are limits to what such a document can be expected to discuss and explain. In many of the more difficult cases, there are good arguments for approving a planning application, and there are equally good arguments for rejecting it. Either decision could be justified on the facts, though only one will be.

In these circumstances, what it is that makes a man plump for one choice rather than another is perhaps a question for psychologists rather than students of government. To say that in the last resort it may be no more than 'intuition' is not to suggest that there is anything untoward or irrational about this final step; however thorough the preliminary analysis, logic and reason alone can never settle the issue for *ex hypothesi* neither decision is more logical than the other. The result is that whilst the reasons given for a decision do indeed set out the case for that particular verdict, at a deeper level they do not necessarily explain *why* it was reached. If a Minister rejects a planning proposal because he thinks the damage it will inflict on amenity, or the strength of local feeling, outweigh any economic advantages it may have, his decision-letter will tell us that these were indeed among the factors which he took into account. It will not tell us why he gave them as much weight as he did. That is something he may not always be able to explain even to himself.

If these reservations are kept in mind, Inspectors' reports and Ministers' decision-letters do provide a certain amount of information about the standard drill in important planning disputes. Assuming that the developer can establish the need for his project (not usually a difficult test for him to pass, because major capital investments are not proposed without good reason), it is the objectors and their case that now comes under scrutiny. If there is little or no substance in their claims, the development can be allowed to proceed without much soul-searching on the part of those responsible for the decision. However, where the objectors have pressed their opposition to the point of a public inquiry or a petition against a Private Bill, it is hardly likely that there will be nothing at all in their fears and criticisms. In that event, the decision-makers must next ask themselves if the developer's requirements can be met in some other way that is less objectionable to their opponents. If not, that is the end of the matter. But, as we have seen, there usually are alternatives, acknowledged as such by the developer and strongly urged by the objectors. At this point, the final and crucial judgement has to be made. Accepting that the project has to go ahead in some form or another, and knowing what they do about the probable merits and demerits of the alternatives, those who recommend and decide have now to ask themselves whether it is in the public interest to approve or reject the particular application before them. The public interest is, of course, an elusive concept. In this situation, what are the relevant criteria?

What they ought to be is clear enough. Whether or not planning decisions are in fact based on the kind of analysis that follows is another matter. Official descriptions of the decision-making process are certainly couched in a language quite different from the terminology used in the next few pages, though of course it does not necessarily follow that something akin to the approach outlined here is not in practice adopted by Ministers and their officials. In our context, where the point of departure is the need to provide a specified benefit, the public interest plainly requires that this given objective should be achieved at the least possible cost to the community's resources. As we have seen, both the developers and their opponents are inevitably preoccupied with minimising the costs that fall upon themselves, whether in terms of money or loss of amenity. The Government and the legislature, however, have wider responsibilities; it is their business to take into account all the costs involved, private and social, quantifiable and unquantifiable, and to withhold consent for a development if it appears to them that a less costly alternative is available that would fulfil the same purpose equally well. As politicians, of course, Ministers and M.P.s may legitimately have their own views as to *how* the costs of development ought to be distributed, and this is a complication to which we will shortly return. But leaving the problems of allocation aside for the time being, there are clearly formidable difficulties involved in assessing and comparing the total cost to society of major physical projects.

It is true that in recent years the wider application of cost-benefit analyses has reduced the scope for sheer guesswork and unsubstantiated assertion. The object of these complex exercises is to supplement the usual methods of commercial accounting, so as to ensure that when important investment decisions are made it is not merely the costs and benefits incurred by or accruing to the organisation sponsoring the project that are taken into account. Put simply, the technique is first to identify and enumerate all the physical consequences of a proposed scheme; then to quantify the consequences in the appropriate units of measurement and to express these quantities in terms of money values; and finally to aggregate all the resultant money costs and benefits.[1] When it is a question of choosing between alternative projects (as opposed to deciding whether a project is worth undertaking at all), there is clearly a strong prima facie case for simply selecting whichever possibility maximises the margin between costs and benefits, gives the highest rate of return on capital invested, or minimises the cost of securing a given benefit. Naturally, the practicalities of the situation determine which is the most suitable basis for the choice. In the type of situation that we are concerned with, the alternative which entailed the least cost would be the obvious selection.

The advantages of a thorough cost-benefit analysis need no

[1] For the techniques and uses of cost-benefit analysis, see for example Martin S. Feldstein, 'Cost-benefit Analysis and the Public Sector', *Public Administration*, XLII (winter 1964); A. R. Prest and R. Turvey, 'Cost-Benefit Analysis: A Survey', *Economic Journal*, LXXV 300 (Dec 1965); and Nathaniel Lichfield, 'The Evaluation of Capital Investment Projects in Town Centre Redevelopment', *Public Administration*, XLV (summer 1967).

emphasis. As enthusiasts for this approach rightly point out, only
if all the 'spillover' effects (or, as the jargon has it, 'external
economies and diseconomies') of competing proposals are carefully enumerated and evaluated can we hope to be sure that
scarce resources are put to the most efficient use. And since
amenity is a resource like any other, ideally a money figure for
losses or gains under this heading ought to be included in the
analysis along with all the other costs and benefits. Unfortunately,
it is at just this point that the difficulties become most acute, for
not surprisingly cost-benefit studies are least convincing when
they purport to quantify and evaluate 'intangible' or 'non-
material' items in the analysis. True, there are some intangibles,
such as loss of human life or intensification of noise levels, that
can be measured in homogeneous or standard units. Everything
else in the analysis being equal, if it were established that one
scheme or project would save more lives or cause less noise than
others, the choice among them would be simple enough. But
whilst there are some intangibles that can be quantified and
therefore 'ranked' in order of desirability or offensiveness, there
as yet exists no universally accepted technique for taking the next
step and converting these quantities into monetary values. And
to make matters more difficult, other important intangibles, such
as natural beauty or scientific interest, are neither readily quantifiable nor reducible to cash values.[1]

---

[1] For practical purposes, it is often necessary to establish simple scales of
value for some of these intangibles; these scales are based upon the subjective judgements of those considered best qualified to assess the relative
importance of the amenity in question. Qualitative ranking of this kind
occurs, for example, when particular parts of the countryside are designated as National Parks, Areas of Outstanding Natural Beauty, Areas of
Great Landscape Value, Nature Reserves and Sites of Specific Scientific
Interest. It is also true that a good deal of ingenuity has gone into efforts
to quantify and 'price' some of the more intractable items that frequently
come into the reckoning. For a suggested technique for appraising and
ranking landscape values, see J. D. Fines, 'Landscape Evaluation: A Research Project in East Sussex', *Regional Studies*, II 1 (Sep 1968); and for a
critical reaction, D. M. Brancher, 'Critique of J. D. Fines', in *Regional
Studies*, III 1 (Apr 1969). The problems involved in assessing the value of
human life are discussed in J. E. Hayzelden, 'The Value of Human Life',
Public Administration, XLVI (winter 1968). And for an attempt both to
quantify and put a money value on wild life, see D. R. Helliwell, 'Valua-
tion of Wildlife Resources', *Regional Studies*, III 1 (Apr 1969).

Among cost-benefit practitioners there are evidently differences of opinion as to the wisdom of attempting to measure and evaluate intangibles like amenity. Some take the view that in this area there is little to be gained from trying to incorporate numerical data in the arithmetic of the analysis; as they see it, the most sensible course is simply to itemise and describe probable consequences that cannot be readily quantified or priced, leaving it to the judgement of those who make the decisions to attribute to them whatever weight they think appropriate. On the other hand, there are others who reject this attitude as altogether too defeatist; they insist that the area of subjective evaluation can and should be much further reduced, and argue that reasonably realistic 'shadow prices' can be derived for intangibles from careful surveys and calculations of the prices that people are in fact paying in order to avoid the loss or enjoy the benefit of various kinds of amenity.[1]

Doubtless this debate will become increasingly important. But the fact remains that in the circles responsible for making decisions which commonly involve intangibles, there is still a good deal of scepticism about the reliability of any techniques so far devised for imputing monetary measures to amenity values. And rightly or wrongly, it is widely felt that the methods currently on offer do not as yet produce conclusions robust enough to be wholly trustworthy. Comprehensive cost-benefit analyses are also expensive and time-consuming. In the immediate future it is hard to see

[1] For the former approach, see for example Feldstein, 'Cost-benefit Analysis': 'We may try to find shadow prices by asking what people would be prepared to pay for these benefits. Often it is better not to use such obviously weak evaluations but rather to admit the incommensurable nature of the benefits and discuss the benefits and costs of alternative projects in terms not only of money but of these other physical effects.' By contrast, the research team employed by the Roskill Commission on the Third London Airport maintain that 'this method of approach merely substitutes implicit for explicit evaluation', and comment that judgement cannot act *in vacuo*, 'unless it is to be debased into at best mere intuition or at worst mere prejudice'. So far as intangibles are concerned, they subscribe to the view that a reasonably accurate guide to the value of amenity is provided by changes in the freehold value of property. Where this yardstick is not applicable, they argue that the aesthetic, cultural and recreational value of land is reflected in the costs that people are willing to incur in order to take advantage of these benefits. See Commission on the Third London Airport, *Papers and Proceedings*, vol. VII (June 1969).

Governments, developers, or their opponents commissioning them at the drop of a hat. Of course, it would always be open to the Government to require developers to support their applications with the results of such analyses. That day may come. But for some years at least, the chances are that all but a handful of the most important and controversial decisions will continue to be made in the same way as those described in the following chapters.

In a rough and ready fashion the familiar public inquiry and Private Bill procedure does partially reproduce some of the features of a cost-benefit analysis. On the one side, the developers will produce the straightforward commercial costings, both for the project under application, and (more sketchily) for the alternatives which they have rejected. Because it suits them to do so, they will also bring out the side-effects and social costs that these rejected alternatives would entail: as we shall see almost *ad nauseam*, in the battle of arguments they quite naturally try to unearth everything that might possibly tell in favour of their own proposal and against whatever is being advanced by their opponents. And on the other side, in their efforts to establish that the social costs of what is being proposed are so substantial that planning consent ought to be refused (however great may be the strictly financial advantage), the objectors naturally do their best to bring to light every possible ramification and disadvantage that could conceivably result from the developer's scheme. In other words, in these circumstances there is no central intelligence unit methodically thinking out and listing all the possible consequences of a proposed development; rather, the enumeration of relevant considerations arises out of the conflict of interests, with both sides drawing attention to all the costs and benefits in the process of playing for their own hands. The pebble is dropped into the pond, so to speak, and those with the decision to make watch the results, as opposed to working out for themselves, in advance, how far the ripples will travel.

There is also something to be said for the adversative procedure in cases of this kind, even though counsel inexperienced in planning cases do sometimes marshal their evidence as relentlessly as at important criminal trials. As we shall see, in their passionate hostility to development schemes, objectors frequently come close to arguing that a project hardly makes sense even in terms of the developer's own objectives and criteria. At first sight, it might seem a hopelessly over-ambitious strategy for local authorities, amenity societies and individuals to challenge industrialists and statutory undertakers on their own ground, because what they appear to be suggesting is that the developers and their experts do not really know their own business. But in fact, the objectors' approach is not so absurd as it looks. It is true that they will rarely succeed in totally demolishing a developer's case. That would be too much to expect. On the other hand, at the end of the day and as a result of their efforts, a case may well look a great deal less impressive than at the beginning of the controversy. The reasons are not far to seek.

To begin with, there may be divisions of opinion among the acknowledged experts. The developer does not always have a monopoly of the relevant expertise; and in fields where there is no universally accepted wisdom, the objectors may be able to find reputable specialists of their own, ready and willing to challenge the judgement of fellow professionals. Engineers and economists in particular seem to be prepared to take issue with each other, and in public if need be.

In the second place, the developer's case may be tenable, but by no means as completely watertight and invulnerable as he would like it to appear. Capital projects frequently have long gestation periods, and a decision that might have been impeccably sound when it was taken may be a good deal more questionable a year or two later when it has to be defended under challenge. As most observers with experience of decision-making within large organisations agree, there is always a reluctance to change direction after a course has been set. Once taken, a decision tends to acquire a momentum of its own, an inertia that rolls it forward even though circumstances may change or new information come to light. Secondary decisions may be based upon the first, and beyond a certain point, when enough people are committed to a particular line of action, there is a tendency to treat fresh evidence selectively, emphasising what supports the conclusions already reached and playing down the significance of what does not. It is not so much a question of wilful blindness; it stems more from a natural aversion to the prospect of going back to the beginning, reopening old arguments, and undergoing the intellectual anguish of thinking out complex problems all over again, possibly under the pressure of a rapidly approaching deadline. Because the forces of inertia are so powerful, and because there is this disposition to push aside unpalatable facts and arguments, there are obvious advantages in a process that subjects costly investment projects to the critical, and indeed hostile, scrutiny of antagonists with a vital interest in detecting and enlarging upon anything that could possibly be represented as a flaw or weakness in the developer's calculus.

What is more, at least one group of warriors involved in these planning battles is only too familiar with the contrast between the confident face that an organisation turns to the outside world and the interior uncertainties, doubts and disagreements that are never betrayed. Over the years, eminent members of the planning bar regularly appear both for developers and objectors. Confronted with what is at first sight an unshakeable case, counsel may well recall occasions in the past when in their own skilful hands a passable, but by no means irrefutable, set of arguments was totally transformed, emerging as an apparently unchallengeable and unbreakable chain of reasoning.

There is no need to labour the point, for it amounts to simply this: arguments get full justice only when they are advanced by individuals who, as John Stuart Mill puts it, 'actually believe in them, who defend them in earnest, and do their very best for them'. Equally, a case that survives a determined assault from opponents dedicated to destroying it is likely to carry more conviction and command the more confidence as a result.

At the same time, it must be said that public inquiry and Private Bill procedures are not without their weaknesses. It is true that as well as making its own case, each side can and does challenge the policies and decisions of the other. But cross-examination by counsel is no substitute for an independent examination of the technical and financial data produced by interested parties. This is a problem that objectors find especially exasperating. There are cynics who go so far as to suggest that once the developer is committed to a particular scheme, the calculations upon which the original decision was based tend to fade into the background. Doubtless, they say, scheme A was originally selected in preference to scheme B because the sums genuinely did come out that way. But, the theory goes, from that point onwards the developer becomes an advocate, intent upon winning his case. In their more embittered moments the cynics will even suggest that the developer's tactics at this stage are to fabricate whatever figures he believes will best serve his purpose.

Allegations of deliberate falsification may be only the products of an over-excited imagination. Calculated dishonesty is not a widespread feature of British public life. But it should not be forgotten that by the time the battle is joined, both sides are probably convinced that they are on the side of the angels. Estimates and projections are always subject to some margin of error, and most decisions *could* be followed by a whole range of possible consequences. Knowing this, objectors often suspect (and allege) that the developer's evidence is systematically biased in favour of his own scheme, and systematically loaded against anything he dislikes. Whatever the truth of the matter, it would be hardly surprising if, consciously or not, men who believe they are in the right were to resolve doubts in a way that seems most likely to improve their own chances of success in face of what they must sometimes regard as misguided or even perverse opposition. The inquiry procedure may serve to bring to light and enumerate most of the considerations that ought to be taken into account in reaching a decision. It also provides an excellent opportunity for each side to test the quality of the other's arguments. But it is not necessarily the most effective method of establishing an objective and authoritative balance-sheet for the relevant statistical data.

The conventional inquiry procedure is open to another important criticism. Almost invariably, the developer brings forward only one scheme, the scheme that suits him best. It then becomes the business of the inquiry to examine the case for that proposal and the objections to it. But if we assume that the project in question is one of those developments that everyone agrees must eventually go ahead in one form or another – a motorway, a transmission line or a reservoir for example – the object of public policy should surely be to select from among the various alternatives the best method of meeting the community's needs. The ordinary public inquiry is hardly a suitable instrument for this purpose. In the first place, even though other possibilities may be discussed at the inquiry, no one can be sure that they really are the most promising alternatives, because they are usually proposed by objectors without direct access to the necessary technical data. And in the second place, when the object of the exercise is to choose, it hardly makes sense to scrutinise one scheme in isolation. Suppose it is established at the inquiry that there are indeed serious objections to the developer's site or route. On their own, these objections can scarcely provide good enough grounds for rejecting it, because the alternatives may be even more objectionable. Whether or not they are, nobody knows. The point is that unless there has been a reasonably thorough review of all the candidates on the short-list before the final choice is made, a proper comparison is obviously impossible, for the advantages and disadvantages of the alternatives are discussed only obliquely and to the extent that it suits the developer and those engaged in resisting the particular scheme that he is proposing.

Take, for example, a hypothetical situation, in which the developer makes application for a particular site A, having rejected alternatives B and C. We may be quite sure that those who object to A will make it their business to inform the Inspector, and through him the Minister, about any characteristics of B and C which, in their view, make them better sites for the project than A. And, for his part, because he is anxious to secure consent for A, the developer will seek out and put on display everything he can that tells against B and C. But however assiduous the developer may be in gathering incidental information of this kind, it is hardly likely that the full weight of argument against B and C will emerge at a public inquiry into the merits and demerits of A. The reason for this, of course, is that unless they are exceptionally alert or ingenious (in which case they may contrive to be present and make representations in favour of A), the really dedicated opponents of B and C will have no opportunity of voicing their objections at this stage.[1] Consequently, it may be only if and when site A has been rejected that the Minister will be made aware of the full extent of the objections to B, if that is the site which the developer decides is the second best for his purpose.[2] But whatever now comes to light about B, the odds must be very much in favour of approval, and

---

[1] For an example of an interested party appearing in support of a project (when their object was to resist a probable alternative), see the role played by the local branch of the National Farmers' Union in the case described in Chapter 4.

[2] See, for example, the case described in Chapter 3.

not entirely for reasons directly connected with good planning. The only alternatives to granting consent for B are yet another inquiry, this time into site C (which may then prove even more objectionable than A and B), or approving a resubmitted application for A. The reactions of those who have spent their time and money on successfully opposing site A hardly bear thinking about.[1]

In future, and in a limited number of cases, these difficulties will doubtless be overcome by recourse to the Planning Inquiry Commissions provided for in the 1968 Town and Country Planning Act.[2] Although the adversative approach will not be entirely

[1] One method of overcoming this difficulty is for the Minister to insist that the developers should submit details of alternative sites, so that he can examine these other possibilities – and the objections to them – before reaching a decision on the original application. The obvious danger is that a developer may not put himself out to make the best case for what are bound to be his second, third and fourth choices. Of course, if he fails to make a good case for any of the alternatives, and the Minister refuses to approve the original proposal, he does run the risk of winding up with nothing at all. But this possibility would not arise if the project was generally acknowledged to be of vital importance, for then the developer could safely gamble on one or other of the alternatives being approved. In the spring of 1968 the Ministry of Housing and Local Government adopted this approach in relation to an application from the C.E.G.B. for an electricity sub-station at Mop End, near Amersham in the Buckinghamshire Chilterns. See *The Times*, 1 July 1968. And for a variant on this method, see the case described in Chapter 5, where an inquiry was re-opened to examine alternative sites suggested by the Inspector.

[2] See Town and Country Planning Act, 1968, Sections 61–63. Speaking on the Second Reading of the Bill, the Minister of Housing and Local Government explained that Planning Inquiry Commissions, consisting of between three and five members, would deal with 'cases that raise wide or novel issues of more than local significance'. Like the Roskill Commission on the Third London Airport, they will be empowered to employ research staff. In addition, their procedures and terms of reference are designed to allow them to investigate development proposals in depth, as well as providing the opportunity for interested parties to make representations at local inquiries. Of particular importance are the provisions making it possible for Commissions to examine alternative schemes, either at the instigation of Ministers, or on their own initiative, or at the request of the developer. See *H.C. Deb.* (1967–8) 757, col.1371. At the time of writing, more than a year after the Act came into force, no Planning Inquiry Commissions have been set up. Nor would it be appropriate to employ such elaborate and expensive procedures in any but the most important or difficult cases. For a sophisticated apologia for methods of decision-making

dispensed with, a Planning Inquiry Commission, furnished with
the results of a comprehensive cost-benefit analysis covering
several alternative proposals, will formulate its recommendations
at the end of a process clearly very different from that followed
by an Inspector conducting an inquiry into one scheme, and
basing his judgement chiefly on the representations made by
embattled opponents. How often Planning Inquiry Commissions
will be used remains to be seen. But it seems probable that over
the next decade at least, for every case settled by means of this
elaborate new machinery, many more will continue to be decided
by the procedures illustrated in the following chapters.

As we have seen, the more ambitious cost-benefit analysts
attempt to impute a monetary value to intangibles like amenity
in the process of identifying and evaluating all the consequences
and ramifications of an investment proposal. In other words, the
social costs attributable to loss of amenity are incorporated into
the calculations along with all the other numerical data. What
happens in the absence of a cost-benefit analysis (in other words,
almost always), is quite different. Although there may be a certain
amount of disagreement about the figures for costs that are, in
principle, readily quantifiable in money terms, by the close of the
proceedings the Inspector usually has a fairly clear idea of the
magnitudes involved. But neither the developers nor the objectors
will offer anything remotely resembling an objective or precisely
quantified assessment of the amenity values in question. They
will simply assert that these values are, or are not worth the price
of saving them. Consequently, it is left to the Inspectors, and after
them the Ministers, to put their own subjective values on amenity
by way of a judgement. The form that this judgement takes in
the eyes of the parties to a dispute has already been discussed. All
that we need do now is to restate the problem as it looks to those
responsible for the recommendation or final decision.

To take the simplest case, after a good deal of haggling it will
be established and agreed that the developer's scheme is less
costly than any of the possible alternatives. Unfortunately, this
scheme will often be highly objectionable on amenity grounds.
Even without a full investigation, it may be clear that the alter-

that may at first sight appear unsatisfactory, see David Braybrooke and
Charles E. Lindblom, *A Strategy of Decision: Policy Evaluation as a Social
Process* (New York: Free Press of Glencoe, 1963).

natives themselves are not entirely free from amenity objections. But typically, the judgement becomes a matter of deciding whether an intangible amenity, with no determinable money value, is worth a specific price. That price is the difference between the cost of the project under application and that of the possibility generally regarded as the most likely alternative.

Put like this, it might at first sight seem odd that we should leave it to politicians and civil servants to make such decisions. Ministers and their advisers do not go along to size up rare masterpieces as they occasionally appear on the art market and personally decide what price the nation should bid. The difference is, of course, that when Ministers settle amenity disputes they do far more than merely reveal their standards of aesthetic appreciation. They are also taking political decisions. Because 'politics' immediately suggests improper party political influence or bias, planning officials go out of their way to emphasise that politics has no place in their world. At a superficial level this may be true. But if we think of the political process as being essentially concerned with the allocation of values – and costs – in a society, it is clear that planning decisions often have implications that are indeed political, whatever the intentions and mental approach of those involved. This is why it is altogether appropriate that responsible Ministers should make them.

There are always at least three distinct aspects to a major planning decision. In the first place, there is the straightforward determination of the application. Approval is either given or withheld, and after a while the project either physically materialises at a particular spot on the face of the earth or it does not. On the face of things, this is what the dispute is all about, and there is not much politics here.

But secondly, when Ministers and Parliament make judgements of the kind that we are concerned with, they are in effect making decisions about the uses to which the community's resources shall be put. Whenever a scheme is rejected, and the developer obliged to spend more on some alternative project less objectionable on amenity grounds, the result is to channel resources that would have been used for some other purpose into the conservation of amenity instead. To be sure, the power of the Government and Parliament is limited: for the most part they can say yea or nay only to schemes that developers choose to bring forward. But the cumulative effect of these verdicts may be considerable, and the decisions themselves will influence the future thinking of developers pondering upon what will or will not prove acceptable in the eyes of Ministers and Members of Parliament.

It is because the effect of planning decisions is to regulate the allocation of resources between competing uses – and in an area where there are deep feelings as to what is right and wrong – that the element of political judgement may well remain paramount, however comprehensive and ingenious cost-benefit studies become. In time, these analyses will doubtless succeed in establishing beyond reasonable doubt what value the community does in fact place upon intangibles for which there is no market. With rather less certainty, they may also contrive to estimate what value people are likely to set on such benefits in the future. Certainly, findings of this kind will be of great interest, particularly to those whose views happen to coincide with popular evaluations. But does it necessarily follow that political leaders ought to make it their business to see that the community spends precisely as much on something like amenity as would be spent if there were a market for it? No doubt we could discover how much would be spent on education, health, roads, or subsidised arts if the State did not interfere. But we do not, because no one seriously believes that important spending decisions ought to be based exclusively on market research findings. It is of course true that all political decisions are influenced by what politicians sense that the electorate wants or will tolerate. But this is not to say that political leaders ought in principle to surrender or subordinate their own values and priorities whenever they appear to be at variance with popular wishes or demands. To say the least, it is certainly arguable that if Ministers believe that more (or, for that matter, less) ought to be spent on amenity and conservation than the public appears willing to contribute of its own volition, they have the right and the duty to decide for themselves where the public interest lies. A Government, after all, is supposed to be something more than Adam Smith's 'invisible hand'.

And thirdly, planning decisions are political in that they allocate not only resources but also costs that someone has to bear. If a developer's scheme is approved, substantial social costs may fall upon the objectors; if it is rejected, the developer may be obliged to incur considerably higher money costs as a result of having to meet his requirements in some way that is more expensive to himself. In practice, the choice usually lies between inflicting a heavy penalty in terms of lost amenities or other dissatisfactions on a fairly small number of people; or imposing quite small additional charges on the very much larger number of consumers who make use of the developer's services or products. Objectors occasionally draw attention to this aspect of planning disputes; but usually both sides are content to fight the battle on other issues, knowing that the allocative decision will be made automatically and contingently when the verdict is given on the developers' planning application.[1] Nevertheless, behind many of the arguments ostensibly about planning, amenity, aesthetics and civilised values, another equally important conflict is in progress as both sides struggle to avoid a burden that must fall somewhere. For the parties to a planning dispute the rules of warfare may be more formal and ritualised than in the jungle of pressure group or party politics. And from the Minister's point of view, the process may indeed be quasi-judicial. All the same, on any view of what politics is about, discretionary decisions that serve to resolve conflicts of interest and value to the advantage of some and at the expense of others must be regarded as largely political. They are none the worse for that.

Each of the five controversies described in the following chapters has its own special features and its own particular flavour. Yet however much situations may differ in detail, the underlying configuration of interests, strategies and perspectives seems to remain much the same. Having listed and named the parts, we can now begin to see how they fit together in the complicated circumstances of actual cases in the real world.

[1] For an exceptional situation, see Chapter 6, where a probably unrepeatable combination of circumstances resulted in the dispute developing into an overt argument about the appropriate *distribution* of the money costs entailed in preserving the amenity at risk.

2 Oxfordshire Ironstone

The basic duty of the Board is to exercise a general
supervision over the iron and steel industry . . . with
a view to promoting the efficient, economic and
adequate supply under competitive conditions of iron
and steel products, including iron ore. The natural
beauty of an area of contemplated development is
hardly a factor which the Board can properly take into
account, since it does not fall within the criteria laid
down by Parliament.

The Iron and Steel Board, letter to the
Oxfordshire County Council, March 1960

SOUTH OF Banbury the Cotswolds run down into the softer,
rolling countryside of north Oxfordshire. This is an area of dignified manor houses, set in their parks, substantial farms and
picture-book villages. There is East and West Adderbury, Barford St Michael and Barford St John, Swerford, Hook Norton,
Nether Worton and Over Worton, Sandford St Martin, Little
Tew and Great Tew. With their thatched, seventeenth-century
cottages, some of these villages have in fact become celebrated
tourist attractions. It is not dramatic or spectacular countryside.
But the wooded hills, the sunken country lanes, the unexpected
farmhouse or cottage among the trees, and the characteristic
reddish soil of a field under plough, form a landscape of variety
and mellow colour. There is a certain homely and tranquil
beauty about north Oxfordshire.

Roots go deep in this part of England. There are families here
who have farmed this land for generations; others, more recent
arrivals, settled in the district because they liked what they saw.
Newcomers or old, most of them are deeply attached to the
countryside. In counties like Oxfordshire there are also men of
substance and standing, large landowners and independent

farmers, determined individuals prepared to give their time and energy in defence of what they value.

A few feet beneath the folded ridges and meadows lie thick bands of ironstone, an essential raw material for the production of iron and steel. On and off, ironstone has been worked in various parts of Oxfordshire for centuries. One of the prominent ridges near Great Tew is actually named 'Iron Down'. Fifty years ago, a few men working in a quarry might have been regarded as part of the rustic scene; but modern open-cast mining on a large scale can hardly fail to change a peaceful rural environment. Trees must be felled and hedges uprooted; mechanical grabs remove the topsoil; explosives are used to loosen the ironstone; and new roads have to be built for trucks to carry the ore to the railways. It is true that once the ironstone has been excavated, the soil is relaid. But many believe that even the most skilful and conscientious rehabilitation can never wholly restore the countryside to what it was before. As the farmers put it, the bloom goes off the land.

Much of north Oxfordshire is scheduled in the county development plan as an Area of Great Landscape Value. After the war, the County Council decided to confine quarrying to the area near Wroxton, north-west of Banbury, and it was agreed that any attempt to extend mining operations further south should be firmly resisted. In the early fifties, however, the rich, untouched reserves of Oxfordshire iron ore south of Banbury were beginning to attract the keen interest of the iron and steel industry.[1]

IRON ORE: A POLICY AND ITS CONSEQUENCES

When steel was denationalised in 1953, the Conservative Government established a new statutory body, the Iron and Steel

[1] The chief documentary sources for the following account are: Public Inquiry Report (10 Jan 1961), together with verbatim transcript of evidence and correspondence put in; Iron and Steel Board, Annual Reports, and Special Report, *Development in the Steel Industry*, H.C. 214 (1956–7); North Oxfordshire Ironstone Areas Protection Committee, Memoranda; Economist Intelligence Unit Report, *A Survey of Sources of Supply of Iron Ore to the United Kingdom* (5 May 1960); *The Times*; *Oxford Times*.

Board, to exercise general supervision over the industry. Under the Iron and Steel Act of 1953, it was the duty of the I.S.B. to promote the efficient, economic and adequate supply of iron and steel products under competitive conditions. One of the Board's responsibilities was to keep under review the industry's arrangements for procuring and distributing raw materials, including iron ore. Then, as now, iron ore was available from a good many countries, the major exporters being Canada, Sweden, France, Algeria, Tunisia, Venezuela, Brazil, French West Africa and Sierra Leone. From the outset, however, it was the policy of the I.S.B. to encourage the British steel industry to make the maximum use of home-produced ore. In the circumstances of the early and mid-fifties there was a good deal to be said for this policy.

The I.S.B.'s *Annual Reports* covering the years 1953 to 1956 include frequent reference to the difficulties and disadvantages of relying on imported iron ore. Overseas ore had to be paid for in foreign exchange; supplies might be cut off as a result of political instability in Africa; and port facilities, both in the United Kingdom and in the countries of origin, were inadequate. Even more important, competition among the principal steel-producing countries was forcing Britain to look further afield for its iron ore. To make matters worse, there was a shortage of shipping space, and with freight rates going up, the price of imported ore was rising rapidly, a trend which the Board expected to continue into the foreseeable future. According to the I.S.B.'s calculations, the result of all this was that it had become cheaper to produce steel on or near the home orefields than to manufacture it from foreign ore. Since it was their responsibility to see that steel was produced as cheaply as possible, no one at the Board had any doubt that their 'home ore policy' was the right one.

Of course, the I.S.B. were not themselves in the extraction business. But they could, and did, urge the iron ore companies in this country both to expand their existing workings and also to look about for fresh sources of supply. According to the Board's consultants, the areas with the greatest potential for increased output were Lincolnshire, Northamptonshire and Oxfordshire. And as they pointed out, Oxfordshire was an especially promising area because the ore there could be worked by means of shallow, open-cast mining. By 1957 the I.S.B. were clearly setting considerable store by Oxfordshire and the contribution it might make to meeting the future needs of the steel industry. In a Special Report[1] of that year they noted that the total United Kingdom output was expected to rise from 16 million tons a year in 1956 to about 22 million tons a year in 1962. There was a reasonable chance, they added, that surveys currently in progress in Oxfordshire would enable the industry to exceed 22 million tons a year by the latter date, or at least soon afterwards. As on many previous occasions, the Board emphasised that the fullest exploitation of the English orefields, consistent with the maintenance of adequate reserves, was essential for the economic development of the steel industry in the years ahead.

It was at about this time that an important development was afoot in the iron and steel industry. The I.S.B. and the steel companies had begun to consider the possibility of building a new strip mill. Obviously, this would be a project of major economic importance, representing a valuable prize for whichever part of the country was fortunate enough to get it. Naturally, there was a good deal of argument about the most suitable location, the chief contenders being Scotland and South Wales.[2] Among the individual companies in the running for the new plant were Richard Thomas and Baldwins, the largest steel firm remaining in public ownership after denationalisation.

What part the question of ore supplies played in discussions about the location of the strip mill must remain a matter of conjecture. No doubt there were many excellent reasons for siting at least the major part of any additional steel-making capacity in South Wales; and, of course, their experience and reputation gave R.T.B. a good claim on the proposed steelworks. At the same time, with the I.S.B. attaching so much importance to the

---

[1] *Development in the Steel Industry* (July 1957).

[2] In view of what was to happen subsequently, a leading article in *The Times* of 14 June 1957 is of some interest. It acknowledged that there was strong political support for building another steelworks in Scotland. On the other hand, South Wales had better and cheaper coal, and was rather better placed in relation to the market for sheet steel. There was general agreement, it continued, that more use should be made of home ores, so as to reduce the cost of producing steel. Voicing what it obviously thought were obvious truths, it observed that a strip mill in Scotland or South Wales would use imported ore; if the most economic use was to be made of home ore, it concluded, Northamptonshire would be the best place for the new works.

use of home ore, the problem of supplies would almost certainly
have been raised. Whether South Wales can be described as
'near' any of the big English orefields is a moot point. As far as
the I.S.B. were concerned, however, it was near enough. It may
be that the I.S.B. asked R.T.B. if they could and would undertake
to use a substantial proportion of home ore; alternatively, the
company may have volunteered to use home ore in order to
strengthen their claim on the new mill. In either event, it would
have been for R.T.B. to indicate who would supply the ore, and
from where exactly it was to come.

The site proposed by R.T.B. for the strip mill was at Newport,
Monmouthshire. If home ore was to be used at Newport the
obvious source was Oxfordshire, chiefly because it was the nearest
orefield of any size to South Wales. Moreover, Oxfordshire ore is
very easily worked. In some of the other English orefields the
ironstone is more than a hundred feet down; over much of the
Oxfordshire area it is no more than a few feet below the surface.
With only this thin overburden to remove, it would be comparatively cheap to extract. It also enjoyed an important technical
advantage. In order to gain the full benefit of a new steel-making
method proposed for the Newport works, the phosphorus content of the ore had to be below 0·35 per cent. Of all the home-
produced ores, only Oxfordshire ore met this requirement.

As it happened, Oxfordshire ore was already being worked,
on a limited scale, in the Wroxton area, north-west of Banbury.
Under the joint ownership of Stewart and Lloyds and the Guest
Keen steel interests, the Oxfordshire Ironstone Company had
begun operations here in 1917, and by the mid-fifties had worked
about 800 acres. Provided that they could be sure of a market,
there was nothing to prevent the Oxfordshire Ironstone Company
from increasing their output, for the County Council were not
unfavourably disposed towards more extensive ironstone working
in this part of the county. From the beginning, R.T.B. were
prepared to take part of their supplies from Wroxton. But neither
R.T.B. nor the I.S.B. were convinced that the Oxfordshire Ironstone Company could guarantee to meet the full requirements of
the proposed strip mill as production expanded in the sixties and
seventies. Even had R.T.B. been satisfied that all the ore needed
could be guaranteed from Wroxton, it is unlikely that they would
have been happy about relying for their supplies on a company

owned by one of their competitors: as they saw it, it was essential for them to exercise direct control over most of their home ore, so as to be able to regulate the quality of the iron required for their new steel-making technique.

Naturally enough, the I.S.B.'s known policy of encouraging the maximum use of home ore had provided a strong incentive for firms to enter the extraction business. One company that already had the necessary equipment available from their gravel and open-cast coal mining operations was the Dowsett Group. A subsidiary, the Dowsett Mineral Recovery Company, was formed, and extensive surveys were undertaken in the Oxfordshire ore-field south of Banbury. Test borings soon confirmed that substantial reserves were available.

It may be that Dowsetts had gone to Oxfordshire simply on the off-chance of finding markets for any ore that they might find. On the other hand, they may have taken an interest in Oxfordshire because they had learned that R.T.B. were looking for ironstone over and above what could be supplied from Wroxton. At all events, there seems to have been an informal understanding between R.T.B. and Dowsetts: if the new strip mill were allotted to R.T.B., most of the ore would be supplied by Dowsetts from areas to the south of Banbury. There may even have been a suggestion that in due course R.T.B. should buy up the Dowsett Mineral Recovery Company.

A PRELIMINARY SKIRMISH

The Dowsett Mineral Recovery Company submitted their first applications for planning permission in April 1957. They were for two areas, the first of 185 acres east of Adderbury, and the second extending over 973 acres to the east of Bloxham. Both were good examples of attractive, unspoiled English countryside, though by general consent neither area was of really outstanding scenic beauty. However, it was the Oxfordshire County Council's policy to resist the spread of ironstone working into this part of the county. They opposed the applications, which were then called in for decision by the Minister of Housing and Local Government.

Outside of County Hall, these applications would probably

have aroused little interest had they not attracted the attention of Major Eustace Robb, the owner of the Great Tew estate. Convinced that the Bloxham/Adderbury proposals were only the thin end of the wedge, early in June 1958 Robb invited a number of his neighbours to a meeting in Tew House. It was an important conclave, for out of it came a formidable local resistance movement in the shape of the Oxfordshire Ironstone Protection Committee. The original purpose of the Committee was simply to represent individual members of the public who opposed the applications. But as the controversy developed, some of its more active members began to play a far more important role than this description would suggest. Before long, it was decided that the Committee should co-operate with the Oxfordshire County Council in preparing the case against Dowsetts, brief counsel, assemble expert witnesses to appear at the expected public inquiry, appeal for funds, and alert and mobilise other countryside organisations, such as the National Farmers' Union, the Country Landowners' Association, Women's Institutes and parish councils.

A public inquiry into the Bloxham/Adderbury applications was held at Bodicote on 16 and 17 July 1958. By comparison with the battle to come, it was no more than a skirmish. Even so, there was an impressive array of objectors. Apart from the County Council and the Ironstone Protection Committee, they included the Chipping Norton Borough Council, the Chipping Norton R.D.C., the Banbury R.D.C., eighteen parish councils, nine Women's Institutes, a local committee of N.F.U. members, the Oxfordshire Rural Community Council, the C.P.R.E., and two local schools.

Dowsett's case was simple. It was in the national interest to expand the output of home ore. The I.S.B. had said so in their Special Report of 1957. That report had also indicated that the Board were hoping for 2·3 million tons a year from Oxfordshire by 1962, with the possibility of substantial increases after that. The Bloxham/Adderbury areas were by no means exceptionally beautiful, and if the output of Oxfordshire ore was to reach the required level, they would have to be worked sooner or later. Not surprisingly, a representative from the I.S.B. was also at the inquiry to assure the Inspector that Dowsett's applications had the full support of his Board.

For their part, the objectors argued that the Bloxham/Adderbury applications were only the first step. If Dowsetts were given planning permission here, they would soon be back with more applications in this area. Adderbury and Bloxham might not be outstandingly attractive; but some of the adjacent districts, almost certainly next on Dowsett's list, were as beautiful as any stretch of countryside in the Midlands. In any case, not even the Bloxham/Adderbury areas should be worked unless it could be conclusively demonstrated that the requisite supplies of Oxfordshire ore could not be provided from elsewhere in the county. Nothing was worse for a district than to be subjected to mining operations that proceeded by fits and starts, and unless there was the guarantee of a sustained demand for ore from these two application areas, this was exactly what would happen. Far better, the objectors maintained, to confine ironstone quarrying to the Wroxton area, where it was already in progress.

This brought them to their other main contention. As far as they could see, even allowing for a substantial increase in the I.S.B.'s basic figure of 2·3 million tons a year after 1962, the Board's target for Oxfordshire could easily be met from the Wroxton area by the Oxfordshire Ironstone Company. Since that target had been set, the Oxfordshire Ironstone Company had stated that if they were given planning permission for additional areas near their existing workings, they could produce 3 million tons a year, provided that the demand justified such an increase in output. There was unlikely to be any problem over planning permission, because the County Council had no intention of opposing applications in the Wroxton district.

Judged by the evidence that they were prepared to put before the inquiry, Dowsett's case looked decidedly fragile. On the face of things, they had no assured market for their output; or if they had, there was certainly no indication of who they expected to buy their ore. And if, as the evidence suggested, the Oxfordshire Ironstone Company could produce all the Oxfordshire ore for which there was any foreseeable demand, what possible justification could there be for allowing Dowsetts to open up new areas in the attractive countryside south of Banbury? Whatever may have been Dowsett's hopes or expectations, R.T.B. were not mentioned, even hypothetically, as possible customers. Had Dowsetts been prospecting in Oxfordshire on a purely speculative basis, their silence on these matters would have been only natural. But if, as

seems more likely, they had all along been hoping to supply
R.T.B. with iron ore for use at Newport, we can only assume that
both they and the I.S.B. felt that they could not appear to be
anticipating an official announcement from the Government
about the operators and location of the new steelworks.

Soon after the inquiry ended, and before the Minister had
reached a decision, Dowsetts submitted two further applications,
this time for a total of 2,553 acres, south of their first application
areas, in the vicinity of Hook Norton, Swerford, Great Tew and
South Newington. Now they were moving into what was undeniably very attractive countryside. The County Council, of
course, objected, and informed the Minister that in their view the
applications ought to be refused on the grounds that they would
cause 'grave and irreparable harm to the amenities of the district'.

OXFORDSHIRE: THE PENNY DROPS

On 18 November 1958 the Prime Minister, Mr Harold
Macmillan, told the House of Commons that the Government
had authorised two new strip mills. One was to be built by
Colvilles at Motherwell in Scotland; the other was to be constructed by R.T.B. at Newport, Monmouthshire. Both projects,
he said, were to be capable of considerable extension, and this
was particularly true of the Newport works.[1]

R.T.B. could now begin to plan in more detail. As yet, Dowsetts had not secured planning permission to work their application areas south of Banbury; but, rightly or wrongly, R.T.B.
decided to press ahead on the assumption that, in due course,
most of the Oxfordshire ore that they needed at Newport would
be provided by Dowsetts. Work was begun on the installation of
ore preparation plant scheduled to cost about £2 million, and
specifically designed to cope with Oxfordshire ore. British Railways were approached, and asked to make the necessary arrangements for freighting large quantities of ore from Oxfordshire to
Newport.

At this point there is one aspect of R.T.B.'s planning that we
must pause over, for later on it was to assume considerable

[1] *H.C. Deb.* (1958–9) 595, cols 1015–22.

importance. It had never been the company's intention to use
100 per cent home ore. Quite early on, for what were to be
described as 'technical and economic' reasons, R.T.B. decided
that the optimal blend of home and imported ores would be
achieved if they used them in the ratio of 40 per cent from
Oxfordshire and 60 per cent from overseas. Given that they had
to use a substantial proportion of home ore, it may well be that
on their calculations the 40:60 ratio seemed likely to give them
the cheapest and most suitable combination. But what must be
stressed is this: the *principle* of using a high proportion of Oxfordshire ore at Newport had not been dictated by a careful and
open-minded examination of relative costs. As it happened, when
the strip mill was at the planning stage, there probably was some
cost advantage in using large amounts of home ore. But it was
not because they saw the prospect of enormous savings on the cost
of raw materials that R.T.B. were proposing to take more than a
third of their ore from Oxfordshire: they had agreed to go to
Oxfordshire for their supplies in order to conform with the
I.S.B.'s policy. That policy, initiated some years earlier, was based
upon doubts about the wisdom of relying on imported ore, and
upon the general proposition that steel manufactured on or near
the home orefields was cheaper than steel produced from imported
ore. As for the I.S.B., in supporting applications for Oxfordshire
ironstone, it was enough for them that R.T.B. were acting in
accordance with the Board's policy.

Although it was now public knowledge that R.T.B. were to
build a new strip mill at Newport, nobody outside the steel
industry had, as yet, any reason to connect R.T.B. with Dowsett's
applications. But rumours led to private inquiries, and the opposition began to put two and two together. On 29 November 1958,
the Oxfordshire County Clerk referred to these rumours in a
letter to the Ministry of Housing and Local Government. 'It has
come to my notice', he wrote, 'that there may be an association
between the applicants in this case, Messrs Dowsett Mineral
Recovery Limited and Messrs Richard Thomas and Baldwins
and that it may be represented that iron ore from the Dowsett
application areas will be required for the "fourth strip mill" a
share of which has just been allotted to Messrs Richard Thomas
and Baldwins by Her Majesty's Government. Should this in fact
be so', he went on, 'it would introduce a quite new factor into

the situation and I should be glad of the Ministry's assurance
that the County Council would in that event be given the opportunity to comment before any final decision was taken by the
Minister.'

This new development evidently gave the Ministry a good deal
of food for thought. It was not until 30 April 1959, after several
months of consultation with other Departments, that they replied
to the County Council's representations. Following the announcement of the new strip mill, they said, 'certain facts and considerations' not known at the time of the earlier Bodicote inquiry had
come to light. The Minister had been informed that soon after
the new steelworks came into operation in 1963 it would need
1 million tons of Oxfordshire ironstone a year, and the figure
would rise to $3\frac{1}{2}$–4 million tons a year by 1965–6. This compared
with the estimated output for 1962 (from existing sources in
Oxfordshire) of 2·3 million tons a year. It was probable, the
Minister had been told, that beyond 1966 even more Oxfordshire
iron ore would be needed at the Newport works. He understood
that consideration had been given to the possibility of meeting
these requirements from the existing workings in the Wroxton
area. However, the I.S.B. thought it unlikely that the new mill
would be able to rely entirely on supplies from there after the first
stage of development. In the circumstances, the Minister had
decided to reopen the inquiry so that all the interested parties
could make representations on the new information which had
come to light.

When the Bodicote inquiry ended, the opposition had been
uneasy about the outcome, not so much because they believed
Dowsetts to have made out a good case, but because the I.S.B.
seemed to have such an insatiable, yet at the same time incomprehensible appetite for Oxfordshire ore. If it was true that behind
Dowsetts stood R.T.B., the situation looked even more ominous.
It needed only a little imagination to see a sinister chain of influence in the making. R.T.B. had the Government's backing for
their new steelworks. The I.S.B., another official agency, were
apparently telling the Ministry of Housing and Local Government that R.T.B. would have to have a great deal more Oxfordshire ore, far more than the Wroxton area could possibly supply.
Presumably the Ministry of Power, the steel industry's sponsoring
Department, had already accepted this argument. Dowsetts had

by this time submitted applications to work something like 4,000 acres of the north Oxfordshire countryside. It was known that Dowsetts were in some way connected with R.T.B. True, the public inquiry was to be reopened, and the opposition would have the chance to challenge the applications. But in the end the decision would rest with the Minister of Housing and Local Government, a member of the Government which was supporting R.T.B. in their important new enterprise at Newport. As the objectors saw it, behind the scenes the Minister of Housing and Local Government was almost bound to be influenced by the views of the I.S.B. and the Ministry of Power. And as they reflected upon coming events, there were some in Oxfordshire who feared that the outcome was a foregone conclusion.

What made matters worse was the suspicion that far more was at stake than the fate of the areas for which Dowsetts had submitted applications. If, as the Minister had suggested in his letter of 30 April, R.T.B. were eventually going to need $3\frac{1}{2}$–4 million tons of ore a year, then the time would certainly come when even wider tracts of the Oxfordshire countryside would be threatened. Conscious that if planning permission were given for the areas currently before the Minister it would be very much more difficult to protect the rest of the ironstone-bearing land in north Oxfordshire, the County Council decided to press for a thorough and wide-ranging inquiry into the whole question of whether the ironstone deposits south of Banbury ought to be worked. And if the re-opened public inquiry was to decide a major issue of principle, they thought it essential that they should know exactly what development programme was planned for the area, and exactly what arguments Dowsetts intended to deploy in support of their case.

In a letter dated 26 June 1959 to the Ministry of Housing and Local Government, the Clerk to the Oxfordshire County Council pointed out that they would expect to be told (in advance of the inquiry) which areas Dowsetts intended to work in the years ahead, and how they proposed to transport the ore from the quarries to the railhead. In addition, they would need analyses of the ore from a comprehensive series of trial borings covering the whole of the area involved, together with reliable estimates for the cost of producing the ore. Only if this information was available would the inquiry be in a position to judge whether it was likely to be cheap enough, and of the right quality for use in the new strip mill. As the County Clerk observed, nothing could be worse than to grant planning permission, and then to discover that the ore was not quite suitable, or that Oxfordshire ore was, after all, dearer than ore from other districts in England, or from abroad. If that were to happen, the areas in question would presumably be held in reserve indefinitely by R.T.B.; or even worse, they would be subjected to haphazard, small-scale development by Dowsetts or anyone else who succeeded in buying the mineral rights, and who reckoned that there was some prospect of selling the ore at a profit on the open market. As he reminded the Ministry, the County Council had always argued that if an area had to be worked at all, it was important that it should be worked steadily and swiftly, so that the people living there could plan ahead, and so as to limit to as short a time as possible the inevitable disturbance caused by ironstone quarrying. The County Clerk insisted that all the information they were requesting was of vital importance, and he asked the Ministry of Housing and Local Government to 'instruct' the applicants to provide it.

Reaction in the Ministry was cautious but not unsympathetic. They pointed out that after the inquiry the Minister would have to decide the applications taking into account the arguments advanced by both the applicants and their opponents; they could hardly allow themselves to be drawn into collecting information which might be used as a basis for representations put forward by one of the parties to the dispute. On 1 September 1959, however, the Ministry did write to the applicants, telling them that they would be expected to deal with certain specific 'points' in presenting their case.[1] These points bore a strong resemblance to

[1] All correspondence on the applicants' side was, in fact, dealt with by a firm of solicitors. By this stage Dowsetts had been taken over by R.T.B., and it must be assumed that the parent company was now involved in preparing the case for the applications. In the text, the expression 'the applicants' should be taken to refer to R.T.B. and Dowsetts jointly. On the other side, all correspondence was handled by the Oxfordshire County Council, as the Local Planning Authority concerned. After the Bodicote inquiry, however, the chief objectors worked in close co-operation, eventually (in February 1960) forming an advisory committee (consisting of representatives of the County Council, the Protection Committee, the N.F.U., the C.L.A., the Parish Councils Association and the Chipping Norton and Banbury R.D.C.s) to co-ordinate their efforts. In the text, the expression 'the opposition' refers to this united front.

those raised by the County Council. It would be helpful, the Ministry suggested, if the applicants were to prepare a written statement, which could be made available to the Inspector and the Local Planning Authority before the inquiry opened. They were proposing this rather unusual step, they said, because they believed that in this way the case could be dealt with more quickly. If the required information was not produced before the inquiry began, the applicants were informed, the Local Planning Authority might feel it necessary to ask for an adjournment, so as to give themselves time to consider it. The Inspector, added the Ministry, would be bound to take a sympathetic view of such a request. The Ministry also felt that there would be some advantage in dealing with Dowsett's more recent applications at the same time as the inquiry into the original Bloxham/Adderbury areas was reopened.

The applicants provided the information asked for in a letter to the Ministry of Housing and Local Government of 21 September. They confirmed that production at Newport would begin in 1962–3. Within a short time, they said, more than a million tons a year of Oxfordshire ore would be required. By 1965–6 they would need 2 million tons a year, and over the following five years their requirements were expected to rise to about 3 million tons a year. The blast furnaces at Newport had been designed to use 40 per cent Oxfordshire ore. In using this amount of Oxfordshire ore, they said, they were conforming with the stated policy of the I.S.B. They intended to treat the area for which applications had been submitted as an integrated working, quarrying the whole of it simultaneously; that is to say, it would not be worked piecemeal, one part at a time. The estimated life of the areas was twenty-five to thirty years. The ore would be carried by rail to South Wales. British Railways had planned the route, and they were already dealing with improvement schemes on certain sections of the line. And, for the Ministry's information, they added that the Dowsett Mineral Recovery Company was now a wholly-owned subsidiary of R.T.B.

This information the Ministry passed on to the Oxfordshire County Council. The applicants had certainly dealt with some of the relevant factors. But their statement did not go anything like as far as the County Council wanted. They had been told how much Oxfordshire ore the applicants would need at various dates

in the sixties and early seventies. But what were the steel outputs
to which these tonnages related? Had a definite decision been
taken to go beyond the first stage in developing the new strip
mill? Could the new steel-making process at Newport operate
only on the basis of 40 per cent Oxfordshire ore, or would it be
possible for it to use 100 per cent imported ore? If it was true
that the Newport works had to use 40 per cent home-produced
ore, from where did the applicants propose to get their supplies if
planning permission for the current application areas was refused?
The estimated life of the application areas, it had been said, was
twenty-five to thirty years. Where would the applicants find their
ore when these areas were exhausted? In order to form a clear
picture of what the operations in Oxfordshire would entail, the
County Council also asked for a map showing the probable areas
that would be worked in each successive five-year period, mark-
ing the routes by which the ore would be conveyed from the
quarry faces to the railhead. A second map was also requested,
showing the positions of all the test boreholes and setting out
particulars of the ore analyses, the thickness of the seam and the
depth of the overburden at each point.

The opposition were also interested in the reasons that R.T.B.
would give for using Oxfordshire ore. R.T.B. had implied that
Oxfordshire ore was to be used in order to conform with the
I.S.B.'s stated policy. The reasoning behind the I.S.B.'s policy
was something that the opposition could take up with the Board
themselves. Nevertheless, they were anxious to find out more
about the commercial considerations that were involved. At what
price, they asked, did Dowsetts expect to deliver Oxfordshire ore
to Newport, and how did this compare with the probable price of
ore from alternative sources, imported and home-produced?

In retrospect, it is clear that the opposition were feeling their
way, trying to piece together the case that would have to be
answered at the inquiry. And from this point onwards, what will
become a familiar strategy begins to emerge. In the first place,
objectors must try to establish that the proposed development
really will inflict serious damage on the local amenities. Usually
this is not difficult. But it does call for some foreknowledge of
what precisely the developers are planning, so that the objectors
can build up, and put before the inquiry a credible picture of the
disastrous effect that the project in question would have on the

environment. But in the second place, if it looks at all feasible, the objectors may also decide to attack the developers on their own ground, in an attempt to cast doubt on the rationale of their policy or decision. Often, they will suggest that it would be in the public interest (and sometimes, indeed, in the developers' own interests) for them to find some other method of meeting their needs, or an alternative site for their project. This, of course, is a much more ambitious ploy, though if it makes headway it can do a great deal to improve the objectors' chances of success.

Given a reasonable amount of information about the applicants' programme, it would be no problem for the objectors to show that ironstone working on a large scale would certainly disrupt the life of the north Oxfordshire countryside. But what about the other side of the strategy? Would it be possible to mount an attack on R.T.B.'s decision to use Oxfordshire ore, rather than imported ore? At this stage, it looked a very long shot, largely because R.T.B. could always claim that they were merely conforming with the I.S.B.'s known policy. It seemed hardly likely that a County Council and their band of voluntary helpers would be able to shake the fundamental wisdom of that.

To add to the difficulties facing the opposition, by the summer of 1959 a period of economic expansion was well under way. As always in this phase of the business cycle, bottlenecks were becoming painfully obvious, and at one point there were fears that a shortage of steel might hold back the production of cars and consumer durables. It was against this background that in the autumn of 1959, at the request of the I.S.B., R.T.B. agreed to accelerate their construction programme at Newport. Understandably, both organisations were even more anxious to dispose of the problem of ore supplies as soon as possible.

On 24 December 1959 the County Council had asked the I.S.B. to explain why they were supporting R.T.B.'s plans to use 40 per cent Oxfordshire ore. In their reply, on 7 January 1960, the I.S.B. pointed out that it was not their practice to lay down the specific amount, or proportion, of home ore to be used by any individual company. R.T.B.'s decision to use 40 per cent Oxfordshire ore had been taken on technological and economic grounds. The I.S.B. reaffirmed that their policy was still to encourage the maximum use of home ore, consistent with the maintenance of adequate reserves. If Dowsetts were permitted to work their

application areas, they would contribute to the additional production of home ore that the I.S.B. considered desirable. More to
the point, Dowsett's ore would be needed at R.T.B.'s Newport
works, for which the Government had made available a loan of
£70 million. The new strip mill was now expected to come into
operation at the beginning of 1962, or possibly before the end of
1961. Adequate provision must be made for supplying the necessary ore. The Newport project was of great importance to the
national economy because of the continuing and increasing
demand for sheet and other flat rolled products required in the
production of motor-car bodies and in many other industries. It
was essential, they added, that the new strip mill should be
brought into operation at the earliest possible date. The I.S.B.
were confident that there would be considerable expansion beyond
the plans already approved. Right at the beginning, it was vital
to ensure that adequate supplies of iron ore were available as
soon as they were required. If Dowsett's applications were granted,
R.T.B. would be in a position to meet their requirements at
Newport as they arose; they would also have the advantage of
knowing that a large part of their ore was under their own direct
control. As the Board understood it, Oxfordshire ore could be
worked with exceptional ease and cheapness. Dowsett ore, they
claimed, would be among the cheapest in the country, and certainly cheaper than imported ore.

Another letter from the applicants to the Ministry of Housing
and Local Government struck the same note of urgent necessity.
On 13 January 1960 they informed the Ministry that the planned
output in the first stage of the development had been increased
to 1·4 million ingot tons of steel a year. By 1962, they said, R.T.B.
would need more than a million tons of Oxfordshire ore a year.
Previously, they had estimated that they would require 2 million
tons a year by 1965–6; but now they expected to need at least
that much by 1964–5. The Ministry would appreciate that if and
when planning permission was granted, a good deal of preparatory work, including the installation of heavy plant and equipment and the construction of access roads and sidings, would still
have to be completed before they could actually begin to produce
the ironstone. Dowsetts were now estimating that if they were to
be in a position to meet R.T.B.'s needs in good time, they would
have to start production not later than June 1960. It was vital,

therefore, that the Minister should come to a decision on the applications as soon as possible. In much the same vein, the applicants told the County Council in a letter of the same date that they were not prepared to make available any more detailed information because the time taken in putting these written statements together would serve only to prolong the delay in reaching a decision.

'BLOOD FROM THE STONE'

A public local inquiry is very largely a battle of arguments. Both sides are anxious to know, in advance, what evidence their opponents intend to rely upon, for then they can seek expert advice, establish their defence, marshal counter-arguments, and work out promising lines of attack. As the developer's case is almost always the more complex, advance information is usually more vital to the objectors. The Oxfordshire County Council now embarked on a dogged campaign to find out just what case the applicants and the I.S.B. intended to put forward at the reopened public inquiry. From the beginning, it was an uphill task. But in their efforts to elicit more information than the applicants were inclined to provide, the County Council always had one strong card to play. They now knew that R.T.B. were in a hurry; and it was a safe bet that the very last thing they wanted was for the inquiry to be adjourned because they had failed to make available enough information before it began. As the reader will by now have realised, rather less is known about the applicants' thought-processes. But apparently they came to believe, at an early stage, that the objectors were trying to dictate the terms on which the battle would be fought. They saw no reason why they should have their case patterned for them in a way that suited the opposition; nor did they feel themselves under any obligation to help out with information which the objectors seemed to think important for their own purposes.

On 21 January 1960 the Ministry of Housing and Local Government told both sides that, in their view, if the inquiry were held at the end of April this would give the opposition a reasonable period of time in which to prepare their case. Since there was to be this further delay, the applicants relented somewhat, and agreed to provide the further detailed information requested by the County Council 'in so far as it was available and relevant to the issues'. This cautious concession did not go down well with the County Council. In a letter of 1 February the County Clerk observed that *all* the information requested by the County Council must surely be available to the applicants; and as to relevancy, it was all relevant. In any case, it was for the Minister, not the applicants, to decide that point.

And now, for the first time, there appeared an explicit formulation of the crucial question that the inquiry would have to answer. 'The decision whether or not to permit the proposed development', wrote the County Clerk, 'must depend to a great extent on the balance between the resulting loss to the nation of amenity, and the resulting gain to the nation, if any, of working the application areas immediately or in the foreseeable future rather than holding on to them as a long term reserve in case of a national emergency, whether it be military, political or economic.'

As the opposition saw it, there would be no problem about demonstrating the loss of amenity. But what kind of gain for the nation could there be? Not unnaturally, they assumed that the applicants intended to argue that it would be much cheaper to use Oxfordshire ore than imported ore. After all, the I.S.B.'s general policy of encouraging steel producers to use home ore was based very largely on this proposition. And in their letter of 7 January 1960 the I.S.B. had said, quite unequivocally, that Dowsett ore would be cheaper than any other home-produced or imported ore. If the applicants were going to rely on cost advantage, the issue (it seemed) would resolve itself into one of those teasing questions of value that we shall see recurring again and again in this book. Was it worth spoiling this beautiful stretch of countryside in order to save whatever might be the difference in cost between steel made partly from Oxfordshire ore and steel made wholly from imported ore? Or, to put it another way, should the nation pay this price, whatever it might be, in order to save the amenities of north Oxfordshire?

The opposition had to assume that this difference in cost was substantial and demonstrable. Why else should the I.S.B. and R.T.B. be so set upon using Oxfordshire ore? Yet if this *was* to be the applicants' trump card, did it really make sense for the opposition to dwell upon this aspect of the case? It was certainly a question worth asking. But the fact was that apart from drawing attention to the beauties of the countryside and the dismal effects of ironstone quarrying, there was little else they could do. Furthermore, if they could find out what the cost advantage of Oxfordshire ore was supposed to be, and how this figure had been calculated, they might be able to argue, as objectors often do in these circumstances, that the applicants were exaggerating. There must be a significant cost advantage; that went without saying. But the smaller it was, the less would be the justification for impairing the amenities of north Oxfordshire, and the better the opposition's chance of success.

Having decided to probe more deeply into this aspect of the applicants' case, the County Council now began to press for detailed information about the comparative costs of manufacturing pig iron from Oxfordshire and imported ores. On 1 February the County Clerk took up this question with the I.S.B. Recalling the Board's earlier assertion that Oxfordshire ore would be among the cheapest in the country, and certainly cheaper than imported ore, he asked for the figures on which these claims were based. What would be the cost per ton of pig iron, he asked, if Oxfordshire and imported ores were used in the ratios 40:60, 20:80, 10:90, 5:95 and 0:100?

In Oxfordshire the answers were doubtless awaited with some trepidation. For all that the opposition knew, they might well turn out to be crushing. When the I.S.B. replied on 12 February, however, all they had to say was that matters like these went rather beyond what they considered appropriate in the preparatory stages of a public inquiry. Detailed questions of this kind, they said, ought to be put, 'if at all', at the inquiry itself. In the circumstances, therefore, the I.S.B. did not think it right to answer the points raised by the County Council. And in reply to a second request for these comparative costs, on 3 March the I.S.B. informed the County Council that because Section 30 of the 1953 Iron and Steel Act prohibited them from supplying information relating to individual firms, they could not provide the detailed figures that had been available to the Board when they reached their conclusions about the cost of Dowsett ore compared with that of other home-produced ores.

If the I.S.B. were not permitted to disclose this information, the obvious move was to go direct to the firm concerned. On

18 February the County Clerk put the same questions about comparative costs to Dowsetts. The response came several weeks later in a letter of 11 March. In a 'Supplementary Statement' the applicants now dealt with a good many of the points that had been raised in earlier letters from the County Council. R.T.B.'s revised timetable for the Newport works was confirmed. They agreed that it would be technically possible for the new steelworks to use only imported ore. But, they said, the proposed use of Oxfordshire ore conformed with the I.S.B.'s policy, which called for the maximum use of suitable home ore. Oxfordshire was the nearest orefield to the Newport works from which suitable ore could be obtained in the quantities required. All the deposits that they intended to work were near the surface, and close to a railway. Both production and freight costs were therefore expected to be the minimum possible. As they had made clear at the Bodicote inquiry, they were thinking of extending their operations to a further large area round Deddington. They were also carrying out surveys in the districts adjacent to their current application areas. It was expected that in the Hook Norton and Iron Down areas the ore would be transported by heavy-duty dump trucks on specially prepared roads leading to the railheads. In the interests of amenity, they had decided not to use what would have been very conspicuous crusher installations in any of the application areas. Instead, a modern ore preparation plant was under construction at Newport.

This was all very interesting. However, as the County Clerk pointed out in his acknowledgement on 17 March, the applicants had completely ignored the County Council's questions about comparative costs.

The County Council were also anxious to find out more about the I.S.B.'s attitude to another issue that was clearly going to be of some importance at the inquiry. Did the I.S.B. feel any sense of responsibility for the effects of iron-ore-mining on the countryside? Not much, it seemed. In his letter of 1 February the County Clerk had suggested to the I.S.B. that the application areas were of great natural beauty, and in this respect they might be unique among the iron-ore-bearing districts. Since the deposits were scattered, a larger area would suffer loss of amenity than would be the case elsewhere. The I.S.B.'s reply merely pointed out that the Board's statutory duty was to promote an efficient, economic and adequate supply of iron and steel products, including iron ore. The natural beauty of an area of contemplated development, they said, was hardly a factor that the Board could properly take into account.

It was now well past the end of April, the time suggested by the Minister for the public inquiry. The County Council were still not satisfied with the amount of information they had been given, and the applicants were apparently unwilling to provide any more. In an effort to speed up the decision, on 26 May 1960 the Minister himself met representatives from both sides, and as a result of this meeting, a month later the applicants produced another set of plans for the opposition to brood over. This latest dossier included two maps, one showing diagrammatically the probable pattern of areas to be worked in each successive five-year period, and indicating the direction in which the ore was to be transported from the working faces to the railway sidings, and the other showing the positions of all the boreholes in the Hook Norton and Iron Down application areas, together with a schedule setting out details of the analysis, the thickness of ironstone and the depth of the overburden at each borehole.

If the applicants thought that this would satisfy the opposition, they were to be disappointed. On 6 July the County Clerk returned to the attack. The diagrammatic map was dismissed as of little use: to form a clear picture of what was planned, he wrote, nothing less than a six-inch to the mile map was required. More important, he reminded the applicants that they had still not provided any information about the comparative costs of producing pig iron from Oxfordshire and imported ores.

It would seem that until now the opposition had been pursuing this question of costs more in hope than with any real expectation of discovering a serious weakness in the applicants' case. So as to be able to put up a reasonable show at the public inquiry, in March 1960 they had commissioned the Economist Intelligence Unit to examine the economic arguments for using Oxfordshire ironstone at Newport. The report was delivered early in May. It now began to dawn on the opposition that they might well have latched on to something of critical importance.

The opposition would have to assume, suggested the report, that R.T.B. would claim some cost advantage from using 40 per cent Oxfordshire ore. In other words, they would say that this

gave them cheaper steel than any other ratio of home to imported
ore. But, the report continued, the choice of this ratio must have
been based upon calculations made some considerable time before. In the previous few years there had been significant changes
in some of the variables that R.T.B. would have taken into
account. As the report pointed out, the price of imported ore had
begun to go down, shipping freight rates were no longer rising,
and the cost of rail transport within the United Kingdom had
increased. So that, whatever might have been the case for using a
high proportion of home ore at Newport several years earlier, in
the circumstances of 1960 it was almost certainly a great deal
weaker. It might no longer make sense to use as much as 40 per
cent home ore at Newport: the optimal proportion could well be
30 per cent, or even less. And if less Oxfordshire ore was needed,
it might be that the Wroxton orefield would suffice after all.

The Economist Intelligence Unit's report did not merely question R.T.B.'s proposed 40:60 ratio: it also implied that the I.S.B.,
the fount of wisdom, might be wrong in sticking to their policy of
encouraging the greater use of home ore. In 1955, it recalled,
world reserves of iron ore had been put at about 82,000 million
tons; the most recent estimates, by contrast, suggested that
reserves amounted to more than four times as much as had previously been thought. There was certainly no need for anyone to
worry about future supplies from abroad. Moreover, the world-
wide shortage of shipping and the high freight rates of the early
fifties had given way to a surplus of tonnage and appreciably
lower rates than had been expected. These trends might not
continue so markedly in the future; but there was no reason to
fear a recurrence of the type of shipping difficulties experienced
in the previous ten years. If all this was true, why were the I.S.B.
persisting with their policy? The answer, suggested the report,
was inertia. 'In an industry which abounds in joint organisations
and controlling bodies', it observed, 'it may take a long time
before a certain policy, a policy of home ore development, for
instance, is accepted and agreed upon by all parties concerned
and it is to be expected that policies, once adopted, will not be
lightly reversed, even if the reasons which originally led to their
adoption no longer apply.'

For the opposition, this made encouraging reading. It still
seemed too much to hope for; but was there just a chance that

the applicants were reluctant to release the relevant data because they realised that the figures would do little or nothing to help their case?

When he wrote to the applicants on 6 July, the County Clerk repeated his earlier requests for information about R.T.B.'s estimates for the cost of producing steel from home and imported ores. 'Clearly', he wrote, 'these comparative costs were a most important factor in reaching the decision to use 40 per cent Oxfordshire ironstone and 60 per cent foreign ore and, since that decision was taken some time ago, it is presumed that further estimates have been made from time to time to ascertain whether the 40:60 ratio continues to be a sound one from the point of view of the interests of Messrs Richard Thomas and Baldwins Ltd, and of the country.' And in the hope of being able to get to grips with these elusive figures, soon afterwards the County Council retained a chartered accountant to advise them on the economic aspects of the applicants' case. On 13 July the County Clerk wrote again to the applicants, suggesting a meeting between their representatives and the County Council's accountant to examine R.T.B.'s cost estimates.

The reply, received on 28 July, surprised and puzzled the opposition. According to the applicants, cost advantage did not form the basis of their case. Of course, they said, if the County Council wanted to make estimates, that was their business. Most of the necessary information, they thought, would be readily available without reference to Dowsetts or R.T.B. However, if the County Council required specific factual information that only the applicants possessed, they would be glad to consider whether they could provide it. In the circumstances, neither Dowsetts nor R.T.B. thought that a meeting with the County Council's accountant would be appropriate.

This was a disconcerting piece of news for the opposition. Time was slipping by, and now it was being implied that they had failed to understand the case that would have to be answered at the inquiry. When the County Clerk replied on 2 August, a note of desperation began to creep in: 'If the cost advantage of the use of a high proportion of Oxfordshire ore in steel production at Newport does not form the basis of your case, what does?' The answer must have left him as baffled as ever. The policy which dictated the proposed use of Oxfordshire ore had been explained by the I.S.B. in January 1960, said the applicants; the specific proportions of imported and Oxfordshire ores to be used at the new steelworks had been determined by technical considerations which would be explained in detail at the public inquiry.

There it was in black and white. But evidently the opposition still could not bring themselves to believe that, in the end, the applicants would not rely on arguments about cost advantage. On 29 August the County Clerk returned to this point yet again, and asked the applicants to say, quite specifically, whether an alleged cost advantage did or did not form any part of their case. Whatever the answer, he went on, the fact remained that in January 1960 the I.S.B. had claimed that Dowsett ore would be among the cheapest in the country, and certainly cheaper than imported ore. Presumably cost advantage was part of the reason for the I.S.B.'s support for Dowsett's application. And so far as the national interest was concerned, the cost advantage (or disadvantage) of Oxfordshire ore was obviously one of the factors that would have to be taken into account when the application was finally determined. For this reason, the County Council thought it essential to establish in advance of the inquiry the precise extent of any financial savings from using Oxfordshire ore. They were still unable to prepare their case, and time was fast running out. If the applicants were not prepared to provide the necessary information by the middle of September, he wrote, and were not prepared to agree to a meeting with the County Council's chartered accountant, then the Council would feel obliged to ask the Inspector to adjourn the inquiry.

Nor was there much additional clarification on the question of costs to be had from the I.S.B. On 19 September the Board provided the County Council with a draft statement of the evidence that was to be given on their behalf at the public inquiry. The statement explained yet again why the I.S.B. were encouraging the more extensive use of home ore, and why they were supporting R.T.B.'s applications. But so far as comparative costs were concerned, it was couched in carefully guarded language. 'Richard Thomas and Baldwins Ltd have advised the Board', they said, 'that according to their estimates the cost of producing steel at Llanwern (Newport) would be greater if Oxfordshire ore were not used in its production. The Board agree with the Company that there should be a cost advantage in the use of Oxfordshire ore, but cannot say what the precise amount will prove to be.'

Hitherto, hints of further delay had always been followed by additional instalments of information. At this point, however, the applicants dug in their heels. On 5 September they told the County Council that they were not prepared to produce a more detailed map of their development programme. As to the question of costs, whilst Dowsetts and R.T.B. had naturally 'had regard to' the economic advantage to themselves of their proposals, a detailed comparison of costs formed no part of their case in respect of the planning application. A full statement of the technical considerations involved in the 40:60 ratio would be produced at the public inquiry, and not before. If the County Council still felt that they had not been given enough information, they added, no doubt they would refer the matter to the Minister's Inspector as soon as possible.

The opposition needed no invitation, and on 10 September the County Clerk wrote to the Ministry of Housing and Local Government claiming that the County Council had still not been given all the information they considered essential. He emphasised that they attached very great importance to the question of costs. In their view, 'the only factor which could possibly justify the destruction of the amenities of the Great Tew area would be an overriding national need, clearly demonstrated, to use the iron ore in this area, and this must mean that costs must be one of the issues to be fully debated at the inquiry'. It was vital, therefore, that the County Council should know, (in advance of the inquiry) the cost advantage, if any, of using Oxfordshire rather than imported ore at the Newport works. The only way in which they could get this information was for their accountant to discuss the relevant figures with the appropriate officers of Dowsetts and R.T.B. In consequence, they wanted a meeting with the Ministry officials involved, the Inspector, and the applicants' representatives, at which the Ministry could give a clear indication of what information they thought should be made available to the County Council before the inquiry. The Ministry of Housing and Local Government, however, were not to be drawn further into the preliminary arguments, and on 21 September they informed the County Council that the Minister thought it undesirable for him to intervene now that he had appointed the

Inspector to hold the inquiry. He regretted, therefore, that he could not arrange a meeting of the kind proposed. The Inspector, too, felt that it would not be proper for him to join in discussions at this stage.

By now, the date of the inquiry had been fixed for 8 November 1960. While their solicitors and the County Council had been locked in argument about the applications that were already in, Dowsetts had continued with their prospecting in the Oxfordshire countryside. On 25 August they submitted a further planning application for additional land in the Milcombe area. It was subsequently agreed that this application should also be considered at the forthcoming inquiry.

There was still time for one more disagreement, this time about the status of the witnesses that the applicants proposed to rely on. In support of their case, they had decided to call Mr R. A. Hacking, R.T.B.'s Director of Research, Mr W. E. Smith, the General Manager and Mr W. J. A. Knibbs, the Managing Director of Dowsetts (by now renamed R.T.B. (Mineral Recovery) Ltd.). The County Council argued that this was not good enough. They contended that the Managing Director of R.T.B. ought to be at the inquiry, for it was the working programme of the parent organisation – not that of the subsidiary mineral company – that was relevant to the major issues of national policy involved. R.T.B., they maintained, ought to be represented by someone who could speak with authority about the company's development programme, and not by a member of their research staff, supported by representatives of the mineral company. This contention was rejected by the applicants: their witnesses, they said, would be fully competent to speak with authority on all matters that they regarded as relevant to the applications.

A similar exchange took place between the County Council and the I.S.B. The I.S.B. had decided that their spokesman at the inquiry was to be Mr J. R. C. Boys, the head of their Development Division. The County Council wanted a whole-time member of the Board, and not an officer, to give evidence on behalf of the I.S.B. It was clear, they said, that the I.S.B.'s support for the applicants was a matter of great importance. This support, apparently, arose out of the Board's general policy of encouraging the maximum use of home ore. Evidence should therefore be given by a member of the Board, someone who had been respon-

sible for formulating this policy, and who could explain exactly
why it had been adopted. The I.S.B., however, would have none
of this. In the first place, they said, they had been advised that no
member of the Board could be in a position to give evidence as to
why any particular policy decision had been taken by the Board,
since he 'could not take it upon himself to say what particular
factors influenced the minds of other members of the Board
participating in the formulation of the policy decision'. Consequently, they could not agree to the presence of a whole-time
member of the Board at the inquiry. Their second reason was less
metaphysical, but it did suggest that the two sides were approaching the inquiry with very different ideas as to what did and did
not come within its scope. 'The Board do not accept, in any
event', they wrote, 'that it is appropriate that the Inquiry should
constitute itself as an Inquiry into the policies of the Board, and
take the view that the policy of the Board on relevant points is a
matter of fact, and represents a factor to be considered at the
Inquiry with other relevant factors.'

From the I.S.B.'s point of view, this attitude may have been
reasonable enough. After all, *they* were not seeking to extract
ironstone from the Oxfordshire countryside. Why then should
they be obliged to justify and defend their policies to the Oxfordshire County Council at a public local inquiry? On the other
hand, if it was to be one of the mainstays of the applicants' case
that they were conforming with the I.S.B.'s policy, and that policy
was to be beyond challenge, then plainly the opposition were
going into the inquiry with the odds stacked heavily against them.

THE PUBLIC INQUIRY

There was no doubt about the strength of feeling in Oxfordshire.
While the County Council were engaging the applicants at the
official level, leading members of the opposition had been busy in
the villages and hamlets. Throughout the spring and summer of
1960 they were hard at work, addressing public meetings, parish
councils and Women's Institutes, and explaining the effect of
ironstone quarrying on the life of the area. Their efforts were
supported by the local press, particularly the *Oxford Times*,
which gave full coverage to these meetings and ran a series of

feature articles drawing attention to the beauty of the countryside in the threatened districts. From time to time interviews were
recorded with people living in the more picturesque villages.
Some of them held out hair-raising prospects. The vicar of Swerford, for example, predicted that if the applications succeeded,
the effect would be 'to blast Swerford off the map'.

By the autumn of 1960, north Oxfordshire was thoroughly
stirred. Almost every local organisation with any conceivable
interest in the countryside, had lodged an official objection. Apart
from the Oxfordshire County Council, the bodies opposing the
applications included the Banbury R.D.C., the Chipping Norton
R.D.C., the Banbury Borough Council, the Chipping Norton
Borough Council, the North Oxfordshire Ironstone Areas Protection Committee, twenty parish councils, forty-four Oxfordshire
Women's Institutes, the Oxfordshire branches of the N.F.U. and
the C.L.A., the Oxfordshire Rural Community Council, the
Oxfordshire Playing Fields Association, the Oxfordshire Association of Parish Councils, the Banbury Ornithological Society, the
Banbury Historical Society, the Banbury Business and Professional Women's Club, and two local schools. The landowners,
and other owners of mineral rights in more than two-thirds of the
area involved, objected. In addition, a number of national
amenity and recreational organisations, including the National
Parks Commission, the C.P.R.E., the Royal Fine Art Commission, the British Travel and Holidays Association, and the
Ramblers' Association, also came to the support of the local opposition.

On 8 November 1960 the much-delayed public inquiry opened
in Banbury Town Hall. It was expected to take five days; in fact,
it lasted for ten. Held under Section 12 of the 1947 Town and
Country Planning Act, the inquiry was concerned with the applications of Messrs Richard Thomas and Baldwins (Mineral
Recovery) Ltd to mine and work ironstone and other minerals in
six areas in Oxfordshire between Hook Norton on the west and
the county boundary near East Adderbury on the east. Altogether,
the applications covered an area of about 4,700 acres, or nearly
$7\frac{1}{2}$ square miles, though the working areas themselves, from which
the ironstone was to be excavated, covered only 2,871 acres, or
$4\frac{1}{2}$ square miles. The applicants were represented by Mr J. P.
Widgery, Q.C., and Mr G. Eyre; the Oxfordshire County Coun-

cil were represented by Mr R. V. Cusack, Q.C., and Mr B. T. Neill; Mr J. Arnold, Q.C., appeared for the Protection Committee. The Inspector was Mr H. F. Yeomans.

Opening for the applicants, Widgery made it clear that as Dowsetts had now become a subsidiary of R.T.B., to all intents and purposes it was R.T.B., the parent company, who were there seeking planning permission. R.T.B., he said, needed no introduction. It was a company in which Her Majesty's Government had a very substantial interest. Whether it was called a nationalised industry or not was immaterial: the fact was that the Government was a major shareholder. R.T.B.'s works at Newport, he went on, had been designed to meet the growing demand for thin, flat-rolled steel products, which were required for making car bodies and consumer durables such as washing-machines and refrigerators. The new strip mill would also bring more employment to South Wales. It would take fifteen years to complete; but the works had been planned to come into operation in stages. So far as Stage I was concerned, it was hoped to begin production in September 1961, building up to an output of 1·4 million ingot tons a year by April 1962. In Stage II, it was envisaged that output would rise to 3 million ingot tons a year by 1964–5. Beyond that, there might well be further expansion, with output rising to 6 million ingot tons a year by 1975.

To produce steel in these quantities, R.T.B. would need a great deal of iron ore. They hoped to be able to begin feeding ore into the Newport works by March 1961. In Stage I they would need 1 million tons of Oxfordshire ironstone a year, in Stage II 2 million tons a year, and eventually they might well require 4 million tons a year. As yet, no firm decision to go beyond Stage I had been taken; but R.T.B. regarded Stage II as virtually certain.

From the start, Widgery explained, R.T.B. had assumed that a substantial proportion of their iron ore would come from Oxfordshire. Why Oxfordshire? The basic reason, he said, was that it was Government policy to use home ore. This had been a policy decision, involving considerations of foreign politics, foreign exchange, and other questions that went far beyond the competence of any single steel producer, however big. These were matters for the Government to decide. 'It was not our decision', he said, 'and I am not here with evidence to support the rightness

or not of that decision; it was a decision at Government level.'
Given the policy decision to use home ore to the fullest possible
extent, said Widgery, Oxfordshire was the obvious choice for
supplies. It was fairly close to Newport, and its chemical constituents were particularly suitable for combining with foreign
ore in the type of steel-making processes designed for the Newport
works.

It was quite true, he said, that the Oxfordshire Ironstone
Company could provide R.T.B. with half a million tons of ore a
year immediately, and 1 million tons a year three years later. In
fact, R.T.B. intended to take part of their requirements from
Wroxton. But even if they took the full potential of the Wroxton
area, there would still not be enough to meet their long-term
needs. In any case, R.T.B. were anxious to keep a proportion of
their supplies under their own control, so that they could regulate
the quality of the ore supplied to Newport. In order to match
chemical variations in the imported ores, they had to have
at least five ore faces open simultaneously; they could not
just confine themselves to one place at a time. It was for this
reason that they were seeking consent to work over such a large
area.

As to the question of costs, R.T.B. had no intention of disclosing their detailed estimates for the differences that might result
from using imported and Oxfordshire ore in various proportions.
They had, of course, made estimates. But Widgery had been
instructed not to reveal these figures in public because they were
of great commercial importance, and R.T.B.'s competitors would
be delighted to learn about them. However, if the Minister of
Housing and Local Government wanted their costings on a confidential basis, they would be prepared to make them available to
him. They were certainly not going to produce them at the
inquiry.

Developers are as much entitled to try to undermine the
objectors' claims as vice-versa. Turning to the opposition's case,
Widgery conceded that if the applications were granted there was
bound to be some interference with amenity and agriculture. But,
he suggested, it was easy to exaggerate the natural beauty of the
countryside that would be affected. There was a good deal of
difference, he said, between the amenity values of individual
application areas. Judging from afar, some people were under

the impression that the whole area was comparable with Great Tew, which admittedly possessed great charm, and which the applicants would ensure was not damaged by their workings. But, at the other end of the amenity scale, there was the Milcombe area, a relatively featureless plateau adjoining an extremely unsightly installation of wireless aerials on a former airfield. Moreover, it was quite wrong to think, as some people evidently did, that iron-ore workings would destroy all the trees in the area. Trees, he claimed, tended to grow on the edge of the ironstone deposits, and so would not be much affected. 'The effect of mining on the trees', he declared, 'would be so small you would not notice the difference.' Then there was the other popular misconception, that the fall in the level of the land after restoration would leave the farms and cottages on pedestals. 'The idea that homes will be left as castles in the air', said Widgery, 'is quite unfounded.'

The applicants' case was now developed and defended by their four witnesses. First came Mr Hacking, the head of R.T.B.'s central research laboratories. To the surprise of the opposition, he announced that in Stage I of the development at Newport the ratio of Oxfordshire to imported ore would be not 40:60 but 30:70. R.T.B. would revert to the former proportion in Stage II and thereafter. He agreed that it would be technically feasible to use 100 per cent imported ore at Newport. But, he claimed, the ratios that they were proposing would mean cheaper steel. And now, for the first time, there was some precise, quantified indication of what this cost advantage might be. According to Hacking, R.T.B. would be able to produce pig iron 3 per cent (or 12s. per ton) cheaper if they used the 30:70 ratio. Presumably he meant 3 per cent cheaper than if they relied entirely on imported ore, though this was not made clear. In any event, Hacking could not himself explain how R.T.B. had arrived at this figure. It was based, he said, on calculations made by the company's accountant. The accountant was not at the inquiry, for the simple reason, it was implied, that R.T.B. did not attach any great significance to this cost advantage.

Their next witness was Mr Boys, who came to explain why the I.S.B. were supporting the applications. The I.S.B.'s policy, and the reasoning behind it, have already been explained. When it came to cross-examination Boys was hard pressed to justify the

Board's position on several important issues.[1] The I.S.B. advocated the maximum economic use of home-produced ore, he said, because home ore resulted in cheaper steel. But was it not a fact, asked Cusack, that in recent years the price of home ore had increased, whilst that of imported ore had gone down? Boys conceded that this was so; but, he said, there had also been a tendency for inland freight charges to go down, because the railways were prepared to give mineral traffic favourable rates. Then there was the question of maintaining adequate reserves, including strategic reserves. Oxfordshire ore, as everyone agreed, was near the surface, and easily extracted. While foreign ore was

---

[1] Before he gave evidence, there was an argument between opposing counsel about Boys's status as an official of the I.S.B., and the extent to which he was to be cross-examined. For the applicants, Widgery maintained that Boys could not be questioned on the thinking behind the I.S.B.'s policy. He pointed out that paragraph 318 of the Franks Committee's *Report on Administrative Tribunals and Enquiries* had recommended that officers of Government departments should confine their evidence to matters of fact, and should not venture into questions of policy. This, he said, had been accepted by the Government. It was true that the I.S.B. were not, strictly speaking, a Government department. Nevertheless, the principle remained the same: an officer could not be asked to say how his department or organisation had decided upon its policy. To question Boys about the reasons for the I.S.B.'s policy would be to ask him to look into the minds of all the constituent members of the Board, and this would clearly be unfair and impossible. Counsel for the objectors rejected this argument. Cusack argued that the I.S.B. were not a Government department, and Boys was not a civil servant. If Boys was to give evidence-in-chief, outlining the I.S.B.'s policy, then the objectors ought to be able to cross-examine him on it. He reminded the inquiry that the Oxfordshire County Council had anticipated this difficulty when they had suggested that evidence on behalf of the I.S.B. ought to be given by a whole-time member of the Board. If Widgery's contention was accepted, said Cusack, the I.S.B. had a position of immunity enjoyed by no other public or private body in the country. Suppose, he said, the application had come from a private company, and a director had come to the inquiry and said, 'Oh well, it's the policy of my trade federation that such and such a thing should be the case. You must not ask questions why: you must not question the trade federation.' If Boys could not answer questions on policy formation, said Cusack, then the Inspector should require someone else to come from the I.S.B. who could. That person, suggested Cusack, should be Sir Robert Shone, the executive member of the I.S.B. In the end, it was agreed that Boys should be cross-examined in the usual way, and that if Widgery objected the Inspector would rule on the admissibility of the question.

available at reasonable prices, was this not just the type of ore that ought to be kept for use in an emergency, asked Cusack? In an emergency, Boys replied, it would be easier to expand supplies rapidly in an area that was already being worked. But what would happen, asked Cusack, when the Oxfordshire deposits had been used up? They might indeed last for another thirty-five years, as Boys said. But what then? Again, there was the matter of distance between the Newport works and the Oxfordshire ore. Was it not a new departure to have a steelworks using as much as 40 per cent home ore when it was more than a hundred miles from its source of supplies? The Steel Company of Wales had been taking their ore from Oxfordshire, and so had other South Wales firms, said Boys. But then, as counsel pointed out, the Steel Company of Wales had found it so uneconomic to use Oxfordshire ore that they had now stopped.

The third witness for the applicants was Mr Smith, the General Manager of R.T.B. (Mineral Recovery) Ltd. Much of his evidence was concerned with the effect on the countryside of ironstone workings and the methods of extraction that the company intended to use. He denied the suggestion that even after restoration the contours of the area would be completely transformed into a flat prairie. But he agreed that the amount of farmland put out of agricultural use at any one time would be not 60 acres (as Widgery had claimed) but more like 200 in the first five years, rising to 450 acres twenty-five years later. He admitted that it would certainly be possible to see the quarries from public roads in the area, and these quarries, he agreed, would undeniably inflict a temporary scar on the countryside. It was also true that there would be a good deal of noise from detonations. Smith explained at some length how the company would do its best to mitigate the disturbance and shock. The explosions required for loosening the ore would not occur simultaneously; they would be phased out. But as counsel tartly observed, whilst the sound of detonations might be music in the ears of mineral recovery men, even phased-out explosions could hardly fail to disturb and annoy the local residents.

Last of the applicants' witnesses was Mr Knibbs, Managing Director of R.T.B. (Mineral Recovery) Ltd. It fell to him to explain why – if they were so set on Oxfordshire ore – R.T.B. were not making more of an effort to meet their needs from the

Oxfordshire Ironstone Company's Wroxton workings. R.T.B.'s attitude towards Wroxton has already been described. In their view, the Oxfordshire Ironstone Company could not guarantee sufficient ore in the long term; and even if they could, R.T.B. wanted their main source of home ore under their own control. Counsel for the Protection Committee put a much more sinister interpretation on R.T.B.'s policy, though it was an interpretation that reflected a very genuine fear among the local opposition. R.T.B., he suggested, were anxious at all costs to avoid a contract for Wroxton ore. If they once entered into a long-term contract with the Oxfordshire Ironstone Company, he said, they would have to take all the ore that they had contracted for, even though it might have become uneconomic to use any Oxfordshire ore at all at Newport. If R.T.B. were not bound by contract, he suggested, as soon as it became uneconomic to use Oxfordshire iron-stone they would simply abandon their workings. Knibbs could only reply that since he was not a Director of R.T.B. these matters were quite outside his jurisdiction.

It was now the turn of the objectors to develop their case. Their strategy was first to dwell upon the amenity value of the application areas; second, to demonstrate the grave and irreparable damage that the proposed ironstone workings would inflict on the natural beauty of north Oxfordshire; third, to suggest that the preservation of these amenities was in the national interest; and fourth, to argue that these valuable amenities should be destroyed only if it could be proved, beyond doubt, that other considerations outweighed the desirability of preserving them. The onus, they suggested, was on the applicants to show that their case was so watertight, so unassailable, and so proof against criticism, that in this instance it was in the national interest to sacrifice amenity. To a lesser extent, the opposition also argued that there would be a serious, albeit temporary, effect on agriculture.

As to the quality of the north Oxfordshire countryside, the opposition's principal witness was Mr M. W. Robinson, the Oxfordshire County Council's Planning Adviser. The application areas, he said, stretched across several miles of unspoiled and mature landscape. Scenically, this was one of the most attractive districts in the county. And the natural beauty of the countryside was enhanced by its charming villages and ironstone cottages.

The Great Tew area, he emphasised, was of particularly high aesthetic value, consisting as it did of steep-sides valleys, beautifully timbered, and forming an especially pleasing landscape. A large part of central Oxfordshire was scheduled in the County Development Plan as an Area of Great Landscape Value. He had reason to believe that the National Parks Commission was considering the designation of the Cotswolds as an Area of Outstanding Natural Beauty. The eastern boundary of that area came to within two miles of the western extremity of the proposed excavations, and in his opinion, the application areas east of Hook Norton and on the southern slopes of Swerford Heath and Iron Down might well have been included in this Area of Outstanding Natural Beauty, had they been adjacent to it.

What would be the effect of ironstone working on this lovely stretch of countryside? From their experience in the area north and west of Banbury, he said, they knew that open-cast mining, even after restoration, left the countryside bleak, bare and uninteresting. The absence of trees and hedges gave it a desolate and characterless appearance, and he did not see how this effect could be avoided. Even when some timber reappeared many years later, the natural contours of the land would have been distorted into something alien and unattractive. And, of course, in the immediate future the outlook was much worse. Massive pieces of machinery would be left standing about in the countryside; there would be periodic explosions; and trucks and lorries would be continuously shuttling backwards and forwards. Robinson was prepared to admit that so far as agriculture was concerned, in time the land could be brought back to something like full production. But from an aesthetic point of view, the attractiveness of an area worked over for ironstone was invariably destroyed. If there had to be open-cast mining in Oxfordshire, he argued, it should be confined to the area north of Banbury; there were nearly three thousand acres of untouched ironstone land there, he said, and the Oxfordshire County Council had raised no objection to quarrying in that part of the county.

In the course of his evidence, Robinson drew attention to other considerations which, he maintained, ought to be taken into account in cases of this kind. Beauty that nobody ever sees was perhaps of limited value. But one of the characteristics of the north Oxfordshire countryside was its accessibility: the main

roads were chiefly on high ground, and provided excellent vantage points for large numbers of visitors. The English countryside
was a diminishing asset; it was vital, therefore, to preserve what
was left. It was no use arguing that only the acknowledged beauty
spots ought to be saved, for carried to its logical conclusion this
theory would mean that only the beauty spots would remain for
public resort and enjoyment. In those circumstances, he asked,
how long would they continue to be beauty spots?

On the question of trees, the inquiry also heard evidence from
Mr C. M. Harris, the Oxfordshire County Council's Forestry
Consultant. This project, said Harris, would be nothing short of
vandalism. Trees were an accepted part of the Oxfordshire
scene. You could fell a large oak or elm or beech and bulldoze it
away in a day; but no power on earth could replace it in less than
a hundred years. The applicants had suggested that they could
extract ironstone from round the trees without harming them;
even if this was an economic proposition, the effect would be to
lower the water-table, and this alone would probably be enough
to kill trees even as much as fifty feet away from the workings.
After the land had been restored it might prove very difficult to
replace all the trees that had been destroyed, because where the
fresh soil was only a few inches deep the roots of the newly-
planted trees and hedges would soon reach impervious clay strata.
Under these conditions, plants would certainly deteriorate and
probably die.

The Oxfordshire County Council had plenty of allies prepared
to testify to the beauty and interest of the application areas. The
National Parks Commission's witness confirmed that the landscape affected was comparable to much of the Cotswolds, which
the Commission proposed to designate as an Area of Outstanding
Natural Beauty. The loss of natural beauty here, said the Commission's witness, would be grave and irremediable, because
however skilful the restoration it would leave the character of the
countryside permanently changed. The Council for the Preservation of Rural England took much the same line: their representatives had visited areas said to have been restored after ironstone
working, and compared with the surrounding land they looked
bare, impoverished and characterless. It would be a national
calamity, declared the C.P.R.E.'s witness, if Great Tew and
Swerford were spoiled.

The Banbury and Chipping Norton Borough Councils drew attention to the importance of the tourist industry for the area, whilst the Banbury and Chipping Norton R.D.C.'s were particularly worried about the possibility of the workings being abandoned if they became unprofitable in the future. This was a fear that was shared by the Treasurer of Christ Church, Oxford. The college, he said, had had some experience of ironstone operations in the past. He recalled that in 1917 they had signed a lease with Baldwins for certain workings. There was then a reshuffle and the lease was assigned to another company, which had come to the owners in the 1920s with a hard luck story, and offered them a choice between a reduction of 30 per cent in royalties or the abandonment of the workings. The same situation might be repeated here. It was some measure of the intensity of feeling against these proposals, he added, that Christ Church and the other land- and mineral-owners in the area should oppose the applications and voluntarily turn down royalties that might amount to £4 million.

Though clearly of secondary importance by comparison with the amenity objections, there was also opposition to the applications on agricultural grounds. The Oxfordshire branch of the N.F.U. argued that the proposed workings would inflict financial loss and personal hardship on the farmers in the area. They did not claim that restoration was impossible; but it would be many years before the soil was in good heart again. And in the meantime there would be a direct loss of land as a result of the opencast mining, and constant interference with the efficiency of farm working as the quarry faces advanced. The N.F.U. were supported in their objections by the Oxfordshire branch of the C.L.A. and by Major Robb, who pointed out that so far as his tenants were concerned the prospect of iron-ore workings would cast a blight on farming land and would certainly discourage the necessary capital investment.

There was certainly a strong case for preserving this stretch of the north Oxfordshire countryside. And there could be no doubt that local opinion was overwhelmingly against the applications. Nevertheless, as the objectors judiciously conceded, there are times when even the strongest feelings must give way to overriding necessity. Excellent though the case for preservation might be, possibly the applicants had even better arguments, that would demonstrate beyond any shadow of doubt that it really was essential, in the national interest, for them to extract ironstone from this attractive and unspoiled corner of England. The opposition now turned their attention to the case for the applicants.

The attack was based chiefly on the findings of the Economist Intelligence Unit and on the expert evidence of Professor P. Sargant Florence, the former professor of Commerce at the University of Birmingham. Sargant Florence argued that if the new strip mill had been sited in Oxfordshire or the south Midlands, the use of Oxfordshire ore would have been logical enough. But it was more than a hundred miles from Oxfordshire to Newport; and since the port facilities there were so good, the new steelworks was ideally situated to use imported ore. As for the I.S.B.'s policy decision to encourage the maximum economic use of home ore, this (he said) had been overtaken by events. The case for using home ore in large quantities might have been sound enough even as late as 1956 or 1957; but within the previous two or three years the situation had changed so much that the Board's policy no longer made sense, at least as far as the Newport strip mill was concerned.

When they had settled their policy, said Sargant Florence, the I.S.B. must have taken three main factors into account. They were: the price of imported ore, the price of home ore, and railway freight rates. What had happened under each of these heads since 1956?

So far as the price of imported ore was concerned, he said, it was clear that after what had turned out to be a misleading rise in 1957 (the year of the I.S.B.'s Special Report) the trend had been rapidly downward. Taking 1956 as 100, the price index had moved as follows: 1957: 105; 1958: 95; 1959: 86. By contrast, the price of home-produced ore had steadily risen, the index reading: 1956: 100; 1957: 108; 1958: 113; 1959: 123. Within the previous few years, Sargant Florence pointed out, railway freight rates had also gone up. There had been a rise of 10 per cent in August 1957 and another $7\frac{1}{2}$ per cent in October 1958. This upward movement was likely to continue, he said. With the Newport works 115 miles away from the application areas, a small increase in freight charges could make a big difference to the cost of home ore at the strip mill.

As for the availability of foreign ore, he reminded the inquiry that the last United Nations Survey of World Iron-ore Resources had been carried out in 1955. It was now clear, he said, that this Survey had seriously underestimated the extent of world reserves. Yet, presumably, that was the only estimate available to the I.S.B. when they formulated their policy and prepared their Special Report in 1957. And presumably this was the estimate that the Board had had in mind when they decided that R.T.B.'s new steelworks should use a substantial proportion of home ore. 'Whatever justification there may have been in the past', declared Sargant Florence, 'for a greater exploitation of home ore on the ground of difficulties in obtaining imported ore, this clearly does not apply now.'

Then there was the impact on the balance of payments of using imported ore, another argument that was supposed to tell in favour of the I.S.B.'s policy. On the visible side of the trade account, he conceded, it was obvious that there would be some adverse effects. However, any losses there might very well be off-set in other ways. The British Government's policy was to give aid to countries like Mauretania to help them develop their iron-ore industries. But trade was a better policy than aid, he claimed, and if we imported raw materials from underdeveloped countries we would probably open up new markets for our own exporters. Moreover, to assure these underdeveloped countries of a market for their commodities was to improve the prospects for political stability, which, in turn, would help safeguard future supplies of iron ore. There would also be a gain on the so-called 'invisible' side of trade account, he suggested. This would take the form of payments for the use of British shipping together with a financial return on British investment in some of these overseas sources of iron ore. They ought to remember, he added, that this part of Oxfordshire was a favourite resort of American tourists; it was areas like this that attracted them to England in the first place. A good many English tourists also visited north Oxfordshire. Some of them might well choose to go abroad if the local country-side was ruined.

By this point, Sargant Florence was clearly down among the makeweights of his evidence. The Inspector was still thinking about his earlier arguments, and he was evidently anxious to make sure that he had grasped the full import of what the eminent economist was saying. The next few moments were to be

among the most important in the whole of the inquiry, as the
Inspector carefully took Sargant Florence back over the main
points in his evidence. Would it be possible, asked the Inspector,
to draw up a simple balance-sheet setting out the total economic
cost of extracting ironstone from Oxfordshire, and comparing this
with the cost of importing the necessary supplies from abroad?
The answer to that, Sargant Florence replied, depended on
whether the Inspector was including loss of amenity under economic cost. The point was, he continued, that economists like
himself often used the expression 'real costs' to include psychological costs; the loss of beautiful scenery certainly would be a
psychological cost. The trouble was, of course, that costs of this
kind were not easy to quantify. In this particular case, however,
the problem of putting a money value on loss of amenity hardly
mattered, because the applicants had failed to establish that their
scheme had any advantages even on those criteria that were
measurable. Three years earlier, he said, there probably had been
some economic advantage in using home ore rather than imported
ore. But by 1960 the costs of home and imported ore were much
the same. When amenity was also thrown into the scales, there
could be no doubt where the balance of advantage lay. Anyone
could see, he implied, that it did not lie in R.T.B.'s scheme to dig
up the Oxfordshire countryside in order to extract ironstone that
they could get just as cheaply from abroad.

It now remained only for counsel to sum up in their final
speeches. From the opposition there was more criticism of R.T.B.
for not sending better-informed and more authoritative witnesses
in support of applications that were supposed to be so vital to
them. As they reminded the Inspector, only one witness had come
from the parent company itself, and he was a technical expert,
not in a position to deal with matters of policy. He had been
joined by two executives from the subsidiary company, and these
'three musketeers', as Cusack described them, 'had been sent
forth by their superiors, lurking somewhere in Monmouthshire, to
capture this vast stretch of Oxfordshire countryside'. True, there
had been one representative from the I.S.B., and he had been a
fair and helpful witness. But his knowledge and authority were
clearly limited.

From the very beginning, the opposition claimed, the I.S.B.
had maintained that their policy of encouraging the maximum

use of home ore was based primarily on its cost advantage over imported ore. In the light of the evidence heard at the inquiry, the I.S.B.'s policy now looked decidedly suspect. But even if the general policy was sound, the I.S.B. had never instructed R.T.B. to use Oxfordshire ore at Newport. That was a decision for R.T.B., and it certainly did not follow that the company was obliged slavishly to adopt the I.S.B.'s policy even when, patently, there was no cost advantage in their particular case.

As for the applicants' assertion that the 30:70 ratio would mean a 3 per cent saving in the cost of producing pig iron, that claim was totally unsupported by evidence. How could the applicants possibly put forward a precise figure like this? They had admitted that no freight rates had yet been negotiated with the British Transport Commission; they had not yet agreed rents and royalties with about thirty-six landowners in the application areas; and they had not yet entered into a contract with the Oxfordshire Ironstone Company for the quota of iron ore to be drawn from the Wroxton area. With all these unknown quantities, it was quite impossible for the applicants to make a reliable estimate of any cost advantage from the use of Oxfordshire ore. No wonder, it was implied, that R.T.B. had been so reluctant to disclose, far less discuss, how these calculations had been made. And small wonder that there was no one from R.T.B. at the inquiry to be cross-examined on them. The Minister was entitled to conclude that R.T.B.'s costings were sheer guesswork. Even if these figures had any meaning at present, they would be completely unreliable as a guide to costs in thirty-five years' time. The applicants had suggested during the inquiry that figures could be supplied in confidence to the Minister. To do this would be to perpetrate a fraud on the public; if the Minister needed further information the only legitimate way of obtaining it was to reopen the inquiry.

The last word was with the applicants. In his closing address Widgery argued that the Minister had four questions to consider. First, were the I.S.B. right in adopting the policy of making the maximum economic use of home ore? Second, if the policy was right, were the applicants correct in saying that they had to look to Oxfordshire for the ore they needed? Third, could the necessary ore be found in the Wroxton area? And fourth, if the ore could not be found in the Wroxton area, did the amenity arguments outweigh the applicants' case?

The fundamental question, Widgery insisted, was the first. Was the I.S.B.'s policy right in the national interest? When the Newport works were planned, R.T.B. had been asked to conform to the I.S.B.'s policy, and they were content to base their case on the correctness or otherwise of that policy. In the last resort, it was for the Government, and not the applicants, or the public inquiry, to say whether or not the I.S.B.'s policy was sound. How could any steel producer, however important, say whether the national interest required the maximum use of home ore? There was, for example, the question of the balance of payments. To use home ore would save foreign exchange, and only the Minister, in consultation with other Ministers, could decide how much weight should be given to this argument. On a matter of this kind, he said, the final decision could not possibly depend exclusively on the evidence given at the inquiry, because the Government had specialists to advise them on balance of payments questions. The same considerations applied to Sargant Florence's evidence as to the need for 'trade not aid'. The Government was not going to look to a public local inquiry for advice on a policy question like this, and it would have been pointless for R.T.B. to call witnesses to deal with it. Exactly the same could be said of the evidence that the objectors had submitted about the desirability of leaving home ore as a strategic reserve. This was not a matter for amateur strategists in R.T.B. or at the inquiry.

The opposition had argued that it could not be right for R.T.B. to adopt the I.S.B.'s policy in this particular case, because whereas the Board's policy had been adopted in order to save on the costs of producing steel, the applicants had not shown that Oxfordshire ore would mean cheaper steel at Newport. This objection entirely missed the point, he said. It was important to be clear that the I.S.B.'s policy was *not* 'the use of home ore when that produces the maximum of economy'. Rather, the policy implied (in Widgery's words) 'that you use as much home ore as you can until the time comes when it is uneconomic. That is to say, until the time comes when you are losing money as a result.' The first approach, Widgery suggested, would entail that you use home ore only when you can show a substantial cost advantage by doing so. All along, the objectors had been putting this argument into the mouths of the applicants, whilst in reality this was not their position at all. This was why the question of costings was not important. 'Costings become insignificant', said Widgery, 'when our case is recognised to be what it is – namely that we understand the I.S.B. to direct the maximum use of home ore up to the point when it ceases to be economic to do so. For it to be economic in that sense', he went on, 'does not require any specific cost advantage. Indeed, it does not require any cost advantage at all; it merely requires that by and large there should be no cost disadvantage. Anyone who suggests that the use of this ore would be uneconomic must ask, "Why in that case are R.T.B. making such a fuss about getting it?" We are not here for amusement', he declared, 'we are here because we want the ore.'

So, unless the I.S.B.'s policy was misguided (and this was not a matter for R.T.B. or for the inquiry), the applicants were right to use 30 per cent and later 40 per cent home ore at Newport. Once the broad policy was accepted, the choice of Oxfordshire ironstone was virtually automatic, because it was the nearest ore-field to the Newport works, and it also had the necessary phosphorus content. Nevertheless, it might still be said that the applicants should take what they needed from the Wroxton area. Everyone agreed that Wroxton ore would have to be supplied by the Oxfordshire Ironstone Company. The question was, how much could they be safely relied upon to produce for the new strip mill? On 3 March 1960, said Widgery, the Oxfordshire Ironstone Company had told the County Council that they could supply R.T.B. with 500,000 tons of iron ore immediately, and, given consent for their additional planning applications, they could expand supplies to 1 million tons a year by 1963. It was true, as had been said at the inquiry, that since then they had ceased to supply ore to the Steel Company of Wales. Even so, there was nothing to show that the Oxfordshire Ironstone Company could meet the needs of the Newport works. The County Council could have called representatives of the company as witnesses to substantiate their claim that Wroxton could supply the necessary ore. But this had not been done. The fact was that in the near future R.T.B. would require 1 million tons a year, and the Oxfordshire Ironstone Company could guarantee only half that figure. And assuming that the strip mill moved on to Stage II – as there was every reason to suppose it would – the potential output of the Wroxton area would be left far behind.

If the Minister agreed that the basic policy still held good,

Widgery concluded, then Oxfordshire had to supply the ore; and the Wroxton area could not supply anything like the calculated need of the new strip mill in the future. Thus, inevitably, the applicants had arrived at the application areas so vigorously defended at the inquiry. For their part, R.T.B. believed that the objectors were exaggerating the effects of ironstone working on the local amenities. It was only natural that they should. But since every other consideration pointed so inexorably to this particular area, the question facing the Inspector and the Minister was this: would the proposed ironstone workings really inflict so much damage on the countryside that the applicants' case ought to fail at this last hurdle?

On 18 November 1960 the inquiry came to an end. Having toured the application areas to see for himself, the Inspector retired to write his report. The anxious defenders of the north Oxfordshire countryside and the steel men lurking in Monmouthshire now awaited the verdict from Whitehall.

ECHOES IN PARLIAMENT

While the Inspector pondered upon what he had seen and heard at Banbury, rumblings from the Oxfordshire countryside reached Westminster. At Question time on 28 November Neil Marten, the Member for Banbury, asked Mr Richard Wood, the Parliamentary Secretary to the Minister of Power, how much R.T.B. had already spent on capital development specifically designed to handle Oxfordshire ironstone. The company had so far spent £250,000, and it was committed to spending another £1,350,000, Wood replied. He had been told, he added, that if it became necessary, the plant already installed could be used to deal with ore from other sources. Why had this expenditure been authorised before the result of the inquiry was announced?' asked Marten. Was it not true that R.T.B. were trying to influence the outcome of the inquiry? The Minister of Housing was certainly not going to be blackmailed, Wood retorted, if that was what Marten was suggesting. In any event, he added, the Minister had been told that if the decision should go against R.T.B. they would have incurred very little nugatory expenditure.[1]

[1] *H.C. Deb.* (1960–71) 631, cols 11–12.

Soon afterwards, a far more formidable challenge to the Government was mounted in the House of Lords. On 1 December Lord Lucas of Chilworth asked the Lord Chancellor (Lord Kilmuir) if, in view of the widespread concern that had been aroused, he would refer the whole matter of the north Oxfordshire inquiry to the Council on Tribunals. Lucas did not want to influence the Inspector's report, or the Minister's decision. But he thought that there should be a full investigation into what had occurred before and during the inquiry, so that the Council on Tribunals could rule on whether or not the procedure had been in accordance with the spirit and the precept of the Franks Committee's report, which had called for openness, fairness and impartiality at statutory inquiries.

Lord Lucas went on to accuse the Ministry of Housing and Local Government, the I.S.B. and R.T.B. of withholding every scrap of vital information that the objectors needed for the proper conduct of their case. He recalled that at the inquiry counsel for the applicants had begun by claiming that they were only carrying out the policy of the I.S.B. and had then gone on to make the 'fallacious, dangerous and quite erroneous statement', that the I.S.B. 'stood in all regards as a Government Department', and therefore were not answerable for their policy to a public inquiry. He reminded the Lords that the applicants had refused to give any information about their costs, but had said that these figures could be supplied in confidence to the Minister after the inquiry was over. Again, during the inquiry one of the applicants' witnesses had said, or implied, that £2 million had already been spent on equipment specially designed for Oxfordshire ore. That now turned out to be quite untrue.[1] Only a few days earlier, a Minister had told the House of Commons that only £250,000 had been spent, and that there would be very little wasted expenditure if planning permission were refused. If there had been a barrister in charge of the inquiry, a man experienced in taking evidence, none of this would have happened. As it was,

---

[1] In fairness, it should be added that both the applicants and the I.S.B. deny that any such statement was made at the public inquiry. The misunderstanding arose, they claim, because of inaccurate reporting in the press, due in part to bad acoustics. It is certainly true that in the official transcript of evidence several passages are so garbled as to be quite incomprehensible.

added Lord Lucas, the objectors had been obliged to spend
£5,000 in trying to answer a case that had never been put.

He was supported by Lord Salter, the President of the Town
and Country Planning Association. In cases of this kind, he said,
there was usually the problem of weighing the expected economic
advantage against the prospective destruction of the beauties and
amenities of the countryside. But in this instance the applicants
had refused to indicate how much economic advantage they
hoped to gain from their proposals. In his view, the applicants
had been reticent because they themselves were conscious of the
weakness of their own case.

In reply, the Lord Chancellor said that he was distressed to
hear Lord Salter dealing with the merits of the case, even though
he knew that the Inspector had not yet reported to the Minister.
It was quite improper, he went on, to try to put pressure on the
Inspector and the Minister in this way while the case was still
sub judice. Lord Salter interrupted to observe that a public
inquiry was not the same as a court of law: and if critics waited
until the decision was announced it was always too late to express
an opinion. The Lord Chancellor was not impressed. He reaffirmed that the Minister would never be influenced by evidence
that had not been available to both sides in the dispute; that, he
said, would be contrary to natural justice, and he would never be
a party to proceedings of that kind. Until the Minister had the
Inspector's report, it would be premature to consider referring
the case to the Council on Tribunals. In the meantime, he would
look into the criticisms of the way in which the inquiry had been
conducted.[1]

The Lord Chancellor told the House the outcome of his
enquiries in answer to a Parliamentary Question on 13 April
1961.[2] He did not feel that a reference to the Council on Tribunals
would be justified. Lord Lucas had suggested that the Minister of
Housing and Local Government was under pressure because
R.T.B. had already committed themselves to considerable expenditure. There could be no question, said the Lord Chancellor,
of the Inspector's or the Minister's judgement being influenced

[1] *H.L. Deb.* (1961–2) 226, cols 1226–48.
[2] By now, the Minister of Housing and Local Government had been in
possession of the Inspector's Report for something like three months. The
Minister's decision had not yet been announced.

by the fact that expenditure had been incurred before the inquiry, or by the statement made by counsel for the applicants that the Government had a financial interest in the parent company. 'The developer who embarks on expenditure in such circumstances', he went on, 'is assumed to be aware of the risk he is running, and developers often refer to commitments of this sort, particularly in mineral cases. On such matters the manner in which they present their case at the inquiry is for the developers themselves to decide, but no weight is given to arguments of this sort in reaching a decision.'

Lord Lucas had maintained that vital information had been withheld by the I.S.B., R.T.B. and the Ministry. It was obviously in the applicants' own interest, said the Lord Chancellor, to support their application by making available as much relevant information as possible. But it could not be held against them if they took the view that there was a limit to the information they were prepared to give. So far as the Ministry of Housing was concerned, when an application was called in the Minister could elicit before the inquiry only as much information as the applicants were willing to supply. They could not be required, before the inquiry, to elaborate their description of the proposed development. This was their task at the inquiry itself, and the view taken by the Inspector would depend largely upon the applicants' ability and willingness to justify their proposals. In this particular case, the Lord Chancellor went on, the company had prepared a written statement which had been made available to the County Council and to the Inspector. They had gone further, and entered into correspondence with the County Council. If the applicants had failed at the inquiry itself to support with detailed evidence their generalisations on comparative costs, this should not be regarded as depriving their opponents of an opportunity to attack them in cross-examination, but rather as reducing their own chances of obtaining planning permission. In short, he said, the applicants had gained no advantage from not producing further information.[1]

Lord Lucas, however, was not satisfied, and on 20 April he formally asked the Council on Tribunals to consider various unsatisfactory features of the procedure both before and at the inquiry. Subsequently, the Oxfordshire County Council associated

[1] *H.L. Deb.* (1961–2) 230, cols 421–6.

themselves with his request. But long before the Council on Tribunals had looked into the procedural issues raised by Lord Lucas, the anxiously awaited result of the battle of north Oxfordshire was announced.

THE VERDICT AND AFTER

The Inspector's report was presented to Mr Henry Brooke, the Minister of Housing and Local Government, on 10 January 1961. As is usual with reports of this kind, it began with a description of the area involved, and summarised the arguments and counterarguments advanced by both sides at the inquiry. The Inspector then set out his own observations and conclusions. The applicants, he said, had not made out a case on the grounds of cost advantage. True, one of their witnesses had claimed that to use Oxfordshire ore in the proposed proportions would save 3 per cent on the cost of producing pig iron at the Newport works. That witness, however, had not personally been responsible for making these calculations, and he had not been able to say how the company's accountant had arrived at this figure.

As the Inspector saw it, one relevant fact that had emerged from the exchanges on costs was that if there was any advantage at all in using Oxfordshire ore it was very small, and could easily be reversed if economic conditions changed. If the working areas were opened up, and then became unprofitable, there was a risk that they might be abandoned. Or alternatively, if the relative prices of home and imported ore should fluctuate in the future, the workings might be intermittent, and the period of working could be prolonged.

In the Inspector's opinion, there were four arguments in favour of granting the applications. First, there was a demand for Oxfordshire ore in the steel industry. Second, the prosperity of the steel industry was important to the national economy. Third, the potential consumers of the ore at the Newport works expected to make a saving in production costs as a result of using this ore. And fourth, the use of home ore, either from the application areas or from elsewhere, meant a saving on the nation's import bill.

On the other hand, there were two main arguments against granting planning permission. First, the proposed workings would interfere with agriculture over a long period and would impair the efficiency of farming operations. And second, they would certainly injure the amenities of the area. The Inspector had been favourably impressed by the continuity in the character of the villages from Great Tew to East Adderbury, the ironstone walling being the predominant link. The proposed workings would undoubtedly cause severe damage to the rural amenities: there was no question that they would destroy natural features and create a great deal of noise and disturbance. The damage would be more severe in the area south of the river Swere; but the working of any part of the application areas would lessen the attractions of the district as a whole. As the quarry faces advanced across the countryside there would be two sorts of terrain. Ahead of the workings people would see mature farmland; behind them there would be rather bare, restored land at a lower level. What with mechanical face-shovels, 27-ton dumper trucks, the other plant used for removing overburden, railway sidings, and periodic explosions, there would be a considerable amount of noise. The Hook Norton and Iron Down area had specially impressed him. 'It is not exaggeration', he wrote, 'to say that this part of the application areas is beautiful country, and that from an aesthetic point of view, iron ore workings would be a calamity.' The applicants had said that they would restore land progressively as the working faces advanced. But however successful restoration might be as regards reshaping the land, it would be many years before the landscape reached maturity, and even then it would be difficult to disguise changes of level where worked-out land adjoined roads and buildings.

The applicants had established that there was a demand for this ore. But they had conceded that the demand could be met in other ways. There was no evidence, the Inspector added, that the needs of industry made it essential to work these areas. In his view, the balance in terms of economics, including agricultural considerations, was uncertain.

Then came the crucial value-judgement. If there was any small economic advantage to be gained from extracting the ore from all or any of the application areas, the Inspector concluded, it was outweighed by the injury to amenity. He therefore recommended that all the applications should be rejected and that planning permission should be refused, on the grounds that the extraction of iron ore would cause serious damage and loss to agriculture and would inflict severe injury on the rural amenities by destroying natural features and by creating noise and disturbance.

It was not until 8 May 1961 – four months after receiving the Inspector's report – that the Minister of Housing and Local Government announced his decision. Part of the delay may perhaps be attributed to the Lord Chancellor's investigations. The Minister accepted his Inspector's recommendations and rejected all the applications.

In his decision-letter the Minister made it clear that in his opinion the applicants had failed to establish that it was essential to work the areas in question. Since the workings were *not* essential, it was a question of weighing the objections against the economic argument put forward by the applicants. There were two objections. They were damage to agriculture and injury to the amenities. So far as agriculture was concerned, a part of the land (a relatively small part) would be taken out of agricultural use for the full working period. On the other hand, the interference with agriculture caused by the extraction of ironstone would be for the most part of a temporary nature, and in any case would be largely overcome, as working proceeded, by the progressive restoration of worked-out land. In the Minister's opinion, therefore, the effect of the proposed development on agriculture would not have been, of itself, a sufficient reason for withholding planning permission if a strong case for the applicants had been made out.

But taking the agricultural considerations together with the injury to amenities, the Minister thought that ironstone working should not be permitted in these areas (especially in the very attractive areas south of the river Swere) without clear evidence of an overriding economic need. He was not convinced that there was such a need in relation to the whole, or any part of the land in question. Nor did he think that enough attention had been given to the possibility of drawing additional supplies from the Wroxton area.

And there ended this protracted struggle over the use of some four thousand acres of the north Oxfordshire countryside. The Minister's verdict was received with delight and relief in Oxfordshire. The battle was over, and the opposition had won.

Only the postscripts remained to be written. Insisting all along that he had been concerned with the procedural aspects of the inquiry, and not with the merits of the case, Lord Lucas refused to withdraw his reference to the Council on Tribunals. The Council delivered its opinion in the Annual Report for 1961. There were no grounds for serious complaint, it thought, though when the Government had a specific financial interest in a planning application there was something to be said for appointing an independent Inspector, as was usually done with proposals to establish or extend a New Town. But in general, the Council on Tribunals endorsed the arguments put forward earlier by the Lord Chancellor. On the alleged failure of the applicants to make available all the necessary information prior to the inquiry, it suggested that if developers did not produce evidence, that might show the weakness of their case, but it did not demonstrate that there were any deficiencies in the inquiry procedure.[1]

As for the steel industry, it no doubt felt entitled to some guidance from the Government about the policy that it ought to follow in the aftermath of the Oxfordshire decision. This came in a letter from the Minister of Power to the chairman of the I.S.B. in the spring of 1962. It was the Government's intention, wrote the Minister, that the steel industry should use whatever ore was considered, on balance, to be most economic. The producers ought therefore to be free to make use of home ore from a particular site whenever it was clear after a careful examination (if necessary at a public inquiry) that agricultural, amenity, scientific and social objections did not override the case for its use on

[1] This argument is open to two objections. In the first place, any information that the applicant deliberately chooses to keep back is not likely to be evidence that he thinks would help his case. On the contrary, if anything is deliberately concealed, it will be information that might help the objectors. In these circumstances, applications might succeed because the developer has managed to suppress information that would have weakened his case. Secondly, and admittedly this is much less likely, the applicants might simply misjudge the situation. They might conceivably hold back evidence, either because they wrongly judge that it will harm their case or because they think it unimportant, when, had it been available, it might have improved their chances. In these circumstances, the applicants would not be the only losers, for it is clearly not in the public interest that objectors should succeed because a developer has misguidedly or inadvertently failed to produce all the evidence necessary to enable the Minister to reach the right decision.

economic and balance of payments grounds. The Government did not accept the argument that our national resources should be reserved for an emergency. Foreign ore could be drawn from widely separated parts of the world; and furthermore, the Government had been told that it was easier to increase production quickly from areas already being worked than to open up new quarries. Though the Government did not wish to make light of the inconvenience of ironstone working to individual farmers, from the national standpoint arguments drawing attention to the loss of agricultural production did not appear to carry much conviction. From a narrowly economic point of view, iron-ore mining was a more profitable use of land than growing crops or raising stock. And in any case, ironstone extraction involved only a temporary loss of agricultural output, because the land could soon be restored to its original use after the ore had been taken out. But, said the Minister, 'the real possibility of doing irreparable damage to beautiful parts of the country must certainly be avoided'.[1]

And what of R.T.B., deprived of their Oxfordshire application areas? The heavens did not fall. According to the I.S.B.'s Annual Report for 1961, R.T.B. had begun negotiations for increased supplies from the Wroxton area. As compared with what had originally been intended, they also expected the Newport works to be able to use rather more imported ore.

[1] *H.C. Deb.* (1961–2) 658, cols 52–3.

3 Holme Pierrepont and the Power Station

If a station is in an urban area they say it is not safe.
If it is in the country they say that the best agricultural
land in England cannot be spared, and if it is in a
wilderness like Dungeness that is the last breeding
ground of some strange insect, and the station must
not be built there.

Sir Ian Horobin, Parliamentary Secretary to
the Minister of Power, June 1959

COMING SOUTH over Trent Bridge, and taking the Grantham
road out of Nottingham, the traveller soon finds himself in comparatively open country, for between the residential suburbs of
Carlton and West Bridgford a wedge of farmland pushes in to
within a mile or so of the city centre. This wedge forms part of
the Nottingham Green Belt, and through it the river winds east-
wards, before turning sharply north at the village of Radcliffe-on-
Trent. On the south bank of the river, some three miles
downstream from Trent Bridge, stands the hamlet of Holme
Pierrepont, where a solid Tudor hall and a tiny church, set in
surrounding parkland, look across the water meadows and down
to the Trent. Between Holme Pierrepont and the built-up area of
West Bridgford there are flat, open fields, broken only by a few
country lanes and a certain amount of gravel-working near the
river. In the summer, this is a popular place for sailing and riverside walks, and during the winter a local rugby club has for some
years played its matches in these agreeable surroundings. Aesthetic
judgements are always highly subjective, and there were to be
differences of opinion about the scenic beauty of this particular
stretch of countryside. But no one could deny that it was a quiet,
secluded and attractive spot, and all the more pleasant for being
so close to the heart of a great industrial city. It was here, early

in 1960, that the Central Electricity Generating Board proposed to build a 2,000-megawatt coal-fired power station.

Modern power stations are among the most massive structures on the face of the earth, and this was to be the largest coal-fired generating station in Europe. It was to occupy a site of more than 500 acres, with a frontage of one and a half miles along the north side of the A52, the Nottingham to Grantham road. Altogether, the complex was to consist of a boiler house 900 feet long, by 190 feet wide, by 200 feet high; a turbine house of very nearly the same dimensions; eight reinforced concrete cooling towers, each 370 feet high, with a diameter of 300 feet at the base and 200 feet at the top; two chimneys each 650 feet in height; an open compound of something like 1,300 feet by 600 feet, to house the switchgear; a total of more than six miles of railway sidings; and 45 acres of reserve coal stacked to a height of 30 feet. In case the mind is numbed by a catalogue of measurements, it is worth recalling, for purposes of comparison, the height of a few other well-known buildings. St Paul's Cathedral is 365 feet, Salisbury Cathedral 404 feet, and the Blackpool Tower 525 feet high. True, the 650-foot chimneys would be almost needle-like in appearance. But the same could hardly be said of the eight 370-foot cooling towers, each more than sixty yards across at the top. Nor is the effect of a power station on the local environment confined to its visual impact. Very large quantities of coal must be brought by rail every day to the site, and considerable quantities of ash taken away. There is also the question of chimney emissions. What exactly comes out of a power station's chimneys is a matter of argument; but whatever it is, it certainly does nothing to sweeten the surrounding atmosphere.

When the C.E.G.B.'s plans were made public there was astonishment and anger in and around Nottingham. How could a responsible public body even contemplate building a power station in a Green Belt and so close to the city? But change the perspective, look at the situation from the C.E.G.B.'s point of view, and it is not difficult to see what had brought them to Holme Pierrepont.[1]

[1] The chief documentary sources for the following account are: Public Inquiry Report (17 May, 1961), together with verbatim transcript of evidence; *Hansard*; *The Times*; *Guardian Journal*; Nottinghamshire County Council, Minutes and Reports.

No sector of British industry has been more stretched to keep pace with the requirements of post-war economic growth and personal affluence than electricity supply. Between 1945 and 1960 the consumption of electricity more than trebled; to meet the demand, over sixty new generating stations were built during this period, and the capacity of more than sixty others extended. As laid down in the Electricity Acts of 1947 and 1957, it is the duty of the C.E.G.B. to develop and maintain an efficient and economic supply in England and Wales, generating electricity in bulk for the Area Boards to distribute. Side by side with their responsibility for providing electricity as cheaply as possible, under Section 37 of the 1957 Act the Board also have a statutory duty to take into account the effect of their activities on local amenities. These two obligations are often in conflict. Pylons and overhead transmission lines, for example, are never popular additions to the landscape: the cables can be laid underground and out of sight, but only at very considerable extra cost. In most parts of the country, power stations are also unwelcome; and it sometimes happens that the cheapest available site is at the same time open to serious objection on amenity grounds.

Reviewing their future needs in the late fifties, the C.E.G.B. estimated that in the six-year period from 1960 to the end of 1965 work would have to start on two or three new power stations every year. There were clearly going to be problems, for by this stage the Board's extensive construction programme since the end of the war had already used up many of the less contentious sites. Generating stations can hardly ever be built in cities and towns, because sites of sufficient size are simply not available. The choice therefore lay between fairly remote rural districts and the outer fringes of built-up areas. What with National Parks, Areas of Outstanding Natural Beauty, Areas of Great Landscape Value, Green Belts, Nature Reserves, and Sites of Special Scientific Interest, it was becoming increasingly difficult to find sites that did not provoke opposition from one amenity interest or another. To make matters worse, the number of possible sites for coal-fired power stations was in any case very much restricted by reason of economic constraints that confined the search to certain parts of the country. And within the areas that were broadly suitable, technical considerations still further reduced the range of effective choice.

By the late fifties the post-war shortage of coal was over.
Indeed, as a result of growing competition from oil and nuclear
energy, within a few years the industry was to be hard pressed to
sell all the coal it produced. As the National Coal Board well
knew, the long-term prospects for coal were largely dependent
upon the C.E.G.B. and upon their willingness to go on building
large coal-fired power stations. For their part, the C.E.G.B. were
satisfied that coal *could* remain competitive with other sources of
energy, but only if the sites for new generating stations were carefully chosen to minimise capital and operational costs.

There was obviously a great deal to be said for siting power
stations as near as possible to the coal they would burn. For this
reason, the important Nottinghamshire and Derbyshire coalfield
was naturally an area of considerable interest to the C.E.G.B.
Apart from coal, generating stations also require very large
quantities of water for cooling purposes. In the east Midlands the
one really reliable source of water all the year round was the
river Trent. Drawn to the Trent valley by this combination of
coal and water, in 1958 the C.E.G.B. began to look for two large
sites for power stations needed in the mid-sixties. As we shall see,
securing ministerial consent for power stations can be a time-
consuming and even hazardous business;[1] in order to reduce the
need for more new sites in the future, the Board hoped to be able
to find areas that were large enough both for first, or 'A' stations,
and also for second, 'B' stations, at a later date.

Within the Trent valley area, the number of available sites was
strictly limited. Any location on which tall chimneys might interfere with flying from nearby airfields could be ruled out at once.
The ground itself had to be level, with satisfactory foundation
conditions to support the immense weight of the generators and
boilers. If it was eventually to house two power stations, the site
had to be at least 500 acres in extent. It had to be as near the
river as possible, but above flood level. To keep to a minimum
the need for new transmission lines, the site had to be conveniently
placed in relation to the existing grid system. Coal had to be
brought in, and at least part of the waste ash taken away by

[1] For a full account of the consents procedure for power stations and
overhead lines, see Appendix 72 to the *Minutes of Evidence* given to the
Select Committee on Nationalised Industries (Electricity Supply), vol. III
(May 1963).

train; the site therefore had to have reasonably good rail connections.

By the spring of 1959 the Station Planning and Development Branch had drawn up a short-list of the more promising possibilities, and in March the C.E.G.B. announced that the five sites which they thought warranted further examination were at Market Warsop, West Burton, Cottam, Holme Pierrepont, and Ratcliffe-on-Soar. Market Warsop (some four miles north of Mansfield) was hardly a serious contender, and was quickly eliminated. It was well placed for coal, but as it was so far from the Trent, its feasibility depended on the successful development of dry cooling towers. The C.E.G.B. were still awaiting the results of experimental trials with one of these towers at Rugeley in Staffordshire, and at this stage they were not sure whether they could be used in a large-scale generating station. This left the four riverside sites. Cottam was in open country and about thirty miles north-east of Nottingham. West Burton was still further north, near Sturton-le-Steeple. On the other side of Nottingham, Ratcliffe-on-Soar was about nine miles south-west of the city, and on the outer edge of the Green Belt. Though close to the main-line railway from London, it lay within what was then a secluded fold of countryside near the confluence of the Trent and the Soar. (Subsequently, the M1 motorway was extended to run almost alongside the site.) Holme Pierrepont has already been described.

There was only one cloud on the horizon. At a meeting in March with Mr R. A. Kidd, the Nottinghamshire County Council's Director of Planning, the C.E.G.B. learned that the two sites in the Green Belt – Holme Pierrepont and Ratcliffe-on-Soar – were likely to stir up a good deal of local opposition. At a second meeting, on 30 June 1959, Kidd repeated his warning. By now, the County Council had consulted District Councils and other local organisations in the area, and it was quite clear that there would indeed be strong objection to both Holme Pierrepont and Ratcliffe-on-Soar.

The C.E.G.B., it will be recalled, were looking for two sites. The next step was to rank their four possibilities in order of preference, taking into account technical features, comparative costs and amenity considerations. It cannot have been long before Holme Pierrepont stood out as an admirable choice. Well over

500 acres were available, so that the site would be large enough in due course for a second 2,000-megawatt station. Set between the Trent and the A52, it would be well served for cooling water and for bringing plant and labour to the site during construction. The rail connections would be excellent, for a new branch line to the recently opened Cotgrave colliery, three miles to the southeast, ran past the site. Because the existing overhead line from Staythorpe to Castle Donington passed nearby, only comparatively short lengths of transmission line would be needed to link the station with the national grid. Foundation conditions were good, and the site was well protected by the river floodbank. Most important of all, it would be ideally situated to draw large quantities of coal from the expanding No. 6 Area of the east Midlands coalfield. As a spokesman for the C.E.G.B. was later to observe, the site was unique because 'to all intents and purposes it was akin to a large-scale pit-head generation on a major river'. Indeed, the Board soon came to the conclusion that they could probably produce electricity here more cheaply than at any other coal-fired power station in the country.

More detailed calculations and investigations were to confirm the C.E.G.B.'s first impressions. Construction costs naturally differed as between the four possible sites. But of much greater significance to the Board were the operational costs over the lifetime of the power station. A 2,000-megawatt generating station consumes something like 5 million tons of coal a year, the equivalent of twenty train loads a day; the crucial differential between various sites was therefore their position in relation to the supplying collieries and the resultant cost of coal haulage.

Calculating comparative transport costs was not relatively straightforward exercise that it might appear, for the Board's objective was to identify the sites that would minimise their total transport bill over a wide area containing many collieries and many power stations. Each of the possible sites for a new power station would mean a different cheapest pattern of supply. The object of the exercise was to calculate and compare the total cost of hypothetical supply patterns, each of which was itself the cheapest pattern for a power station on each of the possible sites. This was a complex task, made practicable only because in 1958 the Board had developed a new computer technique designed to solve the complicated problem of finding optimal patterns of distribution. The two new generating stations were planned to come into service in 1968–9. By then, it was expected that 147 collieries in Yorkshire and the east Midlands would be supplying 38 million tons of coal a year to 75 power stations in the area. Using figures provided by the National Coal Board for the output of coal from each of the collieries involved, the C.E.G.B. were now able to rank the four sites in order of cheapness.

As a result of their calculations, the C.E.G.B. established that on economic criteria the sites should be ranked in the order: (i) Holme Pierrepont; (ii) Ratcliffe-on-Soar; (iii) West Burton; (iv) Cottam. Had the appraisals gone no further, the C.E.G.B. would have sought consent for Holme Pierrepont and Ratcliffe-on-Soar without more ado. But now there was the question of amenity. The Board had a statutory duty to take into account the effects of their proposals on local amenities; and whatever detractors may say, there is no reason to believe that they did not take their obligations seriously.[1] Holme Pierrepont and Ratcliffe-on-Soar were both in the Green Belt and, as the C.E.G.B. were by now well aware, both would be highly unpopular with the Nottinghamshire County Council. How much the prospect of opposition worried the Board is hard to say. They had never yet been defeated by a Local Planning Authority over the siting of a power station, and a run of successes had no doubt given them confidence in their powers of judgement and persuasion. Even so, there was no point in becoming involved in a fight if it could be avoided; and if there had to be a battle, it was only prudent to choose the ground carefully. To apply for *two* Green-Belt sites might be to tempt providence; and if it should come to defending such a proposal at a public inquiry, the Board might be hard put to it to explain how exactly they had interpreted their statutory duty to 'have regard for' local amenities. If they gave any thought to the probable reaction of the County Council, the Board may well have thought it unlikely that, at the end of the

---

[1] See, for example, two papers read to the Royal Society of Arts on 25 November 1959 by Sir Christopher Hinton, the chairman of the C.E.G.B., and Sir William Holford, Professor of Town and Country Planning at the University of London, and a part-time member of the Board; published under the title *Power Production and Transmission in the Countryside: Preserving Amenities*, 4th reprint (London: C.E.G.B., 1963).

day, a coal-producing county like Nottinghamshire would resist an important new power station, even though it was in the Green Belt. But to present them with a package of both the sites they were known to dislike most would obviously be to invite trouble.

Holme Pierrepont was thought to be altogether too good a prospect to pass over. But instead of applying also for Ratcliffe-on-Soar, the second best choice on economic grounds, the Board decided to substitute West Burton, one of the two more expensive sites in the north of the county.[1] Ratcliffe-on-Soar, it should be said, had one important drawback from the C.E.G.B.'s point of view, in that the site was too small for a second power station at a later date. But there could be no denying that it was an attractive spot, and the C.E.G.B. must have reckoned that, when they came to justify their plans, they would be able to claim some virtue in leaving it alone, and incurring extra costs as a result of their forbearance. On 4 March 1960 the Board told the Nottinghamshire County Council of their decision. Their intentions were made public on 9 March, and on 31 March the C.E.G.B. formally applied to the Minister of Power for his consent to two new generating stations, one at Holme Pierrepont and the other at West Burton.

THE VIEW FROM NOTTINGHAM

Coal-mining is by far the most important industry in Nottinghamshire, and the miners constitute easily the largest occupational group in the county; in 1960, of the total population of about 600,000, no fewer than 50,000 men were mineworkers. With their livelihoods and the prosperity of thousands more in the county dependent on the mining industry, a string of coal-fired generating stations in the Trent valley was exactly what the local coalfield needed to provide an assured, long-term market for its output. In the spring of 1959, when the C.E.G.B. announced that they were looking for sites for two 2,000-megawatt power stations, this had been welcome news indeed. The County Council had always encouraged the Board to build new power stations in

[1] West Burton was a comparatively uncontroversial site. The Nottinghamshire County Council did not object, and the Minister of Power gave consent for a generating station here in February 1961.

Nottinghamshire, and they at once agreed to co-operate in the search for sites.

However, the appearance of Ratcliffe-on-Soar and Holme Pierrepont on the C.E.G.B.'s short-list was a disturbing development that caused considerable anxiety in the County Planning Department. Holme Pierrepont was a particularly obnoxious possibility. The County Council set great store by their Green Belt round Nottingham, and in the eyes of the Director of Planning that section of it which included Holme Pierrepont was sacrosanct. As he saw it, a green wedge so close to the centre of Nottingham was particularly valuable, for it brought the countryside nearer the homes of town dwellers and let a breath of fresh air into the heart of the city.

The idea of a Green Belt round Nottingham had first been discussed by the County Planning Committee as far back as 1944. In March 1956 the County Council had defined their proposed Green-Belt area, designed to limit the outward growth of the city and to prevent Nottingham from merging into the surrounding towns and villages. At this time, the Minister of Housing and Local Government had made it clear that until the proposed Green Belt could be formally incorporated into the County Development Plan, all applications for planning permission should be dealt with in the light of the advice given in the Departmental Circular 42/55. The gist of this advice was that inside a proposed Green Belt, planning permission should not be given for new building 'except in very special circumstances'. Between 1956 and 1960 the County Council had received over a thousand applications to develop land falling within their proposed Green Belt, but only those which amounted to infilling, or which rounded off existing settlements, had been allowed. And when disappointed applicants had appealed to the Minister of Housing and Local Government, his decisions had consistently reaffirmed the existing policy of stringent control. It was true that one major development had been permitted. The N.C.B. had been given consent for a new colliery at Cotgrave, three miles south-east of Holme Pierrepont. The County Council did regard this as a special case, because they were satisfied that geological conditions made it almost impossible to put the colliery anywhere else. They also thought it very much in the interests of the county to develop a new pit here, so that coal available in this part of

Nottinghamshire could be fully exploited. But the construction of a 2,000-megawatt power station could hardly be described as infilling, or rounding off an existing settlement. And so long as there were other possible sites in the county, the County Planning Department saw no reason to count it as a 'very special' case either.

The Nottinghamshire County Council were not the only local authority alarmed by the prospect of a power station at Holme Pierrepont. The Carlton and West Bridgford Urban Districts are two fashionable suburbs of Nottingham that contain some of the most expensive property in the county. Carlton occupies high ground across the Trent from Holme Pierrepont, and the local residents enjoyed uninterrupted and extensive views southwards over the Green Belt. A power station for open countryside was not an attractive exchange. West Bridgford was even closer to the site that the C.E.G.B. were investigating at Holme Pierrepont. Both Urban District Councils were concerned about chimney emissions and their possible effects on health, about loss of visual amenity, and about the impact of a generating station on property values in the area. The other District Council to make their opposition known to the County Council was the Bingham Rural District Council. This was the District within which the site was actually located, and the local council were worried about the effect of a power station on the village of Radcliffe-on-Trent. They were also afraid that it might interfere with their sewerage and drainage system, which was linked with the brooks and dykes that ran across the Holme Pierrepont site and into the Trent.

As we have seen, both in March and again in June 1959 the County Director of Planning had done his best to steer the C.E.G.B. away from Ratcliffe-on-Soar and Holme Pierrepont. In March 1960, when the Board announced that Holme Pierrepont was one of the two sites for which they were going to seek consent, the Nottinghamshire County Council at once registered an objection, and asked the Minister of Power to hold a joint public inquiry with the Ministry of Housing and Local Government.

Anxious that the new generating station should be built in Nottinghamshire, yet determined to keep it out of the Green Belt, the County Council had not yet given up hope of persuading the C.E.G.B. to look elsewhere in the Trent valley. A hurried search for alternative sites was now begun, and soon the County planners had a list of counter-proposals for the Board's consideration. The alternative sites put forward by the County Council were at Averham, Rolleston and Upton (all near the Board's existing station at Staythorpe), at Holme (near Newark), and at Ragnall and Woodcoates (near the High Marnham power station). Possible locations that were in effect extensions of the sites examined by the C.E.G.B. at Cottam and West Burton were also suggested.

Some of the County Council's suggestions the C.E.G.B. dismissed at once, either because they were quite impracticable or because the technical problems could have been overcome only by incurring extra expenditure of a scale that the Board considered totally unjustifiable. Averham was out of the question because it fell within the river washlands, which had to be left undisturbed. Holme was rejected because it would have been necessary to bring coal across the main railway line by means of a level-crossing, and this was something that British Railways would not countenance. At Rolleston, major flood prevention works would have been required. And at Rolleston, Averham, Upton and Holme, the Air Ministry would have insisted on restrictions on chimney heights in the interests of aircraft safety.

Where the County Council's sites looked feasible, the C.E.G.B. did make broad assessments of their costs, to see how they compared with Holme Pierrepont. According to the Board's estimates, Ragnall and Woodcoates would have entailed extra transport costs of about £800,000 a year. At Cottam, the foundation conditions were unsatisfactory and the site was frequently flooded; the necessary civil engineering works, the C.E.G.B. calculated, would cost almost £2 million more than at Holme Pierrepont. More important, the Board reckoned that coal haulage to Cottam would have added £1½ million a year to their transport bill. As for West Burton, the cost of transporting coal to a second station there would have been almost as high as for Cottam. From the C.E.G.B.'s point of view, the least objectionable of the County Council's alternatives was probably Upton. But even Upton, the Board calculated, would have cost £600,000 a year more than Holme Pierrepont for coal haulage.

When the C.E.G.B. made it clear that none of the Planning Committee's counter-proposals was acceptable, the Nottinghamshire County Council were brought face to face with a highly disagreeable dilemma. On planning grounds it was no doubt very important to protect this valuable stretch of Green Belt. But for the County Council to lead an army of objectors into a major battle with the C.E.G.B. was not a step to be taken lightly. It was true that they had gone to some trouble to show the Board that their opposition was confined to Ratcliffe-on-Soar and Holme Pierrepont. They had stated repeatedly that they were anxious to help find other sites in the county. Nevertheless, the C.E.G.B. were thought not to take kindly to Local Planning Authorities that crossed them, and even though not everyone could yet foresee what a difficult period lay ahead for the coal industry, even in 1960 it was questionable whether a coal-producing county like Nottinghamshire could afford to run the risk of diminishing the Board's interest in the Trent valley as a home for new power stations. In their situation, did it really make sense for the County Council to put planning considerations before coal and electricity?

What with working miners, miners' officials, ex-miners and miners' wives, at least twenty members of the Nottinghamshire County Council were personally connected with the coal industry, and six or seven others represented districts in which there was a sizeable mining vote. In other words, about half of the controlling Labour group's fifty-two members had a very direct interest in the market for local coal. For many of them, security of employment was considerably more important than the sanctity of Green Belts; it was no secret that some thought it would be less than a catastrophe if a smart area like West Bridgford had to put up with a little of the dust and grime that are common enough in colliery districts. Agreed, planning committees have a special responsibility for amenity; but the planners had made their protest, and that (they thought) should be enough. In their view, it would be absurd for a County Council dominated by miners to try to prevent the C.E.G.B. from building a new coal-fired power station on the cheapest available site.

However, the next move lay not with the Council as a whole, but with the Planning Committee. It was for them to recommend whether the County Council should bow to the force of economic argument or persist with their objection to Holme Pierrepont. As it turned out, everything was to depend upon the attitude of the

Committee's chairman, Mr W. H. Foster. A dramatist could hardly have contrived a more painful conflict of loyalties. Like many long-serving chairmen, Foster had become deeply engrossed in the business of his Committee; for many years he had worked closely with the County Director of Planning, learning to respect his judgement and at the same time absorbing much of the professional planner's outlook and scale of values. The planners had made it quite clear where they stood on Holme Pierrepont. But it so happened that Foster was also a miner, a checkweighman and a lodge secretary. Among the miners, sectional loyalties go deep; not unnaturally, many of his fellow miners thought, and said, that when a project of such importance to the coal industry was at stake, it was Foster's duty to put their interests first. In situations like this, chairmen are expected to give a lead, and that alone would have placed Foster in a difficult enough position. But when fate hounds a man, it often makes a thorough job of it. The Planning Committee divided equally on the line they should take, and their recommendation hung upon the chairman's casting vote. Taking his union and political life in his hands, he came down on the side of good planning, and the Committee recommended that the County Council should continue to oppose Holme Pierrepont. Committee decisions can be reversed, but not without a great deal of dissension. The Labour group and the County Council accepted their Committee's recommendation, and from this point onwards all the resources of the Local Planning Authority were swung into action against the C.E.G.B.

It was only an objection from the County Council (as the Local Planning Authority) that could oblige the Minister of Power to hold a public inquiry. But in the circumstances, an inquiry would almost certainly have been ordered whatever the County Council's final decision, for throughout the summer of 1960, as the possible implications and consequences of a power station at Holme Pierrepont began to sink in, the number of objectors steadily mounted. The attitude of the West Bridgford, Carlton and Bingham Councils has already been described. So hostile were they to the Holme Pierrepont site that they eventually decided to brief counsel of their own, rather than rely on the County Council to represent them at the public inquiry. They were now joined in their opposition by a powerful new ally.

Holme Pierrepont lies outside the boundaries of the City of

Nottingham. However, the Corporation felt that it had a legitimate interest in the C.E.G.B.'s plans and a clear duty to object. A power station here would spoil a pleasant rural area that was much frequented by Nottingham people for recreation and riverside walks. There were some parts of the city from which it would dominate the view. Though it was not yet clear exactly which lines British Railways would use to take coal to Holme Pierrepont, the chances were that more trains would have to be routed through Nottingham itself. Quite apart from creating extra noise and smoke, some of these trains might well have to use an already busy level-crossing, thus adding to the serious traffic congestion in the city. Even more important, there were the medical implications of a new generating station so near a built-up area. The Trent valley is notorious for fogs; fog and atmospheric pollution together tend to make life unpleasant and even dangerous for those who suffer from respiratory diseases like bronchitis. For some years the City Council had been greatly exercised by this problem of pollution, and they had tried to cope with it by establishing smoke control areas and by rigorously enforcing local by-laws that required new heating appliances to be capable of burning smokeless fuel. As it happened, they already viewed the C.E.G.B.'s activities with suspicion, because over a period of time the Public Health Department had been measuring the level of sulphur dioxide in the atmosphere and the amount of dust and grit deposited in the city. Between 1952 and 1957 the Corporation's clean-air policy seemed to be bringing about a distinct improvement: in 1958, however, there had been a sudden deterioration. This marked increase in sulphur dioxide, grit and dust occurred in the year after the C.E.G.B. had brought a new 'E' station into operation at North Wilford, south-west of Nottingham. Since there had been no other change for the worse in fuel-burning equipment in the city, the culprits – in the Corporation's eyes – were almost certainly the C.E.G.B. The City Council certainly did not relish the prospect of another and much larger power station to the south-east of Nottingham.

A variety of sectional and local organisations now joined the united front presented by the local authorities. When they learned which sites the C.E.G.B. had under review, the Council for the Preservation of Rural England concluded that all except Market Warsop would be open to objection on amenity grounds. In their judgement, Ratcliffe-on-Soar was the least acceptable. They were disappointed when Market Warsop disappeared from the Board's short-list, and they fully supported the County Council in their opposition to Ratcliffe-on-Soar and Holme Pierrepont. As they saw it, Holme Pierrepont was not in the highest class for sheer quality of landscape; but it was in the Green Belt, and it was of very great scenic and recreational value to the people of Nottingham. But like the Nottinghamshire County Council (though for different reasons) the C.P.R.E. did not oppose Holme Pierrepont without forebodings; there was always the risk that if the C.E.G.B. were refused permission there, they might turn their attention to some other completely unspoiled rural spot that was even less acceptable. As the C.P.R.E.'s representative was to put it a few months later: 'If – which I do not think is likely to be the result – we were to succeed in the objections we are raising to Holme Pierrepont only to find that we were saddled with a power station at Ratcliffe-on-Soar instead, we should not feel that we had done a very profitable day's work.'

The local agricultural and landowning interests also objected. The C.E.G.B.'s partiality for Nottinghamshire represented a considerable threat to the farmers; in 1960 alone the Board were proposing to appropriate more than a thousand acres of Nottinghamshire farmland. Of the sites examined by the C.E.G.B., Holme Pierrepont might not be the best from an agricultural point of view. But it was still excellent land, and as the National Farmers' Union pointed out, left alone it could go on producing for centuries. This view was shared by the local branch of the Country Landowners' Association. To build a power station at Holme Pierrepont, they claimed, would be an indefensible misuse of good farmland. Before taking over additional land in the county, they argued, the C.E.G.B. should make more intensive use of the sites they already possessed.[1]

[1] Even more than is usual in cases of this kind, the Holme Pierrepont controversy presented organisations and individuals with agonising dilemmas. At the public inquiry the C.L.A. were to be represented by the chairman of the Nottinghamshire branch, Mr G. F. Seymour. On a personal level, he found himself in much the same difficulty as the C.P.R.E. As he realised only too well, if the C.E.G.B. were prevented from establishing the new power station at Holme Pierrepont, they might well turn to their other Green-Belt site. His Jacobean country house, Thrumpton Hall, was adjacent to the site investigated by the C.E.G.B. at Ratcliffe-on-Soar.

It was not unusual for farmers and amenity societies to oppose the C.E.G.B.'s plans. But in this instance an existing and highly profitable commercial activity was also affected. Under the proposed Holme Pierrepont site there were extensive deposits of gravel, and close to the site these deposits were actually being worked by the Hoveringham Gravel Company. The Company objected to the Board's proposals on the grounds that once a generating station had been built, this gravel (the reserves were estimated to amount to about 2 million tons) would be sterilised indefinitely. With the shortage of gravel for building purposes becoming increasingly serious, this was a matter of some importance.

And to complete the catalogue of opponents lining up against the C.E.G.B., there were objections from the Nottingham Sailing Club, the Old Nottinghamians Rugby Football Club, the Holme Pierrepont and Radcliffe-on-Trent Parish Councils, the Nottingham No. 2 Hospital Management Committee, the Radcliffe-on-Trent Ratepayers' Association, and numerous individuals in Radcliffe-on-Trent and West Bridgford.

THE PUBLIC INQUIRY

In London it was by now apparent that the C.E.G.B. had stirred up a hornets' nest. The two M.P.s for constituencies in the area directly affected – William Clark (Conservative, Nottingham South) and Sir Kenneth Pickthorne (Conservative, Carlton) – had been drawn into the controversy at an early stage, and their representations and agitated demands for interviews left the Minister of Power in no doubt that feelings were running high in Nottingham and the surrounding districts. On 14 October 1960 the Minister ordered a public inquiry, and appointed Mr H. W. Grimmitt, the Chief Engineering Inspector at the Ministry of Power, to conduct it. When an application from the C.E.G.B. raised important amenity issues, it was usual for a planning Inspector to sit with the Inspector from the Ministry of Power; and in accordance with this practice, Mr D. Senior from the Ministry of Housing and Local Government was also appointed to hear and report on the objections. They were to be joined by a second engineering Inspector, Mr W. L. M. French.

The appointment of two Inspectors from the Ministry of Power was ill received in Nottinghamshire. As usual, said the cynics, the claims of electricity were to be given more weight than those of planning. At a later stage, the Parliamentary Secretary to the Minister of Power was to explain that French would play no part in preparing the report for the Ministers. But the fact that objectors should seize on a small point like this was symptomatic of the atmosphere of distrust and suspicion in which the inquiry opened. Indeed, a story was going about that the decision to develop Holme Pierrepont had already been taken; the public inquiry, it was being said, was only a sop to local opinion, an opportunity for the objectors to let off steam at an expensive but meaningless ritual.

On the other side of the hill, the C.E.G.B. were certainly aware that Holme Pierrepont was one of the most unpopular schemes they had ever proposed. But the C.E.G.B.'s officials, it seems, could not quite bring themselves to believe that this case would, in the end, turn out to be very different from so many earlier encounters with local authorities and amenity bodies. The Board's representatives would arrive on the scene. They would demonstrate the inexorable logic that had led the C.E.G.B. to select Holme Pierrepont. The objectors' claims and fears would be shown to be exaggerated or groundless, and at the end of the day, the Board would emerge victorious, their choice of Holme Pierrepont vindicated by the Inspector and by the Minister of Power. Of sixteen joint public inquiries previously held under the Electricity Acts, fifteen had lasted for three days or less; to be safe, the C.E.G.B. booked the Church Hall, Radcliffe-on-Trent, for four. As it turned out, the inquiry was to occupy fourteen days, spread over a period of two months, and after the fourth day the hearings had to be transferred to the Shire Hall, Nottingham.

The C.E.G.B. were represented by Mr S. B. R. Cooke, Q.C., and Mr David Trustram Eve. The Board's three chief witnesses were Mr F. Faux, their Station Planning and Development Engineer, Mr F. R. Hunt, Principal Assistant Engineer in the Station Planning and Development Branch, and Mr G. England, their Development Engineer for policy matters. Ranged against the Board, the principal objectors were the Nottinghamshire County Council (represented by their Deputy Clerk, Mr J. T.

]

Brockbank), the Nottingham Corporation (represented by its
Deputy Town Clerk, Mr G. Guest), the Carlton U.D.C. (represented by Mr F. H. B. Layfield), the West Bridgford U.D.C. and
the Bingham R.D.C. (jointly represented by Mr D. Cowley), the
C.P.R.E., the Hoveringham Gravel Company (represented by
Mr M. A. L. Cripps, Q.C.) and the Nottinghamshire branches of
the C.L.A. and N.F.U. The inquiry opened on 22 November
1960. From the beginning the atmosphere was unusually tense.
Much of the evidence was necessarily complex and highly technical, many of the exchanges became decidedly heated, and on
occasions a casual visitor might have thought that he had
stumbled into a major criminal trial, rather than a public local
inquiry. Indeed, by the last day, one of the barristers was referring to the inquiry as 'this court', and nobody corrected him.

In essence, the argument between the C.E.G.B. and the objectors turned upon four main issues. First, there was the crucial
question of the Green Belt. For their part, the C.E.G.B. maintained that the Green Belt boundary south-east of Nottingham
had been drawn too tightly up against the existing built-up area,
with the result that it included land that was not genuinely rural
at all. South of the proposed site there was the Cotgrave colliery.
To the north there were gravel workings, and further north again,
across the river, there were several large factories, a railway
marshalling yard, and an area containing oil storage tanks. The
Holme Pierrepont site, they argued, was by no means a great
beauty spot, and a power station here would do no more than
pinch off a somewhat nondescript wedge that by rights ought
never to have been included in the Green Belt in the first place.
In any case, the Government's policy did permit development in
Green Belts in 'very special circumstances'. It was extremely
difficult to find sites that were suitable for power stations, and
since this new generating station was so important for the prosperity of Nottinghamshire, the C.E.G.B. should be allowed some
latitude. Moreover, if they were given consent for the Holme
Pierrepont site, the C.E.G.B. would see to it that the buildings
were of the very best modern design, with the finest possible
architectural treatment. Nobody would be able to say that this
was an industrial blot on the landscape.

Against this, the objectors argued that the C.E.G.B. were very
much mistaken if they believed a re-entrant on the inner peri-

meter of the Green Belt to be of no consequence. On the contrary, a wedge of open land pushing inwards towards the city centre was particularly valuable.[1] And whilst Holme Pierrepont might have struck the C.E.G.B. as a highly suitable site from their point of view, the fact remained that there *were* other possibilities. A power station was certainly not a special case in the same sense as a colliery, and once the pass had been sold, it would become increasingly difficult to hold the line against other would-be developers. Like the C.E.G.B., they would say that since there was already industry in the area, a little more could do no harm.

Second, there was the question of chimney emissions and atmospheric pollution. The objectors protested that on medical grounds it was dangerous to build a large power station so close to Nottingham and its suburbs. In reply, the C.E.G.B.'s representatives claimed that their precautions were so effective that there could be no possible danger to health. In the first place, they argued, modern power stations burn coal so efficiently that virtually no smoke is produced. Secondly, gas leaving the boilers would have to pass through special cleaning equipment, consisting of mechanical grit arrestors and electrostatic dust precipitators, and this process would take care of any solid matter. The Board planned to spend £2 million on cleaning equipment at Holme Pierrepont, and according to their representatives it would have a collecting efficiency of 99·3 per cent. And thirdly, after the arrestor and precipitator treatment, the hot gas would be projected at considerable speed out of the two 650-foot chimneys. These plumes of hot gas would rise another 600 feet, before returning, diluted and dispersed, to ground level, where the concentration of gas would be far too low to be harmful. To

---

[1] For the thesis that countryside near towns is specially important, the objectors needed to go no further than Sir Christopher Hinton, the chairman of the C.E.G.B. In his paper to the Royal Society of Arts (see p. 95 n.) he had written: 'The site which is chosen for a nuclear power plant to supply the London load economically is also within reasonable weekend travelling distance of London. The fact that it is not outstandingly beautiful is of little importance because by policy it is isolated and undeveloped. It is of immense value because even though it is unbeautiful it is a spot to which the man yearning to free himself from the oppression of the London conurbation (I use the word purposely because it is as ugly as the fact) is able to escape.'

substantiate this claim the C.E.G.B. could point to previous experience. It was the practice of their engineers to test for gas concentration at ground level around their sites for two years before a new power station was brought into operation and for two years afterwards. In no case, the Board claimed, did their records show any change in the level of pollution in the surrounding area as a result of establishing a coal-fired power station.

The problem was not that simple, said the objectors. There is a special atmospheric condition known as 'inversion', which sometimes occurs in combination with fogs. Under these conditions, the air nearest the ground is temporarily cooler than the atmosphere above it; consequently, this surface air does not rise in the usual way, and is not replaced by the usual process of circulation. In these circumstances, pollution discharged at a low level could become trapped in the fog layer and could build up into an unusually heavy concentration. The C.E.G.B., however, maintained that inversion would not be a problem at Holme Pierrepont, because the inversion or fog layer would usually be below the chimney tops. And even when this was not the case, the plume of gas would penetrate upwards, through the fog, because of its heat content. Again, the Board had recorded observations to support this claim. In the winter of 1959 their engineers had flown above London fogs, and on two occasions actually photographed gas plumes emerging from the smog and dispersing in the moving air above.

This was not good enough for the objectors. The C.E.G.B. (they contended) were being much too sanguine about the efficiency of their equipment. In view of the undoubted increase in grit and dust that had occurred after the Wilford 'E' station came into service, could the Board really guarantee a 99·3 per cent level of efficiency for their mechanical grit arrestors and electrostatic precipitators? There was also an argument between the two sides about the sulphur content of the east Midlands coal to be used at Holme Pierrepont, the C.E.G.B. maintaining that the figure was 1.0 per cent, and the objectors suggesting that it would be more like 1·6 per cent. But even if the correct figure was only 1·0 per cent (the objectors pointed out), it would still mean that about 180,000 tons of sulphur dioxide a year would descend on Nottingham and the surrounding districts, and this, they said, would be quite intolerable. Did the C.E.G.B. realise, they asked, that a small increase in dust and sulphur dioxide in the atmosphere could have a marked effect on the mortality rate of people suffering from cardio-respiratory diseases such as bronchitis? Nottingham and its suburbs contained something like 450,000 inhabitants. Could it be right, asked the objectors, to take a chance with the health of so many people?

Taken by surprise at the weight of objection on health grounds, the C.E.G.B. had no expert witness at the inquiry, an omission which left them at something of a disadvantage in the purely medical exchanges. Their line of defence, however, was that if 5 million more tons of coal a year were to be burnt near Nottingham, the most efficient and least harmful way of burning it was in one large, modern power station, rather than in dozens of small factories and thousands of individual homes all with tiny chimneys that would be much less effective than a generating station in dispersing chimney emissions. In informed medical circles, said the Board's representatives, it was agreed that the level of pollution that could be considered dangerous was much higher than anything that could possibly be produced by a brand-new generating station. Since the extra atmospheric pollution would be too small to harm anyone, it mattered not whether there were four or four million people in the vicinity. And from this logically unassailable position (which annoyed the objectors intensely) the Board's witnesses refused to budge.

The third main issue for the inquiry was the question of costs. The C.E.G.B. could hardly deny that amenities would suffer to *some* extent as a result of a power station at Holme Pierrepont. Their object was to show that the objectors were exaggerating the damage that the generating station would inflict on the local environment, for the less significant the health risk and the effect on the Green Belt, the greater would be the justification for building the power station at Holme Pierrepont so as to avoid the additional costs allegedly entailed by any alternative site. The aesthetic value of the area in question was, of course, a matter of opinion, and the Board's representatives naturally had no intention of admitting that there was anything special about it. Arguments about natural beauty tended to become a dogged battle of wills typified in the following exchange between counsel and one of the Board's principal witnesses:

Q: Mr Faux, looking at the photograph there, does that appear to be very attractive landscape?

A: It is countryside, yes.

Q: It would appear largely unspoilt from the view from which that photograph was taken?

A: It is fields – agricultural land.

Q: Mr Faux, will you try to answer the question? If you do not understand any question, please tell me and I will try to put it again. Would that appear to you to be a scene or view from which that photograph was taken of largely unspoilt areas of countryside?

A: Well, there are no industrial buildings there.

Q: Would it appear to you to be an area of largely unspoilt landscape?

A: Largely, yes.

As a counter to these tactics, the objectors set out to demonstrate that because the C.E.G.B. had overlooked, or deliberately ignored, a number of important items, the alleged cost advantage of the Holme Pierrepont site might not be as great as the Board claimed. How much had been allowed, they asked, for the coal and the 2 million tons of valuable gravel that would be locked up beyond recovery for at least thirty years if a power station was built at Holme Pierrepont? An access railway would have to be constructed to the site, and this new line would oblige the County Council to modify the design of the proposed Nottingham ring road: these changes, the County Council claimed, would cost at least £200,000. Then there was the question of property values in the area. According to one expert witness, a power station at Holme Pierrepont would reduce the capital value of residential property by something like £3½ million. What had the C.E.G.B. to say to that? Suppose another railway bridge had to be built over the Trent to bring coal to Holme Pierrepont. How much had been allowed for that? What about the cost of traffic congestion in Nottingham as a result of the busy level-crossing at Meadow Lane being closed for almost half the day?

The C.E.G.B.'s reply to questions of this kind was that many of the costs mentioned by the objectors had in fact been taken into account, and the sums involved were trivial by comparison with the differential costs of coal haulage as between the various possible sites. For the rest, they maintained that it was not their responsibility to try to work out the cost of all the side-effects produced by a generating station. If information about such matters as ring roads and property values came to light at the public inquiry, it was for the Inspectors and the Minister to decide whether or not the case for Holme Pierrepont was seriously weakened when secondary charges imposed on others were added to the balance sheet. It would be impossible, they implied, for the C.E.G.B.'s staff to calculate the cost of every single consequence that might flow from their proposals. As one of the Board's representatives protested under cross-examination about property values, he was an engineer, not an estate agent.[1]

Inevitably, the main battle was fought over the central question of comparative costs and the C.E.G.B.'s computer exercise. All along the Board maintained that what really made the difference between the various sites examined was the cost of coal haulage. On this score Holme Pierrepont was considerably cheaper than any alternative, and after Holme Pierrepont the next cheapest site was Ratcliffe-on-Soar. In other circumstances, some of the objectors might well have fastened on Ratcliffe-on-Soar, and urged the Inspectors to rule out Holme Pierrepont on the grounds that another site existed which was far less obnoxious so far as planning was concerned, and which (according to the C.E.G.B. themselves) would cost only £200,000 a year more than Holme Pierrepont to run. Left to themselves, the local authorities to the east of Nottingham – the Carlton and West Bridgford Urban District Councils and the Bingham Rural District Council – would doubtless have thought it expedient to argue the case for siting the new generating station at Ratcliffe-on-Soar, for it is always considered sound tactics for objectors to put forward a

[1] Public inquiries are intensely unpopular with some technical experts, who resent hostile cross-examination at the hands of experienced counsel apparently intent on making them look fools or knaves. The C.E.G.B.'s witnesses seem to have been hardened campaigners, not easily thrown out of their stride, and rarely at a loss for an answer to sarcastic questions. This exchange about the intellectual capabilities of a computer was fairly typical of the aplomb maintained by the Board's representatives:

A computer, you would agree, has not much sense?
Not very much.
It is equivalent to a factory-load of morons?
I have no experience of a factory-load of morons.

plausible alternative to whatever the developers are proposing. And in situations of this kind, it is everyone for himself, with nobody concerned to do more than remove the unwanted project from his own doorstep.

However, the position was complicated for these District Councils because the Nottinghamshire County Council were firmly committed to the defence of Ratcliffe-on-Soar, and it was known that other objectors, such as the Nottingham Corporation and the C.P.R.E., disliked this alternative as much, or even more than, Holme Pierrepont itself. For all the objectors the first priority was to keep the power station away from Holme Pierrepont; consequently, no one dared to suggest Ratcliffe-on-Soar for fear of splitting the grand alliance and thereby reducing the chances of achieving the main object. The result was that in so far as the objectors could unite behind any counter-proposal at all, it had to be not the next cheapest alternative to Holme Pierrepont (Ratcliffe-on-Soar), but the cheapest possibility on the County Council's list of counter proposals. And this, of course, was the Upton site, which according to the C.E.G.B. would have cost them £600,000 a year more than Holme Pierrepont to supply with coal.

The next question for the inquiry was this: how much reliance could be placed on the C.E.G.B.'s estimates? The Board's computer calculations related solely to the year 1968–9, the date when the two new power stations were expected to come into service. The objectors argued that in the years after 1968–9 there might well be substantial changes in the pattern of supplying collieries; these changes might completely invalidate the Board's assessments, leaving them with a site that had been selected for economic reasons that no longer held good. More important, the objectors challenged even the admissibility of evidence based on the computer exercise. They pointed out that the inquiry had only the C.E.G.B.'s word for it that Holme Pierrepont would be £600,000 a year cheaper than Upton. The objectors had no way of checking whether the Board had fed the correct figures into their computer, or whether they had drawn the right conclusions, for no one outside the C.E.G.B. had been allowed to examine the data on which the computer exercise was based. What was to prevent the C.E.G.B. from putting whatever figure they chose (or whatever figure they thought large enough to impress the Inspec-

tors) on the alleged cost advantage of Holme Pierrepont?[1] There
was no denying that this was a highly suitable site from the
Board's point of view. There is a very human tendency, said the
objectors, for everyone to find the answer he wants. If the truth
were known, they suggested, it might well turn out that the
Board had supplied their computer with figures until it produced
the solution they were hoping for, at which point the exercise
had stopped. Their initial preference confirmed, the C.E.G.B.
were now saying that Holme Pierrepont had been selected by the
most up-to-date and sophisticated scientific methods.

These charges were vigorously denied by counsel for the
C.E.G.B. Seen for what they were, he said, the objectors' insinua-
tions were absurd. Was it conceivable, he asked, that the Board
really believed other sites to be as cheap, or cheaper, than Holme
Pierrepont? Were they trying to persuade the Inspectors that a
power station here would be more economic to run, when they
knew full well that there was some other site that would suit them
better? Was there some irrational fascination about Holme Pierrepont that the Board dared not bring out into the open? Was there
some hidden and indefensible motive that they dared not admit
even to themselves? Were they going to an enormous amount of
trouble, and making themselves highly unpopular, simply in
order to do themselves down, and annoy the local authorities in
the area?

[1] For reasons of commercial prudence, and because they felt themselves
under an obligation of secrecy, the C.E.G.B. refused to disclose details of
the confidential agreement which they had reached with the British
Transport Commission over haulage rates. When they are not permitted
to see the developers' calculations, objectors are often understandably
suspicious of the heavy costs sometimes said to be entailed by alternative
sites. This issue was raised in the House of Commons on 20 December 1960
by William Clark, the Member for Nottingham South, in an adjournment
debate on the Holme Pierrepont case. 'My point is this', he said, 'that if
at a public inquiry it is maintained that there will be a saving of £600,000,
£700,000 or £800,000 – whatever may be the amount – and under
questioning that figure cannot be substantiated to the objectors, it is evident
that the witnesses can just as easily say that the saving will be £5 million
or £6 million. It can be put at any figure if the objectors are not to have
the right to question it.' Replying to the debate, the Parliamentary Secretary to the Minister of Power announced that the C.E.G.B. had agreed
that an independent expert, commissioned by the objectors, should have
access to all the relevant documents, including contracts, under a guarantee
of secrecy. *H.C. Deb.* (1960–1) 630, cols 1260–70.

The Generating Board [he said] have no interest whatever in coming here to this public inquiry with figures in which they do not believe for the purpose of making out a case for Holme Pierrepont. The Generating Board in this matter are the servants of the public, although from time to time observations have been made which tend to suggest that the Generating Board are on one side and the public on the other. From the Generating Board's point of view it would be a far happier situation if they had been able to fix on one of the alternative sites in agreement with the County Council, and it would have been much better if the Generating Board had been able to come to the conclusion that to fix on one or more alternative sites was consistent with their statutory duties. But they have been unable to come to that conclusion and that is why they are here.

The fourth and last major issue for the inquiry drew out the essential problem of values that lay at the core of the dispute. Naturally enough, the C.E.G.B. had played down the value of what would be lost in terms of environment if the power station were built at Holme Pierrepont. Similarly, the objectors had challenged the Board's claim that any other site, acceptable to the opposition, would cost at least an extra £600,000 a year to run. But as everyone acknowledged, even had there been agreement about the implications for local amenities and about the precise amount of additional expenditure entailed by alternative sites, facts alone could never have settled the issue, because fundamentally both sides were basing their case upon the assertion of a wholly subjective value-judgement. The question facing everyone involved in the controversy was this: would it be worth spending a very large sum in hard cash, perhaps half a million pounds or more a year, for something which by its very nature could have no determinable and quantifiable value? Again and again, as in the following example, the exchanges returned to this problem:

Q: Do I understand your Board's arguments to be that £600,000 a year is too high a price to pay to preserve the amenities of the Radcliffe, Carlton, and West Bridgford area?

A. In their present form, yes.

Q: So your Board is saying £600,000 is too big a price to pay?

A: To retain those amenities.

Q: What would they regard as a figure which would make the alternative sites a reasonable alternative?

A: That I cannot say.

Q: If your transport economics figures are wrong and, in fact, it cost, say, £100,000 a year more to use Upton, would that alter your view about where the station should go, at Holme Pierrepont or Upton?

A: Clearly, it would have its influence, but I cannot say what the view of the Board would be.

Q: To what conclusion would it lead you, as the technical witness in this matter?

A: It is extremely difficult. It is trying to put a price on amenity.

Q: Someone must put a price on amenity? Would £100,000 a year be too big a price if you were advising your Board?

A: At that sort of figure I should be torn.

Q: Would you think there was a good case for it at Upton?

A: I should be torn. It is still a great deal of money – £100,000. It is £100,000 a year.

Stripped to its essentials, the argument about values was simple. The C.E.G.B. insisted that there could be no possible justification for spending £600,000 a year, or anything like that figure, in order to avoid the insignificant effect that a power station would have on the local amenities. The objectors, on the other hand, maintained that even if Holme Pierrepont would be £600,000 a year cheaper to run than any alternative (which they doubted), this was still a price that was well worth paying in the interests of amenity. A sum of £600,000 a year might sound a large amount, they said; but looked at another way, it would add only 0·016 of a penny to the cost of every unit of electricity produced, and this, they contended, was an insignificant trifle when compared with the harm that a generating station at Holme Pierrepont would inflict on the people of Nottingham and the surrounding area.

Over and above the evidence set before them at public inquiries, Inspectors have also to take into consideration the evidence of their own eyes and ears about the strength of local feeling. It is because the elected council of a major local authority is deemed accurately to reflect the views of those it represents, that Ministers are under a statutory obligation to order a public inquiry if a Local Planning Authority objects to proposals for new development within its area. The presence of the Local Planning Authority (together with four other Councils) among the objectors might alone have been enough to convince the Inspectors that the C.E.G.B.'s plans had stirred up a quite extraordinary degree of resentment in the locality. At the same time, there are occasions when Inspectors come to suspect that local opinion is not quite as united and indignant as those who appear at public inquiries make it their business to suggest. There are also occasions when local opinion is patently divided, even though the elected Councils concerned have lodged objections. Industrial development brings employment, and there are many for whom jobs are more important than planning and amenity.

Only one local ally came forward in support of the C.E.G.B., and this was the Nottinghamshire branch of the National Union of Mineworkers. In a sombre but restrained statement, their representative at the inquiry pointed out that the miners were worried about the possibility of losing an important market for their coal. It was all very well, he said, for the objectors to argue that they were wholeheartedly in favour of a new power station in the county so long as it was not at Holme Pierrepont; but to take this line was to gamble on the C.E.G.B.'s willingness to continue to use coal even if its price was increased as a result of their having to develop unnecessarily expensive sites. As the miners saw it, the stakes were too high for gambling. Coal had succeeded in meeting the challenge of oil and atomic energy only because the C.E.G.B. had made strenuous efforts to use it with the maximum efficiency. 'What we ask', said the miners' representative, 'is that those who are objecting to the Holme Pierrepont site on behalf of the City and County of Nottingham should make it clear to the people in whose names they are making these objections that they are at least running the risk of helping to price east Midlands coal out of the market.'

The objectors, by contrast, were considerably more forceful. Even before the inquiry opened, the Inspectors must have realised that the opposition to Holme Pierrepont was more than usually impassioned. There were certainly signs in the wind. For example, in the middle of his largely factual and descriptive proof of evidence, the County Director of Planning had broken into the following dramatic and colourful warning:

> A great shadow would be spread over the lives of the large number of people living in the near neighbourhood. In substitution for pleasant, open green fields would be this great industrial giant, reaching its arms far skywards, stretching its tentacles far and wide, and snorting fumes and smoke high into the atmosphere to be precipitated on and into the homes of many residents of the County.

And when they arrived in Nottingham, it was not long before the Inspectors themselves were exposed to the wrath of the local inhabitants. In the ordinary way, the man-in-the-street has no opportunity of giving vent to his feelings in person because public inquiries are held during the working day. At the request of the Bingham R.D.C., the Inspectors agreed to attend an informal evening session to hear the views of individuals living in the area, and on the evening of 23 November 1960, after the second day's hearings, between four and five hundred people packed into the hall of the West Bridgford Grammar School for what was to become a highly effective meeting. The Inspectors had gone to the school intending simply to take note of objections that might not otherwise have been voiced at the formal sessions. It is clear from the verbatim transcript, however, that the proceedings soon took on the character of one of those lively political meetings at which the opposition is present in force.[1]

Passionate denunciations of the power station were greeted with enthusiastic applause. The Minister of Power was accused of being judge and jury in his own case, and it was suggested in no uncertain terms that his Inspector was bound to be biased in favour of the C.E.G.B. When Grimmitt tried to explain that the whole purpose of the inquiry was to give due weight to the views of objectors, his remarks were received with a roar of derisive laughter and shouts of 'No, no'. Not everyone understood the role of the Inspectors, and when they declined to answer questions about 'their' power station, and refused to be drawn into an

---

[1] See also *Guardian Journal*, 24 Nov 1960.

argument about the merits of the case, they were subjected to a good deal of noisy heckling and barracking. One man and his wife ostentatiously walked out, shouting that the meeting was a waste of time. Towards the end of the session the atmosphere seems to have become calmer, and a number of speakers, realising perhaps that it would do no good to antagonise the Inspectors, led the rest in thanking them for their courtesy in coming to the meeting at all. By all accounts, the evening of 23 November in the West Bridgford Grammar School made a powerful impression on the Inspectors, and particularly on Grimmitt. Some of the objectors were apparently under the impression, at first, that he personally had selected the Holme Pierrepont site for the new generating station; and even those who knew better were inclined to seize upon him as the only visible target for their anger and resentment.

Next morning the normal hearings were resumed in the Church Hall, Radcliffe-on-Trent. The New Year came and went, and after several adjournments and resumptions, the inquiry ended on 26 January 1961. There followed a period of more than five months' suspense, while the objectors and the C.E.G.B. awaited the Minister of Power's decision.

THE VERDICT

The two Inspectors presented their joint Report to the Minister of Power, Mr Richard Wood, on 17 May 1961. The Report ended with an agreed recommendation, though each of them set out his own analysis and explained separately how he had reached his conclusion. The planning Inspector's half of the Report had a surprise in the tail; and anyone resisting the temptation to turn first to the last page of the electricity Inspector's analysis might have been in doubt until the very end about what recommendation would follow the appraisal that preceded it.

The planning Inspector had concentrated, of course, on those matters that would have been relevant had it fallen to his Minister alone to decide the case. He explained that he had approached the problem by posing and answering what seemed to him to be the vital questions:

(i) Would the proposed power station conflict with the purposes for which the Green Belt had been established? His frame of reference here was the Ministry of Housing and Local Government Circular 42/55, which laid it down that the objects of a Green Belt were (*a*) to safeguard the countryside around towns against the unrestricted sprawl of built-up areas, (*b*) to prevent the merging of neighbouring towns, and (*c*) to preserve the special character of a town.

It requires a close and careful reading of the Report to disentangle exactly what conclusions the Inspector had reached under each of these heads. But the gist of his findings was as follows: (*a*) he doubted whether a power station would conflict with the object of maintaining open countryside round the Nottingham conurbation as a whole; (*b*) in his view, it could not be said that a generating station was the kind of development which would promote residential or industrial expansion in the area, or encourage West Bridgford and Radcliffe-on-Trent to merge together; and (*c*) in the strict sense of Circular 42/55, the proposed power station would not impair any special characteristics of the city of Nottingham.

However, not all sections of a Green Belt were of equal value. In some places, he said, a large-scale encroachment might be permissible, whilst in others the inconsistent development of a small site would do serious harm. The most undesirable feature of the C.E.G.B.'s proposal, he suggested, was its destructive effect on the green wedge north of the A52. 'By any test', he went on, 'it deserves protection, and unless it is entirely certain that there are specially overriding considerations which demand the siting of the station within it, I am disposed unhesitatingly to recommend its rejection.' This sounded conclusive enough. But the next sentence continued: 'It may be, on the other hand, that wider considerations might override the desirability of maintaining the continuity between the countryside south of the A52 and the riverside and that, in the last resort, it might be thought that the wider purpose of maintaining an "appreciable rural zone" round Nottingham would not be impaired by its establishment, so long as the Green Belt south of the A52 remains unimpaired.' If this qualification seemed to leave the door ajar, his final observation made it clear that he was not issuing an invitation: 'There is, nevertheless, great substance in the contention of the objectors that if the station is erected, the open land to its east and west will inevitably fall in for development, in this way materially worsening the environment of West Bridgford and Radcliffe and of the recreational area of the riverside, and a Green Belt which stopped at the A52 would clearly be a poor substitute for the present proposal.'[1]

(ii) Was it true, as some of the objectors had suggested, that a generating station at Holme Pierrepont would not only impair the good aspect of the riverside, but also interfere with public enjoyment of its facilities for sport and recreation? Of itself, wrote the Inspector, a power station would not prevent people from sailing, swimming or playing rugby. But these activities, he observed, were far more thoroughly enjoyed in attractive surroundings than in an area dominated by a massive and overpowering industrial building. To this extent, therefore, the fears expressed by the objectors were well founded.

(iii) Would the buildings and other structures proposed impair the good appearance of the environment? There was no denying, he said, that an edifice as large as a 2,000-megawatt power station was going to present an appearance totally out of keeping with a rural environment. But this objection would have applied even more strongly at all the alternative sites, for they were all deep in the countryside, and some of them were scenically more attractive than Holme Pierrepont. On the other hand, a power station at Holme Pierrepont would be highly conspicuous, and would be visible to far more people than one sited away from a built-up area. In the Inspector's judgement, the objectors were right in maintaining that it would probably impair the outlook from certain parts of the neighbouring residential districts.

(iv) How important was the question of noise? The Inspector noted that the site was comparatively remote from any large residential settlement; he doubted whether the power station itself would produce enough disturbance to be heard outside the boundaries of the site. Noise from the railway sidings would certainly be audible in the hamlet of Holme Pierrepont; but West Bridgford was too far away to be affected, and at Radcliffe-on-Trent there was likely to be more noise from existing railway operations than from new sidings at the Holme Pierrepont site.

(v) Would the power station bring about such a large increase

[1] 'Proposal' because technically it was still only a 'proposed Green Belt'.

in road traffic that the local highways would become dangerous, obstructed or overloaded? It seemed likely that a good deal of ash would have to be taken away from the site by road. But this would be true wherever the generating station was built, and on that score, the Holme Pierrepont site was probably preferable to the alternatives, for it abutted on to the A52 and would be close to the projected Nottingham ring road. Heavy traffic to and from the power station would not have to use secondary roads, and consequently there would be no need for improvements to enable them to cope with the additional loads.

(vi) Did the demand for sand and gravel (known to exist in large quantities under the site) outweigh the arguments for building the station in that particular spot? There was no question, he wrote, that the mineral deposits at Holme Pierrepont were of exceptional value. It was probably true that almost all the feasible riverside sites in the county had gravel under them. But the deposits of sand and gravel at Holme Pierrepont were particularly valuable because they were within easy reach of an extensive and heavily populated built-up area, where the needs of the construction industry were likely to be most pressing. On this question his answer was quite unequivocal; it would be against the public interest to place these minerals beyond reach by building a power station over them.

(vii) Would the diversion of this land from its existing use for farming purposes seriously affect the interests of agriculture? The Holme Pierrepont site was undoubtedly of great agricultural value, he wrote. But so were most of the other possibilities. To assess the relative agricultural merits of all the alternative sites, he noted, there were so many considerations that ought properly to be taken into account, and so much of the necessary information was not available, that he felt himself unable to make any worthwhile comparisons or reach a firm conclusion.[1]

---

[1] The planning Inspector's despairing remarks about the difficulties of grading the various sites in terms of agricultural merit were an apt comment on the whole problem of finding the best site for a power station at a public inquiry concerned to hear local objections to only one of the many possibilities. He wrote:

An exercise applying all the appropriate tests to establish a scale of preferability for all the sites under inquiry would be extremely arduous, detailed and controversial, and it would, indeed, be difficult to define

(viii) If the answers to any of his first seven questions should suggest that Holme Pierrepont was unsatisfactory, could the power station be built at any of the alternative sites considered by the C.E.G.B., or put forward by the Nottinghamshire County Council, (*a*) with less objection than to Holme Pierrepont and (*b*) under conditions equally satisfactory to the C.E.G.B.? All five sites suggested by the County Council seemed to him to be open to various important objections. Of the three other possibilities that had appeared on the C.E.G.B.'s original short-list – Market Warsop, Cottam and Ratcliffe-on-Soar – the first was out of the question until dry-cooling towers had been successfully developed, and the second was unsuitable because it was easily flooded. (When the Inspectors visited the site it had been deep under water.) This left only Ratcliffe-on-Soar, which was vigorously opposed by the County Council because it was in the Green Belt and (as they claimed) in a specially attractive rural setting.

Evidently these objections had not greatly impressed the planning Inspector. In his opinion, the environment at Ratcliffe-on-Soar was not so outstandingly beautiful that the site ought to be rejected out of hand for this reason. And from his inspection of the area he had come to the conclusion that a power station here need not be all that conspicuous. It was true that the site would be large enough for only one generating station; but since the Board had no firm plans to build a second station in the near future, that would be an irrelevant reason for rejecting a site that would satisfy their immediate needs. Ratcliffe-on-Soar, moreover, was exceptionally well placed for railway transport, because the main line ran alongside the site, and it was near the important junction at Trent Station, from which there were direct rail connections to the Nottinghamshire and Derbyshire coalfields which avoided Nottingham itself. To everyone's astonishment, he therefore suggested that Ratcliffe-on-Soar would justify careful consideration as an alternative site.

In the second Report, the Chief Engineering Inspector began

---

an unassailable standard of comparison. An attempt to elicit the information necessary for this purpose at the Inquiry would have prolonged the hearings inordinately and it is doubtful whether it would have been readily available or so unimpaired by cross-examination that it could have been accepted without hesitation or doubt.

by pointing out that the principal objection to a large power station at Holme Pierrepont was the risk of further polluting the atmosphere in and around Nottingham with a possible danger to health. 'Before such a station could operate', he noted, 'it would be necessary for the Board to obtain a "Certificate of Registration" issued by the Chief Alkali Inspector of the Ministry of Housing and Local Government.' This Certificate relating solely to air pollution would not be issued unless the Chief Alkali Inspector was satisfied with the provisions made by the Board for operating the station. 'It is hardly likely', he observed, 'that the Board would contemplate building a station unless they were reasonably certain of obtaining this certificate.'

He went on to commend the C.E.G.B.'s choice of Holme Pierrepont. 'I agree that it has many of the attributes of a good site for a power station. for it would be cheaper to construct and operate than one on any of the other sites. Sites such as this at Holme Pierrepont', he continued, 'are rare in England and Wales and the Board were, in a large measure, justified in coming to the conclusion that the advantages of this site were such as to outweigh the disadvantages.'

As for alternatives, the engineering Inspector agreed that the Board's sites at Cottam and Ratcliffe-on-Soar, and the County Council's counter-proposals for Upton, Ragnall, Woodcoates, West Burton and Cottam were all capable of development, though the last two he thought not very practicable. But he also accepted the C.E.G.B.'s contention that all the alternatives put forward by the objectors would cost at least £600,000 a year more than Holme Pierrepont. It was true that this extra expenditure would add only one-sixtieth of a penny to the cost of a unit of electricity; but, he remarked, 'one cannot overlook the fact that £600,000 per annum is a large amount of money'.

Turning to the question of pollution, the Inspector was satisfied that the highly efficient boilers to be installed in the power station would not make smoke. He agreed that there would be some increase in the amount of sulphur dioxide and fine dust in the atmosphere; but on the whole, he seems to have been inclined to accept the Board's estimates of the quantities that would be involved rather than those of the objectors. He thought the C.E.G.B. were probably right in saying that the coal to be used would have a 1·0 per cent, rather than a 1·6 per cent sulphur content. He did not think that they were being too optimistic in claiming a guaranteed performance of 99·3 per cent for their grit- and dust-arresting plant. Even if occasional breakdowns did temporarily reduce its efficiency, in his opinion there would still be no danger to health or life because of the exceptionally high chimneys planned for the Holme Pierrepont station. In his judgement, the danger of short-term pollution during adverse weather conditions had also been somewhat exaggerated; the C.E.G.B.'s claim – that gas plumes from the 650-foot chimneys would pierce practically all fogs – he considered 'very reasonable'. As to the effect of winds in the locality, he noted that winds which would carry the chimney emissions down the Trent valley into the open countryside, and away from Nottingham, Carlton and West Bridgford, would occur for 60 per cent of the year. In this respect, therefore, the site was well located. Since the proposed power station would not emit smoke, it would not in any way undo the good achieved by local Councils in implementing the Clean Air Act and creating smokeless zones.

So far as health risks were concerned, he also tended to side with the C.E.G.B. It was the ground-level pollution that mattered, he said, and he accepted the Board's view that this would not be materially increased by the power station. He agreed that the less pollution there was, the better. And it was obvious that it ought not to be increased in areas where everyday pollution was already comparatively high. But he thought it was going too far to say that the extra amount likely to be produced by the power station would lead to more illness and deaths in Nottingham and the surrounding district. There might indeed be *some* medical risk; but, he commented, 'one can hardly subscribe to one objector's view that any risk, however small or remote, should not be taken, for this view is rather impracticable in this day and age'.

In his summing up, the engineering Inspector repeated that there was an urgent need for good sites for power stations, and that Holme Pierrepont was a particularly good site. One serious drawback, however, was its proximity to Nottingham and to the best residential suburbs of the city. Nottingham was already overburdened with traffic, and a power station at Holme Pierrepont would add to the congestion. He did not think for one moment that the proposed generating station would create all the nuisance envisaged by the objectors; but the fact remained that there were other sites where there was less chance of these nuisances materialising. Holme Pierrepont would be £600,000 a year cheaper than the other sites proposed by the County Council, and this was an appreciable sum of money. However, he was inclined to the County Council's view, 'that too great a stress should not be laid on the economic factor'. Air pollution, and its effect on health was a very difficult problem, he wrote. But if coal had to be burnt it was best that it should be burnt under efficient boilers with tall chimneys and no smoke, rather than in small fireplaces with low chimneys and much smoke. Here again, though there would be very little risk of the proposed power station seriously polluting the atmosphere, if at all possible it was better to have a power station sited away from an urban residential area. Keeping the reader in suspense until the very end, he added the final sentence: 'There are, however, many who hold the view that power stations should be sited in industrial areas and not in the open countryside.'

The Inspectors' conclusions, set out in full, were as follows:

Although we are satisfied that of all the sites brought to our notice the site under application is technically and economically the most suitable, and (subject to any advice which may be given by the Ministers of Health and of Housing and Local Government) although we are not entirely convinced that the operation of the proposed station would materially increase the atmospheric pollution and/or danger to health, we are, nevertheless, unable to advise that the application be granted for the following reasons:

(a) all the alternative sites considered are capable of development without the disadvantages which would attend the erection of a generating station of the size proposed near a large urban residential area;

(b) the proposed station would seriously impair the value of the green wedge between West Bridgford and Radcliffe-on-Trent as part of the Nottinghamshire Green Belt; and

(c) it would promote a large increase in road and rail traffic in an urban area in which there is a serious traffic problem.

They therefore recommended that the C.E.G.B.'s application to build a power station at Holme Pierrepont be refused.

It is sometimes said that a well-understood form of Whitehall shorthand enables administrators to couch their appraisals in language which to outsiders seems to betray thought-processes that are unconvincing or even downright crude. Was there a more sophisticated message to be read between the lines of the Inspectors' Report? If there was, it may have been this: Holme Pierrepont is a first-rate site, and in any other circumstances we might well have recommended consent. But in this instance the sheer intensity of local hostility has convinced us that economic and technical considerations ought to take second place.

Be that as it may, for the purposes of this study it is the question of values that is of special interest, and there is no doubt that, as drafted, the Inspectors' recommendation was framed in a way calculated to mask the essential value-judgement that they were making. Whatever may have been said by way of advocacy, not even the C.E.G.B. would have denied that there were drawbacks to the Holme Pierrepont site. But the whole basis of their case was that the unquantifiable value of what would be lost as a result of building the station at Holme Pierrepont did not warrant the expenditure of £600,000 a year more on the least costly alternative acceptable to the objectors. The loss of amenity, in other words, was not (in their view) worth this extra expense.

What conclusion had the Inspectors reached about this question of values? A cursory reading of their recommendation might suggest that they had rejected Holme Pierrepont simply because in their opinion it was open to serious objections which ought to rule it out while there were other feasible sites that did not suffer from the same drawbacks. But it needs only a moment's thought to see that this cannot have been the whole story. They can hardly have meant to say that Holme Pierrepont ought to have been avoided *whatever* the additional costs of an alternative site; there must have been *some* price that they would not have considered it reasonable to pay. Though it was not put in so many words (and perhaps they themselves never reflected on the issue in quite this way), what the Inspectors were saying was this: in the public interest it is worth adding £600,000 a year to the country's electricity bill in order to avoid the incalculable cost of extra traffic congestion, and the loss of the unquantifiable amenity value of the wedge of Green Belt that would be impaired if the power station were built at Holme Pierrepont.[1]

What the reactions of the Minister of Power and the Minister of Housing and Local Government were to the Inspectors' Report must be a matter of guesswork. At the political level, they had been left in no doubt that if they approved the power station at Holme Pierrepont they would certainly bring a great deal of odium upon the Government. A massive generating station would be a physical and permanent monument to a highly unpopular decision. By comparison, the prospect of making electricity a tiny fraction dearer than it would otherwise have been, seven years later, cannot have held much terror for them. On the other hand, there was the morale of the C.E.G.B. to consider, and had the Inspectors recommended *consent* for Holme Pierrepont there might have been a certain amount of heart-searching in Whitehall. As it was, this difficulty did not arise. To ignore the advice of officials because it is politically unacceptable is one thing; to reject politically welcome recommendations from impartial Inspectors is another matter entirely, and few politicians indulge in such quixotic behaviour.

On 3 July 1961, in answer to a Parliamentary Question, the Minister of Power announced that he had decided to refuse consent for a power station at Holme Pierrepont. The news was

[1] There was, of course, the complication of Ratcliffe-on-Soar. We know that at least one of the Inspectors had this site (and not Upton) in mind as the best alternative. The additional running costs here were acknowledged to be a good deal less than £600,000. However, to change the figures is not to alter the fact that by implication the Inspectors were saying that there was a money price which the C.E.G.B. ought to pay in order to spare the amenities threatened at Holme Pierrepont. Whether the planning Inspector thought that no significant amenity costs would arise at Ratcliffe-on-Soar is not clear. Because the decision-making process entailed the examination of one site at a time, no one was in a position realistically to assess the loss of environment at Ratcliffe-on-Soar, because as yet there had been no opportunity or occasion for anyone to enlarge on the objections to that site. Yet the apparent assumption that there were no really substantial environmental costs at Ratcliffe-on-Soar may well have played some part in persuading the Inspectors to recommend the rejection of Holme Pierrepont. Difficulties of this kind may arise less often in future, because the Planning Inquiry Commissions provided for in the 1968 Town and Country Planning Act will enable Inspectors dealing with major planning applications to examine several alternatives before making their recommendations.

greeted with delight and relief in Nottingham. In an editorial entitled 'Stillborn-monster' the local newspaper commented that the verdict would be received with grateful thanks by the people of a city that had progressed in a hundred years from squalor to a degree of attractiveness that would have been permanently blighted by the arrival of such a totally objectionable neighbour as a power station. The Minister's decision, it declared, 'asserted the priority of human values over technical data'.[1] In a more down-to-earth way, the secretary of a local ratepayers' association was probably as near the truth when he observed that this episode demonstrated the effectiveness of 'collective opposition'. Amidst the general rejoicing there was only one note of dissension. The chairman of the Nottinghamshire County Council, a miner, remarked that as far as he was concerned, to lose the cheapest site in the Midlands was a 'sad business' for the miners in the county.[2] He might have added that the County Council's problems were not over yet. If the power station was not to be at Holme Pierrepont, where was it to be built? The 'monster' was far from dead; it was merely looking for another home.

POSTSCRIPT

The Nottinghamshire County Council had always insisted that they would be only too pleased to help the C.E.G.B. find sites in the county, provided the Board would rule out Holme Pierrepont and Ratcliffe-on-Soar. Immediately after the Holme Pierrepont decision was announced they therefore offered to co-operate with the C.E.G.B. in the search for another site. Talks began in December 1961. The C.E.G.B. asked the County Council to suggest possible sites on or near the Trent, in the corridor between the Leicestershire border to the south-west of Nottingham, and Staythorpe, fifteen miles or so north-east of the city. Only within these limits, the Board maintained, could the costs of coal haulage be kept reasonably low.

Naturally, the County planners turned their attention first to those stretches of the river that fell outside the Green Belt; that is, to the six or seven miles of the river between Staythorpe and

---

[1] *Guardian Journal*, 4 July 1961.   [2] Ibid.

Hoveringham. It soon became apparent that the only feasible site here was at Upton. Upton, of course, was the site that the C.E.G.B. had rejected once before on the grounds that it would cost £600,000 a year more than Holme Pierrepont. The Board evidently made it clear to the County Council that they were no more prepared to consider Upton now than in 1960. If Upton was not in the running, only the stretch of the Trent between Hoveringham and the Leicestershire border remained. The whole of this area lay within the Green Belt.

The County Council had just emerged successfully from a long and expensive battle to keep the Green Belt intact. But the hard-won victory at Holme Pierrepont had not been achieved without a twinge of apprehension, for there was no guarantee that the C.E.G.B. would be good losers and come back to Nottingham-shire for the second site they needed. The County Council, in fact, had been frankly relieved when they were asked to propose alternatives. If they had hesitated to oppose the C.E.G.B. over Holme Pierrepont, they relished a second clash even less, particu-larly now that competition with oil and nuclear energy was putting the coal industry under increasing pressure. Reluctantly, therefore, the search was switched to the Green Belt.

To the acute discomfort of the County planners, it was not long before they realised that the only possibility remaining was none other than Ratcliffe-on-Soar, the site that they had so vigorously opposed in the past. This site, it will be recalled, was about nine miles south-west of Nottingham and on the outer edge of the Green Belt. Situated in an angle between the Trent and the Soar, it was much more of a rural beauty spot than Holme Pierrepont. However, the Planning Committee felt that they now had no option but to ask the County Council to endorse their decision to accept a power station here. Though this apparently dramatic change of heart could to some extent be justified by reference to the planning Inspector's *obiter dicta* (if one of the Minister of Housing and Local Government's planning Inspec-tors was prepared to recommend it, clearly the site could not be dismissed as totally outrageous on planning grounds), nevertheless it did not go unchallenged in the County Council, and only after a lengthy debate was a reference back defeated by 44 votes to 24.

From the C.E.G.B.'s point of view Ratcliffe-on-Soar was not quite such a suitable site as Holme Pierrepont; however, it was a good second best, if only because it was exceptionally well placed in relation to the existing railway system. No doubt pleased to have secured the County Council's acquiescence, on 29 June 1961 the Board applied for consent for a 2,000-megawatt station on a 380-acre site at Ratcliffe-on-Soar. But if the County Council were no longer leading the opposition, some of the Board's former opponents, like the Nottingham Corporation, objected just as strongly to Ratcliffe-on-Soar as to Holme Pierrepont; while others, like the C.P.R.E., disliked it even more. And naturally, in shifting their ground, the C.E.G.B. had now stirred up an entirely fresh set of objectors, local authorities and organisations which had taken only a passing interest in the earlier controversy, but which were aghast at the prospect of finding the power station on their own doorstep as a direct result of the famous victory at Holme Pierrepont. Thus, the Carlton and West Bridgford Urban Districts, and the Bingham Rural District had left the ranks of the objectors; but their places were taken by two other outraged local authorities, the Long Eaton and the Beeston and Stapleford Urban District Councils. They were joined by the University of Nottingham, the Society for the Protection of Ancient Buildings, the Gotham Parish Council, and the local branches of the N.F.U. and the C.L.A.

This time, however, the C.E.G.B. were not without allies. All the mineworkers' unions in the area expressed support for the Ratcliffe-on-Soar site. The N.C.B., too, entered the fray. Assuming perhaps that the C.E.G.B. would, as usual, emerge victorious, it had remained silent during the earlier controversy. On this occasion, in his alarm at the possibility of losing a market for 5 million tons of coal a year, Lord Robens publicly appealed to the objectors to think again. If Ratcliffe-on-Soar was turned down, he said, the N.C.B. might well have to reconsider its plans to expand production in the east Midlands; if the project was approved, on the other hand, the new power station would provide steady work for 10,000 miners for many years to come.[1]

On 8 January 1963 the C.E.G.B. contingent returned to the Shire Hall, Nottingham, for what was to be another fourteen-day inquiry. Suitably modified, many of the old arguments were rehearsed again at length; and for those who took the trouble to study the evidence given two years earlier there was a ready

[1] *The Times*, 2 Aug 1962.

supply of awkward questions.[1] The C.E.G.B. were now saying that there would be hardly any loss of visual amenity at Ratcliffe-on-Soar, because the power station would be virtually hidden by a convenient fold of land. But at the Holme Pierrepont inquiry, had the Board's representatives not said that Ratcliffe-on-Soar was originally passed over because the C.E.G.B. realised that it was open to serious amenity objections? And what of the County Council and their attitude towards the Green Belt? At the earlier inquiry, the County Director of Planning had painted a lurid enough picture of a power station and its effect on the surrounding area: was he now prepared to see 'a great industrial giant, snorting fumes and smoke' in the precious Green Belt? Witnesses from Long Eaton and Beeston and Stapleford had calculated that it would take a fresh wind from the south-west about five minutes to waft chimney emissions from Ratcliffe-on-Soar to their houses and streets: if atmospheric pollution was intolerable in West Bridgford and Carlton, why was it acceptable in Long Eaton, Beeston and Stapleford? One of the reasons given for rejecting Holme Pierrepont had been the effect on traffic congestion of closing an important level-crossing in Nottingham: but what about the chaotic traffic conditions that would be caused in Beeston if the level-crossing there had to be closed for longer periods during the rush hour?

Long before the end of the hearings, however, it had become clear that the central issue at the inquiry was precisely the same as in the Holme Pierrepont case. Some of the objectors suggested that the Board ought to go to Cottam or Woodcoates, or add a 'C' station to their existing plant at Willington. The C.E.G.B. did not deny that these proposals were technically feasible; the difficulty was that they would cost a great deal more than a power station at Ratcliffe-on-Soar. According to the Board's estimates, the extra capital cost at Cottam would have been £5·3 million, and the running costs would have amounted to something like £1·2 million a year more.[2] At Woodcoates the additional capital

[1] For the Ratcliffe-on-Soar case, see Public Inquiry Report (29 June 1963), together with verbatim transcript of evidence.

[2] In May 1963, before the Inspectors had reported on Ratcliffe-on-Soar, the C.E.G.B. in fact applied for consent for the Cottam site. It would appear that the Board refused to consider Cottam as an 'alternative' to Ratcliffe-on-Soar not only because it was dearer but also because they foresaw that this northern site would be needed as well as Ratcliffe-on-Soar.

cost was reckoned to be £4·1 million and the extra running costs £500,000; and at Willington the figures were said to be £676,000 more on capital costs and an extra £600,000 a year for running expenses.

The Inspectors presented their Report to the Minister of Power on 29 June 1963. They agreed that there were drawbacks to the Ratcliffe-on-Soar site, and for this reason they had looked carefully at some of the alternatives suggested by the objectors. According to the C.E.G.B. these alternatives were all considerably more expensive, and they accepted the Board's estimates. This time, however, it was explicitly acknowledged that what confronted the Inspectors was a question of values: were they prepared to recommend payment of a stated cash price in order to save whatever a power station at Ratcliffe-on-Soar might destroy? In two succinct and unequivocal sentences they spelt out their answer:

> On grounds of cost we doubt if the alternative sites are justified. We do not think the worth of the proposed site as pleasant, good agricultural land, forming part of a proposed Green Belt, is so great as to justify extra costs on the scale indicated by the C.E.G.B.'s estimate.

On 28 August 1963 the Minister of Power announced that he had accepted the Inspectors' recommendation. The result is that the power station now stands at Ratcliffe-on-Soar, a massive landmark, visible to users of the M1 motorway from many miles away. At Holme Pierrepont, of course, there are still open fields. But now that the dust has settled on this long-drawn-out controversy, some of those involved look back and wryly reflect on what might have been. Had the C.E.G.B. applied first for Ratcliffe-on-Soar, the Nottinghamshire County Council and many others would have objected. And with Holme Pierrepont still in the wings, its disadvantages not yet explored at a public inquiry, who can say that consent for Ratcliffe-on-Soar might not have been refused? If the C.E.G.B. had then switched their attention to Holme Pierrepont, it is arguable – to say the least – that in those circumstances the Nottinghamshire County Council would not have felt able to oppose that site. In which case, the power station might now stand there instead.

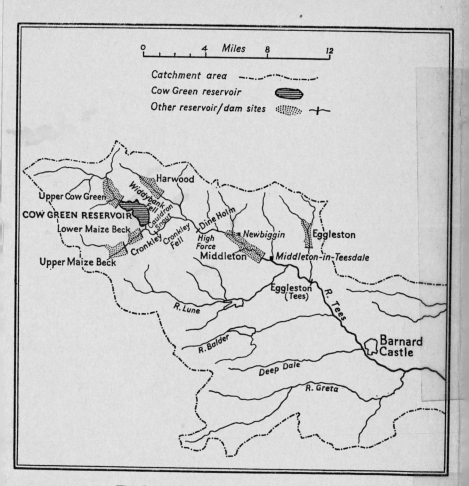

3   The Cow Green reservoir and the alternative sites

4 The Cow Green Reservoir

> We are here as a jury. We are here to calculate, on
> the one hand, the benefits, and on the other the
> drawbacks of this scheme. In my own simple way I
> am asking whether I should decide between flowers
> on the one hand, and people on the other – people
> and their prosperity, Britain and its industrial prosperity.
> I come down solidly against the flowers.
>
> Lord Leatherland, on the Third Reading of
> the Tees Valley and Cleveland Water Bill,
> House of Lords, February 1967

UPPER TEESDALE is one of the wildest and loneliest parts of
England. Extending over about eighty square miles, it stretches
from the town of Middleton-in-Teesdale up into the Pennines, to
the source of the Tees high on Cross Fell. In the upper reaches of
the valley there are few signs of human life, far less of modern
civilisation. It rains a good deal, and the clouds sit like a mist on
the bleak, peat-covered fells. Look at a map of Upper Teesdale,
and the names of the natural features come from a world of
myths and fairy tales. There are the two great waterfalls of High
Force and Cauldron Snout; there are streams with names like
Slapestone Sike, Swarth Beck, and Black Sike; there is Cronkley
Fell and Widdybank Fell, High Cup Nick and Holmwath, Merry-
gill Moss, Falcon Clints and Cronkley Scar. And a mile or so
upstream from the boiling torrent of Cauldron Snout, where the
river runs deeper and quieter, there is Cow Green. The name
refers to an area of land on the western flank of Widdybank Fell,
above the abandoned workings of the old Cow Green lead mine,
and half a mile from the river itself. Although it appears on
maps, until recently 'Cow Green' conveyed little even to those
who knew the area well, for it is not a name that local people, or
anyone else, commonly use to describe this particular patch of
Widdybank Fell.

Remote though they are, the hills and valleys of Upper Tees-dale have never been entirely empty. The area has long been prized by climbers and walkers, country-lovers and naturalists. And for more than a hundred years the rare plants that survive in Upper Teesdale have made it an area of great interest to botanists. This is the home of the Teesdale Violet and the York-shire Milkwort, the Hoary Rockrose and the Bog Asphodel, the Teesdale Sandwort and the Spring Gentian, the False Sedge, the Common Seathrift, the Bird's Eye Primrose, the Yellow Moun-tain Saxifrage, and many others. In the unusual combination of sugar limestone and acid peat soils found on Widdybank Fell, climate and geology between them have nurtured what some eminent botanists consider to be assemblages, or 'communities', of rare plants that are unique in the United Kingdom. These communities may well have been there undisturbed since the period immediately after the last ice-age, more than 10,000 years ago. When the Cow Green mine closed in 1954 it seemed that no one but naturalists and country-lovers would ever again come to this out-of-the-way and inhospitable corner of Upper Tees-dale.[1]

A BREAKTHROUGH AT BILLINGHAM

Seventy miles downstream the river reaches industrial Tees-side. In the depression between the wars few areas suffered worse from unemployment, and more than thirty years later the region still has an air of convalescence. Not surprisingly, Tees-side has always been intensely preoccupied with the problems of getting and keeping industry. In recent years it has been reasonably successful in attracting new firms, and in encouraging those already there to expand. Even so, in the harsh winter of 1962–3 the unemploy-

---

[1] The chief documentary sources for the following account are: Tees Valley and Cleveland Water Bill, verbatim transcript of proceedings before the Select Committee of the House of Commons, May and June 1966, and before the Select Committee of the House of Lords, November and December 1966; *The Times*; *Darlington and Stockton Times*; *Hansard*; D. H. Valentine (ed.), *The Natural History of Upper Teesdale* (Newcastle: Northumberland and Durham Naturalists' Trust, 1965); *The Threat to Upper Teesdale* (London: Botanical Society of the British Isles, 6 July 1965).

ment figures for Tees-side were among the highest in the country. It was a painful reminder of the past: full employment was not something that could ever be taken for granted in the North-east.

Tees-side was vulnerable because it depended so heavily on the iron and steel industry. What was needed, as everyone recognised, was diversification. Consequently, the arrival between the wars of new firms like Shell and I.C.I. was seen as a godsend. I.C.I. were particularly welcome, for with their wide range of activities, even at the worst of times they seemed never likely to be in trouble on all their products simultaneously. By the early sixties they were employing something like 30,000 men, more than a tenth of the entire work force on Tees-side. Providing thousands of jobs, and making a massive contribution to the rate income of the local authorities in the area, they were far more than just another firm; they had become a stable and comforting presence, a valued institution whose needs and wishes were matters of great consequence on Tees-side.

At their Billingham works I.C.I. have been producing ammonia since 1925. For many years coal was an important constituent in the manufacturing process; but in the late fifties, as high-quality coking coal became more expensive, and as other countries developed production techniques based on the use of natural gas that was both plentiful and cheap, the competitive position of the British ammonia industry steadily worsened. At one time there were fears that it might go out of business altogether. It was a depressing outlook, not least because there is a considerable export market for the fertilisers produced from ammonia.

The situation was saved, and the industry rescued, by the persistence of I.C.I.'s research chemists. Early in 1960 they began to develop a new process for converting naphtha, a readily available and cheap oil fraction, into the gases that are needed for ammonia synthesis and the production of hydrogen. By the middle of 1963 it appeared that this new technique, the 'naphtha steam reforming process' as it was called, might have extensive commercial possibilities. Technical breakthroughs of this importance have to be exploited as quickly as possible, for once lost, overseas markets are not easily regained; the pace of technological change being what it is, hesitation and delay can easily fritter away a hard-won competitive advantage.

At the beginning of 1964 two questions faced I.C.I. Were they to go ahead with the new process on a large scale? And if so, should the new plant be added to the company's existing installations on Tees-side? On technical and commercial grounds, they were satisfied that full-scale production was feasible. And so far as Tees-side was concerned, all the signs seemed favourable. It was known that a new port was to be built at Teesmouth; road and rail communications in the area were good enough; oil was available at the Tees-side refineries; there was plenty of skilled labour; and from the Ministry of Housing and Local Government's Hydrological Survey of 1961 the potential supply of water in the area appeared to be adequate. Moreover, it was at about this time that the Government was beginning to take an interest in the North-east and its economic problems. In February 1963 Tees-side had been declared a Development District, and soon afterwards Lord Hailsham made a highly publicised visit to the North-east. In November 1963 there followed a White Paper – the 'Hailsham Report' – announcing that new financial incentives were to be given to industrialists prepared to set up or expand in the region.

Against this background, in January 1964 I.C.I. decided to build two of the largest ammonia plants in the world, each capable of producing a thousand tons of ammonia a day. In September 1964 it was decided to add a third plant of the same size. At their Wilton works the production of hydrogen was also to be increased to permit a large expansion of the output of nylon and similar petro-chemicals. It is a fact about expansion in the chemical industry that new products and new techniques often require water in very substantial quantities.

The authority responsible for providing Tees-side with water is the Tees Valley and Cleveland Water Board. As constituted in 1964, the Water Board had been in existence for only six years, though various forerunners trace their history back to the establishment of the Stockton, Middlesborough and Redcar Water Company in 1851. The chairman of the Board was Alderman Charles Allison, a member of the Stockton Borough Council for almost fifty years and a powerful and well-known public figure on Tees-side. Like a good many other trade unionists of his generation, Allison had never forgotten the misery of the thirties; the dole queue, the means test, victimisation and the soup kitchens, were among his sharpest memories. As he was later to observe, 'all these things have happened in our lifetime, and those of us who have grown old in administration feel that we should do everything we possibly can to avoid a repetition'. There were other veterans of the depression on the Tees Valley and Cleveland Water Board who shared Allison's memories and attitudes: when it was a question of jobs, men of their age and background were rarely in doubt about what was important. The Water Board supplied a large rural area covering more than 500 square miles, and served about 450,000 people, the bulk of them in Middlesborough, Stockton-on-Tees, Thornaby-on-Tees, and Redcar. In one respect, however, their clientèle was unusual; considerably more than half their water went not to domestic consumers but to industry. By far the largest customer was I.C.I. By the late fifties this preponderance of industrial users was making long-term planning increasingly difficult, for as we shall now see, technological innovation can drastically change an industry's water requirements with very little warning.

As late as August 1963 I.C.I. had assured the Water Board, at officer level, that in the immediate future they would need no extra water beyond their existing allocation. Within twelve months, in July 1964, the Water Board were told that as a result of the new ammonia plants which were planned, I.C.I. would, after all, require additional water quite soon. Those in I.C.I. responsible for organising the supply of water were as much taken by surprise as the Water Board. Since it takes only about two years to build a fertiliser plant, but usually between five and seven years to plan and build a reservoir, the makings of a problem were built into the situation from the very beginning. Later on, I.C.I. were to be accused of not making their requirements known early enough, and of not starting the search for extra water sufficiently far in advance of their need. The truth of the matter is that if water is to be available as soon as it is required, the search must be started and the supply organised long before there can be any guarantee that it will ever be needed. Looking for water that may never be required is not a task that anyone in private industry undertakes with enthusiasm.

By August 1964 I.C.I. were in a position to state their requirements more specifically. They would need an additional 11 million gallons a day (m.g.d.) by 1966 for the installations already under construction; for the new nylon and fertiliser plant to be

built between 1965 and 1970 a further 14 m.g.d. would be
required. The Water Board now made inquiries of other large
industrial users on Tees-side, such as Shell and Dorman Long.
Their replies indicated that a further 10 m.g.d. would be needed,
over and above I.C.I.'s 25 m.g.d. It was, of course, the responsibility of the Water Board to provide the water; but since I.C.I.
were guaranteeing most of the capital for what was clearly going
to be a major project, and one in which they had a vital interest,
from now onwards the company and their advisers were to work
closely with the Board and their consultant engineers.

Thus, in the summer of 1964, the problem confronting I.C.I.
and the Tees Valley and Cleveland Water Board was that of
finding an extra 35 m.g.d., a formidable task considering that at
this stage the entire output envisaged by the Board from their
Teesdale sources amounted only to 65 m.g.d. In August 1964 the
Water Board instructed their consulting engineers, Sandeman
Kennard and Partners, to prepare a report and make recommendations for increasing their safe reliable yield – the volume of
water that can be supplied from reservoirs under drought conditions – from 65 to 100 m.g.d.

There were several possibilities. One was a large impounding
reservoir, well upstream on the Tees, from which the water could
be piped to the consumer. This was rejected because of its relatively low reliable yield and because of the expense of pipeworks.
Another possibility was an artificial storage reservoir, near the
consumers, into which water could be pumped from the river and
stored until it was needed. This, too, was rejected, chiefly because
a lowland reservoir of this kind would have been very expensive
in terms of the agricultural land flooded. A borehole scheme, for
the abstraction of water from underground sources in the area
between Darlington and Hartlepool, was also briefly considered.
But the consultants decided that only a carefully designed pilot
scheme, phased over a number of years, would show conclusively
whether or not sufficient water could be provided in this way.
The remaining possibility, and the one favoured by the Water
Board's consulting engineers, was to build a river-regulating
reservoir on the upper reaches of the Tees, or on one of its tributaries.

The principle of river-regulating reservoirs is simply to store
surplus water in the winter, releasing it into the river for abstrac-

tion at a suitable point on the lower reaches when it is needed during the drier summer months. Reservoirs of this kind have many advantages. The only construction work required is the dam, behind which water from the higher reaches of the river collects. The channel of the river, itself serves as a natural aqueduct, carrying water from the upland gathering grounds to the point of abstraction downstream. This technique avoids the expense of a pipeline, secures a higher reliable yield from the river's tributaries, and improves the regime of the river. For these reasons, river-regulating reservoirs were coming very much into favour with River Boards and water engineers in the early sixties. In the circumstances, the Water Board's consultants had no hesitation in opting for this type of reservoir, particularly as in 1959, on the last occasion when the Board had needed to increase their supply, they had been strongly pressed by the then Wear and Tees River Board and by the Ministry of Housing and Local Government to install a regulating reservoir.[1]

There were many possible sites for a river-regulating reservoir in Upper Teesdale. But in their search for the most suitable, the consulting engineers had to take account of a number of important constraints limiting their freedom of choice. The site had to be large enough to yield sufficient water, and it had to be geologically sound, in the sense that water would not leak away through the floor or sides of the valley. It had to be reasonably accessible, otherwise there would be difficulties during construction. Obviously, the Water Board and I.C.I. wanted the reservoir built as cheaply as possible. It was also a point of some importance that the reservoir should not provoke serious opposition, for it had to be ready by 1970. Battles over reservoirs can consume a great deal of time, and whilst money can buy most things, it cannot buy the time taken up by determined objectors, intent on using all available means to fight a project they dislike. And this brings us to the botanists.

Official conservation policies in this country really go back to 1947. In that year the Ministry of Town and Country Planning recognised the importance of conserving wild life for scientific purposes when they adopted a special report from the Wild Life Conservation Committee calling for the establishment of National

[1] The site chosen was at Balderhead. The reservoir had been authorised by Private Act in 1959; at this stage it was still under construction. See p. 141.

Parks and National Nature Reserves.[1] This report actually singled out the rare flora and fauna and the bogs and grasslands of Upper Teesdale for particular attention, and recommended that the whole of Upper Teesdale should be made a Conservation Area. In 1949 the Nature Conservancy was set up,[2] and one of its earliest decisions, three years later, was to establish the Moor House Nature Reserve, on the south side of the very highest reaches of the Tees. In 1957 it proposed another reserve – the Upper Teesdale Nature Reserve – to cover a large area on the Yorkshire side of the Tees, to the south of the river between the Cauldron Snout and High Force waterfalls. The Conservancy opened negotiations with the local landowners in 1959, and the area was eventually declared a Nature Reserve in 1963. Though it was planned to extend the reserve to take in Widdybank Fell, this had not been done in 1964. And oddly enough, even as late as 1966 the map of the proposed Nature Reserve still did not include a stream named Slapestone Sike. It was later to be said that the section of Cow Green on either side of this stream was of the very greatest scientific importance. Whether the omission of Slapestone Sike – described by one prominent botanist as a 'staggering oversight' – was due simply to a clerical error (as the Natural Environment Research Council was to allege), or whether it indicated that very little scientific research of any significance had been carried out there (as I.C.I. and the Water Board were to suggest), must remain part of the argument. Though it did not fall within a Nature Reserve, in 1950 Widdybank Fell had nevertheless been notified to the Durham and Westmorland County Councils by the Nature Conservancy as a Site of Special Scientific Interest, a status it shared with a further 50,000 acres of Upper Teesdale. Clearly, finding a reservoir site acceptable to the scientists in an area like this was not going to be easy.

As it happened, I.C.I. and the Tees Valley and Cleveland Water Board had crossed swords once before with the scientists over a reservoir in Upper Teesdale. In 1956, as a result of an earlier expansion programme, I.C.I. had asked the Water Board to find them additional water. The Board had examined several

---

[1] *Conservation of Nature in England and Wales*, Cmd 7122 (H.M.S.O., July 1947).

[2] For a history of the conservation movement, see Sir Dudley Stamp, *Nature Conservation in Britain* (London: Collins, 1969).

possible sites for a reservoir, including one at Cow Green. At that time they were still thinking in terms of a piped supply reservoir, and when Mr Edgar Morton, the geologist retained to advise the Board, reported in September 1956 that a reservoir here might leak, the Cow Green site was abandoned. There were two other possibilities, at Dine Holm and Balderhead. Eventually, the Board chose Dine Holm, some little distance upstream from High Force. The news of this decision had immediately provoked an outcry from the scientists, and in February 1957 a letter appeared in *The Times*, signed by fourteen eminent botanists, deploring this incursion into an internationally acclaimed area of scientific interest. The area below Cauldron Snout was described by Professor D. H. Valentine of the University of Durham as probably the worst possible site for a reservoir in the Tees Valley from the scientific point of view. In due course, the Nature Conservancy too came out against Dine Holm, and in the autumn of 1957, when it was learned that the Water Board intended to promote a Private Bill seeking permission for a reservoir here, the Conservancy informed I.C.I., the Water Board, and the Durham County Council that it would strongly oppose the project.

The widespread scientific opposition to Dine Holm made a powerful impression at the very highest level within I.C.I. The company spent about £6 million a year on scientific research, and was anxious not to appear an unenlightened and philistine juggernaut. It seemed that the botanists had a case, and it was clear that Dine Holm was by no means the only practicable site. In the circumstances, I.C.I. decided that they ought not to be associated with this scheme, and withdrew their support for the Bill. As a result, in December 1957 the Water Board gave up the Dine Holm project, and instructed their consulting engineers to re-examine the other possibilities. Finally a site on the river Balder, a tributary of the Tees, was selected, and in 1959 a Private Act empowered the Board to proceed with a new reservoir at Balderhead.[1]

[1] It was the commissioning of the river-regulating reservoir at Balderhead which had brought the Board's output up to 65 m.g.d. In arguing the case for Balderhead in 1959 the Water Board had assured Parliament that a yield of 65 m.g.d. would certainly be enough to meet their requirements until 1983. This estimate was to be falsified embarrassingly quickly as a result of the new developments at Billingham in 1963.

Well aware that Upper Teesdale was a highly sensitive area, and having run into trouble with the conservationists once before, this time I.C.I. decided to feel their way carefully. In fact, they set out with the deliberate intention of making this new reservoir project a classic illustration of the virtues and rewards of prior consultation with those affected. But, of course, there were many scientists and scientific bodies interested in various aspects of Upper Teesdale. Who precisely was to be consulted? To I.C.I. it seemed that the organisation best placed to speak authoritatively for the scientists and conservationists must obviously be their official voice, the Nature Conservancy.

'THE BEST LAID SCHEMES . . .'

Intent on avoiding a repetition of the Dine Holm affair, in August 1964 Mr Julius Kennard, the Board's consultant engineer, approached the Nature Conservancy to sound out its views. On 1 September, at the Conservancy's offices in Belgrave Square, he met Mr Max Nicholson, the Director General, for what was to be the first of several informal talks between the two men. Kennard brought with him a map showing the location of no less than seventeen sites in Upper Teesdale that looked possible on the basis of the Hydrological Survey of 1961. Among them was Cow Green. When he examined the list, Nicholson apparently said that on botanical grounds the Conservancy would object very strongly to some of the sites that were included. Kennard, however, formed the impression that Cow Green was not likely to be among those that would be most objectionable. Other members of the Conservancy's staff were present at this meeting, but it was left to Nicholson to do most of the talking. According to Kennard, nobody threw up his hands in horror at the mention of Cow Green, which of course was hardly surprising, because the name meant nothing in scientific circles.

Together with Dr J. L. Knill, an expert on reservoir geology, Kennard then visited Upper Teesdale to inspect the seventeen possible sites. In October Kennard received Knill's geological appraisal. In Knill's opinion none of the possibilities was wholly free from geological problems, but Cow Green, Lower Maize Beck, and Harwood seemed to be the safest. Knill was aware of the earlier adverse report on the geology of Cow Green, but disagreed with Morton's findings.

On 20 October Kennard returned to London for a second meeting with Nicholson. This time he had with him Mr R. Hetherington, I.C.I.'s technical adviser on water supplies. They were now in a position to eliminate a good many of the initial possibilities. Seven had to be ruled out at once because they would not have provided enough water. To four others – at Cronkley, Cronkley Bridge, Holm Wath, and Dine Holm – Nicholson expressed strong opposition. The six sites left in the running were at Upper Maize Beck, Harwood, Langdon, Eggleston Burn, Middleton and Cow Green. Two of these, however, were not acceptable to Kennard. Eggleston Burn was a very doubtful proposition on geological grounds. And from what he had seen of the Middleton site, Kennard realised that a reservoir there would flood several hundred acres of agricultural land, besides probably submerging part of the village of Newbiggin. As he well knew, I.C.I. and the Water Board were as anxious to steer clear of a fight with the farmers as they were to avoid a battle with the conservationists. It would indeed have been ironic had I.C.I. outraged the agricultural interest in order to increase their output of fertilisers. So, there remained four sites. Arranged in Nicholson's order of preference they were at Langdon, Harwood, Upper Maize Beck, and Cow Green.

From Kennard's point of view, the first three sites were certainly feasible. But by comparison with Cow Green, they all had serious disadvantages. The catchment area for Langdon was smaller, and the geology less sound. A reservoir at Harwood would have flooded a good deal of farmland, and would have required a much higher dam than at Cow Green. Upper Maize Beck was a very remote and inaccessible site, and the dam would have been even higher. As Kennard saw it, therefore, Cow Green looked very much the best proposition, and before leaving he told Nicholson that he intended to recommend the Water Board to carry out a detailed site exploration there. For his part, Nicholson was noncommittal. The Nature Conservancy would have to arrange an onsite investigation, he said, in order to assess the degree of objection. The late autumn was hardly the right time to begin a survey of this kind, and in any case, he added it would be for one of their committees to make the final decision as to the Conservancy's attitude.

I.C.I., the Water Board and their advisers were well pleased by Nicholson's attitude. He appeared to appreciate their problems, and he seemed to be concerned to strike a balance between the needs of industry and the claims of conservation. Even so, Kennard was agreeably surprised when on 23 October, only two days after their meeting, he received a letter from Nicholson which seemed to put Cow Green in the clear so far as the Conservancy was concerned. Nicholson wrote that he too believed in quiet negotiations. This was a far more civilised way of settling problems than what he called 'an open fight in the chaotic conditions of a public inquiry'. He had been trying to gauge the probable reaction of the Conservancy to Cow Green, and what he had discovered he set out in his letter to Kennard. As this letter was to assume some significance, part of it must be quoted in full:

> Since your call here [wrote Nicholson], I have been able to find an opportunity which I had not expected so soon for sounding out the opinion of our members who will be responsible for determining the Conservancy's attitude, and as a result of this I think that you could safely go a little further and inform the Board that you now have reason to believe that if the difficulties on your side of the Cow Green site could be overcome [a reference apparently to the possible geological problems] it would be most unlikely to be objected to by the Nature Conservancy. Indeed, if the Board felt able to put up proposals for this site embodying a similar approach to that adopted at Diddington so that it would form a point of attraction for visitors who would otherwise be straying on the more scientifically vulnerable areas of Upper Teesdale, then the Conservancy might feel justified in actively supporting such a project in face of the opposition from certain quarters which would be inevitable for any reservoir above Middleton.[1]

[1] Which members of the Nature Conservancy Nicholson consulted was never publicly disclosed. Nor were the 'certain quarters' ever identified, though it was to be suggested that Nicholson was referring to members of the Botanical Society of the British Isles and the Botany Department of the University of Durham. Informal feelers from I.C.I. to the Durham botanists produced results that were not so reassuring. Nevertheless, the company comforted itself with the reflection that it was, after all, the Conservancy which was the official voice of the scientists.

Kennard and Hetherington could not believe that Nicholson would have written in these terms had he not been sure of his ground. He was saying, so it seemed, that not only would the Conservancy not oppose Cow Green, they might even support it. As Kennard was to remark, when he and Hetherington discussed the letter they both thought that they had achieved a remarkable success. It now appeared that the Water Board had been given the green light for Cow Green. Had they known what lay behind Nicholson's letter they might have been less sanguine. The S.S.S.I. in Upper Teesdale covers a very wide area, and the Conservancy possessed only the sketchiest scientific maps of parts of it. In a general way, the importance of Widdybank Fell was well understood, though how far the rare flora on the fell impinged upon Cow Green was by no means clear. In any case, if (as seemed possible) Kennard was proposing to build the dam at Cow Green, the reservoir itself would be upstream from Widdybank Fell and the vegetation there would not be much affected. Nicholson also had at the back of his mind the recollection that Cow Green had been passed over in 1956 on geological grounds: the geology of the site had not changed since then. And, as luck would have it, none of the three members of the Conservancy consulted by Nicholson had reacted strongly against Cow Green, either because they themselves were not specially interested in the particular type of vegetation found there, or because from what they could understand of it, the Water Board's scheme seemed to be reasonably acceptable from a botanical point of view.

However, it quickly became apparent that in his efforts to be helpful, Nicholson had been over-confident. Immediately after the meeting with Kennard he instructed Dr Derek Ratcliffe, then a Nature Conservancy botanist concerned with vegetation surveys, to carry out a systematic investigation of the Cow Green site on behalf of the Conservancy. But as the weather during the winter of 1964–5 was unsuitable for survey work, it was not until well into 1965 that Ratcliffe was able to produce his report. In the meantime, Nicholson asked the Conservancy's Northern Regional Officer to make contact with scientists known to have first-hand experience of Upper Teesdale, to assess their reaction to the alternative sites mentioned by Kennard. One of the botanists consulted was Professor Valentine of Durham University. From this and other quarters Nicholson was soon made aware that he had seriously underestimated the hostility that a reservoir at Cow Green would provoke.

On 2 November 1964 the Tees Valley and Cleveland Water Board officially informed the Nature Conservancy that they had been advised to undertake further explorations at Cow Green. If the site proved to be geologically feasible, they said, discussions with the Conservancy would be reopened. When Nicholson wrote back on 3 November he was a good deal more cautious. The Conservancy, he replied, could not commit itself until a definite scheme came forward. The helpfulness and candour of the Board's consulting engineers had been much appreciated, and further talks about Cow Green would be welcome. Nevertheless, the Conservancy was disappointed that none of the less objectionable sites had proved technically feasible, for there could be no doubt that any site in Upper Teesdale, Cow Green included, would inevitably give rise to a considerable amount of opposition in various quarters. If the geological report on Cow Green should be favourable, the Conservancy would not be able to give its view on the site at short notice, though it would approach the problem with a desire to be as helpful as possible.

Just over a month later, on 8 December, the Water Board announced that they intended to build a new reservoir in Upper Teesdale. Nothing was said about a specific site. By this stage, however, the Nature Conservancy's attitude had become much more distant, and on 11 December its Northern Regional Officer wrote to the Water Board pointing out that 'beyond reasonable investigation of certain sites' the Conservancy was 'entirely uncommitted about reservoir proposals in Teesdale'. The green light was now at amber.

If Cow Green was no longer certain of as smooth a passage as had seemed possible in October, the Water Board still had no inkling of the storm that was soon to break about them. Speaking at the Board's meeting in January 1965, for example, Alderman Allison could scarcely credit that anyone would be perverse and misguided enough to impede a project so vital to the prosperity of Tees-side. 'Are we going to have the position arise', he asked, 'where people who think more of flowers and plant life than of industry can impose their will?' Another member of the Board advised his colleagues not to panic. He was satisfied that public opinion would not permit idealistically minded people, or cranks, to hinder such an important development. Opposition was irritating, he admitted. But then, so was a flea, and that could be quickly settled with a puff of insecticide.[1]

By February 1965 the consulting engineers had completed the first stage of their exploratory work on the Cow Green site. The geological survey had been considerably more thorough than the 1956 investigation, and they were satisfied that a reservoir at Cow Green definitely would not leak. It was known that of the 770 acres needed for the reservoir about twenty were part of the S.S.S.I. But since so much of Upper Teesdale also had this status – if indeed it was not part of an even more sacrosanct National Nature Reserve – I.C.I. and the Water Board concluded that on this score Cow Green would probably be no worse than anywhere else, for the chances were that there would be protests from the conservationists, whichever site was chosen. In any case, I.C.I. had by now made their own inquiries about the scientific importance of Cow Green and about the value of the work in progress there. A company like I.C.I. has well-informed scientists of its own, with their own contacts in the research world; from them it learned that there were many botanists who knew nothing of Cow Green or of any significant field work in this particular area. And when they found out more about the nature of the research that *was* in progress in Upper Teesdale, I.C.I.'s scientists were not impressed. Accustomed as they were to systematic experimentation, under rigorously controlled laboratory conditions, they saw the Upper Teesdale botanists as being engaged upon the somewhat dilettante Victorian pursuit of labelling and categorising rare flora. There were scientists in the universities who shared this view; but as I.C.I. were to discover, when some of the doyens of the academic world took their stand on the unique value of Cow Green, other botanists were not easily persuaded to come forward to contradict these eminent men in public.

In May the consulting engineers handed over their final report to I.C.I. and the Water Board. They recommended, as a temporary measure, that the Board should apply to the Northumbrian River Authority for a licence to abstract more water from the Tees to meet any immediate deficit in the next few years. More important, they also recommended that the Water Board should

[1] *Darlington and Stockton Times*, 9 Jan 1965.

build a river-regulating reservoir at Cow Green. So far as I.C.I. and the Board were concerned, the die was now cast.

The next move was up to the Nature Conservancy. In fact, it had little choice but to oppose Cow Green, because by this point Ratcliffe had reported on the results of his survey of the area threatened by the reservoir. According to Ratcliffe, the western slopes of Widdybank Fell were of very special scientific interest, and in his view the loss of even twenty acres would be a very serious matter, for each part of this highly diversified complex of species was almost totally dissimilar from the rest. On 22 July, therefore, the Nature Conservancy told the Water Board that it intended to object to the choice of the Cow Green site. At the same time it asked the Board to investigate another possibility on the confluence of the Tees and Mattergill Sike, further upstream. This site, which fell within the Moor House Nature Reserve, was to be known as Upper Cow Green. Presented with a new alternative, the Board's consulting engineers did ask for a geological report; but they refused to consider it seriously, partly because they felt sure it would not provide enough water, and partly because they calculated that it would cost about twice as much and would take something like two years longer to build.

At this stage in the proceedings, everyone concerned with the case was under the impression that the final decision on Cow Green would lie in the hands of the Minister of Housing and Local Government under Section 23 of the 1945 Water Act, possibly after a public local inquiry if there was substantial opposition to the project. In accordance with the usual procedure, on 27 July the Board submitted to the Minister for his informal comments a Draft Order empowering them to go ahead with the reservoir at Cow Green. For their part, the Ministry evidently knew enough about the situation to sense that there was a controversy in the air, and it seemed to them that this was just the kind of scheme that the newly created Water Resources Board might be asked to advise upon. Set up under the 1963 Water Resources Act to advise the Government on the conservation and provision of water in England and Wales, the Board looked to be the ideal body to produce an impartial and authoritative report on the range of possibilities. Accordingly, on 3 August, the Water Resources Board and the Tees Valley and Cleveland Water Board were asked to collaborate in an urgent examination of the problem of how best to provide Tees-side with additional water.

The need for this water was too pressing for the Water Resources Board to carry out an exhaustive survey of all the possible sources in the Tees catchment area. Nor was there enough time for it to assemble its own data. Consequently, it had to rely on the Tees Valley and Cleveland Water Board and their consulting engineers for most of the factual information that was needed to make a recommendation. As it appeared to the Water Resources Board, the problem was this. On existing policies, and with existing sources, there would be a deficiency of 23 m.g.d. by 1971, of 50 m.g.d. by 1982, and of 110 m.g.d. by 2000.[1] The Water Resources Board could see no possibility of finding the additional supplies outside the Tees catchment area in time to meet the extra demand in 1971. Nor was there any chance that desalination would come to the rescue in time. In the short run, it might be possible to fill part of the gap between demand and supply by pumping about 6 million gallons a day from the magnesium limestone area north of Darlington.

As a solution to the Water Board's problems, the Water Resources Board considered both river-regulating reservoirs and the idea of a pumped, storage reservoir downstream from Darlington. A regulating-reservoir, it thought, was much to be preferred, chiefly because the river would benefit from increased flows during dry weather.

If the answer was a river-regulating reservoir, where should it be built? On the available information, seven of the sites previously investigated by the Water Board seemed to be worth a second look. These were at Eggleston, Harwood, Middleton, Lower Maize Beck, Upper Maize Beck, Cronkley and Cow Green. In addition, the Water Resources Board also examined the Upper Cow Green site, the possibility now being advocated by the Nature

[1] For the year 1971 there was no difference between the estimates of the Water Resources Board and the Tees Valley and Cleveland Water Board. But for 1981 the Water Resources Board estimated a deficiency of 21 m.g.d. more than the Water Board. This discrepancy arose because the Water Board had made no allowance for increased demands by major industrial consumers beyond those to which these industrialists were committed under existing agreements, whereas the Water Resources Board had allowed for what they thought was a reasonable rate of growth in industrial demand up to the end of the century. For the water industry's arrangements for financing new capital works, see pp. 175–6.

Conservancy. The significant variables taken into account in each case were: the probable date of completion; the cost; disturbance – such as the extent and nature of any damage that would be inflicted on scientific interest, farming, houses, and roads; and technical factors, that is, the yield and capacity of the reservoir, the size of the area to be flooded, and the length and height of the dam. The Water Resources Board's findings for each of the possible sites can be conveniently set out in tabular form (see p. 151).

When it reported to the Ministry of Housing and Local Government on 20 October the Water Resources Board thought that three of these sites warranted further discussion. Upper Cow Green would produce a significantly smaller yield than Cow Green; it would require a much longer and higher dam; it was estimated to cost £3 million more than Cow Green; and it would probably not be ready until 1971. If the geology proved to be sound, Middleton would provide a larger yield than any of the other sites investigated, and in relation to the very large quantity of water that it would supply, the cost would be quite reasonable. (It was later revealed by Kennard that owing to a typing error in the consulting engineers' office the Water Resources Board had accidentally been led to believe that Middleton would cost £1 million less than the true figure.) On the other hand, Middleton would mean flooding 1,000 acres of agricultural land, including two complete farms and parts of twelve others. About ninety other properties of various kinds would also disappear beneath the water, and a reservoir here would take three years longer than at Cow Green to construct. And if the Water Board were to commit themselves to a large reservoir at Middleton in the 1960s, they would be saddled with an inflexible pattern of supply in the 1980s and 1990s, by which time sources outside the Tees catchment area might have become available.

This left Cow Green. On the debit side, it was strongly opposed by the Nature Conservancy. However, it would cost £2–2½ million (a reservoir at any of the other sides on the list would have cost at least £1½ million more),[1] and it seemed to be the next

Margin note: Middleton – 1,000 acres ag land flooded

---

[1] As the report put it, a decision to use Upper Cow Green or Middleton would involve 'considerable extra costs in money, labour and materials which could otherwise be used elsewhere'. A phrase of this kind was a salutary reminder that the cost of anything is the alternative that is foregone in order to have it. If either of these other two reservoir sites were

WATER RESOURCES BOARD REPORT:
RIVER-REGULATING SITES

	Capacity (m.g.)	Yield (m.g.d.)	Dam			Water area (acres)	Disturbance	Probable completion date
			Length (ft)	Height (ft)	Cost (£m.)			
Cow Green	9,000	35	1,725	72	2–2½	825	Area of S.S.S.I.	1969
Upper Cow Green	7,800	29–30	5,100	152	6	850	Nature reserve	1971
Cronkley	8,000	30–32	1,700	175	4	500	Nature reserve	1971
Upper Maize Beck	5,500	19–20	3,120	159	4	675	Nature reserve	1971
Lower Maize Beck	5,500	18–20	3,880	184	4.5	300	Nature reserve	1971
Middleton	18,000	75	3,860	177	6	1,000	Farmland, roads, houses	1972
Harwood	8,000	30–32	4,310	143	5	360	Area of S.S.S.I., agricultural land, houses, roads	1971
Eggleston	8,000	30–32	3,330	192	5.3	425	Road diversion	1971

logical step in the development of the water resources of the Tees Valley. But the decisive factor, as the Water Resources Board saw it, was that of all the sites under review, Cow Green alone could be completed by 1969; if either Upper Cow Green or Middleton were chosen, industrial developments already under construction might go short of water, with a consequent threat to output and employment.

By this stage, an important new fact about Cow Green had come to light. About 300 acres of the site, it turned out, were common land. This discovery gave rise to legal complications that were now to change the whole character of the case.

In the normal way, the Water Board would have sought to acquire the land by means of an Order, authorising compulsory purchase, under the Water Acts of 1945 and 1948. But because common land was involved, the Acquisition of Land (Authorisation Procedure) Act of 1946 would have applied, and the Order would have been subject to special Parliamentary procedure, unless the Minister of Land and Natural Resources gave his certificate that an equivalent area would be given in exchange for use as common land. Moreover, the Minister had been advised that his consent under Section 22 of the Commons Act of 1899 was necessary for the grant or enclosure of common land, even when the Order authorising the compulsory purchase was subject to special Parliamentary procedure. In giving or withholding his consent under the Act of 1899, the Minister was required to have regard to the same considerations, and if necessary hold the same inquiries, as were directed by an earlier Commons Act of 1876. This meant that before determining the application the Minister had to be satisfied that the grant or enclosure was expedient, having regard to the 'benefit of the neighbourhood' and to 'private interests', as these expressions were defined in the Preamble to the Act of 1876.

Normally, the Minister would have ascertained the views of

---

chosen, something else would not be done. But nobody could be sure what that something was. And even if anyone had known, there would still have been a value problem, for to express the additional costs of Upper Cow Green or Middleton in terms not of money but of the most likely alternative use foregone, would have settled nothing in the absence of general agreement about the value of these other purposes as compared with the value of what would have to be sacrificed if Cow Green were flooded.

people in the neighbourhood by means of an advertisement in the local press and, probably, by means of a public local inquiry. As neither of these steps had been taken, the Minister of Land and Natural Resources was in no position to say what his view would have been had the Water Board applied to him for consent to the grant and enclosure of this common land.

Anyone who has followed this argument closely will see that nothing in it absolutely ruled out the administrative procedure. But clearly, the interaction of nineteenth-century and modern legislation has produced a situation of some complexity. No one could guarantee that hidden legal traps would not be sprung; and with common land involved, it was clearly going to take the Ministry of Housing and Local Government even longer than usual to reach a decision on the Order. In the circumstances, the Ministry apparently took the view that the Water Board would be well advised to adopt an alternative procedure, and promote a Private Bill.

The situation was explained to representatives of I.C.I. and the Water Board at a meeting in London on 27 October 1965. Not all the arguments favoured going by way of a Private Bill. With the administrative process, the Minister has to be convinced; but this is the only hurdle to clear. It is true that there is often a long delay, of uncertain duration, while the Minister makes up his mind on the Order after a public local inquiry. But at least a water authority can be sure that the Minister's decision will be based upon a rational and well-informed appraisal of all the relevant considerations. A Private Bill, on the other hand, certainly has the virtue of a fixed timetable: if successful, it is bound to be through Parliament by the end of the current session. At the same time, an opposed Bill may have not one but several critical hurdles to clear in its passage through the Commons and Lords. And in the last resort, particularly if it achieves some notoriety, its fate may be settled by the outcome of a vote that owes less to reason than to assiduous lobbying, skilful oratory, and relatively ill-informed sentiment. However, since they attached so much importance to the time factor, I.C.I. and the Water Board decided, not without misgivings, that the wisest course was to promote a Private Bill. The Bill was laid in the House of Commons on 27 November 1965.

THE FRIENDS OF COW GREEN

While the water engineers, administrators and lawyers were at work on their inquiries and calculations, the opponents of the Cow Green reservoir had also been busy. As we have seen, it was not until July 1965 that the Nature Conservancy, the 'official' voice of conservation, came out against Cow Green. When the Water Board had announced on 8 December 1964 that they intended to build a large new reservoir in Upper Teesdale, the Conservancy's response, more than six weeks later, was to issue a statement saying that it had agreed 'without prejudice' to test borings at Cow Green to determine whether or not a reservoir on this site was technically feasible.[1] Since the Conservancy's own survey had not yet started, this was perhaps as far as a statutory body could properly go at this stage. But it was not exactly a clarion call to arms, and to a number of botanists it seemed that the Conservancy might not altogether appreciate the importance of the area. As they saw it, a far more vigorous campaign was needed.

The unofficial resistance movement began to take shape early in 1965. Alarmed by the Nature Conservancy's statement published that morning, on 26 January four members of the Botanical Society of the British Isles – Mr J. E. Lousley, Mr J. C. Gardiner, Mr S. M. Walters, and Mr E. Milne-Redhead – met in London to discuss the situation. This quartet made a formidable combination. Neither Lousley nor Gardiner were professional botanists, though Lousley was one of the best-known amateurs in the country. But in their working lives both had considerable experience of the business world, Gardiner being financial adviser to Mr Charles Clore and Lousley an investment manager by occupation. For them, I.C.I.'s reservoir scheme came to assume something of the character of a City take-over bid that had to be beaten off. Walters was a Cambridge botanist, with a wide range of contacts in the universities, while Milne-Redhead, as Deputy Keeper of the Herbarium at Kew, provided a link with the non-academic professional botanists. They were all familiar with Upper Teesdale – like many others, Lousley's interest in botany

[1] *The Times*, 26 Jan 1965.

had been first aroused as a result of a visit to this area many years earlier – and they were all deeply concerned about the fate of the rare flora there. At this initial meeting they decided to organise a letter to *The Times* and to ask the Council of the Botanical Society of the British Isles to set up a special committee which would launch an appeal for funds and mobilise support for an objection to the reservoir on scientific grounds.

A similar nucleus of objectors had formed in the North-east. Here the leading figure was Dr Margaret Bradshaw, a Staff Tutor in botany in the Extra-mural Department of the University of Durham. As the controversy developed, she was to play an increasingly important part in stimulating and extending the opposition to the Cow Green reservoir. Dr Bradshaw was dedicated to Upper Teesdale and its botanical treasures. She had taken an academic post in the North so as to be able to botanise in Teesdale and had worked in the area for the previous fifteen years. This was her world, and she was a determined woman.

To begin with, the tactics of the successful Dine Holm campaign were repeated. On 4 February a letter appeared in *The Times*, signed by fourteen eminent botanists. Among scientists, they wrote, there was grave anxiety about the Tees Valley and Cleveland Water Board's plans for a reservoir in Upper Teesdale. The Tees Valley above High Force was of unique scientific value in Britain. The scientific research already carried out in this area, embodied in more than a hundred publications, had given the Teesdale vegetation, with its extraordinary assemblages of rare species, an outstanding international reputation. Upper Teesdale was an irreplaceable open-air laboratory and ought to be protected from the gross interference and destruction that would inevitably result from the construction of a reservoir and the impounding of the headwaters of the river Tees. 'Whilst we are not unmindful of the claims of industry in an expanding economy', the letter concluded, 'we cannot believe that the values of our society are so crudely materialistic that we shall consciously permit the destruction of such a splendid heritage, for what can be, at best, only a short-term solution of the problem of industrial water.'

The letter had the desired effect. Public interest was aroused, and letters began to flow into the accommodation address used by the Botanical Society of the British Isles at the Natural History

Museum. A spokesman for the Society declared that if the Cow Green scheme was not modified they would join forces with the Northumberland and Durham Naturalists' Trust in an appeal for financial support from the public, so that the scientific case could be adequately represented at the expected public inquiry. On 25 February, by resolution of the Council of the Society, the Teesdale Defence Committee was formally established. It was agreed that the Durham and Northumberland Naturalists' Trust should be represented on it, and the Defence Committee met for the first time in the following month. Whatever line the Conservancy might decide to take, the irregulars were now organised and clearly determined to make a fight of it.

Indeed, in the North-east the Northumberland and Durham Naturalists' Trust had already gone into action, distributing a polemical leaflet, appealing for donations, and urging people in the area to protest to their M.P.s about the proposed reservoir.[1] This initiative in turn triggered off the hoped-for response, and very soon letters and feature articles were appearing in the local press speculating on the probable effects of the reservoir. It was suggested, for example, that once it was built, never again would the great waterfall of High Force be seen in full spate.

In the North-east there was never any popular ground-swell of opposition to the Cow Green reservoir, and outside of scientific and amenity circles, the objectors' efforts to enlist support were not particularly successful. When it came before Parliament, the Water Board's Bill was to be supported by the North-East Development Council, the Northumbrian River Authority, and the North Riding and South Durham branch of the National Farmers' Union, whilst the Durham, Westmorland and North Riding County Councils, the three Rural District Councils and the three Parish Councils involved had no objection to the reservoir. Nor had any of the landowners or tenants in the vicinity. Not even the Darlington Corporation, an ancient foe which had opposed almost every scheme ever proposed by the Water Board and their predecessors, objected to the Cow Green site.

In the scientific world, however, the Teesdale Defence Committee were making much better progress. Among those approached and asked to help were Professor H. Godwin of Cambridge University (a Fellow of the Royal Society and a

[1] *Darlington and Stockton Times*, 27 Feb 1965.

member of the Nature Conservancy) and Professor C. D. Pigott of the University of Lancaster (formerly one of Godwin's students). Godwin was an authority on plant ecology, and Pigott had carried out a great deal of research in Upper Teesdale. Both were men whose views carried considerable weight in botanical circles, and both were to throw themselves wholeheartedly into the fight against the reservoir. Professor Godwin, in fact, undertook to circularise botanists all over the world, and dispatched a round-robin to elicit help for the Defence Committee on an international scale.

At this stage they were apparently hoping that a forceful demonstration of hostility would persuade the Water Board and I.C.I. to think again, as they had over Dine Holm in 1957. However, when Gardiner and Lousley met representatives of I.C.I. in July 1965, it was evident that this time the company had no intention of backing down. I.C.I. said that they were prepared to make available a sum of £100,000 for an intensive programme of research, to be supervised by the Nature Conservancy, before the valley was flooded. They were also prepared to make special arrangements to ensure that as little damage as possible was done in the area round the reservoir during construction. But on one thing they were quite insistent: the reservoir had to be at Cow Green.

The botanists acknowledged that the financial offer was a well-meant gesture; but in their view, a temporary reprieve was not enough. Clearly, there was going to be a battle over Cow Green, and now, they decided, was the time to launch their campaign in earnest. Organised by Professor Pigott, an Upper Teesdale Defence Fund was set up with a target of £5,000, and before long no less than 3,500 donations had been received. Mr Samuel Silkin, M.P., Q.C., was retained to represent the Committee at the expected public inquiry, and 40,000 copies of a well-produced illustrated booklet entitled *The Threat to Upper Teesdale* were sent out urging people all over Britain to oppose the scheme.[1] The coverage was thorough, not to say lavish. One distinguished scientist who received no less than three copies of the booklet was Mr James Newman, the head of the Biology section at I.C.I.'s Jealott's Hill Agricultural Research Station at Bracknell, and the company's principal scientific adviser on the botanical issues raised by the Cow Green case.

[1] *The Times*, 25 Aug 1965.

By the end of 1965 a formidable range of scientific societies had been mobilised in opposition to the Cow Green reservoir. They included the British Ecological Society, the Council for Nature, the Lake District Naturalists' Trust, the Linnean Society, the Northumberland and Durham Naturalists' Trust, the Society for the Promotion of Nature Reserves, and the Yorkshire Naturalists' Trust. In January 1966, in association with the Botanical Society of the British Isles, these bodies jointly petitioned against the Water Board's Bill, claiming that it would damage the rights and interests of their members, because they visited the area in question for research and study. The reservoir, they pointed out, would fall within a Site of Special Scientific Interest. Because of its special geographical formations and climatological history, the area supported a vegetation that was unique in this country. This had been recognised by the Nature Conservancy, which had declared that much of Upper Teesdale, including the reservoir site, should be managed as a Nature Reserve. The reservoir would destroy a remarkable complex of plant communities, and (they maintained) would severely damage other plant communities on the riverside slopes downstream from the site itself.

Had it not outraged the botanists, the proposed Cow Green reservoir would never have become the international *cause célèbre* that it did. But the scientists were not alone in their opposition, for the prospect of a reservoir had also aroused the wrath of the amenity interest and of all the many organisations that concern themselves with the preservation of the countryside. Upper Teesdale is unquestionably an area of very considerable natural beauty, and for years walkers and climbers have enjoyed this wild and rugged stretch of the Pennines. When they realised what was afoot, the amenity societies and leisure organisations – the Council for the Preservation of Rural England, the Commons, Open Spaces and Footpaths Preservation Society, the Countrywide Holidays Association, the Cyclists' Touring Club, the Holiday Fellowship, the Ramblers' Association, and the Youth Hostels Association – all took their stand with the scientific objectors, and they too presented a joint petition against the Bill.

Their petition maintained that the reservoir would probably be included within an Area of Outstanding Natural Beauty by the National Parks Commission. They pointed out that already the County Development Plan showed it as an Area of Great

Landscape Value. High Force and Cauldron Snout, they contended, were by common consent among the finest waterfalls in England. A dam of the type proposed, just upstream from Cauldron Snout, would be an incongruous and unwarranted intrusion at a scenically high point in the dale. It would be visible not only in the immediate vicinity of Cauldron Snout, but also from a wide area of high ground to the south and south-west. A reservoir at Cow Green would mean diverting the Pennine Way, the long-distance hikers' route that runs from the Peak District to the Cheviots. In addition, the amenity objectors alleged that when the water level in the reservoir fell during the summer, or at times of low rainfall, a wide and ugly expanse of shore would be exposed, much of it littered with mud and bare peat. In dry weather, the reservoir would be a blot on the landscape.

Like the Nature Conservancy, the two sets of petitioners were prepared to argue that if there had to be a reservoir in Upper Teesdale (and this they doubted), it should be built at Upper Cow Green. Botanically, this was not such an important site as that chosen by the Water Board. The area was very little visited, the scenery was not so dramatic, and a dam here could be blended into the landscape.

It is always sound tactics for objectors not simply to oppose, but also to try to undermine the developer's case. They can do this by suggesting that his scheme has intrinsic weaknesses, even on his own criteria and in terms of his own objectives. If they can bring forward a credible and workable scheme of their own, their chances of success are even better. Early in 1966 the petitioners approached Mr P. R. Jeffcoate, a well-known water engineer. Julius Kennard, the Water Board's consultant, was one of the foremost experts on reservoirs in the country: Jeffcoate was an authority on borehole schemes, and he was asked to look into the possibility of alternative arrangements that would avoid the need for any reservoir at all in Upper Teesdale.

As we have seen, there was now a formidable list of organisations petitioning against the Bill. Almost every naturalist and amenity society of any standing was in the field against the reservoir. To judge from appearances, the prospect of a reservoir at Cow Green had provoked a spontaneous, independent, and horrified reaction within more than a dozen specialist and well-informed societies and associations, all familiar with the scientific riches of Upper Teesdale and all capable of seeing at once (or of working out for themselves) what exactly the effects of the reservoir would be.

The reality was perhaps less dramatic but more interesting. It is unlikely that the resistance movement was quite the unprompted and spontaneous expression of consternation that its leaders and organisers claimed. Societies and associations are dignified by impressive titles; but in the last resort they are only structured collections of individuals, temporarily or permanently united in the pursuit of a particular interest or objective. There are certain interests that go naturally together; individuals who are members of one society are likely to belong to other organisations concerned with similar or related activities. Through their multiple and interlocking memberships and affiliations, a small but dedicated group of energetic people may be able to activate centres of opposition across a whole range of institutions. Bearing in mind the inventory of bodies that petitioned against the Bill, the affiliations of a few of the leading objectors are of some interest. The following lists are no doubt far from comprehensive.

Dr Bradshaw's role in the controversy has already been mentioned. She was a member of the Council of the Botanical Society of the British Isles and of the Northumberland and Durham Naturalists' Trust, the British Ecological Society, the Society for the Promotion of Nature Reserves, the Yorkshire Naturalists' Trust, and the C.P.R.E.; she was also an Associate of the Council for Nature. Professor Godwin was not only Treasurer of the Botanical Society of the British Isles, but also a member of the Northumberland and Durham Naturalists' Trust and the Society for the Promotion of Nature Reserves. The President of the Ramblers' Association, Dr A. Raistrick, was Vice-President of the Yorkshire Area of the Y.H.A., and a member of the C.P.R.E., the Commons, Open Spaces and Footpaths Preservation Society, and the Yorkshire Dales (West Riding) National Parks Planning Committee. And among others who took a prominent part in the fight against the reservoir, Dr K. R. Ashby was a member of the Northumberland and Durham Naturalists' Trust, the C.P.R.E., and the Ramblers' Association, and Mr Tom Stephenson, the Secretary of the Ramblers' Association, was a member of the C.P.R.E. and of the executive of the Commons, Open Spaces and Footpaths Preservation Society.

The objectors were to claim that seldom had a proposal of this kind aroused such unanimous opposition from so many scientific societies and bodies concerned with protecting the countryside. This was certainly true. Yet as the exchanges before the Select Committees of the House of Commons and the House of Lords were to demonstrate beyond doubt, in the early days, before the battle was joined, there were only a handful of people in the whole country who knew enough about Cow Green and its rare flora to appreciate precisely what was at stake. It was not until the Cow Green case was well under way that most of the naturalists and botanists who had at once rallied to the support of the Defence Committee knew exactly what floristic assemblages were to be found on the western slopes of this part of Widdybank Fell, or how precisely the reservoir would affect them.

Why was it then, that so many learned societies could become so excited and embittered about a project when they possessed so little first-hand knowledge of its implications? How was it that so many responsible and well-known figures were prepared to vouch for the tremendous value of the Cow Green flora in letters to the press and at public meetings? And even if they appreciated the enormous value of these plant communities, how could they be sure that the reservoir would do so much damage?

In part, it was because of the snowball effect created by respect for the word of colleagues and fellow professionals, men whose reputation and position seems to guarantee their integrity, knowledge and sound judgement. Once the resistance movement had started, once two or three eminent authorities had given a lead, and lent their names to the cause, others were soon convinced that something vital must be at stake at Cow Green and were quickly drawn into the pool of opposition. To give but one example, on 6 July 1966 the world-famous naturalist Peter Scott was to write to *The Times*, declaring that the area in danger contained unique scientific material. Later, before the House of Lords Select Committee, he was asked how he knew that this was so. How did he know? Because, among others, Professors Godwin and Pigott and members of the Botanical Society of the British Isles had told him. Professor Godwin himself, it should be said, had visited Cow Green only three or four times in his life. None of this is intended in the slightest to detract from the sincerity of those who led the opposition to the reservoir. They had a cause that was dear to their hearts, and some of them evidently believed in it with a passion and conviction more often associated with religion or politics than botany and conservation. Their campaign was skilfully organised, they worked hard, and they were prepared to give freely of their time and money.

But the influential 'amenity network' of personal contacts only partly accounts for the widespread opposition that was now building up against the Cow Green reservoir, and it certainly does not entirely explain why the petitioners were so successful at the national level in recruiting well-wishers, raising money, and engaging public sympathy. The fact was that the objectors had caught a favourable tide just when it began to run steadily in their favour. By the middle sixties the importance of conservation and ecology was becoming far more widely understood and acknowledged than a decade earlier; and by now, industrial development that threatened amenity was more likely than in earlier years to attract the attention of the mass media. Many of those drawn into the Cow Green controversy neither knew nor cared about the minutiae of the dispute. It was the principle that mattered. Upper Teesdale was undoubtedly an area of exceptional scientific interest and of great natural beauty. As a matter of principle, it was wrong to despoil or disturb areas like this. A stand had to be made somewhere, and if industry were permitted to build a reservoir at Cow Green, if this case was lost by default, nowhere else would be safe. The Water Board and I.C.I., it is true, could count on the support of local trade union leaders and of M.P.s for industrial constituencies in the North-east. But there are naturalists and country-lovers all over the country, and many of them are articulate people who will take the trouble to write to their M.P.s – and they all have M.P.s. There was, too, an element of David and Goliath in the situation. To be smaller and weaker than the giant is no doubt a genuine handicap; on the other hand, in Britain, it is never a disadvantage to be regarded as the gallant underdog.

Nevertheless, in many respects the dice still seemed to be loaded against them. In I.C.I. they were taking on not just a rich and powerful industrial giant, but an institution that enjoys a considerable public reputation for enlightened and responsible behaviour. And in this instance, I.C.I. were themselves about to embark upon what everyone agreed were good deeds. If their plans went ahead, they would be expanding industrial output, increasing exports, and providing employment in an area where jobs are valued above almost anything else. They had also offered the Nature Conservancy no less than £100,000 for scientific research at Cow Green. In all the circumstances the botanists could easily be represented as selfish eccentrics, jeopardising the economic prosperity of Tees-side, callously endangering men's jobs in the process, and all for the sake of a few obscure plants on some remote and inaccessible hillside high on the Pennines. On the face of things, it was not a promising hand.

The Tees Valley and Cleveland Water Bill was given its First Reading in the House of Commons on 26 January 1966. An unopposed Second Reading followed on 1 February, and the Bill was then referred to a Select Committee for consideration in detail. It was a curious situation, for whereas conflicts between the needs of industry and the claims of conservation are very much a contemporary phenomenon, the Private Bill arena harks back to a Parliamentary process that enjoyed its heyday in the eighteenth and early-nineteenth centuries. At all events, the lines were now drawn and the scene set for one of the most extraordinary conflicts of interest and value in recent years.

WHITEHALL TAKES A VIEW

Private Bills are initiated by local authorities, statutory undertakers or business corporations seeking powers that they need, but do not possess, under existing public law. The Government is not directly involved. But the intentions and objectives of those who promote Private Bills may be of considerable interest to individual Government departments, and these departments will ask, or be asked, to make known their views to Parliament. At least five departments – the Ministry of Housing and Local Government, the Board of Trade, the Ministry of Land and Natural Resources, the Department of Education and Science, and the Department of Economic Affairs – were concerned in varying degrees with the fate of the Cow Green scheme. The convention is that the Government is one and speaks with one voice: consequently in the early months of 1966 there was a good deal of inter-departmental consultation designed to hammer out an agreed governmental view on the principle of the Bill. In the end, however, only three departments – Housing and Local Government, Land and Natural Resources, and Education and Science – were to submit reports to the Select Committee of the House of Commons.

There are situations in which Government departments become the 'representatives' of interests and interest groups; when conflicts of interest occur in the outside world, these disputes are inevitably projected into the central administration. The Board of Trade and the Ministry of Housing and Local Government had known about the problems of I.C.I. and the Water Board for well over a year. At one time, of course, it had been thought that the Minister of Housing and Local Government would decide the issue. The Ministry had by now digested the Water Resources Board's favourable report on Cow Green, and in December 1965 one of the Ministry's own Engineering Inspectors had visited the area. His assessment of the situation reached the Ministry on 13 January 1966; as he saw it, there was an urgent need for a new source, a reservoir at Cow Green was the most economic scheme, and it could be developed more quickly than any alternative source to meet the demands of large industrial consumers in the area. The Minister had been left in no doubt about the feelings of M.P.s representing Tees-side constituencies and about the views of trade unions and industrialists in the North-east. And on 7 January 1966 the Executive Committee of the North-East Development Council, a body made up of representatives of local authorities, industry, trade unions and other public bodies, announced that the Bill had their full support. There was also Government policy for the distribution of industry to be taken into account: it was a cardinal feature of this policy to encourage all forms of industrial development in the North-east. Without an adequate and secure supply of water there would be no expansion.

The Ministry of Housing and Local Government, however, had a responsibility not only for the supply of water, but also for the countryside and the preservation of amenities. On 4 April 1966 they received the observations of the National Parks Commission on the Bill. The Commission, not surprisingly, was flatly opposed to the Cow Green site, pointing out that for some years it had had in mind the possibility of designating Upper Teesdale as a National Park, or as part of one. The Commission told the

Ministry that a reservoir at Cow Green would introduce civilisation and artificiality into an essentially wild area that ought to be kept in its existing state as part of the diminishing reserve of wild country still available to the public for recreation and scientific research.

However, in the Ministry of Housing and Local Government, one important decision had already been taken: amenity objections could not weigh heavily against the need for adequate supplies of water. The National Parks Commission's memorandum, therefore, made little impact on the Department.[1] For their part, the Ministry of Land and Natural Resources shared Housing and Local Government's favourable attitude towards the Bill, and were happy enough with the choice of the Cow Green site. Both departments agreed that it was the botanical objection which was important, and neither rated this difficulty significant enough to justify building the reservoir elsewhere.

By contrast, the Department of Education and Science were by no means convinced that a reservoir had to be built at Cow Green. Within the machinery of Government, the Department naturally felt themselves to be the guardians of scientific research, and their initial hostility to the Cow Green scheme was confirmed and reinforced as a result of the stand taken by the Natural Environment Research Council, which by now had become responsible for the work of the Nature Conservancy.[2] In a formal submission to the Secretary of State for Education and Science it explained why Upper Teesdale was of such great scientific interest, and why it believed that the Cow Green scheme should be opposed.

The N.E.R.C. argued that the scientific value of Upper

[1] In the early days of its existence, the National Parks Commission had been assured by the Ministry of Housing and Local Government that reports of this kind would be automatically attached as appendixes to the Ministry's own submissions to Select Committees on Private Bills. By an oversight, and much to the annoyance of the Commission, on this occasion its memorandum was not put before the Select Committee of the House of Commons.

[2] Under the 1965 Science and Technology Act the newly created Natural Environment Research Council formally took over the functions of the Nature Conservancy, reconstituting the Conservancy as one of its constituent committees. In the interests of consistency and continuity the term 'Nature Conservancy' has sometimes been retained in the text when it refers specifically to this committee of the N.E.R.C.

Teesdale was determined by a combination of unusual physical conditions. The rare plants in the area formed unique communities of great genetic and evolutionary interest. For the elucidation of late glacial conditions in Great Britain, and for the study of plant migration to this country, Upper Teesdale was nowhere equalled. It was true that research on the soil and vegetation was still only in the early stages; but if continued, it might well lead to knowledge that would have an important bearing on upland use in the United Kingdom. According to the N.E.R.C., a reservoir at Cow Green would destroy 20 acres of the special vegetational complex there. As a result of damage that might occur during construction it would endanger up to a hundred acres of land of the highest scientific interest. And it would cause changes in the vegetation near the margins of the reservoir by reason of wave erosion, spray and slight localised alterations in the climatic conditions. The reservoir would also create 'visitor pressure', which could interfere with much that was of value, through picnicking, flower-picking, plant collection, pollution and fire. In the N.E.R.C.'s view, if there had to be a reservoir in Upper Teesdale, the Upper Cow Green alternative would be acceptable, and this site ought to be thoroughly investigated before there was any question of approving Cow Green.

Now that a specific alternative to Cow Green was in the running, backed by a responsible body like the N.E.R.C., the essential nature of the dilemma began to emerge. It was a problem that was later to tease two Select Committees. But for the moment it was Whitehall that had to come to grips with the intractable questions of value that lay at the heart of the case.

The difficulty was succinctly and clearly analysed in an interdepartmental memorandum of 28 February 1966. There was now support for Upper Cow Green. As opposed to Cow Green, however, it would take longer to build, the capital cost was estimated to be more than twice as much, and 240 acres of the reservoir site would fall within the Moor House Nature Reserve. On the other hand, to flood the Cow Green site might be to deprive the nation of a unique scientific area, with great research and educational potential, the value of which could not be quantified. But, whilst it was true that nobody could put a money value on this potential, the cost of preserving it could be measured. The cost of preservation would be the additional construction charges incurred at Upper Cow Green (estimated to be an extra £12 million in loan charges spread over a sixty-year period), together with the risk of lost industrial output in the event of a dry or drought year between 1970 and 1972. The value of the output that might be lost could be anything from £8½ million to £35 million, depending on the level of rainfall. Up to 25 per cent of this lost output might have been earmarked for export.

Whilst the N.E.R.C.'s plea for the preservation of Cow Green made no impression on the Ministry of Housing and Local Government, the Department of Education and Science was more receptive, and the Secretary of State took the view that the Bill ought not to be supported unless the alternative site at Upper Cow Green proved on further investigation not to be feasible at all. He agreed that Upper Cow Green would indeed be more costly; and it would mean taking a chance on the possibility of drought conditions for a year or two before it was built. As against this, however, there was the irrefutable argument that the scientific damage arising out of the Bill was absolutely certain and irreversible for all time.

There was thus a clear difference of opinion between the two Government departments chiefly concerned with the Bill. If there was to be a common governmental line, it had to be decided whether the scientific objections to Cow Green were to carry the day, or whether the Bill should be given the Government's blessing. This was a crucial point in the case, for whereas Government support could not ensure a safe passage for the Bill, Government hostility would almost certainly have killed it. Precisely how, or at what level, the difference was resolved is not known outside Government circles. But eventually it was the view of the Ministry of Housing and Local Government, backed by the Board of Trade and the D.E.A., that prevailed. Towards the end of April 1966 the Minister of Housing and Local Government and the Minister of Land and Natural Resources were able to report on the Bill, and both supported it without reservation. The Secretary of State for Education and Science also supported it, though he made it quite clear that only the compelling economic and social arguments had forced his hand, and that he had reached his decision with great regret and reluctance.[1]

[1] At a later stage, when an argument developed as to whether a spokesman for the N.E.R.C. should be called before the Select Committee to

PARLIAMENT DECIDES:
ROUND 1 – THE HOUSE OF COMMONS

In the meantime, the Select Committee had been set up under the chairmanship of Clifford Kenyon (Labour, Chorley). The three other members were Lieut. Cmdr. S. L. C. Maydon (Conservative, Wells), Paul Hawkins (Conservative, S.E. Norfolk), and George Perry (Labour, Nottingham South). Kenyon and Hawkins both had strong links with the agricultural world, Perry was chairman of the South Derbyshire Water Board, and all except Maydon had considerable experience of local government. When they assembled for the first time on 4 May 1966 they can hardly have foreseen what a gruelling course lay ahead. Over the next three weeks they were to sit for twelve full days, much of the time listening to highly technical arguments on subjects as diverse as industrial chemistry, water engineering, water finance, geology, botany and ecology. Even studied at leisure and at the reader's own pace, a good deal of the verbatim transcript is difficult enough to follow; what the committee were able to make of some of the more recondite exchanges between counsel and specialist witnesses must be left to the imagination.

The Tees Valley and Cleveland Water Board were represented by Mr P. Boydell, Q.C., and Mr F. H. B. Layfield (who, it will be recalled, had appeared for one of the local authorities objecting to the C.E.G.B.'s proposed Holme Pierrepont power station). Counsel for the petitioners were Mr H. Marnham, Q.C., and Mr M. Fitzgerald. On the promoters' side, the principal witnesses were Messrs Kennard, Knill, Hetherington, Allison and Newman, together with Mr G. M. Thompson, the Water Board's engineer, Dr J. Newberry, an engineering geologist, Dr P. G. Harvey of I.C.I., Mr N. A. F. Rowntree, the Director of the Water Resources Board, Mr S. F. Jones, the secretary of the North Riding and South Durham branch of the N.F.U., Dr S. Gregory,

---

give evidence that favoured the petitioners' side of the case, the Department took the view that a Research Council had a public function independent of the Government, and ought to be heard independently and publicly on matters involving that function. If the Department had had to give way at ministerial level, plainly they were still prepared to do what they could to help the interest they represented.

a climatologist at the University of Liverpool, Mr B. S. Furneaux, a soil surveyor, Dr A. S. Thomas, a botanical consultant, Mr F. Gibberd, the architect, Mr E. A. Morris, the Water Board's Chief Executive Officer, and Mr S. W. Hill, an expert on water finance. For the petitioners the chief witnesses were Mr Gardiner, Dr Bradshaw, Professors Godwin and Pigott, Mr Stephenson, and Mr Jeffcoate, together with Dr M. W. Holdgate of the Nature Conservancy, Dr G. A. L. Johnson, Lecturer in Geology, and Dr A. Raistrick, Reader in Applied Geology, both of the University of Durham.

In essence, the case made out by I.C.I. and the Water Board was this. The extra water to be provided by the reservoir was needed, it was needed urgently, and there was no reasonable alternative to Cow Green. It was true that other sites in Upper Teesdale were technically feasible. But some of them would not yield enough water, some of them would cause a great deal of disturbance to agriculture and amenity, and all of them would be considerably more expensive than Cow Green. None of them, moreover, could be brought into service as quickly as Cow Green. This was a consideration of great importance because until the reservoir became operational, a drought year of anything like the severity of 1949 or 1959 would seriously interfere with production at the I.C.I. works, with a consequent loss of output, much of which would have been exported.

They conceded that if the Bill went through, a small area containing flora of some scientific interest would be flooded. The reservoir might also detract somewhat from the natural beauty of this part of Upper Teesdale. But, as I.C.I. and the Water Board saw it, both the naturalists and the amenity societies had wildly exaggerated the extent of the damage to their interests. This was particularly true of the botanists. All the rare flora on Cow Green could be found above as well as below the proposed top water level of the reservoir. In fact, they claimed, only three of the plant species on the proposed site could be described as genuinely rare. They were the Yorkshire milkwort, the Teesdale violet, and the Teesdale sandwort. The Yorkshire milkwort could be disregarded, for it also grew on nearby Cronkley Fell, where it could not possibly be affected by the reservoir. There was no point in becoming excited about the Teesdale violet, they said, because it was quite widespread in other parts of the world;

indeed, if the botanists would look carefully enough it might also be found on limestone elsewhere in England, for it could easily be mistaken for the common dog violet. Only the Teesdale sandwort seemed to be seriously at risk, and even that would probably survive, given reasonable care while the reservoir was being built.

Some of the Water Board's witnesses were even to suggest that the Cow Green vegetation was not made up of relict ice-age flora at all, but had arrived in relatively recent times. This particular part of Upper Teesdale, it was implied, had become unique rather suddenly, just when the reservoir was proposed. No doubt some botanists were deeply interested in Cow Green; but they had been carried away by their enthusiasm, and were trying to give an altogether misleading impression of the scientific significance of the site. Anyone who looked carefully at the scientific literature on Upper Teesdale would find that very little of it bore directly on Cow Green, or even on the wider area of Widdybank Fell. The botanists and the Nature Conservancy were arguing that pure research, unrelated to any specific objective, had often produced applications of great practical importance in the past, and might well do so again here. But this was a specious argument that could be used in support of virtually any piece of academic research, however improbable the chances of any useful application. Experience does indeed show that unforeseen results of practical value frequently do come out of pure research; but the likelihood of such an occurrence in respect of one particular piece of pure research is very slight. And the fact was, they said, that the rare flora on Widdybank Fell were not even remotely related to crop plants of any economic importance.

In short, the case for the Water Board rested upon three propositions. First, Cow Green was the best site in terms of the Board's obligations and objectives. Second, the petitioners had exaggerated the scientific importance of what would be lost if Cow Green were flooded. And third, by comparison with all the alternatives, the quantifiable value of Cow Green's advantages was so substantial that it easily outweighed the unquantifiable scientific and aesthetic value of anything that would be destroyed.

On the other side, the petitioners were at pains to emphasise that this was no case of a handful of botanists whipping up synthetic indignation in a desperate campaign to preserve a stretch of countryside that happened to be of passionate interest to themselves and to themselves alone. What happened at Cow Green, they said, was of great concern to scientists all over the country, and indeed all over the world. The Water Board and I.C.I., moreover, had either misunderstood or deliberately misrepresented the scientific issues involved, for when the Bill's promoters went to such lengths to show that this or that rare plant on Cow Green was also to be found elsewhere, they were very largely missing the point.

It was perfectly true – the petitioners would be the last to deny it – that some of these rare flora were of great interest in themselves. So far as some of them were concerned, the proposed reservoir would destroy a significant proportion of the total population known to exist in the United Kingdom. And, despite what I.C.I.'s witnesses had said, a study of these plants might well yield results of great genetic and evolutionary interest. Professor Pigott, for example, argued that experiments on wild plants of this kind, surviving as they did at the limits of their tolerance, in an extremely harsh environment, could in time help mankind understand why the properties of crop plants permitted them to live only within specific environments. Yet it was not so much the presence of individual rare plants on Cow Green that fascinated the botanists. Rather, it was the unique *communities*, or assemblages, of these ancient relict species that made the western slopes of Widdybank Fell an area of such outstanding scientific interest. As Professor Godwin and Dr Bradshaw pointed out, species that were only to be found separately in the arctic, or in alpine regions, or in widely scattered parts of Europe, were here growing together. To study the ecology of these extraordinary communities the botanists needed to be able to examine the *whole* of each complex or series of plants, and they needed to be able to compare one assemblage with another. Twenty acres might not sound much. But to flood these twenty acres would be to slice off the lower end of several natural series. This would very much reduce the range of varying conditions that made these slopes an area of such enormous scientific potential. On Widdybank Fell botany students were able to test ideas and hypotheses of fundamental importance. Once destroyed, this valuable stock of scientific capital could never be replaced. It certainly ought not to be sacrificed for the kind of short-term economic advantage that would be conferred by the Cow Green site.

How much of an impact the botanists and their arguments

made on the Select Committee must remain a matter for conjecture. In their own line of country they were professionals and
specialists, and they doubtless genuinely believed Cow Green to
be of first-rate importance. But few experts relish the unfamiliar
hazards and trials of the witness stand at a public inquiry or
before a Private Bill committee, and university professors are in
some ways worse off than most. They are accustomed to lecturing
ex cathedra; their professional pronouncements are rarely challenged or contradicted, at least not by laymen. Nothing in their
training fits them to undergo with equanimity a sustained and
hostile cross-examination at the hands of a skilful barrister, adept
at leading them on, provoking their anger, occasionally catching
them out, and extracting the apparently damaging admission.
Theirs was a voluntary effort, and they had their own jobs to
attend to. When they were first drawn into the controversy some
of them may not have realised how much time and work would
be entailed. Both Professor Godwin and Professor Pigott were
criticised by Clifford Kenyon, the chairman of the Select Committee, for not spending more time at the hearings, and for rush-
ing away after giving their evidence. If Cow Green really was of
such vital importance to botanists, Kenyon observed, then Pigott
ought to have been prepared to spend as much time at Westminster as the members of the committee. Pigott apologised, but
pointed out that he was paid to teach and could not neglect his
students. The chairman was not impressed. A week's teaching, he
said, was not much when the petitioners were arguing that the
outcome of this case would affect generation after generation of
students in the years ahead.

It has already been suggested that very few botanists were well
enough acquainted with Cow Green to know for certain exactly
what was there, or precisely what would be lost if the reservoir
were built. The Teesdale Defence Committee's skill lay in attracting support from a considerably wider circle, some of whom were
by no means experts on this particular corner of Upper Teesdale.
Under pressure, this sometimes became uncomfortably apparent.
Here, for example, is Boydell drawing together the threads of
cross-examination, and suggesting that even Professor Godwin,
one of the petitioners' principal botanical witnesses, was not as
knowledgeable about the flora on Cow Green as he might have
been:

Q: First, you have not been able to tell us, have you, what plants as individual plants are in the area which will be inundated? You have not been able to tell me, have you?

A: I have been unwilling to commit myself here and now to doing so, knowing that it is within the Committee to find this directly from Dr Pigott.

Q: I understand you to say you were unable to supply them?

A: Very well.

Q: Secondly, you are unable to give me any congregation or grouping of plants in the inundated area: this is right is it not?

A: The same applies as before. I am unwilling to do this.

Q: Last time you said 'unable'.

A: Yes, very well.

Q: Are you both unable and unwilling?

A: I am afraid I am unable to do a great many things.

Q: Thirdly, since you are unable to give the details under those two heads you cannot possibly say how plants as individual plants, or with others, in the seventeen areas (on Cow Green) compare with other areas in Upper Teesdale. It must follow, must it not?

A: Not entirely; partially that is true.

The petitioners, however, had another string to their bow. One of their objectives was to demonstrate the loss of scientific and amenity value that the reservoir would entail. The other was to show that, even in terms of the Water Board's own obligations and objectives, Cow Green was in many ways an unsuitable site, and inferior to at least two alternative possibilities. When they see an opening, objectors often adopt this strategy of attacking developers on their own ground: but it is always a difficult and ambitious tack, for to succeed the objectors have to show that they and their expert witnesses know the developers' business at least as well as the developers themselves.

Initially, the objectors attacked the Cow Green site on geological grounds. Whatever the Bill's promoters might say, there was no escaping the fact that the geological survey carried out in 1956 had suggested that a reservoir on the cavernous limestone at Cow Green would not be watertight. I.C.I. and the Water Board maintained that subsequent investigations had cleared the site on this score; but, the petitioners argued, there must still remain an element of doubt. If these fears were realised, grouting would be required on an extensive scale; that is, liquid cement would have to be injected into the floor and sides of the valley in order to seal it. And if grouting did prove necessary, the cost of the reservoir would be increased, the completion date would be pushed further forward, and even more damage would be inflicted on the vegetation in the vicinity of the reservoir.

As a more suitable alternative, the petitioners began by urging the merits of Upper Cow Green, about two miles upstream from Cow Green. This was the site, it will be remembered, that was favoured by the Nature Conservancy. Although it fell within the Moor House Nature Reserve, the botanists were prepared, or said they were prepared, to see it flooded if Cow Green would thereby be spared.[1]

The Water Board and I.C.I. had rejected Upper Cow Green at a very early stage. Nor did it ever appear a strong contender once the hearings opened. For one thing, the case for Upper Cow Green was hardly developed in a way calculated to impress the Select Committee with the thoroughness of the petitioners' preparatory studies. According to Kennard, the petitioners had at first proposed a reservoir there with a top water level of 1,725 feet. On this assumption, the reservoir would have cost £6 million (Cow Green: £2–2½ million); it would have required a dam 5,100 feet long (Cow Green: 1,725 feet) and 152 feet high (Cow Green: 72 feet); and it would have been completed in 1971

---

[1] The Nature Conservancy divides National Nature Reserves and Sites of Special Scientific Interest into two categories. Sites in the first category are important, but often typical of many similar areas; if a sufficiently good case can be made out for an alternative use, they are considered expendable. In its second category, the Nature Conservancy includes areas that it considers unique and not negotiable under any circumstances. The Moor House Reserve was in the first category. Now that it knew more about what was to be found on Cow Green, the Conservancy placed this area in the second, sacrosanct category. The Water Board and I.C.I., however, argued that if they were to switch their attention to Upper Cow Green, they would probably encounter just as much opposition there. It was all very well for the petitioners to give assurances that they would not object to that site. But what was to prevent some new society springing up, asked counsel for the promoters. In his mind's eye, he said, he could already see the cars with their rear-window stickers urging men of good will everywhere to 'Save Upper Cow Green'.

(Cow Green: 1969). Shortly before the Select Committee proceedings began, however, it was discovered that a reservoir with these dimensions would yield only 29–30 m.g.d., as opposed to the 35 m.g.d. that were needed. The specifications were hastily altered, and the top water level raised to 1,750 feet. The effect of this modification would have been to increase the capacity of the reservoir, bringing the yield up to 39–40 m.g.d. Unfortunately, in solving the problem of yield, the cost of the reservoir would have risen to £9 million, the length and height of the dam would have increased still further, and (according to the Water Board's experts) the completion date would have receded to 1974.

As the proceedings continued, the petitioners realised that they had a much more promising alternative in the Middleton site. To understand the case for Middleton we must digress for a moment in order to explain the water industry's arrangements for raising capital for major works. Under Section 27 of the 1945 Water Act, the Tees Valley and Cleveland Water Board, like other water undertakings, had a statutory obligation to supply water for industrial purposes 'on reasonable terms and conditions'. On Tees-side, the arrangement was that industrial consumers should make a reasonable offer to bear, or to contribute to, the cost of any new works needed to meet their requirements. And so far as the Tees Valley and Cleveland Water Board were concerned, this obligation had been reinforced as a result of being written into several Private Acts. In practice, the industrialists would make their contribution by helping to pay off the loan charges over a period of forty or sixty years. So long as it is ready to pay its share of the capital cost, industry is entitled to demand more water. But there is a corollary: so far as industrial consumption is concerned, the effect of this arrangement is to restrict water undertakings to whatever level of capital expenditure industry is prepared to guarantee.

Consequently, even if a Water Board believes that local industrialists may be underestimating their future requirements, they cannot plan to provide more water than industry says is needed, for then the firms concerned could and would refuse to contribute towards the necessary capital expenditure. And in this event, the money could be raised only by placing the whole burden on the domestic consumer, something the Minister of Housing and Local Government would not permit even if a Water Board were minded to launch a capital project on this basis. In any case, before giving his consent for the development of new sources, the Minister requires proof that there is a real need; and proof is established by the willingness of the firms involved to make a financial contribution, or provide an appropriate guarantee. No other policy makes sense, for the country's water resources are limited, and if one water authority builds reservoirs that are not really necessary, someone else, with a genuine need, may have to go without.

With such a high proportion of their output committed to industrial consumers, this system of capital financing had on several occasions placed the Tees Valley and Cleveland Water Board in difficult and embarrassing situations. The Board had never been able to spend money on new sources until their industrial clients were prepared to guarantee their share of the capital expenditure required. And the industrialists, naturally, always erred on the side of caution, because they were anxious to avoid saddling themselves, for years ahead, with loan charges incurred in providing more water than they needed. By the time they were certain enough of their future needs to give firm guarantees, the unfortunate Water Board were likely to be faced with the problem of providing a great deal more water at very short notice.

In 1966 I.C.I. were prepared to forecast (for guarantee purposes) only a small and gradual annual increase of 2 million gallons of water a day after 1970, that is, after the proposed Cow Green reservoir had solved their immediate problem. The petitioners argued that this projection, as usual, would turn out to be a gross underestimate of the demands that would eventually be made on the Tees Valley and Cleveland Water Board. If the Cow Green reservoir were built, then within three or four years of its completion the search would be on again for another major source. At that stage, inevitably, Middleton would be the choice. It was perfectly true that with a yield of 75 m.g.d. a reservoir at Middleton would provide far more water than was needed in the immediate future. It was also true that it would cost more than twice as much as Cow Green, besides taking a good deal of agricultural land and displacing a number of farmers. Nor could it be completed until 1972. But if the Middleton site was bound to be flooded anyway at some future date, how much more sensible to build a reservoir there to begin with, rather than come back to it after the botanical treasures of Cow Green had disappeared beyond recall. It was not a question of *either* Cow Green *or* Middleton. Rather, the alternatives were either Middleton only now, or Cow Green now *and* (inevitably) Middleton later. Either way, a reservoir would eventually be built at Middleton. But whereas Middleton could save Cow Green, Cow Green could not save Middleton, at least not for more than a few years. It would be nothing short of a tragedy if Cow Green were flooded partly because of the arguments against developing the Middleton site, and then Middleton had to be submerged too.[1]

As the petitioners acknowledged, finding enough water to meet I.C.I.'s needs before Middleton could be brought into service in 1972 would be something of a problem. The solution here, they argued, was for the Water Board to follow up a suggestion made by the Water Resources Board and abstract water from the magnesian limestone and bunter sandstone area between Middlesborough and Darlington. Agreed, the Water Resources Board had put a figure of only 6 m.g.d. on the reliable yield from this source. But this figure apparently related to a daily rate over the *whole* year. The borehole scheme now put before the Select Committee by Jeffcoate, the petitioners' water consultant, envisaged the abstraction of much larger quantities of water, but over short periods of time. In Jeffcoate's opinion, far more than 6 m.g.d. could be abstracted from the magnesian limestone and bunter sandstone if intensive pumping were confined to three or four months during the summer when the extra water was really needed. If a start were made quickly on a scheme of this kind, it would certainly meet the urgent short-term need, and it would also provide a breathing-space, so that a careful and considered view of alternative sources could be undertaken.

The case for the petitioners, then, also rested upon three propositions. First, the Cow Green site was of outstanding scientific importance. Second, by comparison with the petitioners' counter-proposals, the advantages claimed for the Cow Green reservoir were largely illusory. And third, even if there was some

[1] This was a persuasive line of argument. But the petitioners at no time made it clear who was to be responsible for paying for Middleton, and for that part of its potential yield which nobody as yet needed. As an expert witness on water finance put it, 'The Minister has no power to require an industry to pay for more water than it says it wants'.

short-term advantage in developing the Cow Green site, this advantage was easily outweighed by the enormous, though un-quantifiable, value of what would be destroyed if the reservoir was built. The Water Board and I.C.I., they implied, were taking altogether too blinkered and jaundiced a view of the alternative possibilities, and altogether too rosy a view of the Cow Green site.

Naturally, the Water Board would have none of this. So far as the technical suitability of Cow Green was concerned, they pointed out that the recent geological survey had been much more thorough than in 1956, and this time the report was favour-able. Would I.C.I. really be prepared to spend several million pounds on a reservoir, they asked, if there was a serious possibility of it leaking? As for the petitioners' alternatives, Upper Cow Green would take too long to build, and the extra expense could not be justified. In any case, Upper Cow Green itself was open to some of the same botanical objections as Cow Green. As the botanists admitted, any site upstream from Cauldron Snout would even out the river flow and put at risk the riverside com-munities of rare flora below the torrent. If the Middleton site was developed, there would be a justifiable outcry from the farmers. According to the National Farmers' Union, neither Cow Green nor Upper Cow Green was of any agricultural value, whereas on their reckoning a reservoir at Middleton would flood 1,300 acres of farmland, and would affect 39 smallholdings which currently supported about 250 dairy cows, 700 other cattle, 1,000 sheep, 100 pigs, and about 2,500 head of poultry.[1] Moreover, to build a reservoir at Middleton that could provide far more water than would be needed for years ahead was to tie up capital unneces-sarily. And taking the long view, the Middleton scheme would irrevocably commit the Northumbrian River Authority to this method of supplying water to Tees-side, even if less objectionable means of providing it were to become feasible in the future.

[1] The North Riding and South Durham branch of the N.F.U. were thrown into great consternation whenever there was any talk of building the reservoir at Middleton. It will be recalled that Middleton had been mentioned (though dismissed) in the Water Resources Board's Report of October 1965. Thereafter, the N.F.U. became an ardent supporter of the Cow Green site. They also made it abundantly clear to the Select Com-mittee that if I.C.I. and the Water Board should be misguided enough to turn their attention to Middleton they would meet determined and bitter opposition from the farming interest.

On 27 May 1966 the hearings before the Select Committee came to an end. The four M.P.s had a great deal to ponder, for the verbatim record of the complex and conflicting evidence for and against Cow Green fills 700 pages of typescript. Usually, it is not known how M.P.s vote on Select Committees, or what arguments weighed with them. In this case, we know a little of what occurred, for one of the four, Paul Hawkins, took the somewhat unusual step of explaining how he had made up his mind, at the same time disclosing how the voting went.[1] Apparently, Kenyon, Maydon and Perry voted to report favourably on the Bill, whilst Hawkins was against. Hawkins had evidently been impressed with the scientific case for preserving the rare flora at Cow Green. But his main concern had been with the threat to Middleton and the rest of the Tees Valley. He believed that the Bill ought to be rejected, and the Water Board told that they could take no more land in Teesdale for reservoirs. Instead, they should look for underground sources, and investigate the possibility of desalination. In fact, Hawkins seems to have accepted the argument that if Cow Green fell, Middleton would not be far behind. As we have seen, others who sympathised with the agricultural interest were taking the view that if I.C.I.'s thirst could be quenched at Cow Green, something would turn up to save Middleton.

Although the Select Committee had approved the Bill in principle, they decided that they wanted more time to consider two of the issues that had arisen during the hearings. They wanted to know more about the possible need for grouting, and they wished to consider further the question of removing from the Water Board their power to reach agreement with large consumers for the payment of contributions towards the capital cost of new works. At their final meeting on 21 June, however, the Committee decided to take no further action. On the financial question, they received a supplementary report from the Ministry of Housing and Local Government, pointing out that the power to enter into these arrangements had proved to be of great value to water undertakers, and that there was no intention of removing it from the public general legislation covering such statutory bodies. On the matter of grouting, the Bill's promoters let it be known that they intended to sink experimental boreholes on the site so as to establish, once and for all, whether or not grouting

[1] See letter to *The Times*, 9 Nov. 1966.

would be necessary. If the Bill were opposed in the House of Lords, they said, the results of these tests would be available in time to be considered there.[1]

As amended, the Bill now came downstairs from the Committee for its Report stage. Over the next four weeks there was a good deal of lobbying from both sides. The Botanical Society of the British Isles sent out a memorandum to all M.P.s reiterating the case against the reservoir, and the promoters countered this with their own document, explaining why it was vital that the Bill should be enacted.

The motion that the Bill should be further considered eventually came before the House on the evening of 28 July 1966, though the actual debate took place on a blocking amendment moved by Marcus Kimball (Conservative, Gainsborough), which read:

> That this House declines to consider a Bill which would involve irreparable harm to a unique area of international scientific importance, fails to have regard to the proper long-term planning for the water requirements of the area, and is contrary to the declared advice of the Nature Conservancy and the National Parks Commision.[2]

The Cow Green controversy, Kimball declared, was the most important conservation issue ever to come before Parliament. The Select Committee had done a thorough job of work on the Bill; but they had to remember that the Committee had not been unanimous. If the House failed to take a stand over Cow Green, no other area in the country would be safe. The complex community of rare plants at Cow Green was irreplaceable, and every

---

[1] At the request of the Select Committee the Water Board also agreed to omit from the Bill a clause empowering them to provide recreational facilities on the reservoir. The Water Board had never been particularly enthusiastic about this idea and willingly accepted the Committee's recommendation.

[2] For the debate, see *H.C. Deb.* (1966–7) 732, cols 1979–2034. Kimball was a farmer and represented an agricultural constituency. Most agriculturalists favoured Cow Green, if only because the most likely alternative seemed to be Middleton. But, like many Englishmen, he also succeeded in combining an enthusiasm for field sports with a keen interest in conservation and the preservation of the countryside. Kimball had been a member of the Select Committee that considered the Balderhead reservoir in 1959; he knew, therefore, how quickly I.C.I.'s earlier forecasts had gone astray.

botanist in the United Kingdom and in Europe subscribed to this view. If the Bill was approved, he said, they would be setting the worst possible example to the underdeveloped countries, where properly planned conservation and the proper use of natural resources were desperately important. The House might ask why, if it was so important, Cow Green had not been included in a National Nature Reserve. The answer was that in 1959 the Water Board had said that they did not expect to come back for more water until 1983. The Nature Conservancy was therefore justified in thinking that there was no urgent need to give the site further protection by bringing it into a Nature Reserve. Scientists, he said, were notoriously bad at giving evidence to Parliamentary committees, for they are reluctant to speculate and say what they *think* will happen. Consequently, their words may carry less conviction than they feel. He had the greatest admiration for the Botanical Society of the British Isles in taking on 'the Goliath of I.C.I.' on this important issue. Had there been proper long-term planning for the needs of the area, the problem facing the House would not have arisen. If the Bill was not rejected, they would be setting an appalling precedent.

He was supported by Arthur Blenkinsop (Labour, South Shields), a former member of the Nature Conservancy. He argued that if the House approved the Bill it would in effect be saying, as so often in the past, that nothing else mattered in the North-east except industrial development. It was time that they grew out of this attitude. He was not satisfied that the promoters had made their case adequately, and he doubted whether all the alternatives to Cow Green had been thoroughly examined. Much the same position was taken by Sir David Renton (Conservative, Huntingdonshire) and Sir John Eden (Conservative, Bournemouth West), who objected to the Bill chiefly on the grounds that Cow Green was only a short-term solution to the Water Board's problem. Perhaps the most spirited attack came from Eldon Griffiths (Conservative, Bury St Edmunds). He conceded that they were choosing not between right and wrong but between right and right. But he had come down against the Bill because he believed that I.C.I. would suffer only inconvenience if the Bill were rejected, whereas if Cow Green were flooded its unique and invaluable vegetation was quite irreplaceable. 'In effect', he declared, 'it is a choice between a dip in I.C.I.'s profits, which they would have to accept [Hon. Members: 'No'], or it is the destruction of ten thousand years of unique natural history.' Coming from a Conservative M.P. this was certainly a surprising interpretation of the problem, though a number of Labour Members probably shared this attitude. Warming to his theme, Griffiths remarked that he had the impression that if a mighty company like I.C.I. wanted water it tended to assume that no power in England could stop it. Why else had I.C.I. gone ahead with their new developments at Billingham without bothering about Parliament? In his view the greater right lay with those who wished to retain a precious portion of our national heritage rather than with those who admittedly needed more water, but who, with a little more expense and a good deal more ingenuity, could obtain their supplies from elsewhere.

As the debate went on, it became clear that Cow Green was an issue that cut right across party lines. As with Parliamentary business in the eighteenth and early nineteenth centuries, it was the politics of interest and of personal conviction that structured the dispute. Most of those who spoke in favour of the Bill were Labour Members, but they were not without support from the Conservative benches.

R. W. Elliott (Conservative, Newcastle-upon-Tyne North) emphasised the value of I.C.I. to an area that faced the problems associated with the declining shipbuilding and coal-mining industries. M.P.s on both sides of the House, he claimed, had done their best to bring employment to the North-east, and I.C.I. had been encouraged to develop on Tees-side. He believed that if water were not made available quickly, and drought conditions occurred in the 1970s, the effect on the national trade figures and on employment in the area would be disastrous.

Ted Leadbitter (Labour, The Hartlepools) claimed that 'in this region the primary thing at this stage is employment' and later observed that 'it is important to stress the point that in my region we cannot evaluate beauty and the scientific interest of flora until we have the social conditions for all those who live there to enjoy it'. They ought to look very seriously into the issues raised by the objectors: but he thought that they had exaggerated their case. If the Bill was not approved, the House might well inflict serious economic loss on the area.

Fred Willey (Labour, Sunderland North), the Minister of Land

and Natural Resources, said that he was personally in favour of the Cow Green site, and so was the Minister of Housing and Local Government and the Secretary of State for Education and Science. He had been advised by the Water Resources Board that any of the alternative sites would mean taking a grave risk, for a succession of three or four dry summers would seriously interfere with output and employment. He acknowledged that if more time had been available the Water Board might have been able to choose from a wider range of alternatives. But the matter was urgent, and 'very reluctantly' he had to recommend the House to support the Bill.

Other Members also drew attention to the economic consequences of rejecting the bill, among them Ernest Armstrong (Labour, N.W. Durham) and James Tinn (Labour, Cleveland). As the former put it, 'The determining factor for me is that if the Bill were defeated, industrial development on Tees-side would be impeded and delayed'. The latter argued that I.C.I. had taken a justifiable gamble in going ahead with their new installations before making sure of the water they needed. British technology had given us a lead in world markets, and a heavy responsibility would lie on the House if they squandered it. They ought not to neglect the scientific case, but a careful study of the Select Committee's Report made it clear that the effect of the reservoir on the local flora would be minimal. Another Member to speak in favour of the Bill was Timothy Kitson (Conservative, Richmond, Yorks.): Cow Green was his choice, largely because the most likely alternative was Middleton, and if Middleton were flooded the reservoir would have a very serious effect on the forty or fifty of his constituents who farmed in that area. But he, too, was concerned with the wider issue of employment on Tees-side. 'When one remembers that the Hailsham Plan was largely responsible for encouraging I.C.I. to extend its development programme on Teesside', he said, 'and bearing in mind the high unemployment figures we had not many years ago in this area, we must try to do everything possible to continue industrial expansion on Tees-side.'

At the end of the debate nearly 200 M.P.s went into the division lobbies. It was, of course, a free vote.[1] Considering that

[1] Fred Willey, the Minister of Land and Natural Resources, was the only member of the Government to intervene in the debate, and he merely expressed his personal views. From the Opposition front bench Graham

the Bill had been approved by the Select Committee, and was
known to have the support of the Government departments concerned, the result was perhaps closer than might have been
expected. The blocking motion was rejected by 112 votes to 82.[1]
In party terms, 100 of the 112 M.P.s in favour of the Bill were
Labour Members and twelve were Conservatives. Of the 82
M.P.s supporting Kimball's motion (that is, opposing the Bill)
44 were Conservatives, 29 were Labour Members, and 9 were
Liberals.

Labour support for the Bill came predominantly from Members
representing industrial constituencies in the North, the Midlands
and Scotland. The bulk of them were trade unionists, or connected in other ways with industry. The opposition was much
more of a mixed bag. Of the 44 Conservatives against the Bill,
33 represented constituencies south of a line from the Wash to the
Severn. The 29 Labour Members voting against the Bill were
equally divided between northern and southern constituencies,
and a fair proportion of them were younger Members with an
academic or professional background. Nine of the 12 Liberals in
the House voted, and all 9 voted against the Bill.

The motives of Members on both sides must be a matter for
conjecture. Doubtless many who voted for the Bill, particularly
among the Labour Members, simply reacted instinctively in
favour of a proposal that seemed to safeguard men's jobs. Understandably enough, for some of them conservation and amenity,
and indeed almost anything else, would always take second place
when the emotive issue of unemployment came into the question.
Others may have looked one move ahead and calculated that to
reject Cow Green would be to endanger Middleton and the
agricultural interest. Others again may simply have been prepared to take a lead from the Government departments involved,
though presumably very few Members would take the trouble to
be present for a free vote on a Private Bill unless they were themselves genuinely interested in the outcome and had reasonably

---

Page (Conservative, Crosby) did no more than set out the merits and
drawbacks of Cow Green in finely balanced cadences. Willey thought that
he was in favour. But Dame Irene Ward (Conservative, Tynemouth) – who
was against the Bill – interjected 'Nobody knows what he thought'.

[1] The Bill was later given an unopposed Third Reading on 20 October
1966.

firm convictions of their own. On the other side, among the Conservatives voting against the Bill there was probably much less of an emotive reaction on the unemployment question to set against the claims of conservation and amenity. Some Conservatives, perhaps, thought that if the Government was for the Bill, then they ought to be against it. Some Members of both parties may have reckoned that important though I.C.I. were to Teesside, in this instance industry could well afford to pay a little more for its water in the interests of civilised causes like conservation and amenity.

But to judge from the tone of the speeches, it was emotion and sentiment, rather than a cool and open-minded appraisal of the issues involved, that dictated the attitude of most M.P.s. Contrary to what James Tinn said in the debate, the Select Committee at no time produced a summary of their findings or their reasons for approving the Bill. Most Members must have relied most exclusively on simplified, abbreviated and *ex parte* versions of the arguments put before the Select Committee. If the conservationists (or *mutatis mutandis* the industrialists) seemed to have a good case, that was enough. Instinctively and spontaneously, they plumped for either employment or conservation, either industry or amenity. Yet the Cow Green case, like many other disputes of this kind, was never simply a question of this or that, all or nothing.

In essence, the dilemma was this. The plant communities and wild countryside above Cauldron Snout undoubtedly had a certain value, which could not be quantified in money terms. Although there were differences of opinion as to the importance of the area to be flooded, everyone agreed that the reservoir would to some extent detract from its value, both scenically and scientifically. This loss of value was, of course, just as unquantifiable as the value of the area left unimpaired. But if the *value* of what the reservoir would destroy at Cow Green could not be quantified, the *price* of preserving the area intact was calculable. An alternative site was feasible, and by general consent the next best alternative was at Middleton. The price of saving Cow Green was simply the difference in cost and risk between Cow Green and Middleton. This difference was £3–3½ million for certain, a possible threat to men's jobs and to exports, and the loss of good agricultural land. The problem, mercifully, was not so much to put a value on what would be sacrificed at Cow Green as to decide whether an established, specific price was worth paying in order to avoid that sacrifice. In the end, a decision of this kind is bound to rest upon subjective evaluations. And since this was a value-judgement *par excellence*, who better to give a collective verdict than the elected representatives of the people?

Yet not everyone would agree that decisions of this kind are best made in the division lobbies. Whether or not the rare flora on Widdybank Fell were worth the price of preserving them was not a question that could ever be satisfactorily answered on the basis of facts alone. Two honest men, both in possession of all the relevant information, could obviously have come to opposite conclusions. But faced with the question 'to buy or not to buy', a prospective purchaser, if he is to make a rational decision, must surely appreciate what precisely he is being asked to pay for, and he must also understand precisely how much he is being asked to pay. How many M.P.s who voted on the Cow Green Bill really had the time or the patience to find out exactly what plants grew on Cow Green, why they were so important, to what extent they would be affected by the proposed reservoir, and how much it would cost in terms of money, risks and other sacrifices to build the reservoir elsewhere and keep Cow Green as it was? Those M.P.s who spoke in the debate were presumably better informed than most of their colleagues. Some of them even claimed to have read all or most of the evidence. But even allowing that they were speaking to persuade rather than to inform, many of them appeared to have only the loosest grasp on the facts of the case. Anyone listening to the debate might have been excused for thinking that if the Cow Green reservoir were built, the conservation movement in the United Kingdom (and probably overseas too) would collapse in ruins; alternatively, he might have concluded from the arguments on the other side that if the reservoir was not built, I.C.I. would soon be on the verge of bankruptcy, and in no time mass unemployment would return to Tees-side.

ROUND 2: THE HOUSE OF LORDS

The Bill had now to go through the House of Lords. During the summer it had become apparent that the friends of Cow Green were still full of fight. In August there had been a renewed appeal for public subscriptions to support the efforts of the Defence Committee, and on 1 September Dr Bradshaw read a paper to the British Association at Nottingham, roundly condemning the proposed reservoir. To coincide with the formal First Reading of the Bill in the Lords, on 20 October the petitioners organised a mass meeting at the Caxton Hall, London, and borne up on a wave of enthusiasm many of the objectors were talking confidently of defeating the Bill in the second chamber.[1]

In the North-east there was alarm and exasperation at the petitioners' refusal to lie down. When the Bill had emerged successfully from the Commons, some members of the Water Board, in their relief, had jumped to the conclusion that all would now be plain sailing. Sir Charles Allison, for example, magnanimously declared that he regarded the vote in the House of Commons not as a political success, but as a 'real victory for commonsense', and a triumph over prejudice. I.C.I., he said, could now go ahead with their plans, and everyone on Tees-side would rejoice.[2] By October, however, it was apparent that the triumph of commonsense was far from assured, and Allison was again bitterly denouncing the selfishness of the Bill's opponents. Any delay in building the reservoir, he said, would hit Britain's chemical exports at a time when all sections of the community were being asked to make sacrifices because of the economic situation. 'The naturalists and botanists', he said, 'should realise that while they may have very devoted interests in this matter, other people's interests are omnipotent.'[3]

On 8 November 1966 the Bill came before the Lords for its Second Reading.[4] In a debate lasting nearly five hours, the speakers against included Lord Molson, Lord Hurcomb, Lord Strang, Lord Methuen, Earl Waldegrave and Lord Ritchie-Calder: among those in favour were Lord Lindgren, Lord Hawke, Lord Ilford, the Earl of Swinton, and Lord Blyton. By now there was little to be said that had not been said before, though the quality of debate was somewhat higher, and many of the speeches showed a better grasp of the problem than in the Commons.

[1] *Daily Telegraph*, 21 Oct 1966.
[2] *Darlington and Stockton Times*, 30 July 1966.
[3] Ibid., 8 Oct 1966.
[4] For the debate, see *H.L. Deb.* (1966–7) 277, cols 786–868.

There was a strong current of opposition to the reservoir, and it is possible that had the objectors forced a division, they might have been able to defeat the Bill there and then. However, it is the invariable practice in the Lords for the chairman of Committees to advise the House to give opposed Private Bills a Second Reading, so that the evidence for and against can be investigated in detail by a Select Committee. This advice is usually taken, on the grounds that it would be wrong for uninformed Members to obstruct a Bill before the House has had the opportunity of considering the Report of a Select Committee.[1] On the understanding that a special Instruction would be given to the Select Committee, the objectors agreed not to oppose the Second Reading, though they reserved the right to vote against the Bill when it came back to them, whatever the Select Committee's views.

The terms of this Instruction (moved by Lord Molson) were clearly designed to focus attention on what the objectors thought were the more vulnerable aspects of the promoters' case. The Select Committee were instructed to give special consideration to (i) the need to provide a supply of water that would meet the foreseeable requirements of Tees-side for at least the next twenty years, and (ii) other sites for reservoirs, and other methods of supplying water to meet the needs of the more immediate future.

Lord Molson argued that if I.C.I. were prepared to spend £100,000 of their shareholders' money on a crash programme of scientific research, that surely was conclusive proof that what was to be submerged at Cow Green was of great scientific value. The Cow Green reservoir, he said, was only a short-term expedient. Before a final decision was made, they should allow more time for the Water Resources Board to carry out a thorough review of all the alternatives, taking into account the water needs of Tees-side over the next twenty years. As to the risk of drought, no one who had lived through the previous few summers could really feel that there was much danger of three or four dry summers in

---

[1] It is rare for the House of Lords to refuse a Private Bill, or any part of it, a Second Reading. However, on a celebrated occasion on 8 February 1962 a notable speech from the late Lord Birkett was largely responsible for persuading the Lords to reject the clauses in the Manchester Corporation Bill authorising the abstraction of water from Ullswater and the building of a reservoir at Bannisdale. See *H.L. Deb.* (1961–2) 237, cols 209–354.

succession in the near future. The fact was that I.C.I. would be paying only 1s. 1d. per thousand gallons for their water from Cow Green, as compared with the average price throughout the country of 3s. per thousand gallons. The company ought to be prepared to pay a higher price in the interests of conservation and amenity.

Lord Hurcomb drew attention to the international repercussions of flooding Cow Green. Many of the leading botanists and ecologists in Europe were dismayed at the proposal. The short-sighted destruction of this unique area, he said, would seriously set back the world movement for the conservation of nature and natural resources. Earl Waldegrave thought that this was one of the few cases where conservation should take priority over industrial development. 'If we feel that there is no case here', he declared, 'then we should be honest about it and repeal conservation legislation and abandon the whole idea.'

On the other side, Lord Hawke pointed out that every man-made lake arouses intense opposition from some group, and this time it was the botanists. Some of them made great claims, though he had been told that their presence in the area was not particularly noticeable before the Cow Green scheme came to be talked about. 'I sometimes wonder', he said, 'whether we are not in danger of becoming a little bemused by science. After all, what is science? Science is knowledge, and knowledge is all very well . . . but whether the national interest is served by that knowledge depends on whether it conduces to the health and happiness of the human race. Judged on that particular standard, I should have thought that some of the scientific case here looks a little thin.' And in a robust, no-nonsense speech, Viscount Slim observed that 'we earn our living, not by admiring, or even studying botanical specimens, but by keeping ahead of our competitors in the struggle for production and for new methods of production.'

From the Government front bench, Lord Kennet told the House that the Government's attitude was unchanged, and they still supported the Bill. The dispute, he said, was an irreconcilable conflict between two very strong cases. It had so far been marked by confusion, hasty words, and attempts on the part of both sides to discredit the professional competence of the other. The House of Lords, he suggested, was no place for ungentlemanly conduct of this kind. 'I hope that we shall be able to say later', he added, 'that from the moment when the Teesdale Bill went before the Lords such unseemliness ceased, and the thing was thenceforth considered calmly and on its merits.'

As in the Commons, some of the peers who took part in the debate reacted to the Cow Green scheme in a predictable way. Theirs was almost a reflex action. This was a conflict between industry on the one hand and conservation and amenity on the other. Spontaneously and instinctively, and by reason of their background and interests, their hearts were on one side or the other. Peers like Lord Hurcomb and Lord Strang, who were associated with the conservationist or amenity world, were against the Bill,[1] while others, like Lord Blyton and Viscount Slim, who were connected with industry, were for it.[2] In the Lords, however, there were signs of a more thoughtful approach. To judge from their speeches, several peers with no known predisposition one way or the other, had adopted a more rational and open-minded attitude, asking themselves what really would be the cost to industry of not building Cow Green, and what really would be the cost to scientific research of going ahead with the reservoir. Speaking against the Bill, Lord Henley pointed out that if the reservoir were not built at Cow Green there was little likelihood of throwing thousands of men out of work; the worst that could happen was that I.C.I. and one or two other companies would be put to more expense and some inconvenience. On the other side, the Earl of Swinton emphasised that the reservoir would affect only a very small area of scientific interest. But had it come to a vote, the chances are that most peers would have voted on

[1] Lord Hurcomb, an ex-civil servant, had once been chairman of the British Transport Commission and of the Electricity Commission; but he was a former President of the Society for Nature Reserves, former chairman of the Nature Conservancy, former Vice-President of the International Union for the Protection of Nature, the Founder-President of the Council for Nature, and President of the Royal Society for the Protection of Birds. Lord Strang, the former Permanent Under-Secretary at the Foreign Office, was a member of the Nature Conservancy and a former chairman of the National Parks Commission.

[2] Lord Slim was best known as a soldier. He was also a former director of I.C.I. and had a variety of other business interests. Lord Blyton had been secretary of a Durham miners' lodge, a member of the executive of the Durham Miners' Association, and M.P. for the mining division of Houghton-le-Spring.

the basis of principle and instinct, and not as a result of a careful assessment and comparison of the arguments on both sides.

Select Committees of the House of Lords usually consist of five peers. In view of the controversial nature of the Bill, and because of the widespread interest that it had aroused, two further peers were added on this occasion. Under the chairmanship of Lord Grenfell, the Committee was made up of the Lords Crook, Raglan, Clwyd, Croft, Granville-West and Boston. Lord Crook was a man of wide experience in central and local administration. He had taken an interest in the problem of water supply for many years, and had been chairman of the Select Committee that examined the Water Board's Private Bill authorising the Balderhead reservoir in 1959. Lord Boston had also been a member of the Select Committee on Balderhead. Of the remainder, one was a farmer, but none of the others seems to have had any particular connection with industry, water supply, or the conservationist movement. The Select Committee sat for the first time on 22 November 1966. During the next two months they were to meet on nineteen days, and on 19 December they spent a rain-soaked day in Upper Teesdale, inspecting some of the possible sites.

When they appeared before the Committee both sides rehearsed much the same arguments and produced many of the same witnesses as in the Commons. The Water Board's case was still based on the three propositions that they needed extra water, that they needed the water urgently (even more urgently now), and that there was no reasonable alternative to Cow Green. Having heard the botanists before the Select Committee of the House of Commons, I.C.I. and the Water Board were even more convinced that they were exaggerating the scientific importance of Cow Green and the extent to which the value of Widdybank Fell would be diminished if a reservoir were built there. It was very easy, they said, for experts to make too much of the importance of their own speciality. This was exactly what these dedicated enthusiasts had done over Cow Green. In point of fact, they argued, Cow Green had scarcely been heard of until the reservoir was proposed at the end of 1964. In this connection, the ex-manager of the Cow Green mine was produced to testify that in the period from 1940 to 1954 he had never seen anyone scrutinising the vegetation on Cow Green. He also mentioned that in his day heavy excavating equipment had been freely used on the site, and debris and earth had been strewn about quite indiscriminately on what he now learned was virtually hallowed ground.

And this time, the promoters were able to counter-attack the objectors with evidence from an independent scientist. Out of the blue, and to the surprise and delight of I.C.I., a young botany lecturer, Dr K. W. Giles of Birkbeck College, took his life in his hands and volunteered to testify in the Lords that the Cow Green site was nowhere near as important as had been alleged by some of the eminent academics. Apparently, Giles had been incensed by what he regarded as the exaggerated claims made on behalf of the plant communities on Widdybank Fell. 'I would say', he told the Select Committee, 'that roughly 50 per cent of the botanists in this country are completely unconcerned about the fate of Cow Green.' Inevitably, counsel for the objectors suggested that it was presumptuous, not to say impertinent, for a relatively inexperienced botanist to challenge the views of established authorities in their own field. Giles was unabashed. It was the content and quality of an argument that mattered, he replied, not the reputation and standing of the man who put it forward. He contended that the case for the petitioners had been at no time supported by valid scientific evidence directly and positively related to the area in question. To make extravagant claims, on the basis of weak evidence, he suggested, could only do harm to the public image of the science of botany, bringing the discipline into disrepute and at the same time damaging the cause of conservation.

Moreover, the promoters were now able to produce the results of their tests carried out on the site during the summer. These experiments, as the petitioners conceded, confirmed the Water Board's contention that the Cow Green site would not leak and established conclusively that extensive grouting would not be required. The petitioners had made great play with the damage that grouting would do on and around the site; whilst they were no doubt relieved to learn that it would not be necessary, at the same time this news did deprive them of one of their main arguments.

In its essentials, the Cow Green dispute was still a conflict of values. But the terms of reference given to the Select Committee had somewhat changed the character of the argument. In the Commons the onus had seemed to be on the objectors to demonstrate that in order to preserve the rare plants and rugged countryside above Cauldron Snout it was worth spending several million pounds of hard cash and worth endangering jobs in an area where unemployment was a serious problem. It was an unenviable task, though the petitioners had come close enough to success to encourage them to continue their fight. The special Instruction to the Select Committee of the House of Lords altered the situation. In the Lords the Water Board and I.C.I. were on the defensive, for the onus was now upon them to show that Cow Green really was better than any of the alternatives, both in the short run and also considered as part of a long-term strategy for meeting the water requirements of Tees-side.

Whilst Upper Cow Green was never formally abandoned by the objectors, their main effort from now onwards was to be devoted to showing that from every point of view Cow Green made far less sense than Middleton. Tactically, this shift of emphasis was very much to the advantage of the petitioners. Comparing the merits of two reservoir sites is a somewhat less metaphysical exercise than determining whether a particular price ought to be paid to preserve unusual assemblages of rare flora. If the objectors could once establish that on planning grounds there was a better case for Middleton than for Cow Green, then the more chancy question of values – and who could tell what value their Lordships might place on rare plants? – might well fade into the background.[1]

From the petitioners' point of view it became increasingly important that the Select Committee should concentrate upon the comparative merits of Cow Green and Middleton as sources of water, for as the hearings continued the nature of the scientific value attributed by the botanists to Cow Green underwent a significant change. As the petitioners now acknowledged, it was the 'inspirational' value of this area that was really important: it

[1] Organisations that supported the petitioners' cause readily fell in with this strategy. In a Report to the Minister of Housing and Local Government on 18 October 1966 the National Parks Commission specifically advocated Middleton in preference to Cow Green, claiming that the recreational potential of the former would compensate for the loss of agricultural value.

was on Widdybank Fell that Pigott and hundreds of others had first been fired with enthusiasm for botanical studies. Cow Green ought to be preserved because sites like this were becoming more and more precious in an overcrowded Britain. There was nothing trivial or untenable about this argument. But in the Commons, it will be remembered, the botanists had claimed that results of great practical value might very easily come out of pure research on the rare flora at Cow Green.

The case for Middleton had already been set out in the House of Commons; but in view of the special Instruction, the arguments for and against this site became even more important in the Lords. In brief, the petitioners maintained that the additional water from Cow Green would soon be quite inadequate, because the Water Board, as usual, were working on much too conservative an estimate of I.C.I.'s future needs. The reason for this, of course, was that industrial consumers were unwilling to commit themselves to guaranteeing loan charges for water they might never need. Within a few years of completing Cow Green, they said, the water men would be looking for a new source. Inevitably, they would then turn to Middleton; and when Middleton was developed, Cow Green would be superfluous. Since it was bound to be flooded in the end, why not settle for Middleton at the beginning? It was true that a number of Sites of Special Scientific Interest would be affected at Middleton. And it was unfortunate about the farmers. But scientifically Middleton was nowhere near as valuable as Cow Green, and many of the smallholdings there were not really economic. If the Government continued with its policy of encouraging amalgamations in the farming industry, some of these small farmers would, in any case, be leaving sooner or later.[1]

---

[1] In Teesdale itself, the very idea of flooding the valley at Middleton had generated a great deal of anger. On 25 November 1966 the Barnard Castle R.D.C. wrote to the Water Board referring to rumours that were circulating to the effect that if Cow Green was not approved, the reservoir would have to go to Middleton. The Rural District Council reaffirmed that they would strongly oppose the Middleton site. So far as the Water Board controlled the situation, the farmers had no cause to worry. Sir Charles Allison had apparently told the secretary of the local branch of the N.F.U. that so long as he was chairman of the Water Board they would never attempt to build a reservoir at Middleton, whatever the outcome of the Cow Green proposals. Under no circumstances, he said, would

Admittedly, there was the difficulty over the later completion date at Middleton, for it certainly could not be ready before 1973. Between 1970 and 1973, the petitioners argued, Jeffcoate's borehole scheme would fill the gap. If the underground aquifers in the magnesian limestone and bunter sandstone were pumped for only limited periods in each year, as much as 27 m.g.d. could be abstracted in the dry months. This would be quite enough to tide the Water Board over until Middleton came into service.

On the other side, I.C.I. and the Water Board were now to devote much of *their* effort to demonstrating that the 'Middleton plus borehole' scheme ought to be rejected. The Middleton site, they reminded the Committee, would cost about three times as much as Cow Green. It was opposed by the farmers, and it would cause a great deal of hardship and disturbance. Some of the people who lived and worked in this part of the valley were of an age which would make it difficult for them to earn a living elsewhere, and those who were tenant farmers would get very little compensation. If such a large site was developed in the late 1960s, its full yield would not be taken up until the late 1990s, a situation that would make the cost of water unnecessarily high in the meantime. Middleton, in other words, would provide far too much water much sooner than anyone needed it. So far as the critical gap between 1970 and 1973 was concerned, the Water Board – with the full support of the Water Resources Board – argued that it would be wrong to gamble on Jeffcoate's borehole scheme providing enough water by the early 1970s. Even Jeffcoate had conceded that the scheme *might* fail: if it did, and Middleton was not ready, the consequences could be disastrous.

Nor was it inevitable that after and in addition to Cow Green there would have to be a reservoir at Middleton or at some other site in Upper Teesdale. Looking ahead, a variety of possibilities might solve the problem of future needs. Whilst it would be wrong to rely on a borehole scheme to meet the requirements of

he ever contemplate flooding the homes and farms of so many people (*Darlington and Stockton Times*, 24 Dec 1966). In so far as sentiment is always important, particularly when disputes are settled through the political process, the agricultural problem was a serious weakness in the petitioners' case for Middleton. Looked at objectively and dispassionately, no doubt some of the smallholdings on the site were uneconomic. But laymen are not easily convinced that homes and livelihoods should be sacrificed in the interests of plants and botanists. See p. 197.

the immediate future, the Water Board and their advisers were prepared to agree that in the years after 1974 it should be possible to abstract 15 m.g.d. from underground sources. This would help meet the long-term need. Then again, with the passage of time, the Water Board would gain more experience in operating river-regulating reservoirs, and would be able to reduce wastage. There was the possibility of bringing water into the Tees Valley from a reservoir in the Tyne or Wear Valleys. By the 1980s the much discussed barrages across Morecambe Bay or the Solway Firth might have been built; it might then be possible to carry water across the Pennines to the Tyne, the Wear and the Tees. By the 1980s desalination might have become an economic possibility.

The proceedings came to an end on 23 January 1967, and the following morning the chairman of the Select Committee announced their recommendation. They recommended that the Bill should be approved. Because it was such an important Bill, and because of the special Instruction, on 6 February the Committee took the unusual step of publishing a Report explaining how and why they had reached their decision.[1]

The Select Committee were entirely satisfied that the Bill's promoters had established their need for an additional 35 m.g.d., most of which would be required by 1970. They were satisfied that the operations of I.C.I. in the North-east would be severely prejudiced in the early 1970s if this extra water was not forthcoming. There was a considerable market for the fertilisers, nylon and petro-chemicals that I.C.I. would be producing, and if this market was not exploited, exports would suffer, and the national interest would be damaged. On economic grounds, therefore, the Committee were in no doubt that the water ought to be made available to the promoters at the earliest possible date.

Because of the water industry's method of financing capital works, because it was impossible to forecast the effect of the Government's regional policy, and as there was no telling what impact research would have on water consumption in the future, it was very difficult to predict accurately the future needs of industry. For these reasons, the Committee felt unable to make a reliable forecast of water requirements in the area for a period as

[1] *Special Report from the Select Committee of the House of Lords on the Tees Valley and Cleveland Water Bill*, 6 Feb 1967, H.C. 172 (1966–7).

far ahead as twenty years, which was what they had been asked to do.

They had also looked carefully at a number of alternative sites for the reservoir. Only two of the possible sites – Upper Cow Green and Middleton – could be regarded as genuine alternatives to Cow Green. Neither would provide the proven need for water in time, or at a cost at all comparable with Cow Green. Upper Cow Green could not be brought into service before 1974, four years after Cow Green, and it would cost about £9 million, as against £2–2½ million for Cow Green. The dam at Upper Cow Green would have to be twice as high and almost three times as long as at Cow Green, and consequently a reservoir there would constitute a far more serious intrusion into the local scenery than would the reservoir proposed in the Bill. Moreover, the Committee were satisfied that some of the botanical objections to Cow Green would also apply to Upper Cow Green. A reservoir at Middleton would provide twice as much water as Cow Green. But it could not begin to provide water until 1973, and it would cost somewhere between £8 and £9½ million.

It was true that in the late 1970s water supplies over and above the yield from Cow Green would be needed. But the Committee were prepared to accept assurances given by the Water Resources Board that these extra supplies would not necessarily have to come from the Tees Valley. Nor was it certain that they would have to be stored there. They did not believe that in the long run a reservoir at Middleton was inevitable; and to plump for such a large reservoir there at this stage might well conflict with subsequent proposals from the Water Resources Board designed to meet the requirements of the North of England as a whole.

Middleton had other serious drawbacks. If the valley was flooded at this point, some 39 agricultural holdings would be affected, 27 farmhouses would be destroyed, about 1,000 acres of agricultural land would be inundated, and part of the village of Newbiggin would be submerged. The Committee had concluded that as between Cow Green and Middleton, even if everything else had been equal, they would not have been justified in recommending the destruction of houses, farmsteads and farmland at Middleton unless they had been satisfied that an extremely high degree of scientific and amenity disturbance would occur at Cow Green if the reservoir were constructed there instead. On

the evidence, they did not feel that the disturbance to be anticipated was of that nature or magnitude.

The Committee noted, for example, that of the species of rare
plants that would be submerged at Cow Green there was not one
of scientific significance that did not exist elsewhere in Upper
Teesdale. They appreciated that the petitioners were concerned
over certain assemblages of plants, as distinct from individual
specimens, and they accepted that a measure of damage was
bound to occur if the Bill went through. But in view of the need
for the scheme, and since individual specimens existed elsewhere
and similar assemblages might also exist in Upper Teesdale, they
were of the opinion that the damage should be accepted. The
Committee had been impressed by evidence that of 300 acres of
sugar limestone on Widdybank and Cronkley Fells only 20 would
be flooded. This, they felt, was not a sacrifice that could be
reasonably resisted.

They had also considered the effect of the reservoir on the
landscape and amenities of the area. As a result of their visit to
Upper Teesdale they had reached the conclusion that any man-
made scheme would indeed intrude upon the character of the
countryside. But (they suggested) a comparatively shallow reservoir of the type proposed for Cow Green might, in time, merge
into the landscape.

The Committee had given long and careful thought to the
possibility of using underground aquifers instead of building a
reservoir. They agreed that a borehole scheme might make a
substantial contribution to meeting future needs. But there was
some uncertainty about the yield obtainable from these underground sources. The Director of the Water Resources Board had
said that a borehole scheme large enough to provide the quantity
of water required would not be a viable proposition for three or
four years. In any case, a pilot scheme would be needed to show
whether the technical difficulties could be overcome. There would
be the problem of obtaining statutory powers from Parliament,
and arrangements would have to be made with landowners about
wayleaves and sites for the small buildings required. Taking
everything into account, the Committee thought that it would
be hazardous to rely on boreholes alone to provide the necessary
quantity of water by 1970.

In short, the Committee felt that only a reservoir could provide the extra water that was needed, and they were satisfied that the least harmful site for such a reservoir was at Cow Green.

The Bill returned to the floor of the House for its Third Reading on 23 February 1967. Opening the three-hour debate, Lord Grenfell told the House that his Committee had been unanimous in their conclusion that Cow Green alone would meet the needs of the situation. In the light of all the evidence, no other decision had been possible, and he asked the Lords to give the Bill a Third Reading.[1] Reluctantly, the conservationists accepted the committee's verdict. In a speech that clearly made a deep impression on the House, Lord Strang conceded that in the circumstances the Committee probably could not have come to any other conclusion. But the Cow Green controversy had wider implications. There was a lesson to be learned from this case, and they ought to be clear what the moral was. A body of presuppositions governed the development of modern society, he said. When conflicts like Cow Green occurred, these presuppositions served almost universally to resolve the conflict in one way rather than the other. What were these guiding principles? They had been spelt out by J. K. Galbraith in the last of his Reith Lectures for 1966. There he had outlined what he took to be the faith of modern industrial man, the goals and values which determine his conduct, to which everyone, including their Select Committee, was expected to give priority. These were: technology is always good; accordingly, firms must always expand; the consumption of goods is the principal source of happiness; idleness is wicked as an alternative to work; and, finally, nothing should interfere with the priority that we accord to technology, growth and increased consumption. Galbraith himself, as Lord Strang pointed out, did not subscribe to this view. Indeed, he had gone on to argue that through the state, society should assert the superior claims of aesthetic over economic goals, and particularly of environment over cost. If it did not, the industrial system would continue to have a monopoly of social purpose.

Unfortunately, he said, the record of successive British Governments was nothing to boast about. For twelve years, as chairman of the National Parks Commission, he had fought what was often a losing battle in defence of the countryside. They all knew about the Industrial Revolution and its effects on the

[1] For the debate, see *H.L. Deb.* (1966–7) 280, cols 801–65.

environment, and everyone was properly horrified at the desecration of the countryside that had occurred in the days of *laissez-faire* industrialisation. Rightly, they put the blame on the greedy capitalist. Now, in the new industrial revolution, were they not doing the same thing all over again? This time there was a difference, and the difference was that now it was the Government itself, along with industry and the trade unions, that was constantly giving precedence to the claims of development. Unless a halt was called somewhere, the dwindling countryside would continue to be eaten away, and the already damaged coastline would be even more desecrated.

Lord Hurcomb said that he had come to the conclusion that it would not be right to press his opposition further. With better planning and more foresight a less objectionable scheme might have been devised. As it was, under pressure of time, the House would have to take what was essentially a wrong decision. There was little use in setting up agencies to protect sites of scientific importance and to preserve the natural beauty of the countryside if these considerations were in normal departmental practice to be disregarded under pressure from developers of all kinds, advancing the familiar, but often unjustifiable, claim that their proposals alone were practicable, and urgently necessary on some ground of immediate economic advantage. Far too often, he said, the arguments for those interests and values that could not be quantified failed to make an impression on authority.

Right to the end, the underlying proclivities that all along had shaped attitudes to this particular case were still coming to the surface. Lord Nugent of Guildford declared: 'I would say to the noble Lord, Lord Strang, that I feel we are talking about the lives of men and women in this area, which have to be matched against the tremendously appealing considerations of amenity and landscape which turn our hearts over. This is not just a matter of pounds, shillings and pence: it concerns the jobs and the lives of the people who live there.' Those who set a higher value on conservation and amenity naturally took a more sceptical view of the amount of unemployment that would occur if the Cow Green reservoir were not built. As Lord Chorley put it, 'One can be so easily led away by these sentimental appeals of bread and butter for thousands of people.'

The last word came from Lord Kennet on the Government

front bench. He summed up the Cow Green conflict as a 'head-on clash between the quantifiable and the unquantifiable; between industry, which is used to giving precise figures and calculating precise pay-offs, and on the other hand a fortuitous alliance of pure science and the preservation of natural beauty.' He went on: 'I think that whatever posterity comes to feel about the presence of the reservoir at Cow Green it may well remember the passage of this Bill through both Houses as the moment when the British Parliament accepted to the full its duty to examine, regardless of tedium and regardless of cost, the fundamental conflict of interests between one ponderable – industrial and economic progress – and two imponderables – pure research and the preservation of natural beauty.'

Now that all the evidence had been assembled and tested, what was the Government's view?[1] Lord Kennet's final analysis makes it clear that the Minister, presented with the same evidence as had been put before the two Select Committees, would have approved the Cow Green site, chiefly because the objectors would not have convinced him that the sacrifice of unquantifiable values justified the additional cost and risk entailed by any alternative scheme. What the botanists called Upper Teesdale, he said, covered about 7,000 acres. Within this area there were 300 acres where the soil consisted of an outcrop of sugar limestone, mixed with peat. This 300 acres was divided between Widdybank Fell and Cronkley Fell. The Cow Green reservoir would flood 20 of the 165 acres of sugar limestone on Widdybank Fell. The rest would

[1] Had the Water Board proceeded by way of an Order under the Water Act of 1945, the Minister of Housing and Local Government would have given the final decision after both sides had put their case at a public local inquiry. It is one of the odder features of Private Bill procedure that Ministers make up their minds, and Government departments submit their Reports, *before* all the evidence has been collected and tested. Whilst Committees know that these Reports cannot be definitive, they are bound to carry a great deal of weight. It is true that representatives of the departments concerned listen to the Select Committee proceedings, and give their departments' considered view before counsel on both sides sum up. It is open to Ministers to say that as a result of what has come out of the Committee's hearings they have changed their minds. But unless startlingly fresh and important evidence has come to light the odds must be very much against such a change of heart, particularly if several departments have already spent a good deal of time in reaching an agreed governmental view.

not be affected. In other words, altogether there would be a one-sixteenth reduction of the population of glacial relict flora. This was no doubt regrettable, said Lord Kennet; but seen in perspective it was a sacrifice that could hardly justify the very considerable cost necessary to avoid it.

There was no division at the end of the debate. On 22 March 1967 the Tees Valley and Cleveland Water Bill received the Royal Assent, and the fate of Cow Green was settled at last, GOSH.

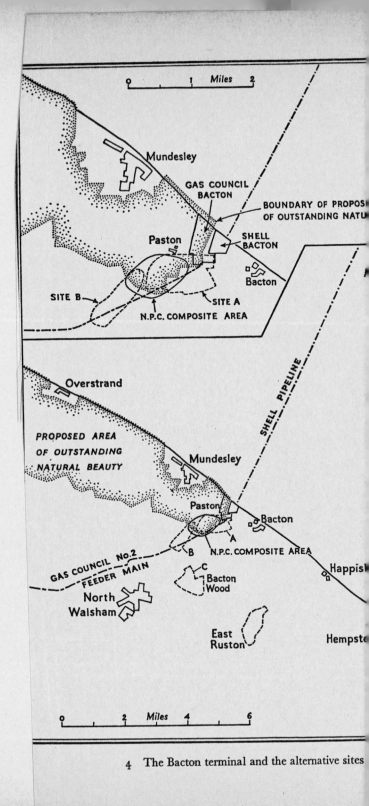

4   The Bacton terminal and the alternative sites

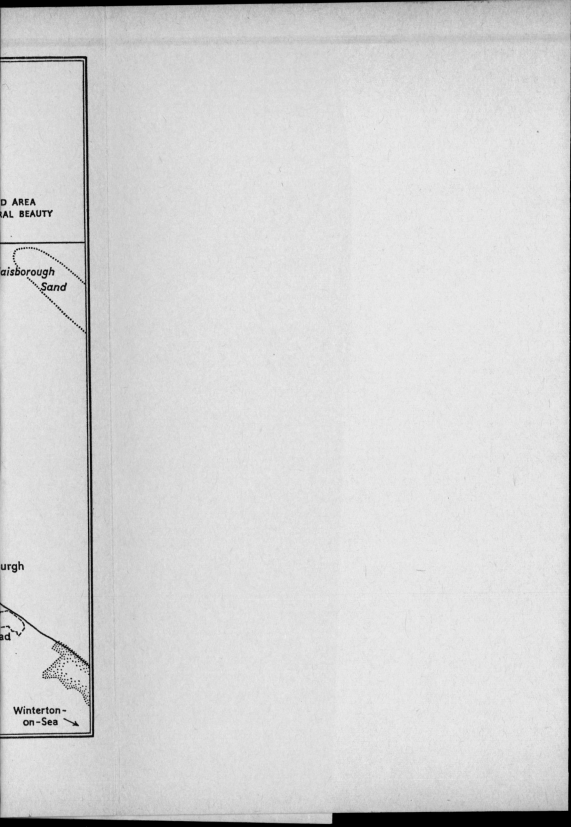

D AREA
RAL BEAUTY

aisborough
Sand

urgh

ad

Winterton-
on-Sea →

5 Bacton and North Sea Gas

You get a place which nobody has ever heard of and
once anybody wants to do anything there, it overnight
becomes a great beauty spot.

Gas Council Scientific Information Officer,
February 1967

Bacton is a seaside village on the Norfolk coast, about twenty
miles north-east of Norwich. It is a popular holiday resort, though
the village is noted more for its setting and surroundings than for
any special attractions of its own. Stretching away to the north-
west, towards Mundesley, there are fine, sandy beaches; and
behind the beaches the cliffs gradually rise from a height of fifty
feet or so just outside Bacton to well over a hundred feet at Stow
Hill. The coast road out of Bacton (B1159) soon turns inland,
running through the hamlet of Paston, a name celebrated in the
history of English literature for the fifteenth-century Paston
Letters. Between Bacton and Paston, a broad expanse of open
farmland reaches back from the cliff top to the coast road; and
beyond the coast road the more undulating countryside that extends inland towards North Walsham provides what many good
judges claim to be a perfect backing for the sweeping lines of the
seaward country. As some saw it, the coast here was 'beautiful
virgin cliff'; others, it must be added, could see nothing but a
'bleak and uninteresting' stretch of undistinguished coastline.
Judgements of this kind almost always depend upon where the
observer stands.[1]

[1] The chief documentary sources for the following account are: Public
Inquiry Report (21 April 1967); Reopened Public Inquiry Report (23 May
1967); Norfolk County Council, Minutes and Reports; Report of a Special
Parish meeting held at Bacton, 21 November 1966, verbatim transcript
made available by the Smallburgh R.D.C.; *The Times*; *Eastern Daily
Press*; Benedict Nightingale, 'Natural Gas at Bacton', *New Society*, 9 Mar
1967.

NORTH SEA GAS

In the 1950s gas seemed to be on the way out. The industry had
all the appearances of a fusty, ailing relic from the nineteenth
century, and few would have given much for its chances of competing successfully with electricity, oil and nuclear energy. Morale
was low, sales were falling, and to make matters worse, for its
raw materials gas was dependent on coal, another industry with
a doubtful future. As late as 1961 a public opinion survey confirmed that gas was widely regarded as 'dirty, smelly, dangerous
and old-fashioned'.[1] True, the industry itself had not yet given up
the ghost, and was doing its best to counteract this unfavourable
image. A vigorous advertising campaign was launched, stressing
the advantages of gas over electricity, and emphasising the bid-
dable nature of gas appliances: 'High speed gas – the heat that
obeys you' was the slogan. The Gas Council was also able to
make some play with the social virtues of its product; unlike the
electricity industry, it had no need to festoon the countryside with
pylons and cables. One of its advertisements, for example, showed
an apparently untouched, golden-brown cornfield, and carried
the caption 'A year ago the gas underground grid was laid
through here'. In a decade that was becoming increasingly sensitive to threats to the environment it was a shrewd thrust, though
a few years later it was to leave the gas industry open to embarrassing ripostes when it became entangled in one of the most
highly publicised planning battles of the sixties (see Chapter 6).

But skilful promotion is no substitute for a good product. The
real salvation of the gas industry was to lie in new discoveries and
technical innovation. In 1962, for example, I.C.I. announced
that they had hit upon a process for making gas from naphtha,
and in 1964 the Gas Council began to import liquid methane
from Algeria, distributing it by means of a high-pressure grid
system to the eight Area Gas Boards. With the industry moving
into the central heating business, and at the same time stepping
up its advertising efforts, there was soon a sharp increase in the
demand for gas. In 1963–4 sales were 5 per cent up by volume

[1] Paul Ferris, 'How High Speed Gas seduced Mrs 1970', *The Observer*,
12 Feb 1967.

on the previous year, and in 1964–5 they were 8 per cent up again on 1963–4.

Above all, the prospects for gas were transformed by the discovery of considerable reserves of natural gas under the North Sea. The first strikes actually occurred onshore in Holland in 1959. Encouraged by these discoveries, the major oil companies then launched extensive exploratory surveys over something like 150,000 square miles of the North Sea. In September 1964 the Shell/Esso Group were granted licences to explore and produce gas from 75 North Sea blocks, each covering about 100 square miles, and from now onwards the emphasis shifted from general reconnaissance to more detailed investigatory work to find suitable points for exploration wells. In April 1965, when Shell U.K. Exploration and Production Ltd drilled the first of their wells, they found no sign of gas or oil; but a year later, in April 1966, they did strike gas in significant quantities, 30 miles off the Norfolk coast, in what was afterwards to be known as the Leman field.

At this early stage, it was widely believed that natural gas would have a profound and dramatic effect not only on the gas industry but on the whole economy of the United Kingdom. When the first discoveries were made there was perhaps a certain amount of unwarranted euphoria. Nevertheless, to find on the doorstep a relatively cheap and readily available source of energy was certainly an unexpected stroke of luck. For at least the next twenty-five years both industry and domestic consumers could look for substantial benefits, as low-priced natural gas met a larger proportion of the nation's steadily increasing requirements for fuel and power. In addition, it was reckoned that the balance of payments would stand to gain considerably as a result of savings on the petroleum products that would otherwise have been imported. Natural gas, then, seemed to provide important opportunities that the United Kingdom could not afford to miss; clearly, this unforeseen bonus had to be exploited as quickly and efficiently as possible.

It was now known that the gas was under the sea. But it still had to be brought ashore, processed and marketed, and it still had to compete with electricity, coal, oil and nuclear energy. Under the Continental Shelf Act of 1964, with certain exceptions concerning the supply for industrial purposes, oil companies are required to offer their gas to the Gas Council (on behalf of the Area Boards) 'at a reasonable price'. Unless this has been done, the Secretary of State for Trade and Industry cannot consent to natural gas being supplied to any other customers. There is no definition of 'reasonable' in the Act, nor are the criteria for assessing reasonableness laid down in it. In practice, a reasonable price is whatever the Minister thinks fair and right, and this is the price at which the oil companies are obliged to sell to the Gas Council. Not surprisingly, when the first contracts were negotiated, buyers and sellers took somewhat different views as to what constituted a fair price, and there followed a good deal of hard bargaining between the Gas Council, the oil companies and the then Ministry of Power. Had the producers refused to sell at the price they were offered, there were no other buyers in the market; but if the Minister had insisted on a price that the producers thought unreasonably low, there was some risk that they might have pulled out of the whole operation, in which case there would have been no natural gas for anyone.

Arguments about pricing aside, the Gas Council and the operating companies shared a common interest in speed and economy. Both were naturally anxious to keep capital costs as low as possible, and their target was to begin supplying consumers in January 1968, with natural gas making a significant contribution to meeting peak demand in the winter of 1968–9. Since pipe-laying under the North Sea is impossible outside the summer months, they were well aware that if work was not started in the spring of 1967 progress might well be held up by the onset of the following winter. This was a tight timetable, with little slack for unexpected delays. According to Shell, their production wells in the Leman field would be able to supply about 500 million cubic feet of gas a day. It was now a question of piping the gas ashore, processing it, and feeding it into the national grid as cheaply and efficiently as possible. And the first step was to find the most suitable landfall for the sea pipes and the best site for the complex of buildings and plant that would make up the reception terminal. Conscious that they were on the threshold of a major development, in the spring of 1966 Shell U.K. Exploration and Production Ltd turned their attention to the cliffs and beaches of Norfolk.

ALL ROADS LEAD TO BACTON

On 17 May 1966 Shell instructed their land agents to survey possible sites for the landfall and reception terminal. They were told to look for an area of up to 75 acres for Shell, with adjoining land for the Gas Council. From the start, it was assumed that the terminal complex would be close to the landfall; the site was to be on, or within a mile of, the coast, and the search was to be concentrated on the sixteen-mile stretch of coastline between Mundesley and Winterton-on-Sea. Two days later, at a meeting on 19 May, Shell's land agents informed the Norfolk County Council's Planning Department of their instructions.

So far as the landfall was concerned, the best spot was obviously the nearest point on the coast to the production wells. The Leman field is more than thirty miles out to sea. Since the cost of laying a 30-inch pipe ten feet under the sea bed was reckoned to be about £200,000 a mile (it turned out to be nearer £250,000), and as Shell were expecting to lay two such pipes to the landfall, their first concern was naturally to make sure that the pipeline followed the shortest practicable route from the gas field to the shore.

The choice of site for the terminal installations was dictated by other considerations. When natural gas arrives at the landfall it contains a number of impurities, such as water and hydrocarbons. These liquids have to be removed before the gas can be passed on to the consumer. The treated gas is then transmitted through measuring and quality control devices before the Gas Council takes delivery into its terminal. Most of the processing is carried out in low-level steel vessels; none of these installations need be particularly conspicuous. But they are of considerable weight, as is the V.H.F. mast needed at the terminal. The site therefore had to be capable of bearing heavy loads.

None of this implied that the terminal necessarily had to be on the coast and adjacent to the actual landfall.[1] However, Shell

---

[1] As a matter of fact, it was not absolutely necessary to build the reception terminal onshore at all. The gas could have been processed out to sea, in which case very little plant would have been needed on the coast. But Shell calculated that off-shore treatment would cost almost four times as much as the same process on land, involving them in some £10 million of additional expenditure over the lifetime of the field. Apart from the

took the view that a coastal site was much to be preferred to one inland for three main reasons.

First, in order to avoid the possibility of radio interference, it was desirable that the telemetric system used to control the off-shore production wells and the gas flow through the undersea pipeline should be operated from as near the coast as possible.

Second, there was a great deal to be said for processing the raw gas as soon as possible after it had come ashore. It is by no means impossible to take gas and liquid together, in the same pipe, for a reasonable distance inland. But there are excellent reasons for not doing so. For a start, the transmission of 'dry', processed gas requires far less pipeline capacity than the equivalent volume in its untreated form. According to Shell's calculations, it would have cost about £400,000 a mile more to pipe untreated gas inland – a wasteful and pointless exercise, since it would result only in the arrival of useless liquid 'slugs' at the terminal. Again, with a two-phase flow (gas and liquid together), an accidental break in the pipeline – though unlikely – would have much more serious consequences than in the case of a line carrying gas only. And the fewer pipes that have to be laid inland, the less disturb-ance there is to agriculture and amenity. Operationally and economically, therefore, there are many advantages in converting to a single-phase flow at the earliest opportunity. From this it follows that ideally the terminal should be as close as possible to the landfall, that is to say, on the coast.

And third, even if the terminal were situated inland, Shell reckoned that they would still have needed to acquire an area on the coast at the point where the pipeline came ashore. In their view, it was essential that they should own this land in order to provide the necessary security and supervision at the vital land-fall; and since they had to acquire land on the coast for this purpose anyway, it obviously made sense to look for a coastal site that would meet both their landfall and terminal require-ments at the same place.

The Gas Council was strongly opposed to the underground transmission of untreated natural gas, and even more in favour

---

question of cost, there would also have been formidable practical difficul-ties in operating plant more than thirty miles off the coast and exposed to some of the worst weather in the world; nor is a platform in the North Sea a popular posting for employees.

of a coastal site than Shell. Its own terminal was to be adjacent to Shell's, so that it could control the gas flow from the production wells and through the No. 2 feeder main into the national grid, established originally to take Algerian natural gas up country from Canvey Island to Leeds. At this stage it was the Gas Council's policy to allow the producers to find their own sites. Subsequently, in order to avoid a proliferation of terminals along the coast, it decided to acquire enough land itself to lease other producers sites for their terminals within the one large area.

When Shell's land agents began their survey of the coastline between Mundesley and Winterton-on-Sea it soon became clear that most of this sixteen-mile section of coast would not really be suitable for the terminal site. Working northwards from Winterton-on-Sea, a good deal of the first six miles between there and Sea Palling is flat, open and marshy. There is a fair amount of wild bird-life in the area, and at Winterton Dunes there is a National Nature Reserve. A site here would also have meant routing the Gas Council's feeder main through the Norfolk Broads. The next five miles, between Sea Palling and Happisburgh, is largely given over to holiday uses. Within this section one possible site at Hempstead was carefully examined; but this was finally rejected because it was vulnerable to flooding both from the Broads and from the sea. It was thought that there would be difficulties in building on low-lying land only marginally above sea level, and in addition the incoming sea pipes would have had to breach the coastal defence works. Further north still, the next two miles between Happisburgh and Bacton were already two-thirds built upon, and part of what remained was occupied by a defence establishment. This left a three-mile section between Bacton and Mundesley. And here, a little to the north of Bacton, in the Rural District of Smallburgh, the surveyors found what looked to be the ideal spot: an extensive cliff-top site, most of which, by good fortune, fell just outside a proposed Area of Outstanding Natural Beauty.

While these surveys were in progress, Shell's hydrographic consultants had encountered an unforeseen complication. Between the Leman field and the Norfolk coast, nine miles out to sea, the Haisborough Sand rises some eighty feet above the sea bed. This shifting sandbank is about eleven miles long and a mile wide, and on it lie a number of charted wrecks. Shell now had to decide whether the pipeline should cross the Haisborough Sand, or alternatively take a longer route round to the north of the sandbank. Eventually, the shorter and cheaper route was rejected because of its technical hazards. The objective now was to find the nearest suitable landfall and terminal site to the northern tip of the Haisborough Sand.

As luck would have it, almost the nearest landfall for a pipeline from the northern extremity of Haisborough Sand was the very suitable cliff-top site that the surveyors had found just north of Bacton. A cynic might be excused for thinking that had the shortest route led to a point near, say, Winterton Dunes, then Shell might have been somewhat less concerned for the sanctity of wild bird-life. Be that as it may, everything now seemed to be falling out for the best. The Bacton site met all the necessary engineering and technical requirements; the land, it turned out, was all in one ownership, and the owners were prepared to sell; and a terminal there would cost less than at any alternative site, either elsewhere on the coast or further inland. Shell and the Gas Council were agreed: this was indeed a highly suitable location for the new terminal, the vital tap through which much of Britain's natural gas would flow into the national grid. On 6 July 1966, in strict confidence, they informed the Norfolk County Council's Chief Planning Officer that Bacton was unquestionably the best site from their point of view.

THE COUNTY COUNCIL IS NOT CONVINCED

Norfolk is primarily an agricultural county. It claims to contain some of the best farmland in England. And if this is an expression that has a familiar ring – it sometimes seems that almost every industrial development ever proposed is fated to encroach upon the finest agricultural land in England – here, for once, the claim is fully justified. In Norfolk, anything that takes land out of farming use is viewed with suspicion and usually resisted. Not far behind in importance comes the holiday and tourist trade. The Norfolk Broads are world famous. The county also has about ninety miles of coastline, dotted with popular and flourishing seaside resorts.

From as far back as 1950, the Norfolk County Council had been concerned about the problem of controlling development along the coast. It was recognised that from time to time new building would be necessary and desirable. But the best approach, the County had decided, was to concentrate development in certain designated areas, keeping the rest of the coastline unspoiled for the enjoyment of the public. To promote this policy, 350 Village Development Areas had been established. Within these areas, proposals for new development were to be given sympathetic consideration; outside of them, the policy was to discourage new building of any kind, unless there was a special need connected with agriculture or other rural activities. In the County Council's consolidated policy statement for the Norfolk coastline, drawn up in 1954, it was envisaged that the three miles of coast between Mundesley and Bacton, together with the countryside behind it, should be protected from anything but agricultural development. Thus, any kind of industrial installation at Bacton would clearly fly in the face of the County Council's planning policy.

There was another important consideration. In the early sixties the problem of protecting the coastline had come to be taken much more seriously both in the world of amenity societies and in official circles. In 1963, for example, the Ministry of Housing and Local Government urged Local Planning Authorities to join forces with the National Parks Commission and the Nature Conservancy in undertaking special studies of their coastal areas. In 1965 the Ministry had asked local authorities for more information about the control of development on the coast, and as a result of the replies, in 1966 a departmental circular called for more determined and effective action to safeguard unspoiled stretches of coastline. The first step, the Ministry suggested, was for each Local Planning Authority to prepare and publish a map, with a brief explanatory statement of its policy. In protected areas the intention ought to be to prohibit all but essential development. At the same time, the Minister made it clear that in considering any planning applications that might come before him for decision, he would take into account these maps and policy statements. Another sign of the times was the National Trust's 'Operation Neptune', designed to buy up and protect stretches of the coastline thought to be worthy of preservation. The

Government itself contributed £250,000 to this voluntary fund-raising effort, which eventually collected £1 million.

These indications of official concern were nowhere more welcome than in Norfolk. And here the coastline seemed to be doubly well protected, for the National Parks Commission was proposing to designate some seventy miles of it, between the Wash and Winterton-on-Sea, as an Area of Outstanding Natural Beauty. The proposed A.O.N.B., however, did not run along a continuous and unbroken stretch of coast: a number of urban enclaves, at Sheringham, Cromer, West Runton, Overstrand and Mundesley, were left out because they had already been developed for holiday purposes. The village of Bacton had also been omitted from the proposed A.O.N.B. Bacton had not impressed the National Parks Commission; a spokesman was later to describe it as an undistinguished huddle of dull brick, pebble, wooden chalet and caravan. When the Commission had examined the coastline here, it had been in no doubt that the proposed A.O.N.B. would have to stop short of Bacton village. But where exactly? The countryside does not suddenly become (or cease to be) beautiful because of a line on the map. But lines have to be drawn somewhere, and as no physical landmark was available, the National Parks Commission eventually decided to bring the proposed A.O.N.B. down to the parish boundary between Bacton and Paston. It need scarcely be said that, in these circumstances, some will take the view that the countryside which falls just outside the A.O.N.B. is really every bit as beautiful as what lies just inside, while others will argue that the countryside just inside the boundary is not really any more beautiful than the immediately adjoining area that has not been thought worthy of inclusion. But fine points of argument aside, anyone proposing a large industrial installation on such a conspicuous and exposed coastal site was clearly touching a very sensitive spot indeed.

In May 1966, when the Norfolk County Council's planning officers first learned that Shell were taking an interest in their coastline, natural gas was very much an unknown quantity. It is doubtful if anyone in Norfolk really understood, at this stage, what a reception terminal was; later on, when Shell's plans were made public, many people jumped to the conclusion that something like an oil refinery was to be built. However, on 17 June the County Council supplied Shell's land agents with a map of the coastal strip between Mundesley and Winterton-on-Sea, showing the proposed A.O.N.B., Areas of Great Landscape Value, Village Development Areas, and areas where policy was under review. According to the map, only a short strip of coastline between Bacton and the Paston parish boundary bore no actual or proposed designation.

As yet, no specific planning application was before the Norfolk County Council, and when the Planning Committee met in June they merely considered, in a general way, the possible implications of natural gas for the county. Since so little was known, they decided to ask for explanatory talks with the Gas Council and the Ministry of Housing and Local Government. On 6 July, it will be recalled, the Chief Planning Officer had been told that Shell and the Gas Council had selected the Bacton site for the new terminal. As the Local Planning Authority responsible for determining the applications when they should come forward, on 21 July the Norfolk County Council opened discussions with other interested parties, and began to take note of their views.[1] Though they were not to be entirely without friends and supporters, it soon became clear that Shell and the Gas Council were going to run into a great deal of hostility, both in Norfolk and at the national level.

For a start, there was opposition to the Bacton site on agricultural grounds. The Divisional Land Commissioner of the Ministry of Agriculture, Fisheries and Food informed the County Planning Department that the land at Bacton was of first-class quality. The deep medium loam there was eminently suitable for all the arable crops usually grown in the district. His Minister, he said, was anxious to safeguard valuable agricultural land as far as possible, and would therefore raise strong objections to the proposed development.

The principal amenity bodies also came out strongly against the Bacton site. The National Parks Commission expressed its concern at the long-term effect of natural gas strikes on the coastline, and in particular on Areas of Outstanding Natural Beauty.

[1] As is usual in the counties, planning powers in Norfolk are exercised jointly by the County Council and the District Councils. In the ordinary way, planning applications are dealt with by the District Councils, with the benefit of advice from the County planning officers. But in the case of a major development, involving a statutory undertaker, the application goes first to the County Council, which then consults the District Council concerned, in this instance the Smallburgh R.D.C.

As far back as 1961 the Commission had begun work on designating this area in Norfolk, and the draft designation map had been produced in November 1966. The National Parks Commission felt entitled to take its stand on the Minister's known policy of discouraging all except essential developments on protected areas of the coastline. The Council for the Preservation of Rural England, alerted by the energetic secretary of their Norfolk branch, told the County Council that in their view Bacton was an unsuitable site, and that Shell and the Gas Council ought to be made to look for an alternative. Protests from the local branch were supported at the national level by the chairman of the C.P.R.E., Sir George Langley-Taylor. As reported in the local press, he sounded a grim warning:

> North Sea Gas should be taken by tanker to appropriate industrial sites for processing. If this is impracticable, it should be piped underground to treatment plants. Once gas and oil installations are built on unspoiled stretches of coastline or in natural beauty spots, there will be no end to it. Chemical and other ancillary plants will proliferate. Vast stretches of countryside and coastal scenery will be ruined for all time.[1]

If the County planning officers were still unsure as to the line they should take, hostile reactions of this kind no doubt stiffened their attitude. As it happened, the chairman of the County Planning Committee, Mr E. J. F. Isherwood, had seized the earliest opportunity to make public his personal opposition to the choice of Bacton. In his view, industrial development would adversely affect the holiday trade and drive away the many holiday-makers who came to north Norfolk to enjoy the scenic beauty of the coast.

By now, Shell were in a position to submit a formal planning application.[2] On 26 October 1966 they asked the Norfolk County Council for outline planning permission to develop a 57-acre site

[1] *Yarmouth Mercury*, 9 Dec 1966.

[2] At the later public inquiry Shell were to be criticised for not coming forward earlier with their planning application. Before the application could be submitted, the company required either an Industrial Development Certificate, or notification from the Board of Trade that an I.D.C. was not needed. Shell applied for an I.D.C. on 2 August 1966; it was not until 25 October that they were informed that a Certificate was not required.

on the cliff top at Bacton. Three weeks later, on 14 November, the Gas Council followed suit and applied for planning consent for an adjoining 60-acre site, part of which fell within the parish of Bacton and part in Paston.

Conscious that early decisions set precedents, the Norfolk Planning Committee were now even more anxious to learn what lay in store for the county and its coastline. Equally important, they were keen to discover what view the Ministry of Housing and Local Government were likely to take. Discussions in November with the Ministry and the Gas Council took them very little further forward. What the County Council wanted was some guidance as to how far normal planning considerations ought to be waived in order to meet the technical requirements of the gas industry. The gas men were arguing that, for operational reasons, a coastal site was essential: the planners were not so sure, and they were not convinced that the Norfolk coastline ought neces- sarily to be sacrificed to avoid the alleged drawbacks of an inland site for the terminal. There was evidently a good deal of talk about the national interest, but so far as the County Council were concerned, no practical guidelines emerged from these discus- sions.

Not everyone in Norfolk thought so highly of the amenity value of the Bacton cliff-top site, especially if the natural gas terminal held out the promise of material benefits. Those who live on the spot are sometimes less concerned about the natural beauty of their locality than others who observe the scene from a distance. The Bacton Parish Council had decided that the villagers ought to be given the chance to hear at first hand what was proposed and to express their feelings at a special Parish meeting. At their invitation, on 21 November 1966 there assembled at the Village Hall a collection of notables the like of which had certainly never before been seen at a Bacton Parish meeting, though within a few months most of the distinguished visitors were to return for a more prolonged stay on the Norfolk coast. From Shell U.K. Exploration and Production came Mr K. Davison, their Opera- tions Manager, Mr H. B. McDowell, their Chief Engineer, and Mr P. C. Spencer, their Personnel and Administration Superin- tendent. The Gas Council was represented by Mr J. Southam, its Legal Adviser, Mr W. H. Walters, Assistant Director of Produc- tion and Supplies, Mr F. E. Dean, its Technical Liaison Officer,

Mr D. Redwood, Deputy Press Officer, and Mr M. Edgar, an Assistant Legal Adviser. Representing the Norfolk County Council were officers from the County Planning Department, the County Councillors from the North Walsham and Cromer Divisions, and Mr Isherwood, the chairman of the Planning Committee. From the Smallburgh Rural District Council came the chairman and vice-chairman of the Council, and the Clerk to the Council. The C.P.R.E. were represented by the chairman of the County branch, Lady Harrod, and the secretary, Mr J. E. Mottram. Also on the platform were the members of the Bacton Parish Council. The total population of Bacton was just over 800; about 170 residents packed into the Hall for the special meeting.

It soon became apparent that the people of Bacton were not greatly concerned with aesthetics. They were much more interested in the rateable value of the terminal, how many jobs it would create, how the waste or effluent would be disposed of, and whether any part of the beach would have to be closed to the public. On all of these counts the Clerk of the Smallburgh R.D.C. had reassurance and encouragement to offer them. There would certainly be a substantial increase in the rateable value of the District, he said. It might be anything from a quarter to half a million pounds. The larger product from a penny rate would enable the District Council to make a good many improvements more quickly than they had expected: the sewerage scheme could be brought forward, more houses and bungalows could be built, car parks could be provided, and open spaces purchased. There would be no problem about effluents. The supply pipes would be sunk to a great depth under the beach and would not interfere with holiday-makers. He thought that about forty men could hope to find employment with Shell; but, of course, if other oil companies were to bring their gas into the Bacton terminal, many more jobs might be provided in later years.

Shell's Operations Manager then explained why Bacton had been chosen, and described the buildings and plant that would be built if planning consent were given. He pointed out that a natural gas terminal does not produce much demand for labour; forty to fifty men, 'fairly skilled', was the very most that Shell would expect to employ. However, it was the company's policy to train local people for skilled jobs as soon as possible. All of this went down well with the villagers, and the mood of the meeting began to run strongly in favour of supporting the Bacton site. The proceedings became a good deal more lively when the secretary of the local C.P.R.E. attacked the applicants and compared them with robber barons, riding roughshod over the rights of the people. Once one industrial installation was allowed on the cliffs, he claimed, there was no valid reason why unlimited expansion should not occur. These remarks were not at all to the liking of the meeting, and at times he was almost shouted down.

Unlike a town or a county, a Rural District is an artefact that rarely generates any special loyalty or affection. The Clerk to the Smallburgh R.D.C., nevertheless, adopted a frankly 'Rural District' and commercial approach to the proposed terminal. 'If this natural gas is to be piped ashore anywhere in Norfolk,' he declared, 'then I am concerned to see that it is in this district, and not to the north in the Erpingham Rural District or to the south in Blofield and Flegg Rural District. Without being offensive in any way,' he went on, 'I think at least some of the audience will agree when I say that Bacton was somewhat spoiled in the pre-planning era, and I cannot see that the bringing ashore of this natural gas in the site indicated will in any way spoil the amenities of that area.' He drew attention to the results of establishing a nuclear power station at Sizewell in East Suffolk. Far from discouraging visitors, the power station had put Sizewell on the map, and ten or twenty times as many holiday-makers and tourists now went there, to the benefit of the local economy. Of course, Shell's project alone would not add half a million pounds to the rateable value of the Rural District; but they might build up to this figure if other companies also came to Bacton. They certainly ought not to allow a proliferation of terminals along the Norfolk coast. All the operations ought to be concentrated in one particular spot, and it should be their object to see that that spot was in the Smallburgh Rural District.

The mood of the Bacton villagers is conveyed by some of the contributions from the floor of the Hall. 'This is the finest thing that can happen to a small place like Bacton', said one. 'I think we have got to look twenty-five years ahead. This will provide jobs on our doorstep and do far more good than visitors', said another. 'The rates are high and the wages are low; now we have the chance to alter that', added a third. At the end of the meeting the villagers voted overwhelmingly (150 votes against 20) in favour of supporting the application. The next evening, a Parish meeting was held in Paston. Here too, at a somewhat smaller meeting, the villagers voted to welcome Shell and the Gas Council to north Norfolk. Some observers, who set a higher value on the natural beauty of the coastline, were disgusted at what they considered an uninhibited exhibition of sheer greed. Not surprisingly, middle-class people in secure professional occupations tend to assign more importance to aesthetics than working-men on low wages in a district that does not even possess an adequate sewerage system.

When the Smallburgh R.D.C.'s Planning Committee met to consider the applications on 29 November they were not quite so taken with the idea of a natural gas terminal at Bacton as their Clerk had been. But it was the loss of agricultural land, more than the destruction of natural beauty, that worried the Committee. They therefore asked Shell to examine a number of inland sites in the Ridlington and East Ruston areas, where the land was of poorer quality. If these sites proved to be unsuitable, the Committee were prepared, reluctantly, to recommend the County Planning Committee to agree to a site of about 100 acres at Bacton.

It was now for the County Council to decide on the applications. When the Planning Committee met on 2 December 1966, they had before them the views of the Ministry of Housing and Local Government, the Ministry of Power, the National Parks Commission, and the Divisional Land Commissioner of the Ministry of Agriculture, Fisheries and Food. The Committee were told that the Gas Council would probably be submitting a further application, for an area of not less than 140 acres. When they met again on 16 December the Committee were clearly on the point of refusing the applications. However, at the request of the Ministry of Housing and Local Government, and on the understanding that a public local inquiry would be held before a decision was reached, they held their hand so as to give the Minister the opportunity of calling in the applications for his own determination. Soon afterwards, on 20 December 1966, the Gas Council's amended application came forward. Altogether, the Gas Council now wanted 135 acres (35 of which were for its own use, and 100 for the use of other producers), and the total area of the Bacton site had grown to over 190 acres. On 3 January 1967 the Norfolk County Council were informed by the Minister that in view of the nature of the development, and its likely affect on the amenities of the area, the applications were to be referred to him under Section 22 of the 1962 Town and Country Planning Act.

Presented with reactions ranging from outright condemnation to wholehearted approval, and confronted with an unfamiliar project for which there were no precedents, the County Planning Committee may well have been relieved to hand over the whole problem to the Ministry of Housing and Local Government. They accepted that the natural gas had to come ashore and be processed in Norfolk. They realised that economic and technical considerations pointed towards Bacton. Nevertheless, there was no denying that on planning grounds (and planning, after all, was the business of the Committee) Bacton was open to serious objections. The terminal would certainly be a substantial intrusion into the landscape; it would constitute a dominant feature in the rural scene; it would run contrary to their established policy of keeping this particular area as open country; in the parish of Paston it would overlap into the proposed A.O.N.B.; and it would sterilise very high-quality land. There was a case for choosing Bacton, to be sure; but the Committee were not convinced that the arguments were so decisive that no alternatives, less objectionable on planning grounds, ought to be considered. If the applicants really felt that the case for Bacton was unanswerable (the Committee concluded), they should be obliged to sustain it under challenge. The County Planning Committee therefore decided to oppose the choice of Bacton at the public inquiry. In the meantime, they urged Shell and the Gas Council to examine other possible sites.

By now, the Committee had a reasonably good idea of what the terminal would look like, for Shell had taken a party of councillors and officials to Holland to see one there. They were not so sure about the technical requirements. However, this did not deter them from picking out two alternative sites for consideration by Shell and the Gas Council. The first was at Hempstead, near the coast, and a little to the north of Sea Palling. So far as agriculture was concerned, Hempstead was admittedly not much better than Bacton. But from a landscape point of view they thought it infinitely preferable. The other alternative was at East Ruston, some three miles inland from Happisburgh. This site was mainly on low-quality agricultural land, and a terminal there (they thought) would be far less conspicuous than at Bacton. The Committee were aware that part of the area was scheduled as a Site of Special Scientific Interest; but, in their view, the terminal installations could be arranged so as to leave at least part of the S.S.S.I. untouched.

How seriously Shell and the Gas Council took all these suggestions is hard to say. Shell's land agents had carefully surveyed the whole area once already, and concluded that no other site was anywhere near as suitable for their purposes as Bacton. Hempstead had been considered and rejected; East Ruston had not been examined because Shell were looking for a site on or near the coast. But whatever the frame of mind, they certainly had to go through the motions of looking again; and of course, if Shell and the Gas Council were going to resist these alternatives at the public inquiry they had to know a certain amount about them in order to be able to say why they were considered unsuitable. As early as 14 December 1966 they were able to tell the Smallburgh R.D.C. that *their* counter-proposals were not suitable. When Shell turned their attention once more to Hempstead and East Ruston they had already decided that these two sites were unacceptable on economic and technical grounds. They were not displeased when they realised that both sites were also open to agricultural, scientific and amenity objections.

If Shell and the Gas Council were clear about what they wanted, there was no such unanimity among their opponents, who found it quite impossible to agree upon an alternative site that they could all support. The Norfolk County Council doubtless believed themselves to be acting in a responsible and constructive way then they suggested alternative sites at Hempstead and East Ruston. The effect, however, was simply to demonstrate the difficulty of finding any site that would not upset someone.

The Smallburgh R.D.C. did not approve of Hempstead or East Ruston. Nor was the C.P.R.E. very much taken with the County Council's suggestions: Hempstead, after all, was a coastal site and therefore just as bad as Bacton. The National Parks Commission, on the other hand, did not object to Hempstead, but disliked East Ruston because of the S.S.S.I. there. The Norfolk branch of the N.F.U. was opposed to Bacton, but it disliked Hempstead and East Ruston even more. The Country Land-owners' Association was against all the sites that had so far been put forward. And the news that Norfolk County Council was suggesting East Ruston at once attracted the attention and dis-approval of the Nature Conservancy, which was becoming increasingly worried at the number of scheduled sites being developed, even though they were often of very great value. A major part of this site had been designated a S.S.S.I. in 1960. The Nature Conservancy had no great interests in Bacton;[1] but it was very anxious to protect East Ruston.

Certain that Bacton was best in terms of their own objectives, and faced with opponents who could not agree among them-selves on an alternative, Shell and the Gas Council approached the public inquiry with confidence. There were individuals with-in the Shell organisation who, in other circumstances, might have put up a fight within the company for a more expensive inland site. But even they could not see that there was anything specially beautiful about the cliff-tops at Bacton. The Gas Council took exactly the same view.

Gas technology is a highly specialist field of knowledge: the world is divided into those who know, and those who do not know. Amenity is an altogether different matter. There are voices that carry weight and command respect; but there are no technical experts who can be refuted (if at all) only by other experts. Aesthetic judgements turn so much on subjective evalua-tion that one man's opinion may well seem to be as good as another's. If it should come to an argument about the aesthetic merits of Bacton as compared with the inland alternatives, a lack of expertise was not likely to place the applicants at any great disadvantage. By contrast, Shell and the Gas Council possessed a near monopoly of technical information about natural gas and its requirements. As it happened (and this is generally agreed by their opponents) Shell were not disposed to conceal what they knew from the objectors, and indeed they provided them with a good deal of the evidence that they subsequently used at the public inquiry. Even so, when it came to arguing about the tech-

---

[1] The cliffs between Bacton and Mundesley had, in fact, been notified as a S.S.S.I. in 1953. But since the scientific value of this stretch of coast-line had diminished, the Conservancy intended to deschedule the site.

nical merits of various sites, the planners and amenity organisations were clearly going to find it very difficult to challenge the
applicants on their own ground.

THE PUBLIC INQUIRY

The significance of the Bacton case was fully appreciated in
Whitehall. Natural gas was new, and so were natural gas terminals.[1] What these large complexes would be like, and what
impact they would make on the countryside and coastline, were
by no means clear. The Gas Council was insisting that it had to
have a coastal site, and though Shell were prepared to be more
flexible, they too were arguing that Bacton was unquestionably
the best location for the terminal. They were also saying that any
undue delay in settling on a site would have serious consequences
for the gas industry. On the other hand, the Norfolk County
Council, the amenity societies, and the agricultural interests were
arguing that Bacton was unacceptable, and that there were
almost certainly more suitable sites if only Shell and the Gas
Council could be persuaded to look for them. These were the
questions that the Minister of Housing and Local Government
wanted thrashed out at the public inquiry.

The inquiry – the longest and most expensive ever held in
Norfolk – opened on 14 February 1967 in Bacton Village Hall.
It was expected to last three days; in fact, it was to occupy twelve,
spread over a period of three weeks. The Inspector was Mr
A. J. Hunt, assisted by an assessor, Mr J. Beighton, of the Alkali
Inspectorate.

The first half of the proceedings was taken up with the case

[1] A natural gas terminal on a 44-acre site at Easington, on the Yorkshire
coast north of Spurn Head, was nearing completion when the Bacton
inquiry opened. This terminal was planned by British Petroleum and the
Gas Council in the spring of 1966, and in the excitement and euphoria
that followed the first gas strikes no one seems to have paid much attention to the possible effects of natural gas on the coastline. It was a small
and not very conspicuous site, there was no local branch of the C.P.R.E.
operating in the area, and B.P.'s proposals went through with little opposition. But for one early warning of the dangers of creating a 'visual disaster
area', see Peter R. Odell, 'What Will Gas Do to the East Coast?', *New
Society*, 5 May 1966.

for the applicants. They were represented by a formidable array of legal, administrative and technical experts. Leading counsel for Shell was Mr S. B. R. Cooke, Q.C. (who, it will be remembered, had appeared for the C.E.G.B. at the Holme Pierrepont inquiry in 1960). Among the witnesses called by Shell were Mr G. Williams, a Director and General Manager, and Mr K. H. Davison, their Operations Manager, together with a chartered surveyor, a chartered architect, a planning consultant and a traffic consultant. The Gas Council was represented by Sir Joseph Moloney, Q.C. Included among its witnesses were Mr D. E. Rooke, member of the Council for Production and Supplies, Mr W. J. Walters, Assistant Director (Production and Supplies Division), Mr F. E. Dean, the Technical Liaison Officer, and a chartered surveyor.

The Shell team first described their search for a suitable site following the discoveries in the Leman field. They explained why they had chosen Bacton, and why it so admirably suited their requirements. Arrangements for purchasing the site had been made, and all that was now needed was planning permission.

Shell and the Gas Council, they said, had examined the two sites put forward by the County Council, and found them both unsuitable. Hempstead, of course, had already been turned down much earlier, mainly because of the additional length of undersea pipeline entailed in bringing the gas round the north of Haisborough Sand. There was also a danger of flooding, and this was not a risk that could be taken with a plant of national importance. And even in terms of the County Council's preoccupations, the applicants argued, there were serious drawbacks to the Hempstead site. From an agricultural point of view, it was no better than Bacton. A number of separate holdings would be affected, and only one owner was willing to sell. Nor was the site entirely free from amenity objections. The nearby beaches were very popular, and the terminal would be close to the proposed holiday town of Sea Palling. It would also be near the fringes of the Broads, and close to an Area of Great Landscape Value.

As for the County Council's other proposal, East Ruston had all the shortcomings of an inland site, plus a few special disadvantages of its own. To convey untreated gas from the landfall to an inland terminal at East Ruston would mean more pipes and extra cost. Because the area was low-lying and marshy, they said, a substantial amount of filling would be required, and this would involve bringing large quantities of material to the site. It might take a long time to acquire the whole of the required area, for part of the East Ruston site was common land, and (as they pointed out) there would be the usual problem of extinguishing commoners' rights. Some good agricultural land would also have to be taken; several holdings would be affected, and none of the owners was willing to sell.

And quite apart from technical and economic considerations, there were other criticisms that could be levelled against East Ruston. Agriculture, amenity and scientific interest were not matters for which the applicants had any special responsibility; nevertheless, they felt in duty bound to draw the Inspector's attention to the disadvantages of the East Ruston site on all these counts. Certainly, their main objection to an inland site was the additional cost. But there was more to it than that. If 'wet' gas had to be carried some distance inland before being processed, the large number of pipes required would cut a wide swathe, perhaps 300 feet across, through the countryside. Within this swathe, equivalent to 35 acres of land in every mile, there was bound to be considerable interference with both agriculture and amenity. There was also the question of scientific interest. A terminal at East Ruston would impinge upon the S.S.S.I., and the applicants did not feel that they could guarantee that the fen and heath vegetation and associated fauna would not be harmed. East Ruston common, the applicants pointed out, was an important reserve of the basic food plant of the British swallow-tail butterfly, which survives only in Norfolk.

Whether the applicants would have been quite so solicitous about the fate of the swallow-tail butterfly had East Ruston suited their book in other respects is a matter for conjecture. However, they now found an unexpected and valuable ally in the Nature Conservancy, which naturally took exception to the idea of a gas terminal on their S.S.S.I., and sent a representative to the public inquiry to say so. The Conservancy's witness told the Inspector that the area in question formed the largest block of reclaimed heathland and acid fen left in this part of Norfolk. It was of great importance for research and field study, and was of special value to ecologists, since it displayed a clearly visible gradation of habitats. The Nature Conservancy, he said, might

conceivably have taken a different view had East Ruston been
the only possible site for the terminal. But patently this was not
the case. As far as the Conservancy could make out, the County
Council had put this site forward only because it was thought to
be of low agricultural value, and even that was not wholly true.

As the hearings went on, it soon became clear that at the heart
of the Bacton case, as in all the other controversies described in
this book, there was a genuine question of values. The problem
was spelt out by the Gas Council's representatives. The figures
must be taken on trust, and no one need agree with their con-
cluding value-judgement. But their analysis of the dilemma cannot be faulted. In essence, the Gas Council's argument was this.
Let it be agreed that the coastal site at Bacton had a certain
beauty. For the sake of the argument, let it also be agreed that a
natural gas terminal would somewhat detract from the beauty of
this stretch of coastline. It was quite impossible to put a monetary
value on attractive landscape; equally, it was impossible to
quantify any loss of value that might result from building the
terminal at Bacton. But the problem could be presented in
another way. It was quite easy to work out what it would cost to
preserve the Bacton site as it was. The cost was simply the additional expense that would be incurred in building the terminal
elsewhere. So that people could see for themselves what was
involved, the Gas Council had worked out the extra cost of the
alternatives that had been proposed. According to its calculations,
in hard cash, the value it was being asked to ascribe to the Bacton
site was this:

(i) if both the landfall and the terminal were at Hempstead,
     the extra cost of undersea pipeline, at about £200,000 a
     mile, would be something like £6 million;
(ii) if the landfall was at Bacton, and the terminal at East
     Ruston, the additional cost of conveying untreated gas
     four miles inland would be four times £684,000, or about
     £2¾ million; plus
(iii) the necessary increase in the length of the feeder main into
     the national grid, which would be about £70,000 in the
     case of East Ruston, and about £350,000 for Hempstead.

This was not all. Even if it was assumed that the costs in terms
of agricultural land taken out of use were identical for Bacton,

Hempstead and East Ruston (which was probably not the case, since the pipeline corridor running inland would almost certainly make East Ruston more costly than the other two sites on this score), there were still the unquantifiable amenity and scientific losses attached to East Ruston and Hempstead. It could very easily be forgotten that Bacton was not the only place where a terminal would result in costs that could not be measured in money terms. And, so far as Hempstead and East Ruston were concerned, there were, in addition, the incalculable costs of any delay in supplying natural gas into the national grid.

In short, it was the applicants' contention that the Bacton site could be preserved only at enormous cost, and the central issue for the inquiry was whether or not it was in the national interest that the resources represented by this very large cost should be used to divert the terminal away from Bacton. The Gas Council and Shell thought not.

Ranged against them were the Norfolk County Council (represented by the County Clerk, Mr F. P. Boyce), the National Parks Commission (represented by Mr M. Chavasse), the C.P.R.E., the National Trust and the Norfolk Association of Amenity Societies (all represented by Viscount Colville of Culross), the Country Landowners' Association (represented by Mr M. Gregory), and the National Farmers' Union (represented by Mr J. Christie). The Smallburgh Rural District Council, which disliked the Bacton site, but was prepared to accept it if the applicants could show that there was no suitable alternative where the land was of inferior quality, was represented by its Clerk, Mr A. E. Crisp.

Everyone now agreed that the landfall had to be at Bacton. What none of the objectors would accept was the terminal on the cliff-top site there. As the Local Planning Authority concerned, the Norfolk County Council led the opposition. They argued that many of the errors perpetrated during the Industrial Revolution had occurred because the pattern of development had been determined solely by commercial expediency. The country should not make the same mistakes again. On this occasion, it would be quite wrong to rush into a hasty decision. Intelligent planning was needed; this called for careful investigation and took time. They believed that the dangers inherent in a short delay had been exaggerated; the applicants were holding a pistol at the head of everyone who opposed them. If there had been any delay up to this point, the fault lay entirely with the developers, and not with the County Council, because Shell and the Gas Council had not submitted their planning applications until well into the autumn, although Shell had begun work on the technical drawings as early as June 1966.

It was perfectly true that pipe-laying could take place only during the summer. But it was misleading to suggest that everything else had to wait on the approval of a site for the terminal. There was nothing to prevent work going ahead on pipe-laying along the route between the production wells and Haisborough Sand, and this accounted for two-thirds of the total distance involved. In fact, since the Bacton landfall was generally acceptable, the pipe could be laid all the way to the coast. The Gas Council, too, could begin the necessary work on its feeder main between the national grid and North Walsham, for this stretch of pipeline would have to be put down wherever the terminal was eventually sited. If the applicants went ahead to this extent, there need be no risk to gas supplies in the winter of 1968–9, even if they were obliged to spend a little longer on the search for a suitable inland site for the processing plant.

According to the County Council, it had now been established beyond doubt that a coastal site for the terminal was not absolutely essential. Canadian experience demonstrated quite clearly that untreated gas could be piped inland for some distance. There was certainly no need to odorise the gas immediately after it had come ashore (this operation was to be carried out by the Gas Council on its site), for a fracture between the landfall and the terminal was most unlikely. Even if one did occur, a gas leak would hardly be a danger to life, for the pipes would here be running under uninhabited fields. As for the extra cost, the expense of bringing the sea pipes four miles inland would be no more than would have been incurred had the production wells been a mile or so further out to sea: and an additional mile out to sea would not have been given a second thought. Furthermore, the County Council could not see why Shell should not use larger, and fewer, pipes to convey the untreated gas from the landfall to an inland terminal. This would reduce the cost of pipe-laying and the disturbance to agriculture and amenity. As the Norfolk County Council saw it, the applicants were taking altogether too tragic a view of the difficulties and drawbacks of an

inland site. And whilst the additional costs of an inland site might
sound impressive, they ought to be seen in perspective: these
extra costs would be very small indeed in relation to the total
expenditure on the project.

As the inquiry went on, the County Council's Hempstead site
gradually dropped out of the reckoning, for even they conceded
its shortcomings. But they were still not persuaded that East
Ruston would be an inferior choice to Bacton. Much of the land
required was of no agricultural value, and although some piling
and draining would be necessary, this, they thought, should not
prove too difficult. Part of the S.S.S.I. could be preserved; or
alternatively, the site could be descheduled. Tree planting would
adequately screen a terminal at East Ruston, whereas (they
claimed) effective screening was simply not feasible at Bacton.

With the Norfolk County Council apparently so favourably
disposed towards East Ruston, there was a certain amount of
surprise all round when, on the eighth day of the inquiry, the
County's Chief Planning Officer suddenly produced a new suggestion. The objectors had been maintaining all along that there
were numerous inland sites if only Shell and the Gas Council
would look again. Where were these sites?, the applicants' counsel
had asked. By this stage the County Council had an answer.
They were now proposing another inland site – later to be known
as site C – about two and a half miles south of Bacton, in the
Witton Heath area near North Walsham. Admittedly, it was
rather late in the day to be bringing forward a new site. But, said
the Chief Planning Officer, largely as a result of what they had
heard at the inquiry, they now had a much better idea of what
Shell and the Gas Council really needed. The applicants, he
suggested, ought to co-operate with the County Council in a
joint search in the Witton Heath district for a site that would be
the best compromise from everyone's point of view.

The Gas Council, it will be remembered, had worked out how
much it would cost to preserve the Bacton site intact. It was left
to the National Parks Commission to present these figures in a
rather different light. The Commission called a scientific consultant who effectively drew attention to the very small incremental cost of an inland site. He argued that if the 30-inch sea
pipe was to be thirty-four miles long, and was to cost £200,000 a
mile, and if the cost of a similar pipe for untreated gas under land

was £50,000 a mile, then the inland extension of such a pipe would add 0·74 per cent per mile extension to the total expenditure. Whilst the Commission agreed that costs had to be kept down wherever possible, an increase of this magnitude was quite insignificant in the context of the enormous sums that were involved in producing and marketing natural gas.

It was not really the responsibility of the Commission to investigate alternative sites. Nevertheless it had evidently done a little exploring on its own account, for it too had a new proposal for the Inspector's consideration. The National Parks Commission's site was on the southern, that is to say, the inland side of the coast road, extending westwards from the site earmarked by the Gas Council for its operations.

The other three amenity bodies represented at the inquiry, the C.P.R.E., the National Trust, and the Norfolk Association of Amenity Societies (an amalgamation of societies representing between them over 3,000 members), all opposed the Bacton site, and drew attention to the damage that the terminal would inflict on this unspoiled stretch of coastline. The amenity objection, they claimed, was by no means flimsy or trivial. Part of the site in dispute lay within an A.O.N.B., and the proposed development would have a much wider impact on the coastal scene than had been suggested by the applicants. The cost of preserving amenity here, they argued, ought to be evaluated against the total cost of exploiting natural gas. And in making this evaluation, everyone ought to pay attention to the diminishing amount of accessible coastline that remained, and the pressure to which it was continuously being subjected. The Bacton case constituted an important precedent, for if on this occasion the Local Planning Authority failed to prevent development in an unspoiled coastal area, it would become increasingly difficult to stop all kinds of further industrial expansion. The coastal site at Hempstead they thought should be avoided. East Ruston was much to be preferred to Bacton, and any extra expense incurred in developing that site would be wholly justified if Bacton could thereby be saved.

Like all the other objectors, the amenity societies claimed that Shell and the Gas Council had exaggerated the consequences of delay. They also criticised the applicants for failing to make contingency plans to deal with the situation if permission for Bacton should be refused. All along Shell and the Gas Council had worked on the assumption that their application was bound to be successful, and that the outcome was a foregone conclusion. If the applicants were really worried about the effect of delay, the remedy was for them to take up the County Council's offer and co-operate in a joint search for an acceptable alternative, either at East Ruston or in the area between Bacton and North Walsham, in the vicinity of the County Council's new proposal.

The other major amenity body represented at the inquiry – the Nature Conservancy – was there not to object to Bacton but to oppose East Ruston. Sites of Special Scientific Interest, the Conservancy claimed, were of immense value to the nation; and theirs was a kind of value that would last a great deal longer than supplies of natural gas.

Finally, voicing the agricultural objections, there were the local branches of the Country Landowners' Association and the National Farmers' Union. They both opposed the Bacton site. But so much of Norfolk is first-class farmland that they found it difficult to suggest other sites that were not equally open to objection on agricultural grounds. The C.L.A. argued that the processing ought to be carried out at sea, an idea that Shell had considered but rejected at a very early stage. They also doubted whether an inland site for the terminal would require such a wide swathe as had been suggested. But if they were wrong about this, and if running the pipes inland really would cause as much disturbance as the applicants had claimed, then they would oppose any inland site. In these circumstances, they said, the applicants ought to choose a site on 'unproductive coastal land'. Further than this helpful suggestion the C.L.A. were not prepared to go. To complete the tangled skein of likes and dislikes, the N.F.U. were so much opposed to Hempstead and East Ruston that it considered even Bacton preferable to either of these two sites.

Positive support for the Bacton site came from the Bacton Parish Council and from the County Councillor for the district, who claimed that he reflected the views of the local people better than the County Council. Most of the people who lived and worked in the locality would welcome the terminal, he said. In his view there was a pressing need for additional employment opportunities in the district, which was far too dependent on agriculture and the seasonal holiday trade.

The public inquiry came to an end on 3 March 1967. To the applicants, who had made great play with the dire consequences of any undue delay, it must have seemed a very long inquiry indeed. Nor were their worries over yet.

'THERE'S NO HARM IN LOOKING'

The Inspector reported to the Minister of Housing and Local Government on 21 April 1967. He began by disposing of the problem of the landfall. No one seriously disputed, he said, that the gas should come ashore at Bacton. The only alternative mentioned had been Hempstead. This possibility the Inspector rejected, mainly because the extra costs of sea-pipes could not be justified, and also because the successive passage of these pipes through the coastal defences would be more difficult and more costly than at Bacton. There was no doubt in his mind that Bacton was the right landfall. By sheer chance, it so happened that on the cliff-top immediately above the most suitable landfall there was a large tract of land admirably suitable for a natural gas terminal. Unquestionably, on grounds of cost, convenience, and technical efficiency this was the best available site.

On the other hand, the Inspector had been impressed with the aesthetic value of this expanse of open farmland between the coast road and the cliffs. He acknowledged that any individual judgement on what is outstanding in the way of natural beauty must necessarily be subjective; but he did not dissent from the National Parks Commission's decision to include much of the area between Bacton and Mundesley within the proposed A.O.N.B. He agreed that the land here merited protection against all but essential development. It was certain, he went on, that the proposed installations would constitute a massive and alien intrusion into the coastal landscape, and that they would seriously affect the local amenities. Bacton, then, was an excellent choice. The difficulty was that there were also excellent reasons for rejecting it.

Turning to the question of alternatives, the Inspector found that a coastal site was not absolutely essential for the terminal. Nevertheless, it had to be recognised that to separate the terminal from the landfall, even if technically feasible, was bound to be more costly and less convenient. And putting his finger upon the crucial problem of values that lay at the centre of the case, he went on: 'In essence, consideration of any inland alternative amounts to setting a price upon coastal preservation'. Value-judgements of this kind are matters more for Ministers than Inspectors, and he quickly moved on to other aspects of the case. But an earlier sentence in his Report, in the section entitled 'Findings of Fact', does provide a clue to the way in which his mind was working. 'Although large in itself', he had written, 'the extra cost of taking the raw gas pipes one mile inland would be a very small percentage of the total pipelaying costs, and an even smaller percentage of the total capital involved in the exploitation of the resources.'

The County Council's alternatives were given short shrift. The Hempstead site was dismissed because it would clearly be inconsistent with a landfall at Bacton. The East Ruston alternative, said the Inspector, had 'little intrinsic merit'; he could not accept that taking a pipeline swathe so far across country would be justified. As to the County's third proposal – the Witton Heath site – this had been introduced so late in the inquiry, and he had been told so little about it, that he offered no comment.

He appreciated that undue delay in finding a suitable site for the terminal would have an adverse effect on the gas industry as a whole, and would postpone the expected savings to be made on imported oil. But since everyone now agreed that Bacton was the right landfall, so far as he could see, there was nothing to prevent the producers from beginning to lay their sea pipes as planned. The Gas Council could also go ahead with laying most of its feeder main from the national grid.

Not convinced that all the practicable inland sites had yet been investigated, the Inspector took it upon himself to suggest that further explorations should be undertaken in the immediate hinterland of the Bacton landfall, in the direction of the route planned for the feeder main. Having toured the area on 7 March 1967, he had singled out two areas that he thought would be worth looking at again. The first was to the south and west of the Gas Council's proposed Bacton site; the second lay somewhat further inland, and south-west of the hamlet of Paston Green.

When they write Reports, Inspectors do not set out to describe their own mental processes. But in this instance, the Inspector appears to have taken the view that whilst the applicants had made out an excellent case for siting the terminal at Bacton, their arguments were not totally conclusive for the simple reason that he had not yet heard all the arguments for and against all the reasonable alternatives. This was not the fault of the applicants, of course; the situation had arisen because the opponents of the Bacton site had failed to put the best of the alternative possibilities before the inquiry. That the Inspector should go out of his way to do part of the objectors' job for them is a clear indication of the importance that he believed the Minister attached to preserving the coastline. It also points to an unfortunate characteristic that public inquiries share with courts of law: the 'right' answer in the public interest may not be forthcoming if one of the adversaries fails to make the best of his own case.

THE REOPENED INQUIRY

On 9 May 1967 the notables returned to Bacton for a further four-day inquiry. This time the Inspector's job was not so much to hear the arguments for and against Bacton but rather to collect information about the two alternatives that he himself had put forward. The reopened inquiry was to underline an important truth about planning problems of this kind. Alternative sites proposed by objectors (or, as here, by Inspectors) may be not only more expensive in terms of money; they may also involve significant, though unquantifiable, amenity costs of their own. It is one thing to argue that X should be preferred to Y if X (though more costly) inflicts no appreciable damage on the landscape or the environment; it is quite another matter if X *also* seems to be open to strong amenity objections, for then there is another, albeit immeasurable, cost to be thrown into the scales against it.

The general location of the Inspector's two new sites – subsequently referred to as sites A and B – has already been described. Site A, which partly overlapped the Gas Council's original application area, was about 360 acres in extent and lay in a shallow valley running up from Bacton Green towards Paston Green. It comprised top-class agricultural land, and was surrounded by attractive developments at Paston, Paston Green and in the vicinity of Bacton Hall. The centre of the site was about a mile from the coast. Site B was further inland, and consisted of an area of some 250 acres extending southwards from Paston Green. This, too, was first-class arable land, with substantial and well-maintained farm buildings and the attractive village of Knapton to the north of the site.

Bacton had been granted a reprieve, and this was welcome news as far as the Norfolk County Council were concerned. At the same time, they had been disappointed to learn that their own alternative (site C) was no longer in the running. Early in April, when they discovered that the farmer who owned 170 acres of this site was willing to negotiate for the sale of his land, site C began to look an even better proposition, and after a special meeting of the Planning Committee on 11 April it was decided to ask the Minister of Housing and Local Government to widen the scope of the inquiry to include an examination of the County Council's proposal. This the Minister agreed to do. Site C was even further inland than sites A and B. Just outside the town of North Walsham, it was about 540 acres in extent, and about half of it consisted of Bacton Wood, an experimental plantation that had belonged to the Forestry Commission since 1953.

Early in the inquiry yet another site was suggested by the National Parks Commission. This was a composite area of about 170 acres, comprising parts of the Inspector's sites A and B. At the first inquiry there had been no love lost between the applicants and the National Parks Commission, and when the Commission produced this new site after the proceedings had opened there were vigorous protests from Shell and the Gas Council. They complained that they had already gone to a great deal of trouble in studying the feasibility of three alternatives, and that it was unreasonable to expect them to investigate a fourth at such short notice. The Inspector, however, decided that he would not be justified in preventing the National Parks Commission from making representations about its composite proposal.

The applicants were not impressed with any of these alternatives. At the outset, Shell's representatives reminded the Inspector of all the disadvantages that would inevitably be associated with any inland site. There would be a considerable delay in making natural gas available, particularly if (as was only too likely) Shell had to secure compulsory purchase orders against landowners who objected to having a pipeline corridor under their farms.

Equally important, there was all the additional expenditure that would be necessary. As compared with Bacton, Shell estimated that the extra costs involved would be £0·75 million for site A, £1·25 million for site B, and £1·5 million for site C. When other producers arrived on the scene these costs ought probably to be multiplied by three. Something like 80 per cent of the extra cost would be accounted for by the additional pipelines that an inland terminal would require. These sums, claimed Shell, were very substantial, even in the context of the total investment in North Sea gas; and they were the more unpalatable for being avoidable. They would fall entirely upon the producers, for the extra expense would not be reflected in the price of natural gas to the consumer.[1]

Even if they did build the terminal inland, the landfall would still have to be at Bacton. They would still have to install a 350-foot radio mast and other equipment on the cliff-top there, and altogether something over 30 acres would still be needed. In other words, now that it had been agreed that the landfall had to be at Bacton, there was bound to be a certain amount of interference with the beauties of the coastline (such as they were) at this particular spot. If they then established the terminal further inland, on sites A, B or C, the extension of the sea pipes would be certain to create a great deal of disturbance, far more disturbance, in fact, than had at first been thought. It now seemed that the sea pipes would have to be laid further apart than they had originally believed, so that the swathe required for five sea pipes might now take up as much as 42 acres in every mile they travelled inland.

Nor were any of the new sites technically suitable. At site A

---

[1] For many years it has been generally acknowledged in the business world that large and well-established private companies ought to behave in a socially responsible way, even when there is no direct gain for themselves, and profits and dividends suffer as a result. Nowadays, the notion that private industry ought sometimes to incur 'avoidable' costs (however unpalatable) in the interests of amenity is widely accepted. In fairness to Shell, it should be said that their protest at this point was hardly characteristic of the company's behaviour throughout the controversy. This unfortunate (and decidedly tactless) *cri de cœur* may have been in part attributable to sheer pique. As the oil companies saw it, the Government and the Gas Council had driven a hard bargain over the price of natural gas. Some of Shell's representatives evidently found it all the more exasperating that additional, and quite substantial, social costs might also fall wholly on the company.

there was a fifty-foot slope on the land, and as this slope ran contrary to the logical flow for the gas, flow reversals within the plant would have to be built at increased cost. Earthworks and terracing would be needed, and a comprehensive drainage system would have to be provided. Site B would create very similar technical problems, for here the slope was if anything steeper than at site A. What was worse, a number of public rights of way ran across the site, and these would have to be closed. The necessary procedures might take up to six months, and perhaps longer if there were objections. Site C was even more unsuitable than A and B. It was three miles from the centre of the site to the landfall, and the site itself was very uneven, full of ridges and hillocks. Those areas that were reasonably level were widely separated, and a great deal of earth-moving would be necessary.

Clearly, it was for these reasons that Shell had rejected the three alternative sites. However, the company's representatives also took the opportunity of pointing out that sites A, B and C were themselves by no means free from amenity objections. Site A, they argued, was no better than Bacton, for more than half of it fell within the proposed A.O.N.B. It was ringed by the hamlets of Paston, Bacton Hall, Edingthorpe and Paston Green, and the physical impact of the plant on these rural communities would be very serious. Site B, they claimed, was, if anything, less suitable than Bacton from a planning and landscape point of view. Included within the site were 35 acres of the proposed A.O.N.B., and to build the terminal here would undoubtedly disturb the amenities of the farming hamlets of Swafield, Old Hall Street, Edingthorpe Green, Edingthorpe Street, Paston Green, and Knapton.

As for site C (the proposal put forward by the Norfolk County Council, the Local Planning Authority), this was totally unsuitable on planning and amenity grounds. Bacton Wood was much enjoyed by the inhabitants of North Walsham; far more people visited it, they claimed, than the cliff-top. With its changing levels of woodland and farmland, and with a canal winding through the valley, this was a most attractive area. To build the terminal here would make it visible over a wide area, and would also detract from the amenities of properties on the fringes of North Walsham.

In sum, Shell's case was essentially unchanged. Planning permission for Bacton ought to be given, because it could not be said that the preservation of this particular stretch of coastline was so vital that it justified the extra cost, inconvenience, disturbance, and loss of amenity that any of the other sites would necessarily entail.

The Gas Council adopted much the same approach. It rejected all the new proposals that had come forward, claiming that these fresh alternatives were just as much open to amenity objections as Bacton. Site C, in fact, was the most beautiful of all those so far considered. The scenery in this area, between North Walsham and the coast, was an attractive blend of first-class agricultural land, interspersed with occasional woodland and heath. Remote from the main lines of communication, and inhabited by a mainly agrarian population, it was an area of great charm and tranquility. By contrast, the Gas Council suggested, the coast itself was rather bleak and uninteresting, and the actual application site was part of a stretch of coastline that was already to some extent marred by holiday development and bungalow sprawl. The Gas Council also drew the Inspector's attention to what it claimed was a significant shift in public opinion. Now that people in the area fully appreciated the implications of an inland location, with all the disturbance that it would create for agriculture and amenity, there had been a surge of feeling in favour of developing the Bacton site.

There was certainly some foundation for this claim. The Smallburgh R.D.C. had never been wholehearted in their opposition to Bacton. When it became clear what the alternatives were, Bacton began to appear an eminently sensible choice. What particularly worried the Smallburgh R.D.C. was the substantial loss of good agricultural land that would inevitably occur, as a result of the pipeline swathe, if an inland site was selected. At their meeting on 14 April the R.D.C. reached the conclusion that all the alternatives put forward fell within an area that was typical of the east Norfolk landscape, and as good an example of rural England as was to be found anywhere. And with the disadvantages of the alternatives looming so large, any aesthetic virtues they might once have been prepared to grant to Bacton vanished without trace. The original application site was now described as a 'windswept plateau', facing the North Sea, and suitably remote from human habitation.

The agricultural and landowning interests had come round to a similar view. The N.F.U. and C.L.A. had never approved of the Bacton site. On the other hand, they now thought that it would be preferable to any of the alternatives, because all the other possibilities would have had a far greater impact on agriculture. The owners of the Bacton site – the East Anglian Real Property Company – also opposed all the alternatives. They had agreed, somewhat reluctantly, to sell their land at Bacton if planning permission were given for the terminal there. Now they were faced with the prospect of having to surrender a small irregular area at the landfall, which would be highly inconvenient, and into the bargain suffering additional disturbance as a result of the pipeline swathe, besides losing even more land if site C was chosen. In the company's submission Bacton was preferable to sites A, B and C because to use the coastal site there would cause least disturbance.

Finally, in written representations, the Paston Parish Council opposed sites A and B because of their harmful effects on agriculture and the rural surroundings, and the parish of Knapton opposed site B on the grounds that it would mean taking more beautiful and better agricultural land than at Bacton, and would disturb more people.

If, to some of the earlier objectors, Bacton looked an altogether better idea, now that the drawbacks of the alternatives were more apparent, the Norfolk County Council had not budged at all. They were still firmly opposed to the Bacton site. In one respect, however, they did see eye to eye with everyone else; they totally rejected the Inspector's sites A and B. It is clear that the overriding priority with the County Council had become the preservation of the coastline, and sites A and B were still much too close to the coast for their liking. Only if the terminal went considerably further inland would they be satisfied, and this was why they were putting forward site C, near North Walsham. Having settled on site C for this reason, there were other advantages to which they could point. Sites A and B were good-quality agricultural land; site C was not, and it was the only one of the three to which the Ministry of Agriculture, Fisheries and Food did not object. Part of it was owned by a willing seller; the rest was Crown property, belonging to the Forestry Commission, which could readily be made available if the Government so wished. It was well clear of the immediate coastal hinterland, so much enjoyed and appreciated by local people and holiday-makers. In any case, the County Council were thinking of permitting North Walsham to expand considerably in the future; if that happened, a gas terminal just outside the town could be co-ordinated with this expansion so as to lessen its visual impact. There was a pleasant wood on the site, it was true. So much the better, for Bacton Wood might well provide a suitable background, as well as completely screening the terminal from the east.

They did not deny that to build the terminal on site C would be more expensive, though they doubted whether the additional cost would be as heavy as had been suggested. Since no figures for the total cost of the project had ever been supplied, they could only guess what the cost of siting the terminal inland would be if it was expressed as a proportion of the total expenditure on the operation. But the chances were that it would make hardly any difference to the producers' selling price for gas; probably the difference would be calculable only in terms of several decimal places of a penny per therm. The Minister of Housing and Local Government would have the relevant statistics. It was his duty to save the coastline from further damage and to conserve good agricultural land. The question facing the Minister, suggested the County Council, was this: in the context of the overall cost of making natural gas available, could some very small incremental cost be justified in the interests of amenity and agriculture? The County Council had reached the conclusion that the extra cost of developing the terminal on site C would be wholly worth while.

The Norfolk County Council's choice of site C was supported by the National Parks Commission. Reluctantly, the Commission now agreed that some installations, including the radio mast, would have to be sited on the cliff-top at Bacton. It was also prepared to concede that Bacton might be the best site for the terminal from the applicants' point of view. But the Commission still thought that the Bacton site was 'both striking and rare'. All three inland sites now under consideration were more suitable, and so far as it could see, the applicants' objections to these three sites were not all convincing. Like the County Council, the National Parks Commission argued that the extra cost of an inland site would be very small as a percentage of the total expenditure involved in bringing North Sea gas ashore. The effects of the swathes, and of pipe-laying operations, had been exaggerated; with proper spacing, and with careful attention to the routing, there need be little damage to amenity and only temporary damage to agriculture.

As the National Parks Commission saw it, there were no insuperable obstacles to building the terminal on any of the three inland sites. Site C, they thought, was the most suitable of the alternatives, even though this would mean sacrificing the recreational and visual amenities of Bacton Wood. If site C was not selected, its second preference was for a composite area, made up of parts of sites A and B. Provided that enough trees were kept, with adequate landscaping the terminal could be built here without serious detriment to holiday or recreational pursuits. The Commission's third choice was site B. Site A it disliked, though even that was preferable to Bacton.

In the interests of a united front, the C.P.R.E., the National Trust and the Norfolk Association of Amenity Societies took a similar line. They, too, were now prepared to accept the County Council's site C. The local preservationists had indeed been forced into a highly disagreeable corner, as they well knew. Had the circumstances been different, they would almost certainly have been fighting tooth and nail to prevent any kind of development on sites A, B or C. If, for reasons of their own, the applicants had originally chosen one of these sites, the C.P.R.E., for example, would certainly have objected. And had there been a public inquiry into sites A, B or C their spokesman would doubtless have described these areas in glowing colours, pointing out that the developers were proposing to desecrate some of the most beautiful countryside in Norfolk. But, of course, circumstances alter cases, and the amenity organisations now argued that all three inland sites suggested were preferable to Bacton, for however charming they might be, they were by no means unique in the Norfolk countryside, and certainly did not merit the same concern as the cliff-top at Bacton. They agreed that Bacton Wood was 'pleasant', and much appreciated by the people who went there; but it could hardly be compared with the value of the Bacton site, which was seen by so many visitors using the coast road.

If the reopened inquiry had demonstrated anything, it was that nobody approved of the two new suggestions put forward by the

Inspector. The applicants had rejected them, and some of the objectors preferred even Bacton to sites A and B. The only alternative acceptable to those who opposed Bacton on amenity grounds was the County Council's site C.[1] However, this was easily the most expensive of the three, it was by no means free from amenity objections, and it was the site that Shell and the Gas Council appeared to like least of all. When the reopened inquiry came to an end on 12 May 1967, the Inspector clearly had a formidable problem of judgement on his hands.

THE VERDICT

The Inspector presented his report to the Minister of Housing and Local Government on 23 May 1967. There was no question, he wrote, that on grounds of cost, convenience, technical efficiency, and availability Bacton was a uniquely suitable site for the terminal. But suppose, for the sake of argument, the treatment plant was built on an inland site: what would be the consequences?

First, there was no escaping the fact that even if the terminal was sited inland, the applicants would still require an area on the cliff-top at Bacton for the landfall installations. The need for such an area would represent an additional claim on first-class agricultural land, though – apart from the radio mast – these installations themselves would have very little effect on the coastal scene.

Second, there was the contentious issue of the pipeline swathes. The Inspector agreed that if a number of pipes had to be laid

---

[1] The Forestry Commission, which stood to lose its plantation at Bacton Wood if the Inspector were to recommend site C, was represented at the inquiry by a spokesman who gave evidence only on matters of fact. The 'facts', as presented to the Inspector, showed clearly enough that the Commission did not take kindly to the prospect of giving up its wood. Bacton Wood, he pointed out, contained fourteen genera of conifer, many of them rare; the replacement value of the plantings was nearly £46,000; and there was an important insect and bird population associated with the district and with the varied flora of the wood. Visitors from North Walsham and Norwich came to Bacton Wood in large numbers; and – an exquisite touch – many who enjoyed its quiet beauty were holiday-makers seeking refuge from the crowded Norfolk beaches.

successively over a period of time there would certainly be considerable disturbance to agriculture. But he did not see why it should result in any permanent damage. So far as the effect on amenity was concerned, a great deal would depend on the nature of the countryside traversed by the pipeline, and the actual route chosen. If it became necessary to fell a large number of trees, the effect of the pipeline corridor would indeed be serious. For these reasons, and also because of the extra costs involved, an inland pipeline swathe would require adequate justification.

Third, there were the agricultural considerations. Little or no distinction could really be made between the arable farmland at Bacton and at sites A and B. But in the case of Bacton, the necessary land could be taken from one farm without affecting the viability of that holding, whereas it was impossible to take land on sites A and B without inflicting serious hardship on the farmers and smallholders there. As to site C, the effect on land of inferior quality and on the farmers, would largely depend on the location of the plant within the area as a whole.

Fourth, there was the question of additional expenditure. An inland site for the terminal would certainly cost a good deal more. Two views had been put forward at the inquiry. The applicants had argued that all unnecessary expenditure ought to be avoided. On the other side, the objectors had suggested that the extra cost would represent only a small addition to the total capital sum invested in the exploitation of North Sea gas, and this was a reasonable price to pay in the interests of preserving unspoilt coastal amenities. The Inspector doubted whether these two views were as divergent as at first sight they appeared. The central question to be decided was whether or not the advantages of keeping the terminal off the coast made it worth moving to an inland site.

Fifth, if the terminal were sited inland, this too would have a detrimental effect on the local amenities. Of the two possibilities which he himself had suggested, the Inspector recognised that site A lay within an attractive valley, and was overlooked from the coast road. It could also be regarded as part of the coastal scene. The nearby hamlet of Paston was well screened, but it would nevertheless be affected. On the other hand, at site A the installations would be set against rising ground, and, as with all the alternatives, adequate landscaping would be much more practicable than on the more exposed application site at Bacton. Site B, in the Inspector's opinion, was outside the immediate coastal environment. But this was a very pleasant rural area, and the western part of the site was relatively high and fairly prominent, though here again adequate landscaping ought to be feasible. Development on the National Parks Commission's composite area, comprising parts of sites A and B, would be less prominent than on sites A and B. Since this possibility had been introduced after the inquiry opened, however, it had not been adequately investigated by the applicants. As to site C, the trouble here was that the longer pipeline swathes could hardly fail to injure the intervening countryside. Within the site, it seemed certain that Bacton Wood would become increasingly significant, both as a feature of the landscape and as a place of public resort. If the schematic layout put before the inquiry was all that was possible, parts of the installations would be prominent, and the value of the woodland as a forestry plantation and for public enjoyment would be prejudiced. Greater use of the woodland itself would make construction more difficult and would virtually destroy the wood and its amenities. On the other hand, in a general way, the Inspector agreed that a screened site on the periphery of North Walsham would have certain advantages.

When all the facts had been set out, and all the arguments rehearsed, there was no avoiding a personal value-judgement. In the Inspector's own words: 'The basic issue is whether preservation in the main of the coastal amenities of the application sites can be justified at the expense of loss of rural amenities, hardship and disturbance, additional costs and reduced technical efficiency, all of which would result from use of any of the inland alternatives.'

In the Inspector's judgement these consequences could *not* be justified, and in his view least harm would be done if all the necessary installations were concentrated at the Bacton landfall. As a footnote, he added that in arriving at this conclusion he had not taken into account the delay that might occur if the applicants were obliged to develop any of the inland sites, though, in his opinion, if the Bacton site was rejected, the chances were that the entire programme for making natural gas available would be disrupted.

The Minister of Housing and Local Government announced

his decision on 15 June 1967. Subject to a number of detailed conditions,[1] he accepted the Inspector's recommendations, and therefore decided to grant outline planning permission for the terminal on the Bacton site.

[1] The Minister expressly excluded from his planning consent any chimney for burning off sulphur impurities from the natural gas. Since the Leman field is relatively free from sulphur, Shell had no need for such a chimney on their site. Subsequently, however, the Phillips Petroleum Company discovered 'sour' gas in the Hewett field; this gas *did* require a sulphur-burning chimney, and a fresh planning application had to be submitted. To the indignation of many of the local residents and amenity societies, in July 1968 the Norfolk County Council agreed to a chimney 175 feet high on the Bacton site. As Lord Molson (the chairman of the C.P.R.E.) pointed out in a letter to *The Times* of 27 July 1968, opposition to the chimney was hopeless because by this time the first stage of the terminal complex had already been built. 'It is most unfortunate', he observed, 'that the first application considered was the one to which the least objection could be raised and that the Minister's decision was issued at a time when he could have only an incomplete appreciation of the facts. If the order of the applications had been reversed the outcome might well have been very different.' It is only fair to add that an independent firm of consulting engineers had advised the County Council that with a stack of this height there would be no hazard or danger to health, livestock, crops or property from chimney emissions. Nevertheless, the original arguments against the Bacton site on grounds of damage to visual amenity would have been considerably stronger had it been known that a tall chimney was to be erected on the cliff top. 'Piecemeal' decision-making of this kind is less likely to occur in future as a result of the provision made for Planning Inquiry Commissions in the 1968 Town and Country Planning Act.

6 Abingdon and the Gasholder

It seems that everyone is prepared to mouth the
cause of amenity; but when it comes to money, no
one is prepared to do anything about it.

The Mayor of Abingdon,
April 1967

ABINGDON is a prosperous old market town on the Thames,
six miles south of Oxford. There was a settlement here in Saxon
times, and the fourteenth-century Benedictine abbey was once
among the most important in England. As late as 1870 it was
still the county town of Berkshire, though in size and importance
it was being steadily outstripped by Reading, further south on
the Great Western Railway. Indeed, the first industrial revolution left Abingdon virtually untouched, so that by the mid-1960s
its population was still no more than about 15,000. The older
part of the town centre, particularly the area near the river, has
a mellow, settled look. In recent years, planning authorities have
become increasingly sensitive to the damage that traffic and unsuitable development can inflict on the mature urban environment of ancient towns like Abingdon.

But the residents of picturesque old towns, no less than anyone
else, require an adequate supply of gas. Abingdon falls within the
district supplied by the Southern Gas Board, one of the twelve
Area Boards responsible for the manufacture and distribution of
gas in Great Britain. Planning ahead, in the course of 1965 the
S.G.B. came to the conclusion that Abingdon was one of the
towns that would need extra storage capacity in time for the
winter of 1968–9.[1]

Storage has always been something of a problem for the gas

[1] The chief documentary sources for the following account are: Berkshire
County Council, Minutes and Reports; *Hansard*; *The Times*; *Oxford
Mail*; *Reading Mercury*.

industry. As between winter and summer, demand naturally fluctuates a good deal; but to cope with changes in demand by varying output is hardly practicable, because this approach would mean installing expensive stand-by plant which would be in use only at peak periods. The traditional method of storage is the familiar gasholder, a structure that could never be described as a thing of beauty. There are alternatives, one of which is to store the gas in relatively inconspicuous high-pressure cylinders. These cigar-shaped cylinders may be as much as 160 feet in length; but their great advantage, from an aesthetic point of view, is that they need stand no more than 20 feet or so above ground level. Unfortunately, this system of storage and supply is considerably more expensive (both to install and to run) than the conventional method. Although the S.G.B. briefly considered putting a high-pressure system in Abingdon, they never gave this possibility serious consideration, because right from the start it was obvious that a high-pressure system would be very much more costly than a standard gasholder.

The choice of site for the new gasholder presented no difficulty, for it happened that the S.G.B. already owned what seemed to them to be the ideal spot. Quite close to the centre of the town, in the middle of an industrial area (zoned as such on the Development Plan), and next to some old railway sidings and an 80-foot-high grain silo, this particular patch of land – known as 'the vineyard' – had long been connected with the gas industry. Over the years, the vineyard had become the nodal point for the whole distribution system in Abingdon. From 1880 to 1930 it housed the old Abingdon gasworks, and there had always been gasholders here until the last was demolished in 1965.

In 1930, under the Oxford Gas Order of that year, the Oxford Gas Company took over the local undertaking from the Abingdon Gas, Light and Coke Company. When the gas industry was nationalised in 1948 the Oxford Gas Company, and with it the vineyard, came under the control of the newly-constituted S.G.B. Soon afterwards, the S.G.B. decided to build a gasholder on the vineyard site. They planned to erect it just outside the area previously occupied by the gasworks; that is to say, the gasholder would not have been built on what was statutorily defined as the S.G.B.'s operational land. The significance of this will shortly become apparent. Discussions were held with the Abingdon

Borough Council, the Berkshire County Council and the Royal
Fine Art Commission, and in 1951 the local authorities granted
planning consent for the proposed gasholder. Apparently, there
was no local hostility, no controversy, and no one suggested a
public inquiry. However, for reasons of their own, the S.G.B.
never built the gasholder, though, of course, they still had planning permission to do so if at some later date they should decide
to take it up.

In its efforts to keep pace with a demand that has risen rapidly
since about 1960, the gas industry in Britain has faced serious
engineering problems all over the country. On occasions, equipment has broken down under the strain. In the winter of 1964–5,
for example, a plant failure in the West Midlands Area led to
industrial chaos and widespread hardship. Painful memories of
this episode only underlined the importance of being ready, in
good time, with the necessary storage and manufacturing capacity.
The demand for gas is settled by factors that are largely beyond
the control of the gas industry itself; but whatever the demand, the
industry's responsibility is to meet it. Nothing excuses failure.
Not unnaturally, there are men in the Area Boards who take
strong exception to anything that looks to them like unreasonable
or irresponsible obstruction on the part of others.

For the gas industry to be late with its capital projects could
well mean disaster. But to be too early is almost as bad; when
costly projects are brought into service before they are really
needed, the effect is to lock up resources that could be better used
elsewhere. Ideally, plans should be kept flexible for as long as
possible. It was calculated that extra storage would be needed in
Abingdon in the winter of 1968–9. The gasholder would take two
years to build. Consequently, there was no need for the Board to
commit themselves and finalise their plans until the late summer
of 1966. Had they required planning permission, of course, the
position would have been quite different. But the S.G.B. knew
that if they finally decided to build on the site chosen in 1951
they already had planning consent; and if they decided to put the
gasholder on their adjacent operational land on the old gasworks
site, then, for reasons that will now be explained, they did not
need planning consent.

The 1947 Town and Country Planning Act instituted a far
more rigorous system of planning control than anything that had

gone before. But both the 1947 Act and the subsequent Town and Country Planning Act of 1962 were, in part, implemented in the form of General Development Orders, which provided for various types of 'permitted development' (development for which planning permission was deemed to have been given automatically). In certain circumstances, statutory undertakers like the S.G.B. benefited from this freedom from local planning control. The 1963 G.D.O., for example, permitted a Gas Board to erect, without specific planning permission, any plant up to 50 feet in height (including gasholders) on their operational land. The gasholder that the S.G.B. planned for Abingdon, however, was a good deal more than 50 feet high, and the Board were proposing to rely on a different provision of the 1963 G.D.O. The Oxford Gas Order of 1930 had empowered the Oxford Gas Company to erect on its operational land any plant – without restriction as to size or nature – that was considered necessary for carrying on the undertaking. The provisions of Class XII of the First Schedule to the 1963 G.D.O. perpetuated powers given under pre-war private legislation and local statutory orders like the Oxford Gas Order. Thus, because the Oxford Gas Company had been entitled to do as it pleased on its own operational land before the war, so was its successor, the S.G.B. In 1950 the Board had been obliged to apply for planning permission for the proposed gasholder because the site had *not* been on operational land. In 1966, when the S.G.B. decided to erect the gasholder on the old gasworks site, they were under no such obligation.

The headquarters of the S.G.B. is in Southampton. In 1965 and 1966, as they went ahead with their plans, the Board's officials had no particular reason to think that the new gasholder would arouse much excitement in Abingdon. It would certainly be quite large: it was to be 128 feet high and 126 feet wide, with a capacity of 1 million cubic feet. But it was to be erected next to a silo 80 feet high, itself no ornament, in an area scheduled for industrial development. And, they recalled, in 1951 the Local Planning Authorities had agreed to what would have been an identical gasholder only a few yards from the spot that the Board now had in mind.

On 28 September 1966 the S.G.B. wrote to the Abingdon Borough Council and the Berkshire County Council, and told them of the Board's intentions. Because of the rapid rate at which the gas industry was expanding, they explained, it was a matter of some urgency for the Board to build a new gasholder in the very near future. The S.G.B. expected to let the contract by the end of October, and it was hoped that work on the site would begin by the end of November. Under existing legislation, they pointed out, the Board did not require planning permission. They could go ahead at once with construction, and they were informing the local authorities of their plans merely as a matter of courtesy.

The news was received in Abingdon with considerable surprise and resentment. Fifteen years had passed since the S.G.B. had been given planning permission for a gasholder on the vineyard, and by 1966 it was half assumed that they were no longer interested in the site. On 6 June Abingdon's Town Clerk had written to the S.G.B. asking them if they were willing to sell the site for redevelopment purposes. The Board's solicitor had replied, very briefly, that the S.G.B. were not prepared to sell any of their land in Abingdon. Nothing was said about a gasholder, though by this time the plans were nearing completion.

The composition of the Abingdon Borough Council, and their attitude towards amenity issues, had changed a good deal since 1951. The highest point in Abingdon is the 150-foot spire of St Helen's church; the proposed gasholder would be only 22 feet lower. A tub almost as wide as it is high makes a visual impact quite different from that of a gracefully tapering spire. Nor was it just the aesthetics of the proposed gasholder that angered the Abingdon Borough Council. They were also upset at the lack of consultation. As we shall see, throughout the controversy that lay ahead, dealings between the S.G.B. and the local authorities were bedevilled by distrust on both sides. In Abingdon the suspicion at once took root that the S.G.B. had deliberately kept silent about their plans until the last possible moment, so as to deny their opponents time to mobilise.

What the man in the Abingdon street thought about the situation will never be known. But among those active in civic affairs in the town there was general condemnation of the S.G.B. and their gasholder. The mayor, Alderman John Jones, denounced it as a 'colossal monster'; and from this point onwards, it was always 'the monster'. The mayor's sentiments were shared on all sides of the Borough Council. As the Town Clerk put it in his reply to the S.G.B., members had 'expressed themselves very forcibly' about the probable effect of the gasholder on the appearance of this part of the town. Others soon joined in the outcry. The chairman of the Friends of Abingdon, the town's civic society, declared that the gasholder would 'completely ruin the look of Abingdon'. The Abingdon Labour Party forwarded a resolution to the Minister of Power, deploring what it called the S.G.B.'s 'authoritarian and peremptory action', and asking the Minister to investigate alternative means of storage and to initiate a review of the law relating to gas supply. The chairman of the Berkshire branch of the C.P.R.E. urged the S.G.B. to site the gasholder at Didcot, near the new power station.

The local newspaper, the *Oxford Mail*, also joined in the hue and cry. As it happened, the editor took a keen personal interest in amenity problems, and over the months ahead he kept up a continuous campaign against the S.G.B. and their gasholder. His tactics often angered the Board; but there can be no denying his persistence and his eye for a telling thrust. In April 1967, for example, the *Oxford Mail* carried a full-page panoramic view of Abingdon with a hypothetical – and hideous – black gasholder superimposed upon it. An illustration of this kind could not fail to make an impact.[1] Thanks largely to the *Oxford Mail*'s campaign – some would say 'crusade' – other national newspapers, including *The Times*, the *Daily Mail*, the *Daily Mirror* and the *Daily Express*, were to latch on to the controversy, and make it an issue of national interest.

The opposition recruited another valuable ally in Mr Airey Neave, M.P. for the Abingdon division of Berkshire. For him, this was partly a constituency matter; his constituents had a grievance and it was his duty to help fight their battle. But like many other M.P.s of all parties, Neave had long been dissatisfied with planning law as it related to statutory undertakers. Any M.P. interested in having the law changed naturally seizes upon a particular case that will reinforce his arguments. Throughout the dispute Neave was to play an active role, prodding Ministers,

---

[1] The S.G.B. claim that this imaginary gasholder was drawn completely out of scale; nor would it have been painted black. Furthermore, the view that was shown (they say) could have been seen only from the roof of the old County Hall, hardly a common vantage-point or a place of public resort.

keeping the issue alive, and advising the local authorities on strategy.

When it comes to competing for public and Parliamentary goodwill in a battle with local authorities, statutory undertakers are frequently at something of a disadvantage. Local authorities are made up of politicians; controversy and propaganda is their business. The local press naturally identifies with the town or county involved; newspapers do not have any similar affinities with a public corporation or an Area Board. And whatever their views on public ownership in principle, few M.P.s feel that any particular statutory undertaking has a claim on their sympathies, especially if it is in dispute with a local authority in their own constituency. On the other side, statutory undertakers are often run by men who have neither the taste nor the aptitude for politics and public controversy. True, they have Government departments to look after their interests, and in the privacy of Whitehall, civil servants no doubt operate very effectively on behalf of their protégés. But so far as open argument is concerned, they must rely on Ministers, for in these circumstances they are the only politicians with the interests of the Area Board at heart. There are usually only two or three Ministers in a Government department, and the time that they can devote to publicising the statutory undertakers' side of a case is necessarily limited. The Minister of Power and his Parliamentary Secretary often had matters other than the Abingdon gasholder to occupy their minds and their speeches.

The Abingdon Borough Council's main concern was to gain a breathing-space, and their first move was to press for talks with the S.G.B. to see if all the possible alternatives to the gasholder really had been exhaustively examined. On 25 October there was a meeting between members and officers of the Borough Council, the Berkshire County Council, and officials of the S.G.B. The local authority representatives suggested that there were five possible alternatives. The first was to find another site for the gasholder outside the Borough, either at Didcot or Cowley. The second was to find another site in Abingdon. The third was to build two smaller gasholders on the vineyard site. The fourth was to install horizontal high-pressure cylinders. And the fifth was to build only one smaller gasholder on the vineyard site to meet the anticipated demand over the next ten years, in the hope that, subsequently, the problem would be solved by new developments in the technology of gas storage and distribution. It was agreed that if the storage capacity had to be installed in Abingdon itself, the high-pressure cylinders would be less conspicuous than anything else. For their part, the S.G.B. officials made it clear that a high-pressure system would certainly be a good deal more expensive than a conventional gasholder. Nevertheless, they readily agreed to look further into all the possibilities that had been suggested.

THE PLOT THICKENS

When the S.G.B.'s plans were first made public, the local press gave the impression that Abingdon and Berkshire had been presented with an irreversible *fait accompli*. This was not the case at all. It was true that under Class XII of the 1963 G.D.O. the Board did not need planning permission for their gasholder. But the Local Planning Authorities were not entirely powerless. In a situation of this kind, it was open to the County Council to make a Direction requiring the developers to submit plans for examination and approval in the usual way. To become effective, such a Direction – made under Article 4 of the G.D.O. – had to be confirmed by the Minister of Housing and Local Government. That, however, was not quite the end of the story. If the County Council concerned were to reject the application, the question of compensation would arise. As the law stood at the time of the Abingdon dispute, under Section 170(i) (a) of the 1962 Town and Country Planning Act, statutory undertakers could claim compensation for any financial loss incurred as a consequence of being refused permission to develop their operational land in the way they chose. This apparently privileged position enjoyed by statutory undertakers was not quite as unreasonable as was to be made out, for, as public utilities, they were under a legal obligation to provide a service in the locality concerned. A private firm could not claim compensation in this way; but a private firm that objects to conditions imposed by a Local Planning Authority can, in the last resort, take its business elsewhere. A statutory undertaker cannot.

The law allowed for one further step. Under Section 22 of the

1962 Town and Country Planning Act, the Minister of Housing and Local Government could call in planning applications for his own decision. And, if the Minister were to refuse the application, the liability for compensation would still fall upon the Local Planning Authority, even though they might themselves have been prepared to grant planning permission, rather than pay the sum asked.

It was against this background that the problem of the Abingdon gasholder came before the Berkshire Planning Committee for the first time on 9 November 1966. The Chief Planning Officer outlined the course of events up to this point, and emphasised that there could be no question about the undesirability of the S.G.B.'s plan. 'It is clear', he reported, 'that a structure of the type proposed, no matter what ameliorative tree screening or colouring devices were employed, would by virtue of its bulk and height in relation to its surroundings dominate the local scene and obtrude into important vistas in the town, particularly from the riverside which forms such an important amenity setting for Abingdon.' For the benefit of the Committee the planning position was also clarified. The only way to ensure that the S.G.B. did not go ahead with their plan was for the County Council to make an Article 4 Direction and risk having to pay compensation to the Board. Just how much that compensation might be was difficult to assess. The only information that he had been able to obtain was that the cost of the conventional gasholder would be about £150,000, and that the alternative high-pressure system could cost up to half as much again. He had also found out (he said) that some years earlier the Aylesbury Borough Council had paid the S.G.B. £70,000 to avoid having a gasholder in the town.

The Committee decided that on planning grounds they ought to oppose the S.G.B.'s plans. If the Board could not be persuaded to abandon the gasholder project in favour of something less objectionable an Article 4 Direction would be made, and (if the Minister confirmed it) planning permission would be refused. Probably not much attention was devoted to the question of compensation, partly because it was not yet clear how much would be involved (on the information available to them the Committee presumably believed that it would amount to about £75,000 – a large, but not enormous, sum), and partly because they assumed that it would be the Abingdon Borough Council, and not the County Council, which would foot the bill. Indeed, the Borough Council were told that if the Article 4 Direction was made, the County Council would expect to be reimbursed for any compensation charge that might be payable.[1]

In the meantime, the S.G.B. had been busy with their review of the alternative possibilities. On 28 December 1966 they wrote to the local authorities setting out the comparative costs of the various schemes that they had been asked to examine. First, there was the possibility of putting the new installations at Didcot or Cowley. The more practicable of the two alternatives (the S.G.B. thought) would be Didcot, about six miles from Abingdon. The cost of building the gasholder at Didcot would be more or less the same as at Abingdon; but as the gas was needed in Abingdon it would be necessary to connect a gasholder at Didcot with Abingdon by means of a 16-inch steel high-pressure main. It would also be necessary to install compressors. The cost of this main, plus the compressors and other ancillary plant, would be about £450,000. And as the Board pointed out, the residents of Didcot too might find a gasholder unwelcome, particularly as it would be solely for the benefit of Abingdon.

Second, there was the possibility of another site in Abingdon. So far as the S.G.B. could see, no alternative site was available. Third, there was the suggestion that the S.G.B. should build two gasholders on the vineyard site, each with a capacity of 0·5 million cubic feet, instead of one gasholder with a capacity of 1 million cubic feet. Each of the two smaller holders would have to have a base diameter of 96 feet and their height, when fully inflated, would be 112 feet. The total cost of the two holders would be £270,000, as compared with that of £210,000 for the gasholder actually proposed by the S.G.B.

Fourth, there was the possibility of a high-pressure installation.

[1] Berkshire County Planning Committee Minutes, 9 Nov 1966. The County Council's insistence that Abingdon should pay any compensation required did not go down well in the local press. On 28 November the *Oxford Mail* declared that it would be quite inequitable to saddle a town the size of Abingdon with such an enormous bill. If the Borough were to borrow £75,000, it pointed out, a twopenny rate would be needed for the following thirty years to pay off the debt. It was soon to become clear that the compensation payable was so large that it would have been quite unrealistic to expect Abingdon to pay the whole sum or even the greater part of it.

There would just be enough room on the site; but the S.G.B. thought that they would be far more cramped for space than was desirable. This high-pressure installation would take the form of three cylinders, each 160 feet long and 12 feet in diameter. They would be raised off the ground, so that the top of the cylinders would be about 20 feet above ground level. It would also be necessary to install compressors, and the total cost of this installation was estimated to be about £310,000.

Fifth, there was the suggestion that the S.G.B. should erect one traditional gasholder, with a capacity of 0·5 million cubic feet. This would cost £150,000; but the idea was hardly a starter, because the Board did not regard a storage capacity of 0·5 million cubic feet as adequate. And sixth, the S.G.B. had been asked to consider building a traditional gasholder of non-standard dimensions. They had looked into this idea and one possibility was a gasholder with a base diameter of 142 feet, and a fully inflated height of 112 feet. Because it was a non-standard article, it would cost about £250,000.

These figures referred only to capital costs. They also had to consider the operational expenses. All of the schemes that the S.G.B. had been asked to consider would mean higher running costs than would be necessary for the conventional gasholder proposed by the Board. These operational costs would be greatest in the case of the high-pressure storage system.

The S.G.B. had not had a great deal of time in which to produce these estimates, they said, and they were not accurate to the last degree. Nevertheless, they did give a realistic idea of the additional costs that any of the alternative schemes would involve. They would be happy to discuss the situation again. But there was the vital question of time. The local authorities were reminded that the Board had originally intended to start building the gasholder in November. It was now the end of December. They were quite prepared to let the matter stand over for a reasonable time; but in the interests of providing an adequate supply of gas for Abingdon, they had to install the necessary storage as soon as possible.

The possible costs mentioned by the S.G.B. were considerably higher than anything that the Berkshire County Council had so far envisaged, and when the Planning Committee met again on 11 January 1967 they decided to ask for a second meeting. They also agreed on another important step. Local Planning Authorities – and individuals – are often at a disadvantage when they find themselves in dispute with statutory undertakers and private industry in that they do not possess the technical expertise to check and challenge the arguments and data put forward by their opponents. In controversies of this kind, half the battle consists in trying to undermine the other side's case. In conjunction with Abingdon, the County Council now decided to appoint an independent expert to advise them on the technical and financial issues involved. The expert appointed was Mr R. W. Beswick, a consultant engineer.

By this stage, the S.G.B. were becoming worried about their timetable. There was also a certain amount of exasperation with the local authorities. It was understandable that Abingdon and Berkshire should want independent, expert advice, particularly as they were evidently becoming suspicious about the Board's costings. But why had they waited until four months after the Board's original letter before appointing their technical adviser? Moreover, as the S.G.B. saw it, the local authorities were an unconscionable time making up their minds as to what they intended to do. Were they going to accept the gasholder, in spite of their aesthetic objections? Or were they going to make an Article 4 Direction and pay the compensation? The S.G.B. felt that one way or the other they had to have an answer soon. On 18 January the S.G.B. informed Abingdon and Berkshire that unless they came to a decision within the next few weeks the Board would have no alternative but to press ahead with their plans. The longest that they could wait before giving the necessary instructions to their contractors was 20 February 1967. If they went beyond that date, they said, they would be running a grave risk of creating a shortage of gas in Abingdon in the winter of 1968–9. The S.G.B.'s overriding responsibility, they stressed, was to safeguard the supply of gas, and this duty took precedence even over their dislike of acting against the wishes of the local authorities.

In the meantime, a meeting between the S.G.B. and the local authorities' representatives had been arranged for 7 February at the Board's headquarters in Southampton. It was preceded by two preparatory meetings. On 3 February members of the Abingdon Borough Council and the Berkshire County Council considered a preliminary report on the S.G.B.'s proposals from their consultant engineer, and decided that their policy should be to press the S.G.B. to install a high-pressure system. On the following day there was a meeting at officer level between the local authorities and the Board. The extra cost of a high-pressure system was now said to be not £210,000, but £250,000. Faced with estimates for a high-pressure system that seemed to be ever rising, and annoyed at the S.G.B.'s letter of 18 January, which they regarded as an ultimatum, the local authority delegation set off for Southampton on 7 February in a somewhat resentful and suspicious frame of mind.

They were led by Mr Richard West, the chairman of the Berkshire Planning Committee. For the first time in the dispute, the local authority representatives came face to face with Mr D. P. Welman, the chairman of the S.G.B. Welman apparently said that in other circumstances he, too, would have preferred high-pressure cylinders, not only for aesthetic reasons, but also because they would have been more easily integrated into the system when North Sea gas became available. But the S.G.B., he said, had an overriding responsibility for ensuring that the necessary storage capacity was installed at the minimum cost. Because of the heavy demand for pressure vessels in this country, said Welman, their price had risen by 30 per cent. On the basis of quotations for other work, the Board were therefore revising their previous estimate for the cost of the high-pressure system from £310,000 to £419,000. And quite apart from the question of costs, it was unlikely that the Board could install a high-pressure system by the autumn of 1968. There was a world-wide demand for pressure vessels, and the manufacturers were often unable to meet delivery dates. Unless the Board were given a firm assurance that the difference in cost between a high-pressure system and the conventional gasholder would be met by the local authorities, they would have to go ahead on 20 February and begin work on the gasholder.

For their part, the local authority representatives argued that if time was short that was the fault of the S.G.B.: they should have taken Abingdon and Berkshire into their confidence earlier. The S.G.B., they thought, were probably being pessimistic about the extra cost of a high-pressure system. Before the meeting it had appeared that the difference in cost between the two systems would be about £100,000. The Abingdon contingent made it clear that they were not prepared to pay that sum, or anything like it. The Berkshire representatives refused to commit the County Council to making any contribution at all.

Before the meeting closed the S.G.B. undertook to provide a written statement comparing the estimated costs of the high- and low-pressure systems. They reminded the local authorities that the statutory basis for compensation would be the *actual* cost (capital and operational) of the high-pressure system, less the estimated cost of the conventional gasholder. It was easy enough to make the latter estimate, they said, because many similar plants had already been built; it was far more difficult to estimate accurately for the high-pressure system, because this technique was comparatively new.

It had not been a particularly cordial meeting, and from now onwards relations between the S.G.B. and the local authorities deteriorated still further. The local authorities had formed the impression that the Board were trying to browbeat them. What they felt was usually reflected accurately in the editorial columns of the *Oxford Mail*, which declared that the S.G.B. were trying to bully Abingdon and Berkshire into paying up. 'The threat is,' it claimed, 'your money or the gasholder.' If the Board went ahead with their plan to ruin Abingdon, it continued, the Gas Council, in its future advertising, ought to show pictures of the town before and after the construction of the gasholder.

Many of those involved in the controversy felt that a difficult situation was made worse by an unfortunate clash of personalities. In the words of one observer, after the Southampton meeting, the dispute was to become very much 'a battle of the princes'. Clearly, there was no love lost between Welman and West. But it might be nearer the truth to say that each of them quickly became exasperated at what he thought was the totally unreasonable position taken up by the other. Conscious perhaps that Abingdon could well set a precedent for many similar cases, the chairman of the S.G.B. felt that it was his responsibility to uphold the Board's legal rights. Had Berkshire been prepared to make an offer – any offer – he might have been prepared to discuss a compromise. But, as far as he could see, Berkshire had no intention of paying anything at all. On the other side, like many others in local government, West no doubt thought that the law was

quite unjust. But considerations of principle apart, as we shall
see, he too had his problems. And as always, if negotiations begin
badly, attitudes harden and it becomes psychologically difficult
to make the first move to break a deadlock.[1]

The local authorities' consultant engineer had been present at
the Southampton talks, and three days later he produced a
further report on the S.G.B.'s case. His observations served only
to deepen their suspicions of the Board and their tactics. According to Beswick, the Board were deliberately exaggerating their
difficulties. As far as he could see, the existing gas main linking
Abingdon and Didcot would be capable of passing enough gas
through to meet peak demand in Abingdon until 1976. He had
been told by the Association responsible for co-ordinating the
manufacture of pressure vessels that it was quite untrue to say
that the industry was overloaded. The Association, in fact,
strongly resented suggestions from the gas and chemical industries
to the effect that the manufacturers were falling behind on
delivery dates. The effect of this report was to confirm the local
authorities in their belief that the S.G.B. had already made up
their mind to install the gasholder, irrespective of the arguments
and alternatives put forward by anyone else. In Berkshire it now
came to be believed that the Board were deliberately inflating
their estimates for the high-pressure system so as to scare off the
local authorities. As one Abingdon Councillor put it, the S.G.B.
had based their figures solely on the question 'How much do we
have to say to frighten them off?'[2]

[1] The local authority view was put on record by the Abingdon Town
Clerk, Mr E. W. J. Nicholson, some months after the controversy ended.
'In my thirty-two years as town clerk in three boroughs', he wrote, 'I have
occasionally had hard, even hostile negotiations with some pretty tough
companies, but never have I encountered a body so uncompromising as
the S.G.B. were in this matter'. *Local Government Chronicle*, 27 Jan
1968.
[2] This Councillor had detected an even more Machiavellian possibility.
If the S.G.B. really wished to install a high-pressure system, they had only
to announce their intention of building a conventional gasholder in order
to provoke a public outcry. In the subsequent furore the local authorities
might feel morally obliged to save their town by offering to pay the
difference, thereby making a substantial contribution towards the cost of
what the Board had wanted all along. This suggestion need not be taken
seriously. But it is indicative of the way in which minds were working
among the Board's opponents. On the other hand, as Welman had

As matters stood after the meeting at Southampton, there was nothing to prevent the S.G.B. from pushing ahead with their plans, regardless of local opposition. The local authorities had managed to keep the S.G.B. talking; but the Board had made it plain that by 20 February the talking would have to stop. Only the Berkshire County Council could now hold up the Board by making an Article 4 Direction.

At the Shire Hall there were mixed feelings about the situation that was now developing. Berkshire extends over a large area, and not every member of the County Council felt passionately about Abingdon. Nor was everyone convinced that the gasholder would be such a catastrophe as was being made out. If the planning enthusiasts wished to fight the S.G.B. they were welcome to do so. But members who neither knew nor cared much about Abingdon were quite determined that the County Council should not pay a penny in order to buy off the S.G.B. Even those who felt most strongly about the gasholder saw no reason why the ratepayers of Berkshire should contribute what was obviously going to be a very large sum in order to save Abingdon from a monstrosity that the S.G.B. had no business to be proposing anyway. Moreover, the County Council had been advised that there was a strong possibility of a change in the law, the effect of which would be to relieve local authorities of the liability for compensation in cases like this. If a new Bill was in the pipeline, there was a good deal to be said for fighting on a little longer, and holding up the S.G.B. until the Government clarified its intentions.

On the face of things, however, it was impossible to avoid the gasholder without paying. As it then stood, the law was quite plain. Only if the local authorities were prepared to compensate the S.G.B. to the full extent of the difference in cost between the high- and low-pressure systems could the gasholder be kept out of Abingdon. At this stage, it seems, Berkshire had no intention of paying anything. Nevertheless, the Planning Committee decided that they ought at least to delay the project, in the hope that some other way of stopping the S.G.B. might be found.

---

observed at the Southampton meeting, the S.G.B. could not afford to underestimate the cost of a high-pressure system, because if the local authorities agreed to pay compensation and then eventually had to find more than they had been led to expect, the Board would have been accused of misleading them.

Accordingly, on 8 February, the day after the Southampton meeting, the County Council took the plunge and made an Article 4 Direction requiring the S.G.B. to apply for planning permission for the gasholder. To become operative, of course, the Direction needed the approval of the Minister of Housing and Local Government, to whom it was now submitted for confirmation. At the same time, the County Council decided to ask the Minister to see a deputation to discuss both the Article 4 Direction and the question of compensation.

ENTER THE MINISTERS

The action now shifted to Whitehall. On 23 February the deputation from Abingdon and Berkshire, led by Airey Neave, saw the Minister of Housing and Local Government. In addition to members of the Abingdon and Berkshire Planning Committees, the deputation also included the chairman of the County Council, Air-Commodore Louis Dickens, and the chairman of the County Finance Committee, Mr F. D. Pickering. The local authority representatives pressed the Minister to confirm the Article 4 Direction, pointing out that if he did not, he would in effect be making himself responsible for the destruction of Abingdon's amenities. There would almost certainly be a public outcry, and he would be the man to take the blame. If, on the other hand, he were to confirm the Direction, he could then call in the S.G.B.'s application and order an independent inquiry, at which the figures put forward by the S.G.B. could be rigorously examined.

So far as compensation was concerned, the local authorities argued that the law was out of date and inequitable. When statutory undertakers were given powers to develop operational land before the war, no one could have reasonably foreseen that they intended building gasholders 128 feet high in the centre of a town like Abingdon. In the circumstances, any liability incurred by local authorities in refusing planning permission for a development of this kind ought to be limited to cases where the refusal would prevent a project that it would have been reasonable to expect when the original powers were granted. In this particular case, the S.G.B. could properly claim that they had the right to erect a gasholder to a height that was normal in 1930. If that proposal was rejected, they would be entitled to demand compensation. But the County Council ought not to be expected to pay compensation if the Board's application for a 128-foot high gasholder was rejected.

The Minister, Mr Anthony Greenwood, was sympathetic. But his officials pointed out that in law the S.G.B. had a perfect right either to build the gasholder or to claim compensation if they were refused planning consent. If the Minister confirmed the Article 4 Direction either the Berkshire County Council would have to give planning consent (in which case there would be no point in making the Direction), or, if they refused consent, they would have to pay full compensation – unless, that is, they could negotiate some more favourable settlement with the S.G.B. It would make no difference if the Minister called in the application. Presumably, the County Council would want him to refuse planning permission; but, if he did so, the County would still be liable for compensation. This could be a very large sum. Whatever happened subsequently, once the Direction had been confirmed, the County Council's liability became automatic. Were they really prepared to pay what might well be asked of them? Would it not be better, the Minister suggested, for the local authorities to hold further talks with the S.G.B., in the hope that the Board would agree to some compromise that would relieve Berkshire of part of the compensation charges? Without a change in the law, this was the best that the local authorities could hope for, and in delaying confirmation for a while, the Minister thought he was doing the County Council rather a good turn.

By this time, the S.G.B.'s deadline for beginning work on the gasholder had come and gone. From their point of view, the situation was becoming serious. Berkshire had made the Article 4 Direction; but the Minister had not yet confirmed it, and it was not clear whether he intended to do so. Nor was there any sign that the Berkshire County Council intended to pay compensation, or indeed to make any offer at all. On occasions in the past other local authorities had objected to gasholders, and the S.G.B. had been able to settle terms with them. The law being what it was, the local authorities had always had to pay if they wanted something other than what the Board proposed. Probably they had not done so with a good grace, because the provision for compensation in these circumstances had always been a sore point with the local authorities. But paid they had. For a local authority to oppose a gasholder without being prepared to offer any contribution at all towards the cost of the more expensive alternative was something new in the S.G.B.'s experience. Why should Berkshire be treated more favourably than other local authorities had been in the past? This attitude, of course, had its counterpart on the other side, where it was widely believed that the S.G.B.'s 'peremptory' attitude arose out of their annoyance at encountering, at last, a local authority that stood up to them.

On deadline day – 20 February 1967 – the S.G.B.'s solicitor wrote to the County Council. He repeated an earlier assurance given by the Board that costs incurred by the S.G.B. up to 20 February would not be included in their claim for compensation should such a claim arise. But as the local authorities showed no sign of accepting liability for the alternative high-pressure system, the Board saw no point in extending the deadline. Any costs that they incurred after 20 February would therefore form part of their compensation claim. It was a letter that contained the seeds of another misunderstanding, which in due course was to embitter still further the already sour relations between the S.G.B. and the local authorities.

The two sides met again at the Shire Hall, Reading, on 4 April, this time with officials of the Ministry of Housing and Local Government and the Ministry of Power present. Everyone agreed that a high-pressure system was the only practicable alternative to the conventional gasholder. The S.G.B.'s final estimate for the additional cost of the high-pressure system was about £250,000, a figure that covered the capital cost of the equipment, the services of outside contractors and consultants (for the Board maintained that their own staff had insufficient technical experience of these high-pressure systems to install one themselves), and a capitalised sum for the running costs.

Berkshire had no intention of finding a quarter of a million pounds and their representatives said so. Since they were not prepared to offer any lesser sum either, the deadlock was complete. The Berkshire contingent understood the representative of the Ministry of Housing and Local Government to say that, in the circumstances, he could not advise his Minister to confirm the Article 4 Direction. If Berkshire was not going to pay the necessary compensation, and if there was to be no compromise, it would have been entirely reasonable advice. Naturally enough, both the Berkshire representatives and those of the S.G.B. assumed that this advice would be given and that the Minister would act upon it, and not confirm the Direction.

When the meeting broke up it seemed that the battle was over. The S.G.B. put out a statement that was a nice blend of firmness and finality:

> The Southern Gas Board recognise that Abingdon is a town of outstanding architectural quality in beautiful surroundings and that there is a special need to preserve the amenities of the town.
>
> Having exhaustively investigated, in consultation with the Borough and County Councils, the possibility of alternatives, the Board find that the cheapest practicable alternative would cost about £250,000 more than the low-pressure gasholder proposed by the Board.
>
> In the absence of a settlement with the County and Borough Councils, on the bearing of this additional cost, the Board feel reluctantly compelled to proceed with the erection of the low-pressure gasholder. The Board will, however, use their best endeavours to operate the gasholder during the summer so that its height is kept to a minimum consistent with the operational requirements of the gas supply system. They will also keep the holder painted and otherwise maintained so that its appearance is as little unpleasing as practicable.

At their next meeting, on 6 April, the Berkshire Planning Committee acknowledged that there was nothing more to be done. The Committee were informed that the County Council's representatives had been told 'verbally' that the Minister was unlikely to confirm the Article 4 Direction (a reference to what had been said at the meeting on 4 April). If the Direction was not confirmed the County Council would be unable to exercise planning control over the gasholder, and the S.G.B. would go ahead with their plans. The Planning Committee's report summed up the situation as they saw it:

> After fully examining all the various factors including the legal position, it is apparent to the Committee that the Southern Gas Board cannot be compelled to substitute high-pressure

storage cylinders for the proposed conventional gasholder, and that this can only be negotiated with them on payment of a sum of the order of a quarter of a million pounds. On the assumption, therefore, that the Minister of Housing and Local Government will not confirm the Article 4 Direction it is recommended:

That (i) The Minister of Housing and Local Government, the S.G.B., and the Abingdon Borough Council be informed that the County Council are unable to contemplate incurring expenditure of the order referred to in the above report in providing an alternative to the proposed gasholder in Abingdon in order to prevent its erection.

(ii) That they be further informed that this decision is taken with the utmost reluctance in view of the damage which will result to the amenities of Abingdon.

(iii) That all possible steps be taken to bring the maximum pressure to bear on the Minister of Housing and Local Government to change the law with the object of preventing similar circumstances arising in the future.

(iv) That the County Councils Association be advised of recommendations (i), (ii) and (iii) above, and be asked to assist.

Even the *Oxford Mail* agreed that Abingdon had lost. And on 7 April when *The Times* and the *Daily Telegraph* reported that Berkshire was not going to find the £250,000 needed for the high-pressure system and that the Minister of Housing and Local Government was not going to confirm the Article 4 Direction, it seemed that the story had indeed come to an end.

Not everyone had quite given up hope of keeping the gasholder out of Abingdon. It was known that the Government had begun a comprehensive review of Town and Country planning law, and that the position of statutory undertakers was being re-examined. In Airey Neave's view it might still be possible to use a putative change in the law as a lever with the Ministry of Housing and Local Government. On 6 April he wrote to the Minister and asked him to intervene. The S.G.B., he wrote, had forced the local authorities into a position where they had no choice but to accept a gasholder that would seriously damage the amenities of the town for a generation. If it was true that there was soon to be new legislation, the effect of which would be to compel the S.G.B. to submit to a proper planning inquiry, the Minister should take steps to find out whether the gasholder really was necessary before the new legislation came into force. He also mentioned that he would be putting down a Parliamentary Question asking the Minister why he had refused to confirm the Article 4 Direction.

At this point, another Government department was to be drawn into the Abingdon controversy. On 9 March Airey Neave wrote to the Minister of Power, Mr Richard Marsh, asking him to use his influence with the S.G.B. The Minister of Power was not directly concerned with planning questions; but he did have a certain responsibility for the nationalised gas industry, and for the policies pursued by the Area Gas Boards. At first, the Ministry of Power approached the problem on a straightforward legal basis. If a high-pressure system was to be installed in Abingdon instead of a conventional gasholder, someone would have to pay the difference in cost. Unless the S.G.B. could be persuaded otherwise, Berkshire would have to pay in full. Ministers have often been criticised for 'persuading' nationalised industries to undertake activities that may be socially desirable, but for which there is no strictly commercial justification or necessity. Social costs incurred on this basis are reflected in higher prices, which the public usually attributes to inefficiency rather than civic virtue. The effect is to undermine morale in the public corporations subjected to ministerial pressure of this kind. As the Ministry of Power saw it, if there was to be a negotiated compromise it was for Berkshire and the S.G.B. to settle the matter between them. However, with feelings apparently running so high in Abingdon and Berkshire, and with the S.G.B. getting such a bad press, the Parliamentary Secretary, Mr Reginald Freeson, began to take a personal interest in the case.

A former leader of the Willesden Borough Council, and vice-chairman of the Planning Committee, Freeson was not without experience of amenity problems. As a back-bench M.P. he had performed in his time the same role as Airey Neave was now playing. At this stage, however, his main concern was to see whether there was anything in the accusation that the S.G.B. had behaved in a reprehensible way in their dealings with the local authorities. When he replied to Airey Neave's letter on 12 April,

Freeson acknowledged that he had been concerned about allegations to the effect that the S.G.B. had acted without proper regard for public opinion. On reflection, however, he did not think that this charge was justified. As soon as the S.G.B. had decided that it was time to implement their plans to meet the growing demand for gas in the area, wrote Freeson, the authorities concerned had been told of the Board's proposals. Since then, he went on, the S.G.B. had gone to considerable trouble to convince the local authorities of the merits of those proposals. Six months had passed since the dispute began, and the S.G.B.'s programme had been set back three or four months. At the last meeting (on 4 April) everyone had agreed that the only feasible alternative to what the Board proposed was a high-pressure storage system, and this, it had been agreed, was prohibitively expensive. Additional expenditure of £250,000 would have been required for this alternative, and the question at issue was this – was it worth it? The local authorities, he claimed, evidently thought not, because they had not been able to agree to incurring this expense. The S.G.B. therefore felt that they had to go forward with the low-pressure gasholder, doing what they could to lessen its visual impact.

Freeson's reply did nothing to mollify Neave or the local authorities. In their view, he was trying to shift the responsibility for the problem on to the Berkshire County Council, misrepresenting their position in the process. Neave claimed in his reply that Abingdon and Berkshire were in no position to find a quarter of a million pounds; it was for this reason, and not because they thought the preservation of Abingdon not worth the money, that they had declined to agree to this expenditure. For his part, Freeson did indeed think that the primary responsibility for finding a solution lay with the local authorities. As he saw it, negotiations had broken down because they were determined not to incur any expenditure on the high-pressure system. It also crossed his mind that Berkshire was probably not the most impoverished county with the most pressing social problems in England. If they were all that horrified at the prospect of a gasholder in Abingdon, he reflected, they could well afford even £250,000, especially if they raised a loan for the purpose.

Neave also made a last-ditch appeal to the chairman of the S.G.B. On 14 April, in a telegram to Welman, he asked the Board to stop work on the site, at least until the subject had been debated in the House of Commons. Welman, however, was not prepared to hold up the gasholder any longer. It would seem, so far as the outsider can judge these matters, that until 20 February the S.G.B. would have been willing, though by no means eager, to install the high-pressure system rather than the gasholder, provided, of course, that the local authorities had agreed to pay the difference in cost, or at least a substantial part of the difference. After 20 February the S.G.B. were much more reluctant to consider the high-pressure system, irrespective of whether the local authorities offered a contribution or not. They had little experience of these high-pressure systems, and they did not relish the prospect of having to install one in much less time than they had allowed for the far more familiar gasholder. When Welman replied to Neave's telegram he pointed out that discussions about the gasholder had been going on for six months already. As chairman of the S.G.B. it was his job to see that there was no threat to Abingdon's gas supplies in the winter of 1968–9 as a result of further delays in carrying out the necessary work. It would be irresponsible for him to hold up construction any longer, he said, because as Neave was well aware the Minister of Housing and Local Government had said that he did not intend to confirm the Article 4 Direction.

ABINGDON MAKES THE SCENE

At their meeting on 6 April the Berkshire Planning Committee had reluctantly conceded that they had reached the end of the road. As they saw it, all that they could do now (short of offering a financial contribution) was to launch a campaign to help change the law, at the same time clinging to the hope that if public and Parliamentary opinion could be sufficiently roused, the Minister of Housing and Local Government might still come to their rescue. At the Committee meeting it was decided that the chairman, Richard West, should write to *The Times*, drawing attention to the gravity of the problem and to the wider implications of the Abingdon case. His letter appeared on 8 April 1967, and set out the main facts of the situation as he saw them. There was no doubt, he wrote, that the law needed to be amended. But the knowledge that it might be amended in the near future was of

little consolation. He pointed out that a high-pressure system
would be perfectly practicable, and would be unobjectionable on
amenity grounds. It would, however, cost Abingdon a great deal
in compensation. 'It seems outrageous', he declared, 'that a
statutory board should be able to ride roughshod over all conceivable planning principles, unless they are bought off.' The
Government and its Boards should not hide behind outdated
legislation; nor should they expect local authorities to pay very
large sums by way of compensation to preserve amenities. In
much the same vein, in a letter of 12 April, the Town Clerk of
Abingdon complained that the Minister of Housing and Local
Government's inaction made nonsense of all the care that the
town had taken over planning in the past. 'The use by the
Gas Board of obsolete legislation', he wrote, 'without any
practical regard whatever to local opinion or amenities shows
that they are every bit as ruthless as private enterprise may have
been.'

These letters had the desired effect. In the course of the next
week or so a series of contributions appeared in the correspondence
columns of *The Times*, attacking the S.G.B. and condemning the
alleged unrestricted planning powers of the nationalised industries. As a result of this correspondence, it came to light that a
number of other towns were also nursing grievances against the
gas industry and its gasholders. Three years earlier, in order to
escape a gasholder even bigger than the one proposed for Abingdon, the County Borough of Grimsby had paid the East Midlands
Gas Board a sum of £66,000, which was half the estimated cost
of an alternative high-pressure system. As Grimsby's Town Clerk
observed, this had no doubt been an enlightened decision on the
part of the Borough Council; nevertheless, in his view it was
wrong that local authorities should be faced with expenditure on
such a large scale, for it might well be beyond the capacity of
smaller towns to meet bills of this size. Statutory authorities, he
argued, ought to be subject to full planning controls; and they
should pay the entire cost of providing installations which would
avoid unnecessary damage to urban or rural amenities.[1] Two
other towns, Canterbury and Oxted, had been less fortunate (or
less enlightened) than Grimsby: as correspondents forcibly pointed

[1] *The Times*, 12 Apr 1967.

out, they were now fully equipped with large, unsightly gas-holders of the traditional type.[1]

By now, the Abingdon gasholder had become something of a *cause célèbre*, and a matter of considerable interest, at least in those circles that concern themselves with planning and amenity issues. On 17 April 1967 *The Times* devoted a leading article to the problems raised by the case, which, it declared, was already 'casting a long shadow'. It was not just a question of the damage that would be inflicted on this lovely old market town – though this alone would be enough to justify all the furore, now that people were more aware of the effect of the surrounding environment on their lives. Important as the preservation of Abingdon was, said *The Times*, this gasholder case had wider implications. The existing impasse, it pointed out, had arisen mainly because public undertakings were largely exempt from planning control, and were empowered to develop their operational land without the approval of Local Planning Authorities. They could be stopped, it was true, on the initiative of the Minister of Housing and Local Government, or by the planning authority with the approval of the Minister. But in either case the undertaking would nearly always be able to claim compensation from the Local Planning Authorities. 'This means', it went on, 'that attempts to regulate the building activities of nationalised industries for the sake of amenity become exercises not so much in administrative control as in commercial bargaining.' In consequence, local authorities were constantly in danger of having to face the question: how much is it worth to buy off this particular piece of desecration? Some of them had evidently paid quite a bit, and presumably the threat to Abingdon might have disappeared had Berkshire been willing to pay the extra £250,000 which the S.G.B. claimed the high-pressure system would cost.

[1] Only one correspondent attacked Berkshire for not offering to spend money in the interests of amenity. In a letter to *The Times* on 17 April, the chairman of the Berkshire branch of the C.P.R.E. compared Berkshire unfavourably with Grimsby. A gasometer, he wrote, would affect the amenities of an area considerably wider than the town of Abingdon. It would, therefore, be appropriate for the County Council to provide most of the compensation. 'Indeed', he went on, 'many people would expect the County Council to jump at this opportunity to use, in the adjacent area, some of the money they will get from the high rateable value of the new coal-fired Didcot power station.'

This state of affairs, said *The Times*, was open to obvious objections. It was quite wrong that the full cost of developing less economically should be borne by the planning authority. On occasions, this cost was obviously more than the authority could pay, and the result then was one more example of urban disfigurement. There was another question, too – why should there be this distinction between public and private industry? The very existence of a system of planning controls was evidence of the country's determination that the narrow dictates of economic profitability should not go unchecked, and this was something that private industry had to live with. Private companies were subject to planning control, even when it cost them money: the same control ought to apply to public undertakings. All public concerns, it concluded, ought to be brought within the scope of a strengthened planning system.

What effect, if any, a stream of hostile letters and a critical leader in *The Times* has upon the men concerned must be a matter of guesswork. The S.G.B. cannot have remained entirely unmoved by the wave of indignation breaking over them, though they resented what they regarded as the very one-sided way in which the controversy was being presented. An industry that sets some store by its public image – particularly as regards its concern for amenity – could hardly have relished, to take but one example, an impassioned contribution from an angry correspondent in Sonning, Berkshire, who declared that it was intolerable that the S.G.B. should have the right to desecrate the amenities of Abingdon, and even more intolerable that it should insist on exercising that right. 'I hope that they realise', he wrote, 'that if they persist in building their gasometer in the middle of one of the most beautiful small towns in England, generations to come will be in no doubt as to who the twentieth-century vandals are.'[1]

It will already have become apparent that the Abingdon controversy was taking a shape quite different from some of the cases described earlier in this book. In three at least of those cases the final decision had turned upon the question 'Is it worth spending a specified sum of money in order to avoid damaging certain amenities?' The argument was not about *who* was to pay, assuming that the amenities in question were thought to be worth

[1] *The Times*, 15 Apr 1967.

the asking price; the law made it quite clear that any costs incurred in the interests of amenity would be borne by the developers, and all the parties to the dispute accepted the law as it stood. As a matter of fact, the law was just as clear in the Abingdon case as in any of the others, except that in this instance it laid the costs of preserving amenities at the door of the Local Planning Authority and not the developers. Nevertheless, the question 'Is it worth spending £250,000 (whoever pays) on high-pressure cylinders in order to avoid spoiling certain views in Abingdon?' was hardly ever asked. Everyone was far too pre-occupied with arguing about the allocation of whatever the additional cost of the high-pressure system might turn out to be.

THE BUCK PASSED BACK

The first public suggestion that the situation might not be quite as it appeared came in a special report on the gasholder controversy in the *Oxford Mail* on 11 April 1967. It recalled that the Berkshire County Council had received no more than an unofficial, verbal indication from a civil servant in the Ministry of Housing and Local Government that the Minister was not going to confirm the Article 4 Direction. The Ministry itself was now denying that the Minister had made any decision either way.

In delaying confirmation of the Direction the Ministry's main concern had been to allow time for Berkshire to try to negotiate a settlement with the S.G.B. The Ministry had nothing to lose by confirming it. For Berkshire, however, the position was not quite so clear-cut. The Planning Committee did not want the gasholder built; and the only way of halting the S.G.B. was for the Minister to confirm the Article 4 Direction. But the Berkshire County Council were unwilling to pay compensation. If the Minister declined to confirm the Direction, the gasholder would be built, and that would be deplorable. At the same time, if events took this course, all the opprobrium would fall on the head of the Minister of Housing and Local Government, as indeed a good deal of it already had. If, on the other hand, the Minister did confirm the Direction, the ball would again be in the County Council's court. Planning powers would be theirs to exercise, and only two options would be open: either they could refuse planning permission (and meet the very large bill for compensation); or they could baulk at the bill and grant planning permission, a move that would make nonsense of the whole campaign against the gasholder. In effect, Berkshire had already indicated that they would see the gasholder built rather than pay compensation; but their responsibility in the matter had been somewhat obscured because the Minister had not so far confirmed the Direction, and therefore the S.G.B. had not been required to submit a formal planning application for the County Council to grant.

At Question time in the Lords on 17 April, the Earl of Lindsey and Abingdon, the High Steward of the Borough, asked Lord Kennet, the Joint Parliamentary Secretary at the Ministry of Housing and Local Government, why the Government had decided not to confirm the Article 4 Direction. To general surprise (for a number of peers had come primed with hostile supplementaries), Lord Kennet replied that the Minister had in fact confirmed the Direction earlier that day.[1]

As matters now stood, the S.G.B. were obliged to apply to the Berkshire County Council for planning permission in the normal way. This they did on 24 April 1967. Work had to stop, and since a further delay was inevitable, the Minister of Power decided to try to bring the two sides together again in the hope that they would be able to find an acceptable compromise. Freeson now volunteered to visit Abingdon to see the situation for himself and discuss the position with representatives from the S.G.B. and the local authorities. On 26 April, in the role of peacemaker, he arrived to inspect the site. Apparently, he formed the impression that the local authorities were not being unreasonable in objecting to the gasholder; provided that the two sides could reach an agreement about the allocation of costs, his personal opinion was that the gasholder ought not to be built. Privately, he was also coming to the conclusion that the S.G.B. ought to be prepared to contribute something towards the extra cost of a high-pressure system, although, of course, there was no legal obligation upon them to do so. Before leaving Abingdon, Freeson offered to take the chair at a further meeting, at which the two sides would discuss the S.G.B.'s estimated costings.

[1] *H.L. Deb.* (1966–7) 282, col. 8.

FROM BAD TO WORSE

Almost from the start, negotiations at member level between the S.G.B. and the local authorities had been conducted in an atmosphere of considerable resentment and suspicion. Relations, it seemed, could hardly get worse. On 22 May, at the S.G.B.'s headquarters, the familiar faces reassembled round the table for what everyone hoped would be the last time. Under the restraining and conciliatory influence of the Parliamentary Secretary, perhaps they could at last reach a settlement. Five hours later, the talks ended acrimoniously and in complete deadlock.

The meeting began amicably enough. For the S.G.B., Welman explained that if the gasholder were not built, the most suitable alternative would be a high-pressure system that incorporated three diesel-driven compressors: electrically powered compressors would have been cheaper, but he ruled them out because of the possibility of a power failure. According to the Board, the capital cost of the conventional gasholder would be £226,000 and the high-pressure system would cost £139,000 more. There would also be additional running costs of £10,000 per annum. Capitalised at 6 per cent over a twenty-year period, this would amount to something like £136,000. In addition, there was the cost of actually erecting the high-pressure system, a job that the S.G.B. said would have to be put out to contractors. For their part, the local authorities argued that various economies could be made, and that in any case they ought not to be responsible for the extra running costs for more than five years. Plainly the two sides were still a considerable way apart; but as the long meeting went on there seemed to be some chance of an agreement.

The S.G.B.'s offer was to pay a third of the additional capital cost of the high-pressure system (that is, about £46,000), plus half the cancellation fee for the conventional gasholder, which, as Welman pointed out, the Board had already ordered. This cancellation fee would amount to about £52,000. On the S.G.B.'s suggested allocation of the additional costs, and leaving aside the cancellation fee, the local authorities would still have been required to find well over £200,000. But it was the cancellation fee that seemed to stick in the throat of the chairman of the

Berkshire Planning Committee. He expressed surprise and indignation at the inclusion of this item, and made it quite clear that Berkshire had no intention of paying anything at all under this head. On this note of heated disagreement the meeting broke up.

It is typical of the whole controversy that the two sides should interpret the significance of the cancellation fee in very different ways. The local authorities' view was that if the S.G.B. had gone ahead and ordered a conventional gasholder, this showed that they had taken it upon themselves to anticipate the outcome of the negotiations. All along they had been determined to install the gasholder, come what might. Suddenly to introduce the question of a cancellation fee at this late stage, just when there appeared to be some chance of agreement, demonstrated once more that the Board's tactics were simply to raise their price if ever there seemed to be any danger of a settlement that would involve a high-pressure system.

As the S.G.B. saw it, on the other hand, the Berkshire County Council had been told quite clearly that the Board would go ahead with the gasholder on 20 February, and would expect compensation for any abortive costs incurred after that date. They could not see how the chairman of the Berkshire Planning Committee could fail to understand the situation. If he appeared surprised and angry, it must be feigned anger and astonishment. From the S.G.B.'s side of the table, it looked as though the cancellation fee was being used as a pretext for breaking off talks that seemed to be all too close to an agreement which would have involved the Berkshire County Council in paying far more than they intended.

Freeson apparently found it hard to understand the local authorities' attitude. It seemed to him that just when the S.G.B. had come round to making a definite offer to pay something in the interests of amenity, Berkshire were being far more rigid and demanding than their legal and tactical position warranted. With some force, he reminded the local authorities' representatives that if they failed to reach a settlement with the S.G.B. there were only two possible outcomes to the dispute, neither of which they would like. One was for the County Council to reject the Board's application for planning consent, in which case they would be liable for compensation far in excess of a negotiated sum. The other was for the County Council to approve the application, in which case the gasholder would be built in Abingdon despite all the efforts of its opponents.

In the meantime, Airey Neave (with the help of other sympathetic M.P.s) was doing his best to keep the gasholder issue before the public eye. On 17 April, in a written answer from the Ministry of Power, he extracted the names of no less than forty-five other towns in which conventional gasholders were either under construction or were proposed. He followed this on 25 April with a Question for the Minister of Housing and Local Government asking if he would introduce legislation requiring statutory undertakings such as the S.G.B. to obtain planning consent before erecting gasholders or other buildings on their land. The exchanges that followed merely went over familiar ground, and the Minister declined to comment specifically on the Abingdon case. But in answer to a supplementary Question from Sir Derek Walker-Smith (Hertfordshire East), he acknowledged that there were doubts as to whether the existing method for solving disputes of this kind was the right one, and told the House that the position was indeed under review.[1]

On 9 May it was the Minister of Power's turn to answer Questions. Ronald Bell (Buckinghamshire South) asked the Minister how many sites in England were occupied by Area Gas Boards upon which they were entitled to erect gasholders more than 50 feet in height without planning permission. There were about 600 such sites, said Freeson; but many of them were already fully occupied by plant and buildings. He pointed out that planning was the responsibility of the Ministry of Housing and Local Government, not the Ministry of Power, and refused to give a general direction to Area Gas Boards ordering them not to erect new gasholders until fresh legislation had been brought in.[2]

It was during this period of apparent deadlock that on 24 May the issues were again discussed in a leading article in *The Times*. Almost for the first time in the controversy, the statutory undertakers' side of the case was spelt out in public. It was perfectly true, observed *The Times*, that if statutory undertakings were prevented from developing in the way they chose on their operational land, they were – unlike private industry – entitled to claim compensation from the planning authority concerned. They had

[1] *H.C. Deb.* (1966–7) 745, cols 1320–1.
[2] *H.C. Deb.* (1966–7) 746, cols 1253–4.

been given this right, of course, because they had a statutory obligation to provide a service, an obligation which was itself a corollary of their monopoly power. Private developers had not been given the right to claim compensation, because they were free *not* to develop if they thought the planning authority was being unreasonable. But without some form of built-in constraint (in this case the liability to pay compensation) there would be no limits at all to the conditions that a planning authority might impose on the statutory undertaker.

There was another aspect of the case that had so far escaped attention. Implicit in most of the criticism that had been levelled at the S.G.B. had been the unspoken charge that the Board were somehow akin to an obstinate, mean, and above all philistine private individual, willing to perpetrate any aesthetic atrocity rather than spend a little more than was absolutely necessary. But, as *The Times* pointed out, a public utility is not in the same position as a grasping individual, or even a private firm seeking to hold down costs in order to maximise profits and dividends. The extra cost of a high-pressure system would not come out of the pockets of members of the Board or their officials. In the end, it would be the S.G.B.'s customers, the gas-consuming public in an arbitrarily defined area in the south of England, who would meet any bill for amenity that the S.G.B. agreed to pay. The fact was that if local authorities were to pay no compensation in cases like this, then the entire cost of preserving local amenities would fall nominally on the statutory undertakers involved, but in reality on their customers, regional or national. And if the public utility in question was an organisation whose losses had to be subsidised by the Exchequer, then these amenity costs would fall on the general body of taxpayers.

Local amenities, *The Times* concluded, were primarily for the benefit of local people. Since they were matters of local pride and satisfaction, at least part of the cost of preserving them ought to be borne locally. This, it argued, was a principle that ought to be developed and not eroded. The real problem arose when the cost of preservation was greater than it was reasonable to expect the local residents to bear, even when the word 'local' was extended to cover the whole area of the county planning authority. 'What is at present lacking', it pointed out, 'is an equitable formula for apportioning a cost which must fall somewhere.'

THE MINISTER TRIES AGAIN

After the acrimonious ending to the meeting in Southampton on
22 May, Freeson was at first inclined to wash his hands of the
affair, and let the normal planning procedures take their course.
After a day or two, second thoughts prevailed and he turned his
mind to devising the 'equitable formula' called for by *The Times*.
On 26 May he wrote to the S.G.B. and the local authorities,
setting out his final proposals for ending the dispute.

He accepted the S.G.B.'s contention that for technical reasons
the most suitable high-pressure installation would be one that
incorporated three diesel-driven compressors. It was possible, he
conceded, that economies might be made, and that the Board's
cost estimates might prove too high. On the other hand, there
was the usual possibility that costs might rise during construction.
These two possibilities, Freeson suggested, should be regarded as
cancelling each other out. In his view, the S.G.B.'s estimate of
£365,000 for the capital cost of the high-pressure system should
be accepted; in round figures, this was £139,000 more than the
low-pressure gasholder. As far as the additional running costs
were concerned, Freeson did not accept the S.G.B.'s claim for
£136,756: in view of the rapid changes taking place in the gas
industry, he thought that twenty years was too long a period over
which to assess this commitment. A realistic period, he thought,
would be ten years, which at £10,000 a year would represent a
capital sum of £70,000.

There remained the cost of erecting the high-pressure system
and the cancellation fee for the low-pressure gasholder already
ordered. The maximum figures under these two heads were
£35,000 and £52,000 respectively. Under Freeson's formula, the
additional capital costs, the erection costs, the cancellation
charges, and the extra running costs would all be shared equally
as between the S.G.B. and the local authorities. On this basis,
Berkshire and Abingdon between them would contribute £69,000
towards the extra capital cost and £35,000 towards the additional running costs. They would also contribute a further sum of
up to £43,000 in respect of cancellation and erection costs. The
local authorities' share of the additional costs would thus be

£148,000; or, if they preferred to make their contributions towards the extra running costs yearly, a capital sum of £113,000 and £5,000 a year towards operating costs. In short, the essential principle underlying this formula was that both sides should share the extra cost on a 50:50 basis.

Freeson's attitude, apparently, was that both sides were equally responsible for the dispute and that both sides had an interest in reaching an early settlement. Looking at the situation from the S.G.B.'s point of view, the law might be on their side, but if the statutory planning procedures ran their full course the ensuing delay could well endanger Abingdon's gas supply. And as far as the local authorities were concerned, if Berkshire refused planning consent, they would be liable for compensation far in excess of the figure that he was now suggesting. Freeson, moreover, made it quite clear that this was the Ministry of Power's last word: if this 50:50 formula was not acceptable they would take no further part in the dispute.

From the standpoint of the local authorities, Freeson's new proposals were certainly an improvement on what they had been asked to pay at the Southampton meeting. Whether these more favourable terms went far enough remained to be seen. The ball was once again in the local authorities' court. Were they now prepared to make *some* contribution? If so, were they prepared to accept Freeson's formula? If not, how much were they prepared to offer?

The problem was discussed at meetings of the Abingdon Borough Council and the Berkshire Planning and Finance Committees at the end of May and the beginning of June. When the Berkshire County Clerk wrote to the Minister of Power on 5 June the local authorities had agreed on their line, though Berkshire's offer still had to be confirmed by a special meeting of the County Council called for 20 June. There had been hints in the press that the local authorities would offer rather less than the Ministry of Power had suggested. They were, indeed, offering a great deal less.

The local authorities had agreed, reluctantly, that as the law stood they had to be prepared to make some contribution towards preserving the amenities of Abingdon. Nevertheless, they still thought that the S.G.B. were exaggerating the costs of a high-pressure system. According to their expert advisers, three electric compressors (which were both cheaper and less noisy) would do the job just as well as three diesel-driven compressors. They had confirmed with the Southern Electricity Board that the possibility of a breakdown in the electricity supply was so remote that it could be ignored. The saving under this head, they reckoned, would bring the estimated additional cost on the capital side down from £139,000 to £109,000. Then there was the £35,000 claimed by the S.G.B. for erection and consultancy charges. In the local authorities' view this figure, too, was unnecessarily high: in fact, they were advised that the work could be done for half this sum.

As far as the additional running costs were concerned, the local authorities were not prepared to make any contribution at all. No other local authority, they argued, had been asked to make any payment under this head, and they thought the claim was quite unreasonable, considering that the S.G.B.'s turnover was about £20 million a year. This, they claimed, was an expense that the Board ought to absorb in their ordinary running costs.

Finally, there was the question of the S.G.B.'s abortive contract for the conventional gasholder. The Board had all along been aware that the local authorities objected to this gasholder, and they knew that there was the possibility of an Article 4 Direction. If, in spite of all this, they had gone ahead with the contract, they could not expect to be paid compensation for what had been a deliberate act on their part. If, on the other hand, they had placed an order for the gasholder before telling the local authorities of their plans, then they were even more open to criticism. The local authorities, therefore, were most certainly not prepared to pay anything under this head either. In their view, this claim was nothing short of an impertinence.

In all the circumstances, the Berkshire Planning and Finance Committees were recommending to the County Council that they should make a payment of £72,000 in complete settlement of the S.G.B.'s claim. This was to be paid, without interest, by half-yearly instalments, over a period of years. And if the law relating to compensation were changed, the instalments were to cease and the amounts already paid were to be returned or the position reconsidered. As the County Clerk emphasised in his letter to the Ministry of Power, the figure of £72,000 was not in any sense a counter-offer. This was the sum the two Committees thought they should pay, and they were not going to pay any more. If the S.G.B. did not accept the figure of £72,000, then the County Council, with the greatest reluctance, would deal with the planning application in the normal way, and would allow the gasholder to be built, in spite of its detrimental affect on the amenities of Abingdon. As the Planning and Finance Committees saw it, they were offering a generous sum. The Minister of Power should urge the S.G.B. to accept it. Berkshire, then, was offering less than half of what Freeson had suggested the local authorities should contribute on the basis of his 50:50 formula.

What view the S.G.B. took of 'their' Minister's intervention is not known. Apparently, the chairman of the Board had himself suggested, informally, to the Ministry of Power that a 50:50 allocation of the final cost might be the answer. But if the S.G.B. were going to forgo half the compensation to which the law entitled them, they thought that the local authorities ought to be well satisfied. As they saw it, Berkshire had been playing a dangerous game of brinkmanship with Abingdon's gas supplies, and there was no justification at all for the outraged air of grievance that they were continuously displaying. On 8 June the S.G.B. wrote to the County Council commenting on their attitude. They could not understand why the Berkshire County Council were so indignant about the cancellation fee. Long before the meeting in Southampton on 22 May, they pointed out, the S.G.B. had made it clear that they were going ahead with a conventional gasholder, and that any costs incurred would be included in the Board's compensation claim. They cited their letter to the County Clerk of 20 February to this effect, and added that, as a matter of fact, the S.G.B. had entered into the contract on 28 February.

The news that the Board had ordered a conventional gasholder nineteen days *after* the County Council had sent the Article 4 Direction to the Ministry of Housing and Local Government on 9 February did nothing to improve the atmosphere. By now the local authorities were ready to put the worst interpretation on everything done by the S.G.B.; to them, it looked like another piece of sharp practice. 'I imagine my Council will be astounded', observed the County Clerk in his reply to this letter.

Now that the local authorities had shown their hand, Airey Neave resumed his efforts on their behalf in Whitehall. On

7 June he discussed the situation with Anthony Greenwood and Fred Willey at the Ministry of Housing and Local Government, and did his best to impress upon the two Ministers the fairness of Berkshire's offer of £72,000. Greenwood, apparently, undertook to help find a solution to the dispute and promised to hold more talks with his ministerial colleagues. Airey Neave emerged feeling quite pleased with his progress. On 15 June he saw Marsh and Freeson at the Ministry of Power, and urged them to ask the S.G.B. to settle on Berkshire's terms. Freeson's proposals, he argued, were quite inequitable. If the negotiations broke down, he said, they would bear the responsibility. The two Ministers were adamant. They flatly refused to intervene again, and refused to appoint an independent arbitrator. As far as they were concerned, Freeson's proposals of 26 May were their last word. They were not specially interested in specific figures; what they wanted was a firm commitment from Berkshire to meet 50 per cent of whatever the additional cost turned out to be. In their eyes, the final decision rested with the Berkshire County Council.

Tidings of this latest impasse were ill received in Berkshire, and the *Oxford Mail* turned its anger on to Greenwood as well as Marsh. It was criminal, the paper observed, that Abingdon should be ruined because Marsh and Greenwood chose to do nothing to stop the S.G.B. 'If the Monster gasholder is built', it declared, 'it will be a monument to the crass lack of sense of these two men as much as to the arrogance of the S.G.B.'

DEUS EX MACHINA

At their special meeting called on 20 June the Berkshire County Council were due to reach a decision on the recommendation from their Finance and Planning Committees: were they or were they not to offer the sum of £72,000 as their contribution towards the extra cost of the high-pressure system? Freeson had by Ministry of Power had said their last word. The S.G.B. had accepted Freeson's proposals. There was now, so it seemed, only one possible outcome to the dispute. Berkshire would confirm that £72,000 was its final offer. The S.G.B., backed by the Ministry of Power, would turn it down. The Ministry of Housing and

Local Government would stay on the touchline. With the County Council unwilling to pay more than £72,000, the Berkshire Planning Committee would then, with great reluctance and distaste, give planning permission for the conventional gasholder and the 'monster' would be built at last.

Events were to take a different course. Just when the tragic dénouement seemed inevitable, there dramatically appeared upon the scene Mr Fred Willey, the Minister of State at the Ministry of Housing and Local Government. Realising that the brinkmanship was over, and that unless something was done the gasholder really would be built, the Ministry of Housing and Local Government had evidently decided that this was the time to take a hand.

On 15 June Air Commodore Dickens, the chairman of the Berkshire County Council, had been surprised to receive a telephone call from Willey suggesting a meeting. The next day, over tea at Dickens's house at Crowthorne, they discussed the situation and talked about the possibility of the Minister of Housing and Local Government calling in the case for decision. Willey had no firm proposals to make, but he promised to consult the Ministry of Power again. When he left, Dickens felt mildly encouraged.

On 20 June, fifteen minutes before the special meeting of the County Council was due to begin, Dickens received another urgent message from Whitehall, asking the County not to come to any decision that day. This news was recounted by Dickens to the Council, whereupon it was agreed that they ought not to reject the opportunity of further talks. After a short debate, the County Council decided to refer back to the Planning and Finance Committees their proposal for an offer of £72,000.

The further talks took place at the Ministry of Housing and Local Government on 28 June, when Dickens and the chairman of the Berkshire Finance Committee met Greenwood and Willey at the Ministry of Housing and Local Government. After further consultation with the Ministry of Power, Greenwood had something to offer. It was not much, but it was a slight improvement on Freeson's original terms. Greenwood's suggestion was that the County Council and the S.G.B. should equally share the capital cost and the capitalised running costs of the high-pressure system, while the Lands Tribunal should be asked to arbitrate on the cancellation fee for the abortive contract. On Greenwood's reckoning, the County Council's share under the first two heads would amount to £104,000. And if the Lands Tribunal's verdict went their way, this was all that they would pay.

As the talks went on, however, it became apparent that there was an entirely new element in the situation. It was now clear that if the County Council stuck to their guns, and refused planning permission, the Minister was going to call in the application for his own decision.

Greenwood had evidently decided that he could not possibly allow the gasholder to be built simply because the County Council refused to pay. He took the view that since they had been largely responsible for turning a local problem into a national issue, they could not complain if he treated it as such. Nor could they complain if he agreed with them that it would indeed be a sin if the gasholder were built. If the application were called in, and the Minister decided that the gasholder ought not to be erected (and, patently, this was going to be his decision), the County Council would be liable to pay the whole of the extra cost of the high-pressure system. There would be no question of sharing the additional cost with the S.G.B. In other words, the Minister had decided that the gasholder was not going to be built, and the County Council were going to foot the bill, whether they liked it or not. The proposition now being put to Berkshire was this: agree to pay £104,000 (rather than the £72,000 which you have said is your final offer), or you will be compelled to pay a great deal more, perhaps twice as much.

The Minister's attitude was perhaps partly attributable to a growing feeling within the Department that whilst the existing law would not remain in force for much longer, if the gasholder were built it would be there for many years to come. On 20 June Airey Neave had asked the Minister of Housing and Local Government what progress he was making with his review of the legal position of statutory undertakings in regard to planning applications and compensation. In reply, Willey had said that consultations were proceeding with the other departments concerned about setting on foot an inquiry, and that he was soon to meet representatives of the County Councils Association, the Association of Municipal Corporations and of the Greater London Council. In fact, these talks took place on 11 July, the day on which the Abingdon controversy was to be settled.

This was the position that was explained to a joint meeting of the County Finance and Planning Committees on the morning of 5 July. After a long debate it was agreed that there were now three possibilities open to the County Council. They could reject the S.G.B.'s application for the conventional gasholder, and accept the Minister's terms. This would mean paying £104,000 for certain, and taking a chance on the Lands Tribunal's decision about the cancellation fee. Or, they could grant planning permission for the gasholder in spite of the Minister's warning that if they did this he would call in the application and revoke their consent, thereby making them liable for the whole of the compensation payable. Or, they could refuse the application without agreeing to the Minister's terms, thus making themselves liable for whatever compensation the Lands Tribunal might fix. On the face of things, only the first choice seemed to make sense. In the event, on a majority vote, the two Committees adopted the second course.

Evidently, some members still took very strong exception to spending over £100,000 of the ratepayers' money on Abingdon. Others probably reckoned that the full compensation would be such an enormous sum that the County Council would never be forced into paying it. The Government must be bluffing. Whatever their reasons, the two Committees were now recommending the County Council to grant planning permission for the gasholder, in spite of the Minister's clear warning that if they did so he would call in the application. In other words, they were not prepared to pay £104,000 to keep the gasholder out of Abingdon; but they were willing to have the Minister oblige them to pay considerably more to achieve the same result. It remained only for this quixotic recommendation to be put before a special meeting of the County Council on 11 July, when the odds must have been very much in favour of its acceptance.

Any notion that the Minister of Housing and Local Government might be bluffing was soon dispelled. Immediately after the joint Committee meeting Dickens spoke on the telephone to the Deputy Secretary concerned. He was told categorically that if the County Council accepted the recommendation from their Finance and Planning Committees, the Minister was certainly going to call in the S.G.B.'s application.

In a last-minute effort to save the situation, on the afternoon before the County Council's special meeting Dickens again travelled to London to see Willey at the Ministry of Housing and Local Government. In the course of a long meeting the Minister had one final concession to offer on behalf of the Ministry of Power and the S.G.B. He had accepted the County Council's argument that electric rather than diesel compressors could be used. Consequently, the contribution required from Berkshire could now be reduced from £104,000 to £89,000 (plus, of course, the Lands Tribunal's assessment of the County Council's share, if any, of the cancellation fee). He also left Dickens in no doubt that the Minister meant what he said about calling in the application and revoking the County Council's consent should they give it at the special meeting on the following day. Later that evening they were joined in the House of Commons dining-room by Freeson. When the three men went their separate ways, Dickens had apparently agreed to use his influence to get the County Council to accept the terms that Willey and Freeson had offered.

At the special Council meeting next day Alderman R. H. C. Seymour moved an amendment to the report from the Finance and Planning Committees, calling on the County Council to refuse consent for the gasholder and to accept the terms of settlement put forward by the Minister of Housing and Local Government. He pointed out that unless a negotiated settlement was agreed upon, there was no doubt that in law the County Council were liable to pay the whole of the difference in cost between the high- and low-pressure storage systems. In his view this difference, even allowing for economies, was unlikely to be less than £220,000. 'It is clear', he said, 'that most, if not all, members of the Council would consider that this figure was too high a price to pay, even for the amenities of Abingdon.' It was true that if they accepted his amendment, they would be giving way to pressure from the Minister. But, as the law then stood, he felt that the Minister's terms were by no means unreasonable from the County Council's point of view. It was better, he argued, to pay what the Minister suggested, rather than to run 'the almost certain risk' of having to pay more than £200,000, which would be about twice as much as the negotiated figure.

Some members indignantly accused the Government of blackmail, and complained that they were taking away the Council's freedom of choice. As one speaker correctly observed, the Minister was proposing to deprive them of the right to accept the gasholder if they thought the price of buying off the S.G.B. too high. But by now cooler counsels had evidently prevailed, and many more members had had second thoughts about the wisdom of cocking a snook at the Minister. A majority agreed with Seymour: £200,000 *was* too much to preserve Abingdon intact, and it would be wrong for them to put the ratepayers of Berkshire at risk for such an enormous sum. At the end of the debate, Seymour's amendment was carried by thirty-eight votes to fifteen.

There followed a number of informal meetings between the S.G.B.'s solicitor and the County Clerk and County Treasurer. On 10 August the S.G.B. offered new terms. The Board were now prepared to accept, in full and final settlement, the sum of £120,000 by six half-yearly instalments. The S.G.B. were to let the County Council know as soon as the cancellation charge was settled, and if this turned out to be less than £52,000, the Board were to pass on to the County, by deduction from the next half-yearly instalment, a third of the amount by which the cancellation charge fell short of £52,000. Subject to that one proviso, the £120,000 was to be paid without any inquiry into the costs that the Board actually incurred, or into the costs that the Board would have incurred on the low-pressure scheme.[1]

So it was that the Berkshire County Council decided to refuse planning permission for the gasholder and to accept the Minister's terms. At their meeting on 13 September the County Planning Committee considered the S.G.B.'s subsequent application for planning consent for a high-pressure system, and subject to appropriate conditions relating to noise control and tree planting, recommended that consent should be granted.

The controversy ended on 21 October 1967 when the S.G.B.'s terms were formally accepted by the County Council. A few members wanted to press the Minister of Power to hold a public inquiry into the whole affair. The general view, however, was that of the chairman of the County Planning Committee. He drew some comfort from the outcome. They had reason to congratulate themselves, he said, because they had drawn nation-wide attention to an inadequacy in the law. They had been commended for

[1] For the sequel, see p. 295, footnote.

their stand by many individuals and organisations, and they had succeeded in saving one of the most pleasant towns in the country. The last word was with the chairman of the Finance Committee: 'no one is happy about this', he said, 'and I am not pretending that it is a satisfactory settlement; but in the circumstances it is the best we can expect.' Privately, there were some who considered that the County Council had been fortunate to come off so lightly, for whatever the moral rights and wrongs of the case, legally they had never had a leg to stand on.

ABINGDON AND THE LAW

Town and Country planning law had been under review long before the battle of the Abingdon gasholder began. The Town and Country Planning Act that was to receive the Royal Assent on 25 October 1968 brought in radical and extensive changes over the whole field of physical planning. One aspect of planning law that the Government had under examination, quite independently of the gasholder controversy, was the position of statutory undertakers. However, there can be little doubt that the storm over the Abingdon gasholder gave added point and urgency to the Government's review. It may well be that the Abingdon case also had some effect on the provisions that Parliament was eventually to include in the new Act.

In the summer of 1967, when the gasholder dispute was at its height, the Association of Municipal Corporations and the County Councils Association urged the Minister of Housing and Local Government to re-examine the position of statutory undertakers in cases of this kind. On 11 July, it will be recalled, a deputation from the two local authority associations saw the Minister. At this meeting the Minister was pressed to change the law, so that local authorities were freed from any liability to pay compensation to statutory undertakers.

Subsequently, an inter-departmental working party was established, including representatives of the Ministry of Housing and Local Government, the Ministry of Power, the Ministry of Transport and the Treasury. The working party's task was to recommend a formula that would be generally applicable, and which could be given statutory force in the Town and Country Planning Bill then in preparation.

Two possibilities were considered. There was the local authority view: statutory undertakers should be given no compensation at all when they were refused planning permission. Alternatively, there was what now came to be referred to as the 'Freeson formula'. On this argument, the compromise finally reached in the Abingdon case should be set up as a general principle, with local authorities paying half the compensation for which they were liable as the law then stood. This solution, presumably, was supported by the statutory undertakers, and their sponsoring departments, the Ministry of Power and the Ministry of Transport. The views that were put forward on both sides can be pieced together from what was later said in Parliament.

The local authorities' case was based upon four main arguments. First, they maintained that the Abingdon case had been settled under duress, and for that reason it ought not to be taken as a precedent. The two local authorities concerned in the Abingdon dispute had agreed to pay half the required compensation only because they had a very weak case in law. It would be absurd to base new law on a precedent that had been established only because the old law was unsatisfactory.

Second, they argued that statutory undertakers should be exposed to the full social costs of their activities, so that they had some incentive to find solutions that were less harmful to planning and amenity. It was wrong that they should be able to claim compensation for not doing what they ought not to do, and ought not to be allowed to do.

Third, Local Planning Authorities should not have to take into account the possibility that a refusal on their part might leave them open to a heavy claim for compensation. This possibility might well influence their judgement; whereas, by rights, their only concern ought to be whether or not the proposed development was appropriate for the land in question. The Freeson formula was much too rigid; 50 per cent of an enormous compensation claim would represent a crippling burden for a good many small planning authorities. In this event, monstrosities would be built all over the country, not because nobody objected, but because the only people with the power to stop them could not afford to do so.

And fourth, the services provided by statutory undertakers might not always benefit the localities whose amenities were threatened by the necessary installations. A gasholder in one town might be used to supply another. In these circumstances, why should the first pay compensation and the second go scot-free? It would be better to avoid complications like this by making statutory undertakers pay the whole social cost of their operations.

On the other side, the statutory undertakers and their departmental spokesmen maintained that Local Planning Authorities ought to pay half the necessary compensation, so that they would take care to exercise their powers of control with a proper appreciation of the financial implications of their decisions. It is all too easy, they implied, to be irresponsible and unrealistic when the bills are paid by someone else.

When the new Town and Country Planning Bill was published and given its First Reading in December 1967 the working-party had not yet settled the argument. In the course of the Second Reading debate on 31 January 1968, however, the Minister of Housing and Local Government told the House that he hoped to introduce new clauses dealing with compensation at the Committee stage of the Bill. He explained why statutory undertakers had originally been given their special position, but acknowledged that the climate of opinion had changed since then. Any modern industrial undertaking, said Greenwood, had to be prepared to accept reasonable costs in order to make its buildings, plant and operations acceptable to public opinion. In consultation with his colleagues, he had decided that in cases where statutory undertakers were entitled to compensation, but private developers were not, the compensation should be shared equally between the statutory undertakers and the planning authorities. That is to say, the entitlement to compensation previously enjoyed by statutory undertakers would be reduced by half. The new arrangement would apply both when planning permission was refused for operational land and when the local authority withdrew planning permission previously authorised by a Private Act or Order. In short, the arguments of the statutory undertakers and their sponsor departments had prevailed, and the 'Freeson formula' was to be given a statutory basis.

The Minister's announcement was welcomed by Fred Willey

(who by now had ceased to be Minister of State). He pointed out that what Greenwood was now proposing followed the pattern charted in the difficult negotiations over the Abingdon gasholder. 'In my view', he said, 'when we set the precedent by experience and hard bargaining, it is better to follow it in legislation.' Airey Neave also gave a 'guarded welcome' to the Minister's decision. In principle, he was inclined to think that local authorities ought to pay something for saving their amenities; but the Freeson formula he found altogether too inflexible. Abingdon, he observed, had won 'a costly victory': even a 50 per cent reduction in their liability might still leave local authorities facing very substantial bills for compensation.[1]

On 25 April 1968, at the twenty-first meeting of the Standing Committee on the Town and Country Planning Bill, Niall Mac-Dermot, Willey's successor as Minister of State at the Ministry of Housing and Local Government, introduced the promised new clauses. Their effect was to narrow the definition of operational land, and to halve the compensation that local authorities had to pay to statutory undertakers, (*a*) where planning permission to develop operational land was refused, and compensation was claimed by virtue of the fact that it was operational land, and (*b*) where there had been a withdrawal of planning consent originally given under Class XII of the General Development Order.

The new clauses were welcomed by Members on both sides of the Committee. The Minister had done something, and that was cause for satisfaction. But clearly the Committee felt that the Minister had not gone far enough. Some thought that the 50:50 formula was too inflexible, while others maintained that local authorities ought not to have to pay anything by way of compensation. Under pressure, MacDermot agreed to look again at the new compensation clauses.

When the Bill left the Commons, however, the Government had not seen fit to make any further changes. Local government has many friends in the Lords, and when the Bill reached the Committee stage, on 26 June 1968, Lord Brooke of Cumnor and Lord Ilford put down amendments designed to benefit the local authorities. Lord Brooke argued that the local authorities should be liable to pay only 10 per cent of the required compensation,

[1] *H.C. Deb.* (1967–8) 757, cols 1361–1482.

and Lord Ilford's amendment relieved local authorities of any liability at all for compensation.[1]

Like his colleague in the Commons, the Minister (this time Lord Kennet, Joint Parliamentary Secretary at the Ministry of Housing and Local Government) was under considerable pressure during the debate, and eventually the two amendments were withdrawn when Lord Kennet promised to reconsider the position.

As before, when the argument shifted from Westminster to Whitehall, the statutory undertakers came into their own again, and when the Bill returned to the Lords for its Report stage, Lord Kennet told the House that the Government had not felt able to go further after all.[2] Aware that Parliamentary feeling was very much against the Government on this issue, the local authority champions again challenged the Minister. With the support of Lord Brooke, Lord Grimston of Westbury moved an amendment taking away from statutory undertakers the entitlement to any compensation from local authorities. The arguments that had been put before the inter-departmental working party were now rehearsed again, but this time in front of a voting audience most of which was plainly out of sympathy with the statutory undertakers' side of the case. Any peers who had forgotten the Abingdon dispute were soon reminded of it.

Changing the law is not always as straightforward as it seems. In opposing the amendment Lord Kennet explained some of the complications that would arise if it were adopted. There had been a good deal of misunderstanding about the Abingdon case, he said. The S.G.B.'s entitlement to compensation had been nothing to do with their being a statutory undertaker. When Parliament in the past had authorised development in the form of a private or local legislation, that right had been perpetuated by Class XII of the General Development Order. These rights were enjoyed by private concerns and local authorities, as well as by statutory undertakers. If these rights were withdrawn, and the would-be developer was prevented from doing what the Order permitted, he was entitled to compensation. The Abingdon case had attracted a great deal of publicity because it was a pretty, old town, and because the sum that had to be paid in compensa-

---

[1] *H.L. Deb.* (1967–8) 293, cols 1502–12.
[2] *H.L. Deb.* (1967–8) 296, cols 105–18.

tion was substantial. But the question of compensation had arisen not because the developers were statutory undertakers but because their General Development Order rights were being taken away.

He went on to explain in detail how the Bill would affect statutory undertakers, and how they would stand in comparison with private developers. When statutory undertakers lost rights given under Class XII of the General Development Order, the compensation to which they were entitled was going to be reduced by 50 per cent. When private developers lost these rights, *they* would still be able to claim compensation in full. On the other hand, under Section 170 of the 1962 Town and Country Planning Act, statutory undertakers had a right to compensation (whether or not they were covered by the General Development Order) if they were refused permission to develop their operational land. Here, too, their compensation was being reduced by 50 per cent. Private developers, of course, had no such rights over operational land, and they would not be entitled to any compensation in these circumstances. Thus, where General Development Order rights were involved, statutory undertakers would be worse off than private developers; where operational land was concerned they would be better off. But since the Government was also proposing to narrow the definition of operational land, a good many developments which might have qualified for compensation in the past would not do so under the new Act.

The effect of Grimston's amendment, argued Lord Kennet, would be not to put statutory undertakers on the same footing as everyone else; it would be to penalise them. For if the amendment was carried, statutory undertakers would not be entitled to any compensation in any circumstances; whereas private developers would still be able to claim 100 per cent compensation when they were not permitted to exercise General Development Order rights.

On grounds of equity, Lord Kennet was also prepared to defend the Government's new clauses:

When they (statutory undertakers) provide their service it is nearly always for the benefit of the local community, and if the local community want it provided in the interests of their area in a way which is more expensive, as they may very rightly want, it is not unreasonable that they should make a contribution through the rates.

It may be hard to put this contribution on communities where the amenities are worth preserving, whereas no doubt in other cases the local authority will not think it worth refusing and paying up the compensation. But there is money also in local amenity. If a town is pretty, and is kept pretty, it attracts tourists and this is reflected in the rates.

Until the new clauses had been introduced, he said, the balance had been tipped in favour of the statutory undertakers. At very considerable expense to them, and wholly to the advantage of the local authorities, the measures proposed by the Government would redress the balance. Lord Brooke and Lord Grimston were not impressed, and refused to withdraw their amendment. On a division, the Lords then defeated the Government's clause by fifty-two votes to thirty-five.

What the reactions were in Government circles is not known. It may be that the Ministry of Housing and Local Government were not heartbroken. At all events, when the Bill came before the Lords for its Third Reading on 15 October 1968, Lord Kennet announced that the Government had decided to accept the amendment. 'We have borne in mind the strong views expressed, in this House and elsewhere', he said, 'about the cumbersomeness of the earlier proposals; about the continuing right of statutory undertakers to compensation in circumstances in which no one else would be entitled to it; and about the effect of having to deal with the kind of case which has focused attention on this issue, for instance, Abingdon.'[1]

Much the same line was taken by the Minister of Housing and Local Government when the Lords' amendments were considered in the Commons in the early hours of the morning of 24 October 1968. Greenwood acknowledged that there had been misgivings about the Government's provisions. In the end, he said, the Government had decided to bow to Parliamentary feeling. The last word was with Airey Neave. Thanking the Minister for his personal intervention in the Abingdon case, he added: 'I do not think that the former chairman, now retired, of the Southern Gas Board can possibly have foreseen the events which he would

[1] *H. L. Deb.* (1967–8) 296, cols 1275–6.

set in train when he attempted to bully the Borough of Abingdon into paying the full amount of compensation."[1]

Whether or not any of the parties to the dispute had been guilty of bullying must be for the reader to judge. But there can be little doubt that as between the two possibilities of 50 per cent compensation or no compensation at all for statutory undertakers, it was the highly publicised Abingdon dispute, and recollections of what appeared to have happened there, that helped settle the argument at the very last stage.

Looked at dispassionately, there was a good deal to be said for the Government's original proposals. The arguments for requiring local authorities to make some contribution towards the preservation of their own amenities are by no means untenable. But for some years Parliamentary opinion had been very much against the statutory undertakers on this issue, and the Abingdon affair made the situation even more difficult for them and their sponsoring departments. In the privacy of an inter-departmental working party their case could hold its own. However, the S.G.B. – rightly or wrongly – were by now firmly cast as the villains of the piece, and the statutory undertakers' cause inevitably suffered by association. Ironically enough, when the dispute left Whitehall and came into the Parliamentary arena, it was left to the Minister of Housing and Local Government to defend their interests. There is reason to believe that he and his Department had all along been arguing that local authorities should be relieved of all liability for compensation. With Parliamentary feeling running so strongly in the same direction, it was hardly to be expected that the Minister responsible for planning and amenity would fight to the last for the developers and their rights. In the end, it seems, the Lords' amendments were accepted because no one in the Government had the heart to fight such an apparently unrewarding battle all over again in the Commons.

[1] *H.C. Deb.* (1967–8) 771, cols 1485–7. As a result of the Government's acceptance of this amendment, the Berkshire County Council subsequently suggested to the S.G.B. that there was now a case for waiving the unpaid instalments of the £120,000 agreed in August 1967. On 22 July 1969, under a new chairman, the Board agreed to reduce their claim by £50,000. *Local Government Chronicle*, 13 Sep 1969.

7 Values for Money: A Postscript

'London decided,' Byrd corrected me gently.
'All eight million of 'em?'
'Our department heads,' he said patiently. 'I
personally opposed it.'
'All over the world people are personally opposing
things they think are bad, but they do them anyway
because a corporate decision can take the blame.'

Len Deighton, *An Expensive Place to Die*

THERE IS a good deal to be said for the view that case-studies
are best left to speak for themselves. The morals that a storyteller
perceives and extracts may not be the only, or even the most
illuminating lessons to be drawn from the events he describes.
And whilst the cases included in this book do have important
features in common, the fact remains that a collection of five
studies, spread over a period of ten years, hardly constitutes a
satisfactory basis for profound generalisations about anything at
all. At most, they prompt a few final reflections about the processes and value-judgements that together do so much to shape
the environment we live in.

If there is one persistent and blindingly obvious motif that
runs through all amenity disputes, it is clearly this: what we are
not prepared to pay for, we cannot have. But who are 'we'? And
how do 'we' decide what is to be spent on preserving or enhancing amenity and the natural environment? There is no central
budget, framed by one man or a readily identifiable group of
individuals. Indeed, no one even knows precisely how much is
spent. What happens, of course, is that the level of expenditure
on amenity is settled as a result of countless separate and unco-
ordinated decisions, each of which stems from a combination of
value-judgement and calculated self-interest. It is a subtle and
complex process. Most of us have no very active part to play.
But this is not to say that public opinion is of no significance, for

such are the linkages and mechanics of the planning system that no one directly involved can afford to ignore the views and values of the onlookers. And given time, all but the most foolish or insensitive of the principal actors will respond to a change in the public mood.

It is, of course, the community itself which sets the whole process in motion with its demands for more and better goods and services at the lowest possible prices. Industrialists and developers answer with their plans to meet these demands, created in part by their own promotional efforts. When they reach the design stage of their project or product, they may simply select the cheapest methods of installation and distribution that are technically feasible and legally permissible, regardless of their likely impact on the environment. Inevitably, they will be more careful with their own, their shareholders' and their customers' money than others would have them be. But single-minded 'economic man', ruthlessly intent on minimising costs and maximising profits, is probably a rarity in Britain. Few leading businessmen or members of public boards are totally unmindful of society's informal sanctions and constraints. Interestingly enough, the C.E.G.B., the organisation which throughout the country spends more on industrial construction than any other, claims that it takes its cue about the proper level of expenditure on amenity direct from public reaction to its proposals.[1] What occurs at this stage in the developer's camp is often of crucial importance. Afterwards, once they have gathered momentum, major projects are not easily headed off further along the line. It should not be forgotten (though it frequently is) that part of what is spent on amenity results not from the outcome of last-ditch struggles at planning inquiries, but from deliberate and voluntary choices made by developers.

How much this voluntary expenditure amounts to every year, nobody knows. But clearly it needs only a small change in the climate of boardroom opinion to add or subtract very substantial sums that are never recorded and added up. As to why unforced expenditure of this kind is undertaken, obviously it would be ridiculous to suggest that it is attributable entirely to finer feelings or a well-developed social conscience. Only a very imprudent

[1] *Report from the Select Committee on Nationalised Industries (Electricity Supply),* H.C. 236-II (1962-3) *Minutes of Evidence,* Q.947.

company or public corporation would fail to ponder the probable reaction of others in the system to their proposals. How will the Local Planning Authority, amenity organisations, Members of Parliament, or the Minister react? What *they* are likely to consider reasonable is something that must always be taken into account.

By its very nature, the control of development is bound to be a somewhat negative activity. But the role of local authorities, as part of the filter system through which schemes proposed by developers must pass, is not wholly passive. Their known attitude cannot fail to exert some influence on the thinking of developers, and on the proposals they see fit to bring forward. If a planning authority acquires a reputation for being comparatively easy to please, there is inevitably rather less incentive for the developer to offer to incur more expense on amenity than is absolutely necessary; if, on the other hand, its standards are known to be more rigorous and exacting, a developer has good reason to go to more trouble and expense in an effort to avoid the delay and uncertainties attendant on a rejected planning application, an appeal, a public local inquiry, and a decision from the Minister. As he well knows, only if the Local Planning Authority refuses planning consent, thereby obliging him to appeal to the Minister, will third parties have the opportunity to come into the case and make their objections known. Clearly, it is in the developer's interests to satisfy the Local Planning Authority, so as to avoid unlocking the gate to all the other potential opponents.

Moreover, if a Local Planning Authority does decide to reject an application, or lodge an objection to a proposal that has gone direct to the Minister for determination, the resources that it can bring into play may well prove decisive. It is hard to believe that the cases described in Chapters 2 and 3 would have taken the course they did had the Local Planning Authorities concerned not decided to fight. It is not always easy for a local authority to know what to do for the best. In Chapter 3 we saw something of the tensions that may develop within a local council while they settle their official attitude to the prospect of new industrial developments in their area. As anyone with experience of local government and politics will realise, it would require another set of case-studies, with an entirely different focus, to do justice to this stage of the planning process. But here again, the same com-

bination of personal evaluation and sensitivity to the likely reactions of others plays an important part in shaping attitudes
and determining decisions. Professional planning officers will have
views of their own as to what ought or ought not to be permitted
in the interests of good planning. But they are also influenced by
the known outlook of their lay masters, the elected representatives. They, in turn, cannot afford to disregard local feeling.
Local issues may affect local elections much less than many
councillors believe. All the same, it is what they believe that is
important, and no politician takes lightly the possibility of an
outcry in the press, stimulated very often by a vocal and well-
organised local amenity society.

It is widely held that amenity organisations of all kinds usually
come on the scene too late in the day to exert much influence
over the outcome of major planning disputes. Sometimes, when
a Local Planning Authority approves a planning application they
dislike, they have no opportunity at all to make their views
known. But there is no telling how frequently it is the activities
of local amenity societies, and their range of informal contacts,
that help sway the decisions taken by local authorities. Left to
fight on their own, it is probably true that very few amenity
organisations carry sufficient fire-power to defeat powerful
developers. But they certainly make valuable auxiliaries. And as
we saw in Chapter 4, in favourable circumstances, the pattern of
interlocking affiliations that is so characteristic of the amenity
world makes it possible on occasions to mobilise formidable
alliances, commanding a good deal of sympathy in both Houses
of Parliament.[1]

This brings us finally to the Inspectors, civil servants and
Ministers, the men who between them settle those cases that come
to an open fight.

Of all the individuals involved in the planning process, few

---

[1] Attempts have recently been made to put informal arrangements for
co-operation on a more permanent footing. At the end of 1969 it was
announced that a Committee for Environmental Conservation (CoEnCo)
had been established. Consisting of a nucleus of eighteen members, representing the principal bodies in the fields of amenity, wildlife, soil, air and
water, noise, archaeology and architecture, and outdoor recreation, its
purpose is 'to act as a liaison body and to take action on environmental
problems which transcend the terms of reference of more than one
society'. See *The Times*, 11 Dec 1969.

have more scope for the exercise of personal value-judgements than the Inspectors. It is true, of course, that in the important and controversial cases, theirs is not the last word. From time to time (though very rarely) their recommendations are rejected. But anyone – be it departmental official or the Minister himself – inclined to set aside their reasoned judgements has to make out a convincing case for so doing. It is also true that in the ordinary run of minor cases there is a known ministerial policy which they must take into account. But as everyone agrees, when an Inspector sets off to preside over an inquiry into what are often unique situations, such as those described in Chapters 2, 3 and 5, there is little by way of prior guidance that the department can give him. He must be left to make up his own mind on the basis of what he sees and hears; and in the last resort, the weight that he attaches to various arguments that are put before him must depend upon his own subjective evaluations.

Yet when this has been said, the fact remains that no more than anyone else do Inspectors work in a complete vacuum. There may be no precisely identical precedent for some of the more difficult cases; and probably no subsequent cases will ever be quite like them in the future. But Inspectors are not launched upon an entirely uncharted sea, for by the very nature of their work they are constantly called upon to make these subjective judgements as to the value of amenity, and they cannot fail to learn how their recommendations are being received by Ministers. Over the years they naturally develop a feel for what Ministers are likely to consider a reasonable sacrifice of amenity in relation to the price of saving it.

Civil servants are in a similar position. In advising their Minister, they too must exercise a measure of personal judgement. If they conclude that an Inspector has given too little or too much weight to the value of amenity, it is their business to say so. But once again appraisals are bound to some extent to be conditioned by the known attitudes of the next man in the line. And now, of course, we have reached the Ministers, the men who stand at the end of the chain. It is not long before a Minister and his senior officials learn a good deal about each other; and civil servants quickly discover how 'amenity-minded' their Minister is. Critics of the civil service have sometimes attacked its readiness to adjust, in advance, to what it thinks the reaction of Ministers will be, without putting issues to the test. How much force there is in this criticism is not a question for discussion here; rightly or wrongly, officials generally take the view that there is no point in making recommendations which they think it virtually certain that their political masters will not entertain.

Except on a point of law, there is no appeal from a Minister's decision. His judgement is final, and cannot be reversed. Ministers' verdicts are important not just because they result in the loss or the preservation of particular amenities, nor even for the cumulative effect of the many such decisions they take every year. Equally influential are the reverberations. What appears to be the prevailing ministerial outlook at the end of the line is something that enters into the thinking of everyone with a part to play in the planning process.

But if their judgements are beyond challenge, and their influence pervasive, in practice not even Ministers enjoy complete freedom to follow their personal inclinations. They too have to consider the reactions of others. Take the position of the Minister with strong feelings about the need to preserve amenity. Faced with a proposal that is clearly open to powerful amenity objections, he can no doubt be relied upon to veto anything that seems to have only small or problematic economic advantages. But much as he may sympathise with the conservationists, there will frequently be cases that raise agonising doubts. It is not always the developers who are being unreasonable; he is bound sometimes to wonder whether the threatened amenity really is worth the price of saving it. He will be well aware that though they talk the language of conservation and amenity, some of those who start or join local preservation societies are in reality (and quite understandably) more concerned about the value of their property than the abstract beauty of the countryside and its value to the nation.

Whitehall is beset with the representatives of good causes and sectional interests, all trying to persuade Ministers to spend money, or cause it to be spent, on worthy objects. Perhaps with good reason, the 'amenity net' tends to couch its appeal in apocalyptic tones. At the highest level, the conservationists certainly look agreeably altruistic and disinterested by comparison with some of the other lobbies that compete for Ministers' attention. But however good the cause, no one in Government wants to risk earning a reputation for softness or gullibility. The Minister who responds generously with other people's money will be extolled among the beneficiaries as the gallant defender of all that is best in our heritage. Elsewhere (as he knows) he may be dismissed as a naïve innocent, easily taken in and swayed by colourful and exaggerated appeals to sentiment. In itself, no single decision adds very much to prices or taxes; usually, the extra cost to each of us of saving some valuable amenity is infinitesimal, a fraction of a penny on our bills. However, if decisions consistently go one way rather than the other, the effect in aggregate may be considerable. And if a Minister shows signs of forgetting it, there will always be colleagues at hand to remind him.

Besides, as every politician knows, the community always finds it hard to stomach the idea of paying for collective benefits, even when the results take the form of tangible and material items like schools, roads or hospitals. In these sectors there is at least something to show for what the public has been obliged to spend. When Ministers look forward to the day of reckoning, when they must defend their record in office, they know that in many fields of Government activity there will be statistics to cite and positive achievements to describe. But when they come to explain what they have done in the interests of amenity, what is there to point to? Where a power station, an overhead transmission line, or a reservoir might have been, there is now pleasant open countryside, still intact and no less (but no more) pleasant than before it was threatened. Where atmospheric pollution might have been higher, it is now lower. Where there might have been noise and disturbance, there is now peace and quiet. These are real and substantial benefits. But not everyone appreciates the absence of evils that failed to materialise; and no politician would bank on getting credit for negative blessings of this kind, even from those who have benefited most.

On the other hand, there are also pressures that push Ministers in the opposite direction. Not even the most philistine of politicians will relish the thought of going down to posterity as the man responsible for assorted monstrosities, or the Minister who permitted the destruction of priceless and irrecoverable treasures, all to save sums of money that are bound to appear unforgivably trivial in ten or twenty years' time. As everyone now realises, amenity is certain to become scarcer, and therefore more valuable, in relation to almost everything else. And once gone, it is obvious that restoration will be immeasurably more difficult and expensive than preservation, if indeed it is possible at all. Ministers, moreover, are only men like any others. Everyone likes to keep the good opinion of those with whom he most often comes into contact. As they themselves well know, the Ministers directly responsible for planning are regarded by local authorities and the amenity organisations as 'their' champions. No one enjoys the scorn or ill-will of disappointed protégés. And increasingly, Ministers who show themselves insufficiently sensitive to the claims of amenity are likely to get a bad press into the bargain.

All politicians worry about public opinion, although exactly what the expression means in this context is not easy to say. Certainly, in the last decade or so amenity societies have become more numerous, more confident, and probably more influential. But this is still a minority movement, and very much a middle-class phenomenon. As we saw in Chapters 3, 4 and 5, working men and their trade unions do not always rally enthusiastically to the cause of conservation; and the cry of bread before beauty' is not uncommon at public inquiries when amenity objections seem to put in jeopardy the prospect of more jobs or higher rateable values. No doubt this is a short-sighted and wrong-headed attitude. But it is not difficult to see what cynics have in mind when they suggest that many conservationists can afford to concern themselves with intangibles because they already have enough of everything else and are appalled at the consequences of extending their own standard of living to the rest of the community. The headlong pursuit of measurable economic growth may indeed be an unworthy and unintelligent activity; but not unnaturally, some of the less affluent have yet to be convinced that the game should be stopped before a few more of the material prizes have come their way.

Some years ago, when he was Minister of Town and Country Planning, the late Lord Dalton declared to a friend, 'My dear fellow, preserving the countryside doesn't win votes, you know.'[1] As we enter the seventies, politicians are evidently having second thoughts. Even the handful of cases described in this book reflect a change of outlook. In chapter 1 an important public authority

[1] See letter in *The Times*, 7 July 1967.

could argue, without turning a hair it would seem, that the natural beauty of the countryside was no business of theirs. A similar avowal today in the same circumstances would be almost unthinkable, even if it was not precluded by the terms of the 1968 Countryside Act. Or, to take the case described in Chapter 6, the Abingdon gasholder that raised such a furore in 1966 and 1967 had been approved virtually without a murmur in 1951.

The new mood has worked a change even in the machinery of government. In the autumn of 1969 it was announced that Mr Anthony Crosland, the newly appointed Secretary of State for Local Government and Regional Planning, would take any decisions which had a clear and widespread effect on the environment. On taking up his post, he observed that he saw it as his role 'to try to ensure that major development does not exact too high a price in terms of the whole environment'.[1] And as a further sign of the times, a few weeks later the Government established a standing Royal Commission on Environmental Pollution.[2]

Whether expressions of concern for 'the quality of life' yet make any popular electoral appeal must be very much open to question. But in the last few years there has certainly been a striking transformation in the milieu within which planning decisions are taken. How much practical effect it will have remains to be seen. Nevertheless, conservationists are no longer brushed aside as cranks and obstructions in the path of progress, and politicians who do have a genuine and personal interest in the preservation of amenity need no longer feel that theirs are lone and unpopular voices crying in a hostile wilderness.

There is no doubt that standards of propriety do change, and almost without our realising it they do influence behaviour and decisions. In the early sixties the then chairman of the C.E.G.B. told a Select Committee of the House of Commons that so far as amenity was concerned, what would have been perfectly acceptable fifty years earlier had become quite inconceivable. It simply

[1] *The Times*, 16 Oct 1969.

[2] Subsequently, in October 1970, the new Conservative Government announced that the former Ministries of Housing and Local Government, Public Building and Works, and Transport were to be unified in a single Department of the Environment, under a Secretary of State. For the rationale behind this change, see *The Reorganisation of Central Government*, Cmd 4506 (H.M.S.O. Oct 1970).

did not enter the heads of his Board members, he said, to do some
of the things that had been considered merely routine in the past.
If, in future decades, wealth that might have been put to other
uses is devoted to the preservation of amenity instead, this diversion will doubtless be in part due to thousands of individual and
voluntary decisions, taken in response to a new and perhaps more
enlightened social ethic that sets a higher relative value on
immaterial goods that cannot be bought and sold. But if society
comes to take the view that as a matter of policy a shift of resources into the conservation of the natural environment is
urgently required, it is hard to see how this can be achieved
within a reasonable time except through the instrument of law.

Although it seems to have gone largely unremarked, existing
Town and Country planning legislation, with its system of development control, has itself been responsible for one such shift of
resources over the last twenty years. Had all land been put to its
most profitable use, irrespective of the social and aesthetic consequences, the face of Britain would now look very different. A
price has been paid, in terms of delays and higher costs. But to
judge from what was done in the absence of controls, few would
argue that the price has been excessive. The question now is
whether the 'disamenity' legislation we have ought to be
strengthened and extended.[1] Visual amenity is important. But
clearly the contamination of water, noise, and atmospheric
pollution represent far more serious threats to the environment.
Clean-air legislation has done something to combat a number of
the more obvious nuisances. And when the possibility of pollution
arises out of proposals to develop or redevelop particular pieces
of land, the ordinary planning controls may come into play. But
the worst menaces are subject to few controls that really bite,
either because they are produced by industrial installations established long before there was any effective Town and Country
planning legislation, or because they are not directly connected
with the use of land. So it is that a man needs planning permission to erect a garage in his garden; but no one requires consent
to pollute the atmosphere with the noise and exhaust of his internal combustion engine.

[1] For a recent exposition of the case for new legislation to protect the
'amenity rights' of the individual, see Edward J. Mishan, 'The Spillover
Enemy', *Encounter*, Dec 1969.

Though it has taken us a surprisingly long time to acknowledge it, there is nothing inevitable about the growth or continuation of these destructive evils. They occur only because they are tolerated. No Government is going to ban motor-cars or aeroplanes in the interests of a better environment. Yet this is not to say that stringent controls could not be placed upon their noxious side-effects.

The dialogue that would follow any such proposal is easily predicted. Those responsible for creating the nuisance would begin by arguing that their goods and services were, unfortunately, inseparable from the consequences of making them available. Modern technology is often attacked as the cause of all our environmental problems; but at least it would soon dispose of this argument. Obliged to concede that it is technically possible to avoid much of the damage that their operations inflict on the environment, the nuisance-makers would then argue that the costs entailed could be so high that it would no longer be possible for them to provide their goods and services at prices which the community is able to afford.

And then, if the legislators remained undeterred, it would very often be found that costs of treatment plant, or anti-noise or anti-pollutant devices, were not, after all, as high as had been feared. The reasons are obvious enough. Once their use became obligatory, an inescapable cost of production and a condition of staying in business, the inventive skills of engineers and chemists would soon be directed towards the problems of developing cheaper prophylactics. And with an assured, large-scale market there would be every incentive for them to succeed. A more satisfactory and less dangerous environment cannot be had for nothing; but the price might well turn out to be less than would at first sight appear. Adapting to necessities, including self-imposed necessities, is after all one of the greatest of human skills.

The object of this book, however, is not to advance a cause or to advocate specific changes in public policy. They are tasks for which others are far better equipped. There can be few who do not now realise, dimly or clearly, that consumer affluence and the second industrial revolution constitute an unprecedented threat to the natural environment. What the direct evidence of our eyes, ears and noses does not tell us, the conservationists will. Undoubtedly, there are some forms of pollution that really are matters of life and death, or will be in the not too distant future. They, of course, are forces of absolute evil, and no price is too great to ward them off. But it would be nonsense to suggest that all threats to amenity and the environment are as serious as this. The conflict between industry and amenity takes many forms; but it is not always a contest between virtue and evil. Nor is the world divided into heroes and villains. The five projects examined in this book were among the most controversial in the last decade. It was clear from the beginning that each in its own way would inflict some measure of damage on the environment. But could anyone reading this collection of stories honestly say that the individuals responsible for launching these schemes were acting out of greed or thoughtlessness? The truth is that they were all reasonable men, simply doing what they thought the logic of their situation required of them. This was as true of those who lost their case as of those who won.

For those who have seen the light, the path of virtue always looks plain and unmistakable. Others grope about more uncertainly. It is easy enough to say that the community ought to devote less attention to producing goods and more to avoiding bads. But when the choice comes at the end of a controversy like those described in earlier chapters 'the community' collectively cannot do anything. Interest groups have a part to play in the planning process, and indirectly the public mood does make itself felt. But, in the end, it still falls to a few individuals to make the final decisions. If more is to be invested in amenity, resources must be withdrawn or diverted from some other use. The preservation of amenity is not the only worthy cause on which more should be spent, and we cannot always be sure that only the trivial alternatives will suffer as a result of increased expenditure on conservation. Nor, under the existing arrangements, is there any guarantee that the financial burden will fall on those best able to pay. There is not much to be said for a system where the price of basic utilities is raised in order to preserve the amenities of the comparatively well-to-do. And added to these problems is the now familiar but still intractable difficulty of judging how much ought to be spent on values that have no money price. In the years ahead there will be no shortage of general exhortation. But of one thing we may be quite certain: making the choices will become an even more perplexing and thankless task.

Index

Milne-Redhead, E., and Cow Green, 154

Mineworkers, National Union of, support for Holme Pierrepont, 116; for Ratcliffe-on-Soar, 130

Ministers, and planning applications, 5–10, 21–3, 30–5, 301–3

Mishan, E. J., 10n, 305n

Modern Law Review, 9n

Modern Political Analysis (Dahl), 15n

Moloney, Sir Joseph, Q.C., for Gas Council at Bacton inquiry, 223

Molson, Lord: and Cow Green, 187, 188; and Bacton, 244n

Moor House Nature Reserve, 140, 148, 166, 174

Mop End (Bucks.), proposed electricity sub-station, 31n

Morris, E. A. (T.V.W.B. Chief Executive Officer), 169

Morton, Edgar, and Cow Green, 141, 143

Motherwell, proposed strip mill at, 44

Mottram, J. E. (secretary, Norfolk C.P.R.E.), 216

Munby, Denys, 9n

Municipal Corporations, Association of, and legal position of statutory undertakings, 284, 288

National Coal Board, 3, 92, 95, 97; supports C.E.G.B., 130

National Farmers' Union (N.F.U.), 4; and Cow Green, 30n; opposes Oxfordshire ironstone working, 42, 48n, 64, 73; opposes C.E.G.B., 103, 106, 130; supports Cow Green site, 156, 168, 178; opposes Bacton site, 221, 226, 230, 238

National Parks, 11, 24n, 91, 139–40

National Parks Commission, 71, 199; opposed to Oxfordshire ironstone working, 64, 72; and Upper Teesdale and Cow Green, 158, 164–165, 193n; and coastal development, 211, 212; and Bacton, 212, 213–14, 218, 220, 226, 228–9; alternatives to Bacton, 229, 234, 239–40, 243

National Trust, and Bacton, 211, 229, 240

Natural Environment Research Council (N.E.R.C.), 140; and Cow Green, 165–7

Natural History of Upper Teesdale, The (ed. Valentine), 134n

Nature Conservancy, 3, 140, 141, 157, 165; and Cow Green, 142–6, 148, 150, 154, 158, 169, 170, 181; alternative proposals, 149, 159, 174; I.C.I.'s offer of finance for research, 157, 163; and coastal development, 211, 221, 231; and East Ruston, 224–5, 230

Nature Conservation in Britain (Stamp), 140n

Nature Reserves, 11, 24n, 91, 140, 158, 174n, 209

Neave, Airey, M.P., and Abingdon gasholder, 250, 261, 265–8, 276, 281–2, 284, 294

Neill, B. T., 65

New Lives, New Landscapes (Fairbrother), 2n

New Society, 3n, 203n, 222n

Newberry, Dr J., and Cow Green, 168

Newbiggin, 143

Newman, James (I.C.I. scientific adviser), and Cow Green, 157, 168

Newport (Mon.), Oxfordshire ironstone for proposed strip mill at, 40, 44, 45, 46, 47, 49–50, 52, 56, 57–8 65–6, 67, 70, 74, 78–9, 84, 88

Nicholson, E. W. J. (Abingdon Town Clerk), 259n

Nicholson, Max (Director General, Nature Conservancy), 2n; and Cow Green, 142–6

Nightingale, Benedict, 203n

Norfolk Association of Amenity Societies: opposed to Bacton, 226, 229–30; alternatives, 240

Norfolk County Council: informed of Shell's Bacton intentions, 207, 210, 212–13; control of coastal development, 211–12; discussion with interested parties, 213–15; planning powers, 213n; opposition to Bacton site, 218–20, 222, 226–8, 238–40; alternative proposals, 219–20, 221, 223, 228, 232, 234, 236, 238–41

316 *Index*